THE PURITAN EARL

Henry Hastings, third Earl of Huntingdon

The Puritan Earl

THE LIFE OF HENRY HASTINGS
THIRD EARL OF HUNTINGDON
1536–1595

CLAIRE CROSS

MACMILLAN
London · Melbourne · Toronto
ST MARTIN'S PRESS
New York
1 9 6 6

MACMILLAN AND COMPANY LIMITED
Little Essex Street London WC2
also Bombay Calcutta Madras Melbourne

THE MACMILLAN COMPANY OF CANADA LIMITED
70 Bond Street Toronto 2

ST MARTIN'S PRESS INC
175 Fifth Avenue New York NY 10010

Library of Congress Catalog Card Number 66–18871

PRINTED IN GREAT BRITAIN BY ROBERT MACLEHOSE AND CO. LTD
THE UNIVERSITY PRESS, GLASGOW

CONTENTS

CONTENTS

LIST OF ILLUSTRATIONS

MAPS

ACKNOWLEDGEMENTS

I FIRST came upon the third Earl of Huntingdon when, still at school, I was looking into the early history of the Leicester Free School and saw how his commanding personality dominated the school's Elizabethan refoundation. With breaks I have worked on his career ever since and I owe very much to the many who have helped me, to Miss Ruth Bird, who inspired my love of history, and to Mrs. A. M. Erskine, who, when Leicester City Archivist, suggested this project. Professor H. P. R. Finberg taught me much about the technicalities of writing and I appreciate the encouragement he at Leicester and the late Professor N. Sykes at Cambridge gave me to start on serious historical research.

To those institutions which enabled me to carry out this research I am most grateful, to my own college, Girton College, Cambridge, for a research scholarship, to the American Association of University Women for a visiting fellowship which made possible a year's work in the United States, and to the University of Reading for a research fellowship there.

I should also like to thank the staffs of the libraries and record offices which all contained material relating to the Hastings family, of the British Museum and the Public Record Office, the Bodleian Library, the Cambridge University Library, the Henry E. Huntington Library, San Marino, California, and the Folger Shakespeare Library in Washington and of the English county record offices especially in the Midlands and the North of England; also the owners and custodians of private collections of manuscripts, the Duke of Rutland, the Marquis of Bath and the Marquis of Salisbury who gave me access to their Elizabethan family papers.

Lastly I acknowledge with gratitude the help of scholars in

various specialised fields: I thank again Mr. J. P. Cooper, Professor L. Stone, Mrs. M. Chibnall and Mr. W. R. B. Robinson for discussing the intricacies of Elizabethan estate management, Dr. P. Collinson, Professor M. Curtis, Dr. G. Owen, the Reverend B. Hall and Miss J. Schenck (now Mrs. Y. Ibish) for much information on Elizabethan puritanism, Mr. P. Tyler and Father Hugh Aveling, O.S.B., for help over the northern high commission and recusancy in the north, Dr. L. J. O. Boynton for elucidating Elizabethan military organisation, Professor F. B. Williams, jun., for allowing me to use his index of the dedications of early English printed books some years before it was published, Dr. R. Strong for freely sharing his knowledge of sixteenth-century portraits. I cannot thank all by name but I must record the encouragement I have always received from Professor Sir John Neale, Professor J. Hurstfield and Professor S. T. Bindoff, from their seminars and from fellow students at the Institute of Historical Research. Dr. P. N. Brooks most kindly read the book in typescript and did much to further its publication. Miss Ann Marshall greatly lightened and enlivened the task of reading the proofs. Finally, I owe an immense debt to my former supervisor, Dr. G. R. Elton, for his continuing help over the years and to Mr. Denis Bethell, whose lively and generous criticism of this whole biography when in manuscript lies behind any order and coherence the book may now contain. This has been a co-operative venture, and I thank all who made it so.

The King's Manor, York   CLAIRE CROSS
27 September 1965

LIST OF ABBREVIATIONS

P.R.O.	Public Record Office
B.M.	British Museum
Lans. MSS.	Lansdowne Manuscripts
Harl. MSS.	Harleian Manuscripts
Eg. MSS.	Egerton Manuscripts
Cott. MSS.	Cotton Manuscripts
Add. MSS.	Additional Manuscripts
C.U.L.	Cambridge University Library
Bodl.	Bodleian Library
Hunt. Lib.	Huntington Library, San Marino, California, U.S.A.
H.A.	Hastings Manuscripts
Leic. Mus.	Leicester Museum, Department of Archives
York, Borthwick Inst.	Borthwick Institute of Historical Research, St. Anthony's Hall, York

CALENDARS AND WORKS OF REFERENCE

A.P.C.	J. R. Dasent (ed.), *Acts of the Privy Council*
C.L. & P. Hen. VIII	*Calendar of Letters and Papers, Henry VIII*
C.S.P. Dom.	*Calendar of State Papers, Domestic*
C.S.P. For.	*Calendar of State Papers, Foreign*
C.S.P. Span.	*Calendar of State Papers, Spanish*
C.S.P. Ven.	*Calendar of State Papers, Venetian*
C. Scot. P.	*Calendar of Scottish Papers*
C. Hamilton P.	*Calendar of Hamilton Papers*
C. Bord. P.	*Calendar of Border Papers*
C.P.R.	*Calendar of Patent Rolls*

H.M.C.   *Historical Manuscripts Commission Report*
D.N.B.   *Dictionary of National Biography*

The place of publication of a book is only given when it is a town other than London. All Elizabethan spelling (except for the spelling of some proper names), has been modernised.

Dates have been quoted according to the modern calendar in which the year begins on 1 January, not on 25 March, as it still did in the Elizabethan period.

References

Since the references are confined almost exclusively to source material these have been grouped together according to the chapters in which they occur and placed at the end of the book.

INTRODUCTION

SOBRIETY and restraint are not fashionable today. In themselves
deliberately unexciting, they were among the virtues most highly
prized by sixteenth-century Protestants, even by Protestant
gentlemen of rank. The third Earl of Huntingdon consciously set
out to exemplify these qualities and in doing so helped to establish
a trend which became a part of the English character. Both for the
creation of the ideal of the Protestant gentleman and for the nature
of the development of English Nonconformity his career is of
very real significance. When writing about the Elizabethan scene,
naturally most historians have concentrated on the star performers,
the queen herself and her most prominent courtiers, the inscrut-
able Earl of Leicester, Essex to whom all things seemed possible
and who lost everything by aspiring too high, Cumberland both a
gallant and a privateer, the handsome and dissolute Oxford. Yet
the nobility could show another face, sombre, conscientious,
serious. Huntingdon belongs with the godly among his fellow
peers, with men like the second Earl of Bedford or the Earl of
Warwick: in some ways he would have resembled the Catholic
William, Lord Howard of Naworth, if he had had the time to
develop his scholarly interests further. Across the centuries these
noblemen find their spiritual descendants among such Victorian
evangelicals as the Earl of Shaftesbury whose zeal springing out
of a Christian family background spread to encompass all types of
social reform. Their influence upon English life may well have
outlasted that of their more glittering Elizabethan contemporaries.

Huntingdon's importance lies first and foremost in that he
furnished a pattern to the Protestant peers. The second half of the
sixteenth century presented reforming laymen with the kind of
opportunity they had never been offered since the conversion of

England from paganism. The national Church had not yet taken shape and the new Anglican clergy had no monopoly over theology: certain godly laymen seized this chance of guiding the Church along the paths they would have it follow. Huntingdon never wearied of promoting piety within his own household, of favouring zealots in the universities and of assisting them to positions of eminence in the Church. Nevertheless to label him a Puritan muddles the issue more than it clarifies it, for their detractors applied this epithet to any Protestant whose religious devotion exceeded that of his fellows. As far as he has left any record, Huntingdon adhered firmly to Calvinism; he did not concern himself particularly over the form the government of the Church should take, and was certainly no Presbyterian. He merely worked towards the apparently simple aim of a more thorough Protestant reformation within the Established Church.

Radical in religion, in other matters Huntingdon exhibited the conservatism which might be expected from one of his station, and in most ways led a life typical of many other members of the nobility. After an education at court during the latter years of Henry VIII and for the whole of the reign of Edward VI, he succeeded his father as third Earl of Huntingdon in 1560, and at once assumed the political and social leadership of his own county, Leicestershire. Elizabeth distrusted Huntingdon because of the claim he could make to the crown on her death, which some zealots openly espoused for the sake of his religion, and she kept him waiting for nine years before entrusting to him the temporary task of helping guard Mary, Queen of Scots in the troubled year of 1569. He proved his unquestioned loyalty in this assignment and she at last rewarded him in 1572 with office in the state worthy of his rank when she appointed him president of the council in the north, a post he held until he died in 1595. As the queen's viceroy over all England north of the Trent (apart from the county of Lancaster) Huntingdon had conferred upon him by this office far more personal responsibility than went with many posts at court, although these have been given more attention. For twenty-two years, during which time the Council in the North reached its maximum efficiency, he had the duty of seeing the region was quietly governed, and protected from hostile forces from within and without. With a foreign country across the border, and with Spain threatening invasion he soon discovered international politics took on a different aspect when viewed from York. Internally he directed his whole policy towards banishing those lawless elements which still survived even after the quelling of the Northern Rebellion of 1569 and creating a peace under which Protestantism could flourish and spread. He proved that a nobleman could perform the often tedious work of an administrator no less diligently than men of lower birth, like Cecil himself or Walsingham, who had been specifically trained for that sort of service.

Yet Huntingdon always remained a nobleman, one of that select band whose numbers, so long as Elizabeth reigned, never rose far above sixty.[1] All the peers knew each other and assembled together formally at court or at the time of parliament and fairly frequently entertained each other in their country houses, as on that grand occasion in 1561 when the Duke of Norfolk played host in Norwich to the Earls of Northumberland, Huntingdon and Surrey, Lord Scrope, Lord Abergavenny and other leading noblemen.[2] In the sixteenth century just as much as in the eighteenth, birth counted immensely in political and social life. Genealogy was a living study: most noblemen were related however distantly and they remembered their kinship. Huntingdon stood at the head of a large family whose members all looked to him for advancement; in exactly the same way he in his turn applied himself to powerful men in other families to whom he was connected by birth or marriage for their help and influence. Such relationships of noblemen with those above and below them have been very little studied.

*   *   *

Because, perhaps mistakenly, many think of Elizabethan history as relatively recent they all too readily overlook the technical difficulties which stand in the way of writing a biography in this period. Thomas Cromwell only ordered the keeping of registers of births, marriages and deaths in every parish in 1538; quite often these registers do not exist until well into Elizabeth's reign and, as is the case with Huntingdon, not even the date of a man's birth can be certainly known. Usually, by the second half of the century, personal letters survive in abundance but they tend to be business letters which rarely reveal much about a writer's personality. Huntingdon wrote innumerable letters about administration in the north to the central government, yet he was most reticent about expressing his personal feelings. He has described what he did, but not what he thought: indeed he worried lest his private correspondence might fall into unsympathetic hands and asked his privileged younger brother to burn the letters which had passed between him and his wife.[3] In this brother, Sir Francis Hastings, who shared his religious beliefs so passionately, Huntingdon had something of an *alter ego*. Hastings, a highly literate country gentleman, imposed upon himself the task of writing a commentary upon his brother's life and his words add much to what can be known about Huntingdon as a man. Nevertheless much still has to be deduced from his actions. Through his own writings Sir Francis made sure that posterity should be left in no doubt of his Protestant convictions, but Huntingdon, though no less committed, recorded almost nothing about his beliefs. Facts of his adherence to the cause have to be gleaned from the type of clerics he presented to livings, from his educational foundations, from the religious works dedicated to him. Again, while a complete list of the books dedicated to Huntingdon can be drawn up and details of books he gave to people and institutions occasionally emerge, no list of the books he owned exists, as one does for the second Earl of Bedford.[4] Although his public life is far better documented, lacunae remain even here: but for a chance statement by the clerk of the Lord Mayor of York nothing would have indicated that Huntingdon had already been created Lord Lieutenant in the north by 1581, for no record of the appointment survives in the Public Record Office. Complete transcripts of legal cases can now very rarely be found, and usually only the pleadings of the plaintiff or the defendant come to light with all the consequent possibilities of misinterpretation. Above all, estate records, particularly concerning the buying, selling and mortgaging of land are open to this fate, and to hope for accuracy in connection with Elizabethan accountancy is to be doomed to disappointment. The evidence, then, though in places overwhelming in bulk, is still fragmentary and fairly often the fragments do not fit together: it serves to hammer home the knowledge that Huntingdon after all lived four hundred years ago.

Although the Corporation of Leicester, in gratitude for his many kindnesses, in 1623 commissioned a portrait of the dead earl for their Guildhall only one portrait of Huntingdon painted in his own lifetime now exists and it hangs in the Tower. Finished in the Armada year, it shows a man already well into middle age wearing armour which probably had first been made for Ambrose, Earl of Warwick when he went to fight for the French Protestants at Le Havre in 1562, and still bore the Dudley emblems.[5] Huntingdon looks out somewhat sadly, his face stern and ascetic, the picture of a man who for a long time had experienced the cares of office in addition to his family worries.

To reconstruct the places where Huntingdon lived is nearly as hard as to breathe life into his personality. During the Civil War the Parliamentarians slighted the castle of Ashby de la Zouch in Leicestershire, Huntingdon's chief residence, which in his time provided lodgings for his family and seventy servants: only its outer walls stand today, a ruin romanticised by Sir Walter Scott. The great house at Stoke Poges which came into the hands of the lawyer Coke has gone, Lubbesthorpe in Leicestershire where Huntingdon's mother lived a widow for sixteen years has long been a depopulated village and nothing of her mansion remains. Only at York have some traces of Huntingdon's handiwork withstood the vicissitudes of time. The lodging of the Abbot of St. Mary's, converted in the reign of Henry VIII into the head-

B

quarters of the Council in the North, after enduring various indignities on the abolition of the council, and after accommodating the school for the blind for more than a century, has become one of the first buildings of the University of York. Newly restored, the wing he built and ornamented with his family crest, houses an educational enterprise surely after his own heart. The very countryside Huntingdon once knew has been no more immune to change: modern agricultural techniques have transformed the remote Yorkshire vales, which he found very difficult to penetrate when ordered to review the musters in wintry weather, almost as much as the gentler hills of Leicestershire or his rich moorland in Somerset.

This then is a biography attempted within the limits prescribed by the surviving evidence. A study of Huntingdon's career supplies some fresh information on less familiar aspects of the age and it has therefore seemed best to present the facts as they are as clearly as possible. At times it might have been easier to gloss over the difficulties and fill in the gaps with elaborate supposition but this perhaps has already been tried sufficiently for the period. The vigorous personality of Sir Francis Hastings still glows through his writings; it is hoped that through them and through this essay the brother he so much admired may also come to life. Huntingdon's biography has been divided into two parts, subjectively not chronologically, between his private life and his public career: again, determined by the amount of material available, the second part exceeds the first in length. As in his life, so in the book, religion makes the connecting link for like most of his contemporaries he believed religion should be lived in public as well as observed in private. To know his religion is in a sense to know the man.

PART ONE

The Man

CHAPTER ONE

Young Lord Hastings

THE MAKING OF A ZEALOT

> In his life I observed these excellent parts in him. He was a
> sincere professor of God's truth and therein most zealous; a
> loyal servant to his sovereign, and for her service would spare
> neither purse nor pains; a careful man for his country being in
> public causes most provident, and in private most upright,
> loathing and detesting to seek gain by either; a most loving
> and tender hearted man to his kindred, for whom he held
> nothing that he had too dear; a most pitiful man to the poor,
> and devising continually how to do them good; a true friend
> to his friends, and ready always to perform the true part of an
> honourable friend to them, and an honest man to all men in
> all actions. Here have you the portrait of as perfect a man as
> flesh and blood can afford, and yet I do not avow him clean
> from all imperfections, but I dare avow him clean from any
> gross corruption or villany. . . .[1]

So Sir Francis Hastings unashamedly wrote in a panegyric upon
his beloved eldest brother, Henry, the third Earl of Huntingdon a
few months after he had died in December 1595 and the circle of
his godly friends echoed his sentiments. Even when a more
impartial audience reads this outpouring of fraternal affection,
Huntingdon still seems something of a paragon among the
Elizabethan aristocracy. His Protestant enthusiasm, as his brother
knew from experience, had informed all his actions as much in his
private life as in his public career. This study aims at showing how
such a man could appear at such a time and how his beliefs affected
all he undertook.

From very early in his life Protestant writers held Henry, Lord Hastings up as a type of the ideal Christian nobleman. His religious zeal, not his birth, in the eyes of these writers made him worthy of honour, for 'true nobility . . . descendeth not to posterity by right of inheritance, nor is it purchased by riches, favour or any worldly means, but is the free gift of God, consisting in the excellency of the mind of the possessor, and not in the opinion of the variable multitude.'[2] They rejoiced that Lord Hastings showed himself a pious Protestant, even more for the influence his example would be bound to have on the rest of society, for while they may formally have discounted rank in their hearts they did not question the nobility's undoubted leadership. Born in 1536, Lord Hastings came of a new generation which had never known a Catholic England, but the experience of his elders was quite different.[3] Protestantism had not become safe and socially respectable until the reign of Edward VI: before then it had been a prescribed sect chiefly associated with the lower orders, and Mary's accession was to thrust the zealots back into danger and dishonour. Propagandists, eager for all the support they could muster, realised the value of a man who combined godliness and illustrious birth. No one could call Lord Hastings a new nobleman, and later in life when Catholics in self-defence ridiculed his devotion to Protestantism they never cast doubts upon his impeccable gentility. Had the government of Elizabeth been as weak as that of Katherine de Medici or Margaret of Parma he might well have become another Henry of Navarre or William of Orange whose beliefs and position in the state so greatly resembled his.[4]

The Hastings family traced its origins back to the somewhat shadowy yet still historical figure of Thomas de Hastings of Gissing in Norfolk whose grandchildren flourished there towards the end of the twelfth century and may well have been a cadet branch of the more famous medieval Hastings family, Earls of Pembroke. The ancestral connection with the county of Norfolk never developed; quietly and unspectacularly the family acquired land around Wistow in Leicestershire and Allerston in the North

Riding of Yorkshire until by the reign of Edward I, Sir Nicholas Hastings stood high enough in his county to be summoned to attend the king at Carlisle on his campaign against the Scots. The son of Sir Nicholas, Sir Ralph Hastings, made the first of the politic alliances which contributed so much to the family's gradual ascent when he married Margaret, daughter of Sir William de Herle, Chief Justice of the Court of Common Pleas and sister and coheir of Sir Robert de Herle of Kirby in Leicestershire. Like his father Sir Ralph fought for his king and he died from wounds received at the battle of Neville's Cross in 1346 leaving his son, Sir Ralph the younger, a competent estate in Leicestershire as well as Yorkshire. In different parliaments this Sir Ralph represented both counties as Knight of the Shire. He died in 1397 and three of his five sons, Ralph, Richard and Leonard, in turn succeeded him: the third Sir Ralph took part in the insurrection of Henry Hotspur and Owen Glendower against Henry IV and was beheaded in 1405, his brother Richard also had no issue and on his death in 1436 Sir Leonard Hastings at the age of forty became the head of the family. As a retainer of Richard, Duke of York he continued the family tradition of loyalty to the House of York, an allegiance which in the next generation transformed the family fortunes.

By 1455 the Hastings family had accumulated a respectable patrimony and was held in repute in Yorkshire and Leicestershire but it still had not risen to political prominence. The friendship between Edward of York and Sir William Hastings, eldest son and heir of Sir Leonard Hastings, completely changed the situation, and with dramatic suddenness the family found itself among the most powerful in the nation. The year after Edward IV had won the English throne he created Sir William Hastings Lord Hastings of Ashby de la Zouch giving him, to support the honour, the manor of Ashby in Leicestershire which had been held by the Lancastrian Earl of Ormond. From this time onwards Ashby became the centre of the family's influence. Lucrative offices followed in rapid profusion: Edward appointed Lord Hastings Master of the Mint, Chamberlain of the Royal Household, Receiver of the Duchy of Lancaster. For nine years he moved from strength to strength until the Lancastrians successfully revolted against Edward and restored Henry VI. In the bad days of 1469, Hastings's loyalty never faltered and when Edward fled abroad he stayed in England to rally the Yorkists and fought again for his master at the battle of Tewkesbury. As soon as he had regained the throne Edward rewarded him by appointing him Lieutenant of Calais and for the remainder of the king's life Hastings continued high in his favour with the fount of patronage open before him. He did not fail to make good use of his opportunities. In the subsequent history of the family, obtaining the wardship of Lady Mary Hungerford, in her own right the heiress to the baronies of Botreaux, Hungerford and de Moleyns, can be seen as one of his most signal triumphs. Hastings married Lady Mary to his eldest son, Edward, and with these great accessions in Buckinghamshire, Wiltshire, Somerset, Devon and Cornwall more than doubled the family lands at one stroke. In the end he paid the price of his meteoric rise; knowing his devotion to Edward IV and his young sons, Richard III dared not trust him and he had him executed in 1483. Yet his political fall did not bring economic disaster upon the family as it might well have done since, in an attempt to regain the support of the widow and her young son, Richard restored to them the confiscated family lands within a month of Lord Hastings's death. The bond, however, between the family and the House of York had at last been broken.

Tudor writers glorified William, Lord Hastings as a hero who had unjustly suffered at the hands of the usurping Richard. In *Richard III* Shakespeare, in order to emphasise his loyalty to Edward IV's heir, made Catesby (whom Richard later commissioned to murder the princes) report how he had sounded Hastings on Richard's proposed assumption of the crown,

> And finds the testy gentleman so hot,
> That he will lose his head ere give consent
> His master's son, as worshipful he terms it,
> Shall lose the royalty of England's throne.

More, upon whose chronicle Shakespeare heavily relied and who probably wrote not much later than a generation after Hastings's execution, also reflected upon his death in similarly edifying terms.

Thus ended this honourable man, a good knight and a gentle, of great authority with his prince, of living somewhat desolate, plain and open to his enemy, and secret to his friend: ethe [easy] to beguile, as he that of good heart and courage forestudied no perils. A loving man and passing well beloved. Very faithful and trusty enough, trusting too much.

So, in spite of former close ties with the Yorkists, fate looked kindly upon the Hastings family when Henry Tudor overcame Richard of York on the battlefield of Bosworth.[5]

Edward, the second Lord Hastings, extended the family fortunes no further but contented himself with husbanding and garnering his father's great gains, in itself no small achievement in a troubled age: by taking up arms for Henry VII against the Yorkists at the battle of Stoke he set an example of allegiance to the Tudors from which his descendants never swerved. He died, still relatively young, in 1506. George, his son, inherited his grandfather's tastes, though apparently not his ability and spent much of his time at court. In 1529 he fulfilled his ambition and the family at last reached a formal dignity commensurate with its great estates when Henry VIII created him Earl of Huntingdon. Again like his grandfather, the first Earl of Huntingdon succeeded in arranging a most significant marriage for his heir: Francis, Lord Hastings married in 1532 Katherine Pole, daughter of Lord Montague and granddaughter of Margaret, Countess of Salisbury, while his younger brother, Thomas, married her sister, Winifred. No connection could have been more honourable, or more dangerous. The Countess of Salisbury, niece to Edward IV, had transmitted to her descendants a good title to the crown should the Tudor line fail, and in 1532 only the sickly life of Princess Mary (in the direct line) stood between it and extinction. Not only their birth but their actions had brought the whole family into the king's displeasure. The Countess of Salisbury had remained

faithful to Katherine of Aragon throughout Henry's campaign for
the divorce and after her death befriended Princess Mary; her son,
Reginald, Cardinal Pole, stayed abroad, in open defiance of the
king, championing the Pope as head of the universal Church at the
very time when Henry had taken England out of the Catholic
communion. Henry did not contain his anger for long: Reginald
he could not reach, but he had his elder brother, Lord Montague,
executed for treason in 1538 and the old Countess of Salisbury
was brought to her death in 1541. Some tried to implicate the Earl
of Huntingdon in their fall but he survived unscathed and retained
his office of servant to Prince Edward.[6] Through this marriage
Huntingdon not only secured a further valuable increase in land
for his descendants (Lady Katherine eventually inherited substantial estates in Devon and Somerset), but also a claim to the
throne itself. By the beginning of Elizabeth's reign, since the sons
of the Countess of Salisbury had either died childless, or without a
male heir, Katherine, now Countess of Huntingdon, had become
her oldest living descendant and she had many sons to perpetuate
the claim.

The first Earl of Huntingdon, despite these moments of anxiety,
succeeded in establishing the Hastings family at the Tudor court
and from an early age Francis, his eldest son, accompanied him
there: at the coronation of Anne Boleyn, Henry dubbed him a
knight and at the christening of Prince Edward and the funeral of
Jane Seymour gave him a small part in the ceremonies.[7] On the
death of the first Earl of Huntingdon in 1544 Francis, the second
earl, immediately inherited his honours but he did not involve
himself directly in politics until after the death of the king; then
on the accession of Edward he came to the fore. Little now
remains among the Hastings manuscripts to reveal the character
of the second Earl of Huntingdon; there are no personal papers
and inevitably the man has to be deduced from his actions. He
emerges as a politique driven forward by his desire for family
aggrandisement, a realist who, like the Marquis of Winchester
knew how to bend with the times. Political expediency, it seems,

led him to join the extreme wing of Protestantism: he appears first among the opposition to Somerset and as a supporter of Northumberland during the last four years of Edward's reign gained entry to the highest councils of the state. On 13 October 1549 Huntingdon helped conduct Somerset to the Tower and on the same day Edward created him a Knight of the Garter; the next month he appointed him lieutenant over the forces setting out for the relief of the besieged city of Boulogne. Once Northumberland had a sure hold on power and Huntingdon had returned from his military duties in France he was brought into the Privy Council and regularly attended its meetings until the end of the reign.[8] Huntingdon reaped from the alliance with Northumberland a profit in proportion to his loyalty; he seized the chance of buying monastic lands in Leicestershire and Somerset, next, the office and fees as keeper of Conway Castle came his way and when the lands of John Beaumont, Master of the Rolls, fell forfeit to the crown through the latter's corrupt practices as a judge, Huntingdon obtained a grant of a very sizeable portion of them.[9] An opportunist on the alert to promote his own interest, Huntingdon can scarcely have comprehended the very different values which his eldest son was being taught to admire.

Henry, Lord Hastings, the future third Earl of Huntingdon, was Edward VI's senior by little more than a year and in recognition of his grandfather's position at court Henry VIII invited him to share the prince's studies. Before the king died he had joined the select group of young gentlemen surrounding Edward which included at varying times Henry, Duke of Suffolk and Charles Brandon his younger brother, Edward Seymour, Earl of Hertford; John, Lord Lumley; Henry, Lord Strange; James, Lord Mountjoy; James Butler, Earl of Ormond and Barnaby Fitzpatrick.[10] Henry VIII, a cultured monarch himself, called some of the most learned men in England to teach his son but, in choosing them, he also selected convinced Protestants. Sir John Cheke, Richard Cox, later Bishop of Ely, Sir Anthony Cooke and Roger Ascham all took a part in the education of Edward VI:

Henry may have desired his son to be a strong king and have seen sound learning as one means to this end; his schoolmasters, however, felt their first responsibility to be to produce a godly prince, supported by a religious magistracy. With alacrity Lord Hastings laid hold upon the training offered, imbibing with his companions the wisdom of the Greeks, growing proficient in the writings of the Romans, above all making his own the new theology for the first time married to Renaissance scholarship. According to Christopher Ocland, who wrote a Latin poem, published in 1582, love of Protestant piety early showed itself in him:

> Hic veterum libros ineunte aetate studendo,
> Qui Graece sophiam, vel qui scripsere Latine
> Voluit; collusor puero post seria Regi
> Magnorum antiqua Regum de stirpe propago.
> Praeconem hic sacrum Satrapas attentior audit,
> Exprimit et vita morum pietate relucens.[11]

Years later Huntingdon recalled an anecdote about his life with Edward VI. Fuller collected the story and told how the old Earl of Huntingdon, bred up in childhood with King Edward reminisced to Sir Thomas Cheke about his grandfather. Sir John Cheke had fallen so seriously ill that all his friends thought him on the point of death except Edward, who felt certain God would spare him to go on with his teaching. 'No, he will not die at this time,' he declared to his courtiers, 'for this morning I begged his life from God in my prayers and obtained it.' Cheke, Huntingdon went on to relate, did in fact recover.[12]

Memories of the high standard of scholarship expected of Edward and his fellow students, of the epistles and themes they wrote in Latin and Greek, of the long excerpts learned by heart, of their carefully compiled commonplace books of classical tags must have come back to Huntingdon when he drew up the statutes for the Free School in Leicester, scrutinising each page before sanctioning it with his signature. At Leicester the scholars of the three highest forms studied much Cicero, *Ad Herennium*, *De*

Amicitia, the orations and other works, a little Caesar, Vergil, Ovid and Horace, and in Greek, Aesop and Isocrates: they wrote their Latin letters and themes, 'repeated' the long passages they had learnt by heart and on Saturday mornings added useful phrases to their notebooks. There, too, a conscious attempt was made to inculcate godliness with good learning: the youngest children learnt to read from Calvin or Nowell's catechism in English, then graduated to Calvin's Latin catechism and Châteillon's scripture dialogues, *Dialogi Sacri*; the seventh form boys for the foundations of their Greek read the New Testament or Calvin's catechism which Henri Estienne had opportunely translated into Greek in 1551. This reflected extraordinarily accurately the scheme of learning pursued in Edward VI's circle suitably modernised by the inclusion of works of Protestant theology written in the subsequent two decades.[13]

Edward VI never finished his education, dying before his mentors decided he could lay his school books entirely aside but Lord Hastings moved on from his grammar learning to get a glimpse of higher matters. For a time, probably in 1548, he studied at Queens' College, Cambridge, though, in common with most young noblemen he did not proceed to a degree.[14] The final stage thought necessary to complete a gentleman's training consisted in a leisurely tour of the Continent to learn French and Italian and gain some knowledge of international politics. Uncertain conditions in England in the 1550's made this the most perfunctory side of Hastings's education and later in his life he regretted his ignorance of French which prevented him from helping entertain foreign embassies. He paid very brief visits to the Continent, and saw a little of France and the Low Countries but never reached Italy, the height of his ambitions.[15]

Nevertheless, in spite of these omissions, contemporaries without an excess of flattery could see in Lord Hastings the model young courtier and Renaissance gentleman. In 1556 Sir Thomas Hoby, married to Elizabeth Cooke, the learned daughter of Sir Anthony Cooke and one of Edward's schoolmasters, sent to him his translation of that textbook for all aspirants to true nobility, Castiglione's *The Courtier*. The book had long been celebrated at the courts of Europe in its original Italian but this was the first time it had been translated into English and Hoby hoped for its favourable reception:

And for so much as none but a noble young gentleman, and trained up all his lifetime in court, and of worthy qualities, is meet to receive and entertain so worthy a courtier, that like may fellowship and get estimation with his like, I do dedicate him unto your good lordship, that through your means, and under your patronage he may be common to a great many. And this do I not for that I suppose you stand in need of any of his instructions, but partly because you may see him confirm with reason the courtly fashions, comely exercises and noble virtues, that unawares have from time to time crept into you, and already with practice and learning taken custom in you: and partly to get him the more authority and credit through so noble a patron. For, no doubt, if you be seen willingly to embrace him, other young and courtly gentlemen will not shun his company.[16]

In the light of his subsequent career it is revealing to see that Hastings had already found a way to unite his love of Protestantism with his courtly accomplishments. In maturity he won renown not for his broad education, not even primarily for his patronage of scholars but because before everything else he placed his adherence to the reformed religion. His zeal appeared while he was still a youth and Thomas Paulfreyman stressed this side of his character in 1557 when he also thought fit to dedicate a book to him.

Although I have been sufficiently persuaded that your honour ever from the cradle have been trained up in the pathway of virtue and according to the profession of a true Christian have received instructions, as well in the sacred scriptures as also otherwise in profane learning: the knowledge of both which, with age, hath so largely grown, that ye need not my help and furtherance for the keeping of those things the better in memory which ye have with such diligence read: yet having an eye to your estate upon whose shoulders in time some charge of this commonwealth is like to lean (as commonly it happeth to all noblemen, but most worthily indeed to those whom God hath endued with the gift of understanding and knowledge) I thought it not unfit to present unto your good lordship this little book, entitled *The Treatise of Moral Philosophy*.[17]

With his father a close confederate of Northumberland and from his childhood accustomed to spending long periods at court, Lord Hastings very early became acquainted with the harsh world of politics: in 1553 he found himself caught up in the intrigues of his elders. As the year progressed and as Edward VI's grasp on life grew increasingly precarious Northumberland strove desperately to ensure that his ascendancy should continue after the king's death. He thought a series of dynastic marriages might buttress his position and bind his supporters more securely to his side so at the end of May 1553, when the death of Edward was daily expected, Northumberland married his son, Guildford Dudley to Lady Jane Grey and, almost immediately after this ceremony, went on to celebrate the double marriage of Lady Katherine Grey to Lord Herbert, the Earl of Pembroke's eldest son, and Lady Katherine Dudley to Lord Hastings.[18] For a few brief months Hastings had Lady Jane Grey for his sister-in-law. They must have already known each other for both came from noble houses in Leicestershire, both had spent much time at the courts of Henry VIII and Edward VI. They shared much in common and together they epitomised the godly and learned young people the Edwardian reformers had laboured to produce. John Aylmer had fostered Lady Jane's aptitude for the classics while Huntingdon had learnt under the royal schoolmasters: in both had been kindled such a burning love of Protestantism that they continued faithful to their religious profession until their death. For Lady Jane, the victim of her father's ambition, the end came soon; Hastings might well have suffered a similar fate. King Edward died on 6 July 1553 and Huntingdon with his son faced an unenviable choice. If Northumberland succeeded in his plan to place Lady Jane on the throne then Huntingdon could hope for some of the highest offices in the state, if he failed and Mary established her right then his rebellion could mean death for him and his heir. Huntingdon decided for the duke and accompanied by Hastings took to the field and advanced with Northumberland into the eastern counties against Mary's supporters.[19] Northumberland burnt Sawston Hall in Cambridgeshire, having failed by a few hours to capture Mary there, and insisted upon marching on in spite of the news of the uncertain allegiance of the council in London and the wavering loyalty of his own men. Lord Grey's hesitation began to affect others and a scuffle broke out among Northumberland's forces in which Hastings was wounded. In two days all was over. The council in London proclaimed Mary queen and Northumberland could do nothing except follow its capitulation: in the presence of Huntingdon, Grey and their sons he declared for Mary at Cambridge. Retribution came swiftly upon their failure and by 25 July Northumberland and three of his sons, Huntingdon and Lord Hastings were all prisoners in the Tower.[20] At this point Mary decided to exercise clemency and within a month gave the Countess of Huntingdon permission to visit her husband, and Huntingdon the liberty of the prison garden: in October he surrendered his Welsh offices to the crown and a few days later Mary released him, though for a time he still remained under house arrest, and Lord Hastings, whose offence in any case had been less heinous than his father's, received a free pardon in November.[21]

In contrast with her husband who had staked a great deal on Mary's exclusion the Countess of Huntingdon stood to gain from her accession to the throne. The Countess of Salisbury, her grandmother, had been the queen's godmother and governess: all through the years of disgrace when Mary had been displaced in her father's affection first by Elizabeth, and then by Edward she had remained loyal, and voluntarily shared her seclusion, indeed her association with Katherine of Aragon and Princess Mary may have provided Henry with an additional reason for desiring her death. Mary forgot neither her godmother's devotion nor the manner of her death. Scarcely had the second Earl of Huntingdon been freed from the Tower before his wife exhibited a bill in

The tomb of Francis, second Earl of Huntingdon (d. 1560) and Lady Katherine Pole

parliament petitioning that she and her sister Winifred, wife of Sir Thomas Hastings, be restored to the blood and estates of Henry Pole, late Lord Montague. The next year the queen granted the request in recognition of the service done to her by the Countess of Salisbury and the sisters were readmitted to the extensive Pole estates in Hampshire, Wiltshire, Devon, Somerset and elsewhere.[22]

At this stage in the family's history the second Earl of Huntingdon opportunely discovered other highly useful connections apart from his wife. His younger brother Sir Edward Hastings, happened to be his exact political opposite: while Huntingdon had associated with the extreme reformers during the reign of Edward VI, Sir Edward Hastings had continued to be an avowed Catholic; while Huntingdon had declared for Jane immediately upon the death of Edward, Sir Edward Hastings had rallied troops in Buckinghamshire to go to Mary's aid. Now he gained his reward. Very early in Mary's reign he became a member of the Privy Council and receiver of royal lands in the Home Counties: in 1554 Mary appointed him Master of her Horse, an office which had been Northumberland's, and also gave him some of the attainted duke's lands. Throughout the reign his power and influence increased and finally a few months before her death Mary created him Baron Hastings of Loughborough, granting him several estates including the manors of Loughborough and Market Bosworth in Leicestershire to maintain his dignity.[23] As a staunch Catholic from the beginning, he supported Mary's determination to reconcile the English Church with the See of Rome, though his loyalty did not prevent him from opposing her plans for a Spanish marriage to such an extent that the queen threatened to dismiss him from the Privy Council.[24] Once the marriage had been carried through no other issue arose to divide him from his mistress. Since he had no legitimate heir and so could not hope to create a subsidiary noble house he turned to his eldest brother's son and furthered to the best of his ability his cause with the queen.

From the end of 1554 Henry, Lord Hastings had an even more

c

influential relative, in this case a great-uncle, at the court. Soon after Mary's accession the Countess of Huntingdon realised that the time was ripe to reopen contact with Cardinal Pole whose allegiance to the Pope had long cut him off from his kinsfolk in England: now his nearest living relative, she sent two letters in succession to her uncle on the Continent. The cardinal read them avidly, they were, as he explained, the first he had received from his family for many years; alluding to the execution by Henry VIII of his brother, Henry Pole, Lord Montague, the Countess of Huntingdon's father, and of his own mother, Margaret, Countess of Salisbury, he described how grief made him unable to read the letters at one sitting for the remembrance of the loss of those whom he had left in good state on his departure from England. He looked forward with touching eagerness to a reunion with his surviving relations.[25] With Mary's marriage safely accomplished the emperor no longer had reason for delaying Pole's return to his own country and the queen at last authorised Sir Edward Hastings and Lord Paget to set out for Brussels in November 1554 to conduct him ceremonially back to England: they found him, they reported to the queen, a 'man of God, full of all godliness and virtue ready to humble himself to all fashions that may do good'.[26] The Earl and Countess of Huntingdon (more than ready to improve the occasion) asked the cardinal to stand godfather to their sixth and youngest son, Walter. Pole found letters from the countess waiting to greet his arrival, he met Henry, Lord Hastings for the first time and rejoiced with his mother over the 'gifts and graces' God had already bestowed upon him.[27]

Despite great occasions of the Church and State, Pole never lost his interest in the domestic affairs of the Hastings family. Naturally he concerned himself particularly with the welfare of his godson; as soon as Walter was old enough he took him into his own household at Lambeth and wrote happily to his niece that he made strides in his studies and he trusted he should grow both in virtue and learning.[28] Walter Hastings bore the marks of his great-uncle's careful training for the rest of his days: throughout Elizabeth's reign he passed a fairly retired life in Leicestershire almost certainly a crypto-Catholic; his wife, Joyce Roper, had definite Catholic connections and his son, Henry Hastings, made the Spiritual Exercises with Father Gerard.[29] Cardinal Pole showed himself no less kind to his eldest nephew: he thought highly of his ability and wrote frequently to his niece in his praise. Lord Hastings on his side spent much time in his great-uncle's company and through him he gained his first taste of foreign travel when in May 1555 he persuaded Pole to allow him to make a flying visit to France. Apologetically the cardinal wrote to the Countess of Huntingdon to explain how it had come about that her son had accompanied him to Calais contrary to his father's wishes. At first Pole had determined his nephew should remain at court but he prevailed upon him to permit him to go with him one stage, as far as Lord Cobham's house; a further concession took him to Canterbury and then he had his desire and went over to Calais. In mitigation, Pole said, Lord Hastings had only stayed there one day though Lord Arundel and other noblemen would gladly have detained him: even the winds had favoured the truant by giving him a fair passage, much better than Pole had had on his return in June. Hastings gained another glimpse of the Continent later that summer when he and his father joined the courtiers conducting King Philip to Brussels.[30] In the midst of the excitements of court life Pole encouraged his nephew to keep up some of his academic attainments. The cardinal continually received small tokens of affection from the Countess of Huntingdon, embroidered pockets and napkins, pasties of red deer: a gift he told her he would appreciate even more would be news of Lord Hastings's 'translation of the book written of nobility in that part I showed him, which I would take for a grateful present as he could give me'. Hastings obeyed and set to work on Osorius's *De Glorie* as well as on his *De Nobilitate*. The manuscript translations he produced were sufficiently well known to be referred to in flattering terms by Metellus in his introduction to Osorius's *De Rebus Emmanuelis, regis Lusitaniae* published a generation later.[31]

In their different spheres both his Catholic uncles exerted themselves to advance Lord Hastings and the behaviour of his father helped to rehabilitate the family. When in the winter of 1553–4 Wyatt rebelled against Mary, and Lord Grey and his brothers tried to raise the Midlands in revolt against the marriage proposed between the queen and Philip of Spain, Huntingdon remained loyal, and with a band of horsemen captured the Duke of Suffolk in Warwickshire. No love had been lost between the Grey and Hastings families poised in an uneasy equilibrium in Leicestershire where only the Greys' new brick mansion at Bradgate could rival the Hastings's massive pile at Ashby. During the reign of Edward VI it had seemed for a time as if Grey would prevail, but he lost all by this last desperate venture which brought both Lady Jane and himself to the scaffold in February 1554 and his whole house into eclipse. For the rest of the sixteenth century Leicestershire became a Hastings preserve. Nothing now seemed to stand in Lord Hastings's way: probably through the influence of his uncle, the Master of Horse, Philip appointed him one of the gentlemen of his chamber in 1554, and he probably owed to the same uncle, rather than to the cardinal whose health was declining fast, the first grant he received in his own right of the office of the Prince's Fee at Leicester which Mary passed three days before she died.[32]

Yet to Hastings all his promotion must have had a bitter taste and he can hardly have avoided reflecting whether he had gained the world at the cost of his soul. Latimer, Ridley, Cranmer, whom he had been taught to revere at the court of Edward VI, suffered death for their faith; other godly ministers, including his former master, Richard Cox, went into exile on the Continent; the Mass had taken the place of the sermons Hastings later delighted to hear. Rather than conform some members of the nobility also fled to Switzerland or Germany: Katherine, Dowager Duchess of Suffolk and her household, the Earl of Bedford, who had sat with the second Earl of Huntingdon in Edward's Privy Council, both chose to leave the country. Henry, Lord Hastings had no such alternative: Huntingdon conformed, and he had to follow his father's lead. Nevertheless his interior resistance proved to be remarkable. The love lavished upon him by Cardinal Pole could not alter his private convictions in the slightest and throughout Elizabeth's reign he displayed an intense revulsion for all aspects of Catholicism. Once he had the means of patronage at his own command immediately he begun to succour the ministers returning from exile. The holy places of Protestantism had been closed to him but he made certain that his heir was not deprived of the blessings of a sojourn in Geneva.

While Mary lived Hastings kept his own counsel, only one or two small incidents reveal where his sympathies lay. When the Spaniards first entered England in the train of Philip to celebrate his marriage with the queen, the Spanish ambassador picked up a rumour that Lord Hastings had been wounded in an affray with Philip's men.³³ More significantly, Lord Hastings maintained his friendship with Edward Courtney, Earl of Devonshire, and some of his earliest surviving letters are those to this hope of the Protestant faction. After a period in the Tower, Courtney had gone into exile on the Continent from which Mary would not permit him to return. Hastings dispatched letters to him there, envying him his chances of seeing Italy:

I hear your lordship hath been at Venice; wheresoever you be I would to God I were with you for that I should both have the sight of the country which I most desire to see and also your company from whom without flattery I would never be absent.

Hastings wrote this letter in January 1556: in May the government discovered a plot to depose Mary and place Elizabeth, married to Courtney, on the throne. This connection might have become very dangerous for him had Courtney not died of a fever in Padua in September.³⁴

What could not be achieved by plots came about through the course of nature: Mary's reign was visibly drawing towards its close and to the Protestants' joy she had no Catholic heir. On her death the career of Henry, Lord Hastings received a redirection

nearly as radical as that which had happened on the death of
Edward. Almost at once he lost his two protectors, for Cardinal
Pole died the very same day as the queen, while Edward, Lord
Hastings, although he lived for another fourteen years, lost all
political influence on the accession of Elizabeth: the Earl of
Huntingdon could no longer sponsor his son in their stead.
Frequently in his letters to his niece the cardinal had commiserated
with her on her husband's ill health and increasingly Hastings had
acted for his father. He supervised the legal confirmation of the
restoration of the Countess of Huntingdon's lands and then
watched over the sale of some of the estates: Pole wrote specially
to the countess in praise of her son's competence.[35] Lord Huntingdon's health did not improve under Elizabeth: he was able to
accompany the new queen from Hatfield to London at the time of
her accession, but when parliament assembled in the new year he
made his son one of his proxies in the Lords and in May 1559, in
the formal commission appointing him Lord Lieutenant of
Leicestershire, the queen specifically authorised Lord Hastings to
perform the office for his father during his sickness.[36] Nevertheless
the Earl of Huntingdon did not lose by the death of Mary:
Elizabeth confirmed to him the lieutenancy over Leicestershire,
the chief office he had held in the previous reign after Suffolk's
fall, and also granted him the court office of Master of the Hart
Hounds and a minor wardship.[37]

His father's weakness meant that Hastings learnt early the
responsibilities involved in caring for a large household. When
the Earl of Rutland considered marrying his son to one of the
earl's daughters, Hastings with his uncle, Edward, Lord Hastings
of Loughborough began the negotiations and reported on their
progress to his father at Ashby.[38] In estate matters, from 1557 he
had held a commission with others to grant leases extensively in
Leicestershire and in 1560 the earl and countess made him the
general surveyor of all their lands with freedom to grant leases, in
order that he might repay their debts.[39] As his illness grew upon
him there remained only one way in which the second Earl of

Huntingdon could forward his son, thrown so soon upon his own resources. Now that Robert Dudley had risen high in the queen's favour he could again afford to remember the marriage he had arranged during Northumberland's ascendancy between Dudley's sister and his own son. He wrote from Leicestershire begging him to further his interests at court but he did not live long enough to benefit from the connection. The second Earl of Huntingdon died in June 1560 and when at the end of the month Dudley suggested a visit to Ashby the third Earl of Huntingdon, his brother-in-law, welcomed him eagerly: his stay, he explained, would coincide with 'the woeful day of burial' appointed for 14 July.[40] The new Earl of Huntingdon at once revealed his strong sense of family loyalty by giving his father a costly funeral and burying him in a splendid Renaissance tomb. The early 1560's, like the 1590's, marked the end and the beginning of an age: the third earl was the contemporary of the queen and Leicester, sixteen years younger than Cecil and a member of the new generation destined to control affairs for the greater part of the reign. His father's death set him free, for the first time in his life, to act as he would and without the least hesitation he chose to advance the cause of true religion.

CHAPTER TWO

The Godly Household

ALTHOUGH only twenty-three, Huntingdon was old for his years when the care of a great noble household fell to him and he took up his responsibilities with the greatest earnestness. His education had taught him, as it had been designed to impress upon Edward VI, the irresistible claims of duty, and his duty in 1560 appeared quite clear; to advance God's true religion, to serve the queen in whatsoever capacity he might be required and to provide for his father's family. He waited for more than twelve years before he received high office in the state: in the meantime, being the man he was, he discovered that the reformed worship of God and the welfare of the Hastings family could be promoted side by side.

The second Earl of Huntingdon left a widow, five surviving sons and five daughters, all except Huntingdon and his eldest sister under age. Behind the family proper stood the retinue composed of all conditions of men from the gentlemen of the chamber, the yeomen and the grooms of the stable to the kitchen domestics: in 1564 after a period of retrenchment the household still included seventy-five servants, as equally dependent upon the earl as his immediate family.[1] Two problems, of religion and of finance confronted Huntingdon. On the one hand the household had outwardly professed Catholicism for the length of Mary's reign and while the link with Rome had again been broken on Elizabeth's accession there had not yet been time to instil in it a lively spirit of Protestantism: on the other the second Earl of Huntingdon had accumulated debts and entered into obligations which it did not seem possible his estates as at present managed could fulfil. True to his own nature, Huntingdon addressed himself first to the spiritual problem where his real interest lay.

Katherine Dudley, the new Countess of Huntingdon, came from a similar background to her husband, she belonged to the same generation and like him had received a Protestant upbringing.[2] Their marriage had been arranged from the most naked of political motives, yet it proved to be a happy one, never disturbed by those janglings which made the household of the Earl of Shrewsbury and Bess of Hardwick so notorious or even by the incompatibility such as divided the easygoing Earl of Cumberland towards the end of his life from Margaret Russell, his devout wife.[3] Huntingdon to his dying day tried to shelter his wife from family worries: she, for her part, frequently intervened with her brother and with the queen to ward off financial disaster from her husband. Religion united them and together they set about creating a godly household.

Although grammar schools were being founded and re-established apace at the beginning of Elizabeth's reign and this interest in public education grew steadily as the century progressed, gentle households still provided most of the training for the children of the aristocracy. The education given there had successfully been adapted to meet the demands of the times: the old instruction in courtly accomplishments remained, but increasingly a new emphasis was put upon religious teaching and scholarly virtues. An able young graduate from Oxford or Cambridge might find a better opening for his talents (as well as greater opportunities for advancement) in a nobleman's family than in a grammar school. Many of the most famous men in the Elizabethan church including Aylmer, Andrewes, and Hooker began their careers as private tutors and chaplains. These great households can be compared with the public schools of the last century for in them the leaders of the coming generation were moulded: they performed a service of vital importance in late medieval and Tudor society. Unfortunately, the new Earl and Countess of Huntingdon left no account of their intentions when they came in possession of their household: what they attempted to do has to be pieced together from scraps of information and certainly neither the names of all the children they received nor of all the chaplains they employed are known. Yet quite enough evidence survives to show the surprising extent of the household's influence: it could be seen reflected in a family in a remote part of Yorkshire, and in the conduct of a great-nephew during the Civil War.

Huntingdon intended his household to be a devout Calvinist one; some idea of its religion can be gleaned from the authors he patronised and the books they dedicated to him. Anthony Gilby, who had fled early to the Continent on Mary's accession and had taken a prominent part in producing the great work of the English exiles, the Geneva Bible, was the first of a line of convinced Protestant ministers to be protected by him. Refusing to compromise himself by accepting preferment in the insufficiently reformed English church Gilby spent the last twenty-five years of his life as Huntingdon's preacher at Ashby de la Zouch and helped transform the household there into a Protestant seminary in miniature. In 1570 he published the translation he had made for his patron of the *Commentaries of the divine, John Calvin, upon the prophet Daniel . . . especially for the use of the family of the right honourable Earl of Huntingdon, to set forth as in a glass, how one may profitably read the scriptures, by considering the text, meditating the sense therof, and by prayer.* All the evidence suggests that the Hastings family did read their way through this and similar Protestant manuals of worship, hearing first two or three verses from the prophet, then Calvin's exhaustive exposition, more verses, more exposition ending with a prayer also of Calvin's composition. The daily round of family prayers, morning and evening, personal meditation and examination of conscience, frequent attendance at sermons and the sacraments on weekdays and Sundays which Lady Margaret Hoby established when she had a household of her own she almost certainly copied from what she had learnt in Huntingdon's family.[4]

Gilby did not content himself merely with translating Calvin's commentary on Daniel for the Hastings family: in 1580 he followed it up with his translation of *The psalms of David truly opened and explained by Theodore Beza*, which Beza himself, Calvin's successor at Geneva, had dedicated to Huntingdon in the Latin original. Gilby offered it to the Countess of Huntingdon,

as a preparative to move your godly mind to the more diligent meditation of these arguments of the psalms, which are very profitable, and to this paraphrasis, which is a brief and a plain declaration of the meaning of the Holy Ghost, who did indite the psalms, and set them forth by his secretaries, David and others, as shall appear in their places.[5]

Time and again Huntingdon and his wife accepted similar translations of spiritual treatises. In 1572 Arthur Golding dedicated to Huntingdon his version of Beza's *Book of Christian questions and answers* to the intent that 'the children of light may learn from it how to withstand the adder's brood of the Romish Antichrist'.[6] John Stockwood, minister of Battle, in the same year, sent his translation of Bullinger's *Commonplaces of the Christian religion*: Gilby's example in publishing the lectures on Daniel specifically for the Hastings family had encouraged him to take this liberty.

I use not many words in excuse of my boldness, and procuring your honour's favour in accepting my travail [he explained to Huntingdon], because that in so doing, I should seem to doubt of that natural clemency and loving mind, that hath always been found in you towards such as have yielded up their labours for the furtherance of Christ his congregation, under your honourable protection.[7]

Huntingdon did not disappoint Stockwood; he subsequently became his 'very good lord and master', and received two further effusions from his pen. One was another translation, this time of a book by Daneau, *A fruitful commentary upon the twelve small prophets* which Stockwood recommended to the favourable protection of Huntingdon and his countess jointly, 'towards whom these many years I have been a faithful devoted servant and poor well-willer, and unto whom I willingly confess that every way I owe far greater duty than any way lieth in my small ability to yield and perform'; the other, Stockwood's own work, *A very fruitful sermon preached at Paul's Cross*. In this he bewailed the lack of 'faithful and painful labourers' in the Church and employed 'a great part of my endeavour to the stirring up of the minds of the godly magistrates to have an especial care and regard that as well the small flocks as the greater charges might be furnished with godly learned teachers'.[8]

Huntingdon quickly gained a reputation for his 'gentleness in accepting as well the good will of them which according to their ability offer but a mite, as also the great learning of those divines, which in their sermons and writings do much excel the most part of those pastors that are not unprofitable instructors of the unlearned', and this emboldened Thomas Brasbridge to present him with his 'short exposition of the prophet Abdias'.[9] John Field, the organising secretary of the Presbyterian movement within the English Church, did not let slip the opportunity to pay tribute to one of the outstanding patrons of zealots, and from him Huntingdon received his translation from the French of *Four sermons of Master John Calvin* which he coupled with the pious wish that God would strengthen him

in that happy course of the gospel, wherein of his singular goodness he hath drawn you: that you may be as a bright star in his Church comfortably shining forth in constancy and maintenance of the same truth, to the stirring up of many: that not only it may be given you (as the Apostle saith) to believe in him, but also to suffer for him. For this is true honour to suffer for righteousness.[10]

Yet further sermons, calculated to increase devotion, came from Bartimaeus Andrews, a founding member of the Dedham Classis: he dispatched to Huntingdon in 1583, *Certain very worthy, godly and profitable sermons upon the fifth chapter of the songs of Solomon*.[11]

The Countess of Huntingdon's religious opinions seem nicely to have echoed her husband's views. Little more than two years after they had moved to York in 1572 she arranged on her own initiative for Matthew Hutton to preach at the wedding of one of her cousins, and later on a visit to the south she spoke with her brother on behalf of the Protestant dean writing to Hutton to let him know of Leicester's good opinion of him.[12] In 1589 she obtained from Elizabeth the bestowing of a prebend in Southwell minster, made vacant on the promotion of Dr. Hutton, but then the queen considered Lady Huntingdon's zeal exceeded her discretion. The countess asked to have Mr. Spark appointed, presumably Robert Spark, her husband's chaplain, yet on his bill coming before the queen she made difficulties about signing it, saying she had heard the man was tainted with Puritanism. Lady Huntingdon enlisted the aid of both the Archbishop of Canterbury and the Bishop of London in an attempt to convince the queen that the rumour referred to another Mr. Spark, for there was indeed a Thomas Spark who had preached several times at Paul's Cross in the 1560's, and had been involved with Lawrence Humphrey in the controversy over vestments: in spite of her efforts, the name seems effectively to have barred the man. Considering the Countess of Huntingdon's intimacy with the queen this is scarcely likely to have been the only time when she tried to influence royal appointments in the Church.[13]

Works of devotion continued to be sent to the Countess of Huntingdon long after her husband's death. Francis Bunny, when dedicating his *Comparison between the ancient faith of the Romans and the new Romish religion* described at first hand Lady Katherine's 'great zeal and fervent desire and love to the truth, and your Christian care to augment your knowledge of the will of God'. She had apparently favoured during his lifetime Richard Greenham, that pattern of Protestant ministers, who so faithfully served his flock at Dry Drayton in Cambridgeshire: after his death Henry Holland published his works posthumously, offering them jointly to the Countess of Cumberland, the late Earl of Bedford's daughter, and the Dowager Countess of Huntingdon, since Greenham, he explained, had been

a man well known unto your honours, and to those most religious patrons of all piety and good learning, the right honourable Earls (of blessed memory) of Huntingdon, Warwick and of Bedford, which now sleep in the Lord. Of them much was he reverenced in his life-time: of your honours much lamented after death, for that you know the loss of such to be no small wrack unto the Church and people of God.[14]

The same two noble ladies, celebrated for their 'Christian carriage and profession of religion' received from Thomas Savile, in 1606, his *Raising of them that are fallen*. The last tribute to the Countess of Huntingdon's 'integrity of heart unto God, manifest by your most virtuous life, and zealous love unto true religion' came from Thomas Collins in 1610 when he published his religious poem, *The penitent publican, his confession of mouth, contrition of heart, unfained repentance and fervent prayer unto God for mercy and forgiveness.*

Into this circle of piety which he and his countess had laboured together to bring into being, Huntingdon eagerly introduced his younger brothers and sisters: some responded enthusiastically in a way which could not have failed to gratify him though two at least found little to attract them in Protestantism. Sir Francis Hastings, who most admired his brother for his religion, described in glowing terms his concern for his family:

The tenderness of his hearty affection in love to his kindred and care to do them good appeared most plainly by many and sundry proofs: for how honourably he did deal with all of us that were his brethren from the day of our father's death to his own dying day we must all acknowledge, and all the world can witness it, and such of us as had children he did double his kindness upon us in them, both in easing our charge and in caring to breed them and bring them up in the fear of God. And for such as were further off to him in kindred, his care was not wanting to do them any good either to train them up in learning or otherwise dispose of them as their inclinations did lead them in the knowledge of God and his gospel, and to this end no cost did he spare at any time: and thanks be given to God, the Church hath the profitable use of some that by his care and charge were brought up in the nursery of true divine learning.[15]

As a guide when planning the future of his sisters and brothers Huntingdon had his father's will which set out each child's material inheritance. Lady Katherine Hastings alone among his sisters did not need his help: she had already secured her place in society when, little more than a child, she had been married by her father to Edward Fynes, Lord Clinton (later Earl of Lincoln), much to the apprehension of Cardinal Pole, who disapproved of early marriages unless the young people lived separately until they reached maturity.[16] In 1560 his four other sisters, Frances, Elizabeth, Mary and Anne, all looked to him for their advancement. The second Earl of Huntingdon had left each of his daughters a yearly stipend of £20 until they married or became eighteen: on their marriage each had a jointure of £1,000, but their brother wished to do more than this. He entered into an undertaking in 1562 with John, Earl of Oxford that his heir, Lord Bulbeck, should marry either Lady Elizabeth or Lady Mary within a month of his attaining his eighteenth birthday provided his sister consented, and offered as a dowry 1,000 marks over and above the £1,000 laid down in his father's will.[17] This scheme came to nothing and, considering the slights the young and feckless Earl of Oxford later put on Burghley's daughter Ann whom he did marry, it would seem that Lady Elizabeth and Lady Mary both escaped an unhappy match. The prospects of all Huntingdon's sisters brightened later in 1562 through another contract he made with their mother which doubled their marriage portions; in return for the Dowager Countess of Huntingdon's leasing the greater part of her lands in Hertfordshire, Hampshire, Wiltshire, Somerset, Devon and Cornwall which she held partly in dower but more largely in her own right, Huntingdon promised to pay her an annuity of £960 and his sisters £1,000 each in addition to the £1,000 left them by their father when they married. Eventually two of the sisters were established in that station in society into which they had been born; Lady Frances Hastings married Henry, Lord Compton (probably in 1567), and in December 1571 Lady Elizabeth Hastings married Edward Somerset, later Earl of Worcester, both, like their sister Lady Katherine, becoming the wives or mothers of earls.[18]

For a brief moment Lady Mary Hastings contemplated a much

more exotic match. To intelligent Englishmen the Muscovites still sounded almost as strange and remote as the Indians of America even though their merchants were trying assiduously to open new contacts with Russia, whose czar on the whole welcomed their pioneering ventures. Ivan the Terrible heard so much praise of the English queen from these traders that, like many another contemporary prince, he contemplated marrying her. Elizabeth considered his aspirations impertinent and outlandish and gave him short shrift, but the czar persisted in his determination to marry an English lady of the royal lineage and heard mention of the name of Lady Mary, the only lady of suitable birth still single. In the autumn of 1582 his ambassador, Pissemsky, who arrived in England to treat for an alliance between Russia and England, also had instructions to open negotiations for his master's marriage. The queen received the proposal with little enthusiasm; she told Pissemsky that Lady Mary had only recently recovered from smallpox and gave this as a reason for not allowing her portrait to be painted and sent to Russia. Only after much procrastination would she agree to the ambassador's actually seeing the lady duly attended by maids of honour and gentlemen in May 1583: then, to the amazement of the English court the Russian prostrated himself before Lady Mary, doing her homage as though she had already become the czarina. The matter went no further. Lady Mary was said to have been frightened by reports of the czar's cruelty, while the ambassador could not deny that the czar already had one wife and she, moreover, had just borne him a son. Later in the year Pissemsky returned to Russia accompanied by Sir Jerome Bowes who had the duty of persuading the czar to abandon the marriage plans, giving as reasons the lady's ill health, her inability to make the long journey and the reluctance of her family to part with her. After these excitements Lady Mary's friends nicknamed her the 'Empress of Muscovia'. She died not long after this, unmarried, like her sister Lady Anne Hastings, who predeceased her by many years.[19]

Convention permitted Huntingdon to leave his sisters' educa-

Lawrence Humphrey, President of Magdalen College,
Oxford, and Regius Professor of Divinity, 1560–89

tion to his mother while their birth assured them a ready entry to court circles, but he clearly felt his duty required him to supervise his brothers' upbringing far more closely and only Sir George Hastings contrived to slip through his fingers. He was, in any case, the least likely of the young Hastings to have been influenced by Huntingdon, for he was only a year or two younger than his brother, in contrast with Edward, Francis and Walter who were all Huntingdon's juniors by more than eight years. When Huntingdon became earl, George Hastings alone among the brothers had already achieved financial independence. The second Earl of Huntingdon had arranged another early marriage for him and in 1556 he had married Dorothy Port, one of the daughters and coheirs of Sir John Port of Etwall in Derbyshire; only two years later Port died and his daughters shared his estates between them and consequently Sir George entered early into his wife's inheritance. Throughout his life he seems to have kept some distance from his elder brother and he certainly never loved Huntingdon with the devotion of Edward or Francis. Religion may have caused the division, for contemporaries knew of the suspicion, voiced by Camden, that the brothers 'while agreeing in brotherly love yet were not of one mind in religion'.[20] In later life George seems to have sympathised with Catholics; his wife had Catholic relations, including Father John Gerard, her nephew and one of the most brave and resourceful priests on the English mission towards the end of the reign; searchers captured a Catholic layman at Hastings's house in 1586, while Catholic plotters favoured George's claim to the throne to the exclusion of his elder brother. When he eventually succeeded his brother as fourth Earl of Huntingdon, Sir Edward and Sir Francis anxiously watched to see whether he would continue to protect the Protestant preachers sponsored by their brother. To their evident relief he conformed and in any case his lack of enthusiasm had no lasting effect since he did not live long as an earl before his place was taken by his undoubtedly Protestant grandson.[21]

Unlike Sir George Hastings, Edward, Francis and Walter

D

Hastings in 1560 depended entirely upon Huntingdon for their promotion. The second Earl had stipulated that up to the age of fifteen each of the boys should receive 20 marks a year for his maintenance, this being increased to 40 marks until he reached twenty-one when manors and rents bringing in an annual income of £60 were to be assured to him for life. Huntingdon dealt with his younger brothers as generously as with his sisters. In 1572 he granted his brother Edward an annuity not of £60 but of £100 and once his fighting days ended Edward established himself, with his brother's goodwill, at Leicester Abbey.[22] Francis and Walter Hastings also became substantial country gentlemen, Sir Francis until the 1580's settling on the manor of Market Bosworth in Leicestershire and Walter spending all his life at Kirby Muxloe in Leicestershire. The brothers' marriages in every case supplemented their inheritance: probably as early as 1567 Francis Hastings married Magdalen Langford, widow of Sir George Vernon and daughter of Sir Ralph Langford, 'the king of the peak'; in the 1570's Sir Edward Hastings married another widow, Barbara, eldest daughter and coheir of Sir William Devereux and previously wife of Edward Cave of Ingarsby, in Leicestershire; and lastly Walter, in the same decade, married Joyce, daughter of Christopher Roper of Linstead in Kent.

Huntingdon amply fulfilled his father's trust, yet he thought first not of his brothers' material prosperity but of their spiritual welfare and for this reason paid the closest attention to their education. Francis and Walter both studied at Oxford: there is no evidence whether Edward did or not; he certainly read law at the Middle Temple, for in 1562 he was sharing a chamber there with Edward Ameredith, later one of Huntingdon's solicitors.[23] It has often been said that at the beginning of Elizabeth's reign Oxford tended towards Catholicism at a time when Cambridge had already committed itself to Protestantism but this is too sweeping a generalisation: neither university bore a simple religious stamp. At Cambridge, so long as John Caius remained master he had room for Catholic sympathisers in his college; Philip Baker, the

Provost of King's and Vice-Chancellor in 1562 was also subsequently charged with popery.[24] These Cambridge colleges at least can be compared with St. John's College at Oxford in the 1560's where Edmund Campion studied in the company of senior members predominantly conservative in religion. Yet Oxford, no less than Cambridge, in the same decade contained some of the leading Protestants, expecting and working for a further reformation in the Church: this makes it easier to understand why Huntingdon chose Oxford for his younger brothers rather than his own university. Lawrence Humphrey who had been a former exile and remained a close friend of Anthony Gilby was President of Magdalen and Huntingdon decided to send Francis Hastings there. Another radical and Marian exile, Thomas Sampson, had been made Dean of Christchurch. In 1562 Huntingdon presented books to the college, the works of St. Augustine and Gregory Nazianzen in Latin and Greek, which had only quite recently become available in print: at this time some of the more learned Protestants had high hopes of using arguments from the Greek fathers against their Catholic opponents.[25] The Hastings boys were in Oxford in the spring of 1565 when the controversy over vestments broke and the High Commission in London called Sampson and Humphrey with other ministers before it for refusing to wear the surplice. Thomas Sampson would not conform and lost his deanery; significantly he found a safe haven for the rest of his life as Master of Wyggeston Hospital in Huntingdon's borough of Leicester: Humphrey, since he had not been appointed by the crown, succeeded in remaining at Magdalen. The boys' tutor there was one Carolus Baldus, who reported to Anthony Gilby in 1566 Francis's great progress in Latin and French and that Walter also showed promise. Later in the year their eldest brother came in the queen's train when she visited the university in state and with other persons of rank made the most of the opportunity of hearing Humphrey read at the Divinity Schools.[26]

Having been subjected to the same education, the Hastings

brothers yet reacted very differently. Sir Edward Hastings, while no scholar by inclination, remained a convinced Protestant for the rest of his life. He chose a military career and first appeared in arms in 1569 'when he went against the rebels in the north': in August 1570 the Earl of Sussex knighted him at Carlisle and three years later he petitioned for a commission to lead a company of men across the border to quell the loyalists holding Edinburgh Castle for Mary. In 1581 he was still a captain up in Berwick, but after this, apart from the Armada year, he established himself in Leicestershire and threw himself into the campaign against local recusants, uncovering with great eagerness the secret 'practices' of the papists to the government. So enthusiastic a Protestant did he become that Sir Francis Hastings thought it necessary to counsel him against the excesses of Martin Marprelate.[27]

Walter Hastings's life could not have been more different: he passed his time in Leicestershire consolidating his estate at Kirby Muxloe and in the Forest. A Catholic sympathiser, if not an avowed Catholic he apparently never forgot who his godfather had been. The Dowager Countess of Huntingdon may have secretly supported her youngest son, for of her, too, Catholics continued to speak kindly.[28] This religious division among the Hastings brothers corresponds to no age division; it cannot be explained by the fact that the older children were brought up as Protestants while the younger children remained loyal to the revival of Catholicism under Mary, nor by motives of rebellion against a strict father or elder brother and particularly not by economic motives, for Walter, the Catholic and youngest brother, because of living a retired life appears to have been far more prosperous than the two Protestant brothers next to him in age. In the case of each of the brothers their religion seems to have been a matter of personal decision and conviction. Many other Elizabethan families must have been split by religion, and especially families with scholarly interests. The totally different ways in which the Reynolds brothers developed caused consternation at Oxford. John Reynolds, a fervent Calvinist, became President of

Corpus Christi and put the case for the Nonconforming ministers
at the Hampton Court conference of 1604, yet one of his brothers
was expelled from Corpus for Catholicism in 1568 while his more
famous brother, William, was received into the Catholic Church
in the next decade; he studied and taught at Louvain and Douai
and died a priest in Antwerp. This was an age when men who
cared deeply about their faith tended to be attracted to one of the
two extremes.

* * *

Huntingdon had failed to impart his enthusiasm for Protestantism to Sir George and Walter: Sir Edward, it is true, grew into a
zealot, but his real and most resounding spiritual success came
with his next to youngest brother, Francis, who received from
Huntingdon such a firm grounding in the principles of Protestant
piety that henceforth they guided his every action and remained
with him until the end of his long life. From his arrival in Oxford,
Francis Hastings applied himself diligently to his work, and
acquired a great admiration for Lawrence Humphrey. The first
fruits of his studies, a Latin exercise in oratory delivered in
Magdalen Hall, he duly dispatched to his eldest brother as a token
of gratitude for the benefits he had conferred on him.[29] From
Oxford he probably went for a time to one of the Inns of Court
like his brother Edward, for in 1574 he was admitted a member
of Gray's Inn.[30] While in London he made contact with the more
radical Protestants and, retaining his close links with his family in
Leicestershire, he provided a useful connection between the
Genevan émigrés in the capital and those others who had settled in
the county. He carried letters from Lawrence Tomson in London
to Gilby at Ashby de la Zouch and came up from Leicester with
letters from Thomas Sampson. A close friendship developed
between Francis Hastings and Sampson and the young man lent
the old scholar books, including a history of the recent colloquy
between the Catholics and the Calvinists at Poissy which Sampson
proceeded to translate from French into English: adding a short
confession of the Christian faith he published it with a dedication

to the 'right worshipful Master Francis Hastings' which included
a graceful compliment to his facility in French.[31] This interest in
languages may well have combined with his love of theology to
attract him to the French Protestants in London: on his own
initiative in 1573 he gathered a collection from the gentlemen of
Leicestershire for the poor of the French Church and brought up
in person £10 4s. to the church deacons.[32] Doubtless the Leicestershire gentry contributed the more readily to Francis Hastings's
appeal because of the widespread sympathy for the Huguenot
refugees newly arriving in England after the massacre of St.
Bartholomew which had so horrified Protestant Englishmen. Sir
Philip Sidney, his near contemporary and Huntingdon's nephew
by marriage, had been staying with Walsingham (then the queen's
ambassador) in Paris when the Catholic mob had been incited to
murder the Protestants assembled to celebrate the marriage of
Henry of Navarre. Neither forgot the terrors of that night and the
shock they received helps to explain the revulsion they ever
afterwards showed towards Catholicism.

In Leicestershire, Francis Hastings did not confine his friendship among the radicals to Sampson and Gilby; Thomas Wood,
the intrepid Puritan layman and former exile who had moved from
London to Leicestershire, by 1570 attached himself to him and
made him one of the overseers of his will.[33] Nor did Hastings
forget his admiration for his Oxford president: in 1573 he wrote
to Humphrey to urge him to take up the bishopric he had heard he
was being offered, since he feared he might decline it for conscience
sake. Humphrey, thanking his former pupil 'for your good advice,
which may seem to proceed even from one that may be not only a
scholar of mine but a master in Israel', assured him he thought 'it
no sin to desire the good work of a true bishop'.[34] More than a
generation later, in the parliament of 1601, Hastings expounded
to the House of Commons his old teacher's somewhat unorthodox
definition of the four types of Puritans:

I learned of Dr. Humphrey who was sometimes my tutor a division of
four sorts of Puritans: first the Catholic which holds that a man cannot

sin after baptism, secondly the papist, which is such a merit-monger, that he would not only save himself by his own merits, but by the merits of others also, a third sort are the Brownists or Family of Love, a sect too well known in England, I would they had never so been, the fourth and last sort are your evangelical Puritans, which insist wholly upon scriptures as upon a sure ground; and of these [Hastings added in parenthesis] I would we had many more than we now have.[35]

In nothing was Francis Hastings more clearly Huntingdon's brother than in his passionate longing to pass on the benefits of his religious upbringing. He sent one of his earliest letters, a moving appeal to remain faithful to the Protestant cause, to his otherwise unknown cousin Anne, who was a Protestant convert in a Catholic household. Anticipating the hostility the girl would encounter, Hastings, 'for the great desire I have of your increase in knowledge and understanding of true religion' felt impelled 'to scribble unto you a few lines' which grew into an extremely long letter. He knew well the moral pressure which would be put upon her.

I know they will say to you, your father, your mother, all your friends and kindred are good Catholics, and in professing this religion you must needs condemn them and all your forefathers which were wise and learned, therefore beware what you too do. But to this you may easily answer, 'Each one is to be saved by his own faith and not by the faith of any other', and with Cyprian you may say, 'We are not to take what they did which were before us, but what Christ did which was before all, and follow that'. As for condemning them, we do not, but leave that to the Lord to whom only it belongeth to condemn or save as it shall please him. I know they will not be ashamed to say, it belongeth not to you to deal in the scriptures, and what should you do meddling in matters of religion, but how absurdly that is spoken the words of our saviour Christ doth manifestly prove where he saith generally to all sorts, 'Search the scriptures, for they bear witness of me.'

Having gone on to attack purgatory, the doctrine of the sacrifice of the Mass, the mediation of the saints, in fact all the distinctive Catholic doctrines, Hastings took leave of his cousin in a great cloud of rhetoric:

Now therefore seeing what great difference there is between the truth of the gospel and the counterfeit religion of popery . . . do you beware, good cousin, how you do harken to any carnal persuasions in this behalf: let neither loss of friends, loss of living, no nor loss of life, draw you to deny the truth, for what can all the friends in the world do for you, if the Lord Jesus forsake you, what can store of living profit you, if the Lord Jesus bless it not, what comfort can you have of life being estranged from Christ, to be short, what benefit get you in gaining the whole world if you damn your own soul? Comfort yourself therefore in Christ, rest upon the Lord, depend on his providence, for he is ready and willing to help all those that put their trust in him.[36]

Through Huntingdon's aid established upon the family manor of Market Bosworth, supported by a wife as pious as himself, Hastings gladly assumed the duties of a godly magistrate. From at least 1571 he appeared regularly on the commissions of the peace for Leicestershire and undertook the office of sheriff in 1572 and again in 1581.[37] When his brother moved to York he supervised for him his favourite educational scheme, the building of the Free School in Leicester; and at Wyggeston Hospital (the other Leicester charitable foundation reorganised by Huntingdon), he helped Thomas Sampson to remove all traces of popery, acting as his intermediary with Burghley for the confirmation of a hospital lease.[38] Hastings shared with Sampson his fierce hatred of Catholicism and early directed his energies to the task of banishing recusants from the county: in 1577 he sat on a commission charged with certifying the number of Catholics in Leicestershire and in the following year the Privy Council singled him out for praise for his diligence in searching out disguised priests.[39] To Walsingham, later, he felt free to confide his fears that this 'viperous brood' of Catholic priests would spread far and wide to contaminate the whole realm unless sterner measures were taken to control them. He besought God to give Walsingham strength to continue his labours for the good of the Church and Commonwealth:

I confess it passeth the bounds of my calling to rip into the diseases of these two, and it is beyond my reach to judge of either, but yet as a poor member of the body I may say . . . that I feel this body is not free from infection of sickness, else might I seem over-senseless, and to be void of that feeling care that ought to be in every good Christian and true Englishman, and feeling this ... my place will bear it to pray that England may long continue an happy nation to possess this great light of the gospel with increase and to enjoy this rare government in peace with great comfort. ... [40]

As a younger son Hastings had not the same means as Huntingdon had for acting as a patron of Protestants but he fell no whit behind him in his intentions. His first-known intervention in Church affairs happened in Leicestershire. The queen had presented Adam Squire to Hastings's own parish of Market Bosworth in 1577 and while his Protestantism could not be called in question his conduct did not conform to Puritan standards. Not only was he a pluralist, and yet frequently in debt, but rumour also gave out that he ill-treated his wife, the daughter of Bishop Aylmer.[41] In 1587 Aylmer, with other high commissioners, ordered Squire's sequestration that his creditors might be paid, and required two local gentlemen, Francis Hastings and George Purfrey to take possession of his property. The directive caused Hastings the greatest spiritual strife, for he in no way countenanced pluralism nor condoned Squire's reputed way of life, yet the sequestration provided merely for the good of the creditors, leaving the people of Bosworth without a minister. He wrote to Aylmer explaining why he could not approve of the sequestration and suggested an alternative course to the bishop; Squire should be made to forfeit his other benefices, tied to his cure of Bosworth, and attached to the Hinckley conference for an exercise to himself and others in learning; or, if his conduct was beyond reform, he should be displaced from his benefice and a worthy minister appointed.

Our days, my lord [he told Aylmer], require rather a continual care how to feed and teach generally the hungry and ignorant people then any care to fill our purses: ... and surely I am persuaded that the Lord's blessing will sooner follow him that seeketh the discharge of his duty in his calling, without regard of high promotion or great wealth, then of him that aspireth to these two latter and neglecteth or little regardeth his calling.[42]

Since Francis Hastings was a friend of Thomas Cartwright who in his Lady Margaret divinity lectures, delivered in Cambridge in 1570, had first set out a scheme to transform the English Church on a fully Presbyterian system, he could scarcely be expected to show an undue reverence to bishops. In the same year as he rebuked Aylmer he submitted a 'Christian Treatise' of his own composition to Cartwright for his criticism: he found in it

matter of thanksgiving unto the Lord for your sound knowledge of our holy religion, and that the blameless walking in the same for which you are commended proceedeth not from an imitation only of those whom you esteem of the better sort but (as it ought) from a certain and ruled knowledge out of the word that the same is acceptable unto God in Jesus Christ.[43]

Hastings never abandoned Cartwright, not even at the time of his greatest disfavour with the Anglican hierarchy. From Guernsey where he had taken refuge in the household of the governor, Sir Thomas Leighton, Cartwright continued to write to him on behalf of a young minister, William Bradshaw whom Hastings had previously maintained at Cambridge and may well have sent to live with him in Guernsey.[44] The intellectual content of Cartwright's Presbyterian teachings would have appealed to Hastings as an educated man: 'popularity' he could not abide and when the Martin Marprelate tracts appeared in the 1580's in common with many respectable Protestants he was horrified, not so much by their savagery as by the vulgarity with which they attacked the Establishment. In great agitation he advised Sir Edward Hastings against these lampoons, arguing that Martin's 'vein of writing seemeth little to savour of a well seasoned spirit'.

Good brother be you warned, and let us all be warned by others perils to keep ourselves every way from consenting to Martin's course: or consulting with any that are known to favour him about that matter, unless it be to endeavour to withdraw them from that humour, for I am verily persuaded he hath no warrant out of God's book for the manner of his dealing. I cannot deny but that our Church hath many defects, and yet dare I not affirm that this is the way to reform them: it is a good think [*sic*] to desire the amendment of things amiss but it cannot be good to seek to amend them by a wrong course, it is a commendable thing to long after reformation, but it deserveth no commendation to seek it unorderly. . . .[45]

One way of working for reform which Hastings entirely approved was the ensuring of a supply of young men well trained in religion ready to enter the Church. From its beginning he supported Mildmay's plan to found a specifically Protestant college in Cambridge, and in June 1585 he presented Emmanuel College with an annual rent-charge of £8 issuing out of his lands in Leicestershire and it was probably he who influenced Huntingdon to give livings to the college later.[46] The type of man presented to a living concerned Hastings greatly and particularly after 1583 when he moved to Somerset to supervise the management of Huntingdon's estates he became increasingly preoccupied with ecclesiastical matters. When spending a night in Exeter on Huntingdon's business in September 1583 he took the opportunity of reproving his remote kinsman, Sir Richard Grenville, for his treatment of 'that godly, learned and painful preacher, Master Eusebius Pagit' who had formerly lived near Hastings in Leicestershire but now held the benefice of Kilkhampton, Grenville's parish. That Grenville should so little value his ministrations much distressed Hastings and he exhorted him to examine his conscience to see whether the root of his objections to Pagit lay in himself or in some faults in the preacher. All men ought to reverence their minister, he went on,

And I know some that show great zeal and will be accounted earnest professors, and will not stick to express the same by diligently frequenting the word preached, and by giving good countenance to the minister thereof, and this have I seen well performed and continued whilst the preacher hath held him in a general course of doctrine, but if by any occasion (as duty bindeth him), he be drawn into particular reprehensions, and the same are felt to touch the quick, then kick they and cannot be quiet till they have hindered themselves of so great a blessing . . . for no sooner is the preacher misliked for his plainness, but then is there such hunting into his doctrine, and such sifting of his life, and so many baits laid for him, that zeal is forgotten, the word hath lost his due regard, and the minister for doing his duty is despised. . . .

Hastings attributed Grenville's resistance to Pagit's attempt at setting up a Presbyterian platform solely to pride: 'The man whom the Lord hath throughly seasoned with humility,' he informed him, 'he falleth flat before the sceptre of the word, and yieldeth to be censured by it, as a mean to reform him.' Yet his pride in the end proved Grenville's glory and he died the Protestant hero of 'The Revenge'.[47]

Hastings's high concept of the respect due to the office of a minister in no way held him back from rebuking individual ministers whom he considered were not living up to their calling, though with them he essayed a more 'loving' manner than he used with the erring laity. When writing to one Mr. Price (perhaps Cadwallader Price instituted to the living of Newton St. Loe in Somerset in 1585), Hastings diplomatically set down his own spiritual shortcomings before reaching the crux of his letter:

There be iii things, Mr. Price, which I will make bold to lay down unto you as faults (in my judgment) necessarily to be reformed in your function and calling: the first is your not instructing of your people in some measure, the second is your admitting them to the Lord's Table without examination, being so far unable to give a reason of their faith as some of them can scarcely say the articles of their belief, the third is your want of care in visiting and instructing those that be sick that if they live they may learn to glorify God by amending their former evils, and if they die they may learn with courage and comfort to leave this wretched vale knowing that death is but their passage to a better life. . . .[48]

Robert Parsons, the Jesuit, had some justification for his accusation that at his house at North Cadbury Hastings had created a 'Puritanical Presbytery'. He had himself presented Robert Sipthorpe, M.A., to North Cadbury in 1593 and, probably, Robert Dike to Holton in the same year while Huntingdon had given the living of Aller to Richard Spicer in 1582: Thomas Crane, M.A., whom Hastings brought to South Cadbury in 1587 seems to have been the leader of this little group of ministers.[49] They liked to think of themselves as Christian philosophers meeting in happy equality and to them Hastings turned for consolation when overwhelmed by grief on the deaths in quick succession of his dearly loved brother, Huntingdon, and then of his own wife, asking in despair, 'Why should we desire ... to live to behold and feel the miseries that befall us?' Philip Bisse, the Archdeacon of Taunton, replied on behalf of Crane, and urged Hastings to return to Cadbury that they all might comfort him personally:

But what do I write hereof or of any former thing to you? I know you had rather, and so would we your poor friends wish rather *coram philosophari* of these things then to commit it to mute and dead papers, the which I beseech almighty God shortly to bring to pass, to whose holy comfort I commend your worship, who ever keep us to be his and to hold fast our holy profession in this backsliding and wayward age.[50]

In spite of the prompting of his clerical friends Hastings could not bear to live at North Cadbury after his wife's death; he sold the house and estate in December, 1596 and thought of returning to the company of his surviving brothers in Leicestershire. His brother George, however, the new Earl of Huntingdon, gave him scant encouragement and in the end Hastings went back to Somerset.[51] By 1599 he had married again: Mary Watkins, his new wife, had been previously the wife of James Hannam of Holwell, and Hastings, whose first marriage had been childless, now found himself with a young family of step-children. A new vista of ecclesiastical patronage opened up for him with the (temporary) lordship over the Hannam and Watkins estates. Impatient to install a Protestant minister at Holwell he persuaded the incumbent to resign and obtained the institution of George Derby, B.A., 'a preacher whom I desire to enjoy both in his neighbourhood and labours'.[52]

Hastings never felt constrained to confine his intervention to parishes where he held the advowson: he took upon himself the charge of advancing worthy ministers whenever the opportunity arose. As he wrote in 1602, 'to further a good people to a good minister, a longing people to hear to a labouring, speaking minister to teach them is a bond of duty I may never forget, and a work of duty I must ever be ready to perform'. Such resolution emboldened him to approach Whitgift himself in an attempt to induce him to grant a preaching licence to his protégé, William Bradshaw. Hastings conceded that Whitgift might find Bradshaw 'fearful to do some things that may be urged on him' but personally undertook, in a gesture hardly likely to have reassured the archbishop 'that he shall not offer any disturbance to the peace of our Church either in word or action, but shall painfully bestow himself in that place to preach Christ crucified and to arm his people with some measure of knowledge to stand Christianly and courageously for the truth of Christ and to resist all errors broached against that holy doctrine'.[53]

Early in his career Hastings's anxiety over the state of the Church in England involved him in national politics and calamities in political life inspired him, as a watcher in the wings, to dispatch long oratorical letters to the chief actors on the political stage. First Huntingdon received his brother's philosophical meditations but with time the circle of his correspondents grew. In December 1581 when it seemed possible that the queen might even yet allow herself to be entrapped into marriage with a Frenchman and a papist and the morale of the godly dropped to a very low ebb, Hastings could do no more than pray 'the Lord in mercy look upon our sovereign . . . and he in mercy deliver her from this snare'. Fears of what might come about at Westminster, Hastings argued, should not deflect Huntingdon from his worthy proceedings in the north:

As the Lord our God hath used you as his good instrument under her majesty to defend his cause and to serve him in this Church and commonwealth, in which calling you have (praised be his name) walked dutifully towards her majesty, comfortably to God's children and carefully in seeking to win and draw the ignorant and obstinate to the knowledge of the truth: so continue your course and I pray God continue you therein, for he it is *qui dat et velle et perficere*, and he it is who I doubt not will perfect in you that he hath begun, but (*in domino mihi charissime et observande*) as it is a matter belonging to every child of

God to watch over his brother, and that I to your lordship am tied by a double true love knot, so I trust with your good favour I may utter those few speeches following only to express my care and show my good will.[54]

Five days after Leicester, a great patron of preachers, died in September 1588, Hastings sent off an exceedingly long exhortation to Essex to inspire him to take up his step-father's mantle: God, he maintained, had blessed Essex greatly by bringing him into a world where the light of his Gospel shone most clearly and in gratitude for these abundant gifts required from him a thankful heart,

which by no means you can better express then by employing your whole forces both in honour and credit to advance his truth and to be a comfort to his people professing the same: and now, my lord, is the time come wherein you should put this in practice, in that he hath taken from us that honourable worthy gentleman, whom God used many times as a notable instrument for the good both of the Church and commonwealth, and if it may please God to put into your lordship's heart not only to succeed him but to overgo him in his care in this behalf, you shall be most happy.[55]

Hastings's epistolary exercises found their natural culmination in publication though his adversaries did not fail to point out that publishing controversial works in his own name little became a well-born knight. The 'Christian Treatise' Hastings submitted to Cartwright and his manuscript 'Discourse of Predestination' never, apparently, appeared in print but in 1598 he published his first tract, *A watchword to all religious and true hearted Englishmen* in which he proclaimed his long cherished belief that a man cannot be a loyal subject of the queen except he be also a sincere member of the English Church. It drew an immediate reply from Robert Parsons in *A temperate ward-word to the turbulent and seditious watch-word*. Referring to Hastings there as 'a barking beagle among the hounds of Huntingdon' and as 'a Puritan in religion' he tried to fasten on him ambitions to overthrow the Established Church: 'No man can doubt but that you would have your Genevan disciplinary form of government, whereby all the bishops in

England must be pulled down, and other ecclesiastical dignities discomposed, the queen's supremacy also must be taken away, and other like points of the English Church overthrown.' Parsons was undoubtedly right in thinking Hastings wished to make the Church more Protestant, but he himself had no greater love for the *status quo*, the only difference being he wanted change in the Catholic direction.[56]

The following year in his *An apology or defence of the watch-word*, Hastings counter-attacked with a point-by-point reply to Parson's argument; he received at the same time unlooked for assistance when Matthew Sutcliffe produced *A brief reply to . . . a temperate ward-word* in support of 'this good knight of right zealous mind toward religion'. Parsons could not be silenced and returned in 1602 with *The warn-word to Sir Francis Hastings wast-word* on this occasion putting forward the routine allegation that Hastings had brought poverty upon himself by squandering his goods 'upon the entertainment of ministers' and, much more seriously, by insinuating that the seduction of Essex had been caused by these very Puritans. The controversy petered to its close in 1604 with Sutcliffe's *Full and round answer to . . . Robert Parsons' . . . foolish and rude warn-word*.[57] Elizabethan religious argument is singularly barren, consisting as it does of insults and counter-charges. The opponent in any controversy seems only too eager to score off his adversary in small details but rarely replies to his thesis considered as a whole. Hastings and Parsons remained content with a statement of their own views and hardly tried to argue in a fundamental way. Since their ideas of religion and patriotism were irreconciliable, and since both thought of religion and patriotism as things inseparable, any agreement between them was impossible.

Aside from his literary exhortation for action against Catholic subversion, the one place where Hastings could hope to influence the government's religious policy directly was parliament: characteristically he lost little time in gaining admittance. He sat in every session of every parliament between 1571 and 1610 (when he died) except for the parliament of 1572: first he represented Leicestershire as Knight of the Shire in 1571, and again in 1584 and 1586; then, having settled at North Cadbury he emerged as one of the knights for Somerset in 1588, and also in 1592. In 1597, since he had sold North Cadbury, he returned to sit for Leicestershire but he then changed his mind about establishing himself in his native county and went back to Somerset on his second marriage the next year. His flittings probably cost him the Somerset county seat in 1601, when, for the only time in his life, he had to be satisfied with a borough seat, Bridgwater. By the accession of James, however, his ascendancy had reasserted itself: he represented the county of Somerset again until his death.

Once he had entered parliament Hastings immediately took an energetic part in its proceedings and despite all disappointments never abandoned his belief that the reform of the Church could come through parliamentary action. His career shows how, unwittingly, religious enthusiasm could lead to political opposition. His first appearance in the *Commons Journals* foreshadowed all his later enterprises: with his kinsman John Hastings, and joined later by his brother Edward Hastings he got himself appointed to the committee conferring with the Lords on the Bill for coming to church and receiving communion, a deliberate attempt to force Catholics into the open. The Bill against corrupt presentations within the church similarly drew his ready support.[58] When next he sat in parliament in 1584 he whole-heartedly approved the Bills for the better observing of the sabbath and for regulating ecclesiastical livings. Again in 1857, during the debate which followed the confiscation of the radical Bill and Book, he could not keep silence, 'but in [a] place of free speech [was] willing and ready to deliver his conscience'. In their assembly, he argued, they should do their utmost for the glory of God and the safety of their country:

We must not thrust God out of doors. Our ministers are blind. There is necessity for preaching. Idleness, duplicity, non-residence hinder salvation. The people are untaught, God dishonoured, the word condemned. Catholic seminarists about. With better laws her majesty would be better obeyed.[59]

Sir Francis for one believed parliament and the queen, not the queen alone, knew what was best for the country and in such a loyal outburst as this in fact did not hesitate to put pressure on the crown.

In the 1584 session, Hastings had sat on the committee considering a Bill for creating a learned ministry and he never failed to condemn pluralism and non-residence in the Church or to advocate Bills for the stricter keeping of Sunday and against blasphemous swearing. His hostility towards Catholics continued throughout his life: a few days after he had added his name to the petition to the queen for the execution of justice upon Mary, Queen of Scots he went on to demand the rooting out of all papists from England. In 1601 he introduced his own Bill for the enforcement of the twelvepenny fine for every absence from divine service on Sundays and holy days, from his own experience illustrating the need for this law to be brought back:

I know some half-parishes, I would not say some whole parishes, perverted by Jesuits and seminaries: these be of the poorer and meaner sort of people, of whom this small tax of twelvepence being duly levied, will more pinch than any law yet devised.

The Gunpowder Plot and then the assassination of Henry IV in France caused Hastings to call more and more stridently for the better execution of the penal laws. He asserted in 1610 that there were more Catholics in the country than there had been for seven years and spent his last weeks of life compiling a petition to the king for more drastic action to be taken against them.[60]

Although religion was so much his overriding concern that by the beginning of James's reign Hastings almost automatically sat on every committee and in every conference considering the state of the Church, he also interested himself in other Bills passing through the house. He voiced his opinions on the Bill for the relief of the poor, for the control of cloth production in Somerset,

on the abuses to which monopolies had led, indeed, at the height
of the agitation against monopolies, rejoicing to see Cecil had
realised the extent of the people's grievances he wrote to tell him
'your very honourable carriage therein hath affected the whole
house much, and will work you great honour and love generally
throughout all parts of the land'.[61] Well before 1601 Sir Francis
saw himself as an authority in parliamentary matters.[62] In the first
parliament of James, the Commons recognised his standing. The
government had decided upon Sir Edward Phelips as the new
Speaker and the Commons received notice of the nomination in
silence, then 'the names of others were muttered, as of Sir Francis
Hastings, Sir Henry Nevill, Sir Francis Bacon, Sir Edward Hoby,
Sir Henry Montague, the recorder of London, and others, but the
more general voice ran upon Sir Edward Phelips. . . .'[63] Not only
members of the Commons respected Sir Francis's opinions, for in
June 1604, Sir George Hume, on behalf of the king, consulted
Hastings over whether he thought the Commons could be
induced to vote the king a subsidy while the one granted to
Elizabeth was still being collected. Hastings pointed out that the
Commons might well hesitate to concede another subsidy at that
time, not out of disloyalty but lest the people might complain and
advised the king to avoid a situation in which the House might be
driven into refusing his request. James took the advice to heart: a
fortnight later he sent word that he would not ask for a subsidy
that session.[64]

Hastings's attainments in public life made his fall the more
catastrophic when, consistent in all things, he risked everything
for his religion. The failure of the Hampton Court conference to
allow a greater toleration for ministers with scruples over ceremonies and the wearing of the surplice bitterly disappointed
Hastings and, since parliament was not in session when the king
publicly decided to retain the government of the Church as it had
been under Elizabeth, Hastings could not make his feelings known
there: he and other radicals were left with only extra-parliamentary
means of protest. On the instigation of Puritan ministers in

London between November 1604 and February 1605 petitions poured in to the Privy Council and the king directly against depriving the Nonconformist ministers in Lincolnshire, Hertfordshire, Lancashire, London, Warwickshire, Leicestershire, Northamptonshire, Essex, Devon and Cornwall in addition to the appeals of individual gentlemen on behalf of particular ministers.[65] Acting for his friends, Sir Francis Hastings composed the petition on behalf of the Northamptonshire ministers, forty-five local gentlemen signed it, and then sent it to Sir Edward Montague, and Sir Richard and Sir Valentine Knightley in London for them to present to the king. James took great offence at Hastings's claim that many thousands of the king's subjects would lose their 'faithful pastors' if the policy of deprivation continued, reading a threat of civil disobedience into this 'combination of many hands against law'. The Privy Council summoned Hastings, Montague and the Knightleys before it, and Hastings's examination alone lasted two days: there he heard his petition was considered 'mutinous, seditious, malicious, factious, tending to rebellion'. Vehemently denying the charge he confessed he had erred in dealing with religious matters outside his own county but refused to abandon the dispossessed ministers. In a speech not unworthy of the Wentworth tradition he defended liberty for Protestants and the subject's right of free access to the crown:

If I should have answered contrary to mine own heart and conscience [he told the Privy Council], God is greater then my conscience to condemn me, and if you yourself should find me to dissemble, you might justly adjudge me dishonest. And now I beseech you give me leave to speak boldly and plainly. If the ministers did refuse the ceremonies upon a humour and disposition to disobey and not upon conscience, none should be more opposite to them then myself. But seeing it is through the tenderness of their conscience, let not me lay a blot upon them, being free and innocent, for that myself have some experience of the tenderness of conscience. Neither do I desire to live to see the king so dishonoured, or his subjects so prejudiced that it should be unlawful to petitionate with many or few hands to him who hath power to grant or deny.[66]

Hastings was sequestered to his house in Somerset, forbidden to deal in any matters relating to the king's service and told that only his rank had saved him from imprisonment in the Fleet where the Privy Council sent Erasmus Dryden, who had collected the signatures to the petition: Sir Edward Montague and Sir Richard and Sir Valentine Knightley all received the same punishment. Hastings felt it a most bitter blow that 'after 37 years painful and faithful service' as a Justice of the Peace and Deputy Lieutenant in Leicestershire, Somerset and Dorset he should close his days in disgrace, yet in spite of his frequent appeals to Salisbury, of the promises he extracted from the Earls of Northampton and Worcester to work for his restoration he was never put back on the commission of the peace.[67] He remained permanently in the king's displeasure, he held no official positions in Somerset or Dorset but he could not be denied his place in parliament. He took his seat unchallenged on 5 November 1605 and, as soon as the House had reassembled after the excitement of the Gunpowder Plot, impenitently he introduced a Bill for restoring the deprived ministers. Undeterred by his failure in the parliamentary session of 1606, Hastings threw himself into the work of the committee in 1607 which drew up an omnibus petition to James against Jesuits, non-residence and pluralities and for the silenced ministers. Not so long as he lived would he give up the fight and in April 1610 he supported yet another petition to the king on behalf of the Puritan ministers.[68] On 16 September 1610 he died, full of years, and was buried beside his first wife in North Cadbury church.[69]

That none might doubt his religious profession, decades before his death Hastings had composed lengthy confessions of faith in two draft wills which exactly summarised his whole attitude to life: in his second will, made before 1596, he declared,

Almighty God . . . in his foreknowledge and before I was to work either good or evil hath chosen me to be his child and predestinated me to eternal salvation . . . in his time appointed hath framed me to serve him, and hath allotted me to live here in this wretched vale for a time to the glorifying of him, so that my days are not given me to be spent securely and carelessly, as though I were at liberty to live as I list but religiously and soberly which must give assurance to myself and yield testimony to others that I am one of the number of those who are chosen to be children of so holy a father who commandeth us to be holy as he is holy.

Here indeed was a creed which led to total commitment, which proclaimed itself in all Hastings's actions and for which he sacrificed his prestige. In this will, while expressing his assurance of his own salvation, he also laid emphasis on the more negative and repressive aspect of Puritanism: he left small bequests to his neighbouring Somerset parishes of North Cadbury, South Cadbury, Maperton and Holton 'upon condition that they never use again their church ales, to the prophaning of the Lord's sabbath, the abusing of his creatures in drunkenness and riot and the corrupting of their youth by training them up in gaming and lascivious wantonness'.[70] Like many another eager Protestant, Hastings objected to being called a Puritan, with its overtones of human perfectibility, and towards the end of his life he wished 'that such as profess one Lord, one faith and one baptism with me should forbear so to style me for longing to carry a sincere heart in my bosom towards my God and labouring to attain to a holy conversation before men'.[71] Yet no Elizabethan gentleman surely deserves the name in its later connotation more than he. So Hastings lived and died a zealot, transmitting into the second decade of the seventeenth century that enthusiasm for Protestantism he had learnt from Huntingdon in the early years of Queen Elizabeth.

*   *   *

Having striven to furnish his brothers and sisters with resources of the mind and spirit for a useful and satisfying life the Earl of Huntingdon still had only half performed his family trust. Hard on the heels of the first generation followed the second. The earl and countess had no children of their own and consequently turned their attention to the education of their many nephews and nieces and more distant relatives. Naturally the upbringing of the second Francis Hastings, the eldest son of Sir George Hastings and the heir presumptive to the earldom demanded pride of place. Huntingdon's fear must have been lest the lukewarmness of the father towards Protestantism should be visited upon the son and he did all in his power to counteract the early influences surrounding the child: on Sir George's part his sense of family overcame his conservatism and apparently he had no hesitation in entrusting his son to his brother's care. Once he had reached an age of discretion, Huntingdon sent young Francis to drink deep at the fountain head of the Reformation at Geneva itself and confided him to Beza who took advantage of the occasion to dedicate to Huntingdon his Latin translation of the psalms in appreciation of Huntingdon's bounty towards those in exile for the Gospel's sake: in this younger Francis Hastings he recognised a worthy representative of the noble family.[72] By an irony of history, Edmund Campion and Robert Parsons setting out from Rome to begin the first Jesuit mission to England determined to view Geneva in disguise on their way and discovered Francis Hastings there. They had some talk with his tutor whom Parsons, not surprisingly, thought 'seemed an earnest Puritan'.[73] While in Switzerland he matriculated at the University of Basle and may well have met the Frenchman, Simon Patericke, soon after he had first reached the Continent. Already in 1577 Patericke could refer to him as his 'dear friend' when offering him his translation of Gentillet's *Discourse upon the means of well governing*: he must have been but one of many to call upon Hastings to 'tread the steps of your uncle, the right honourable Earl of Huntingdon, a man most admirable and illustrious, as well for godliness and other noble virtues, as for noble parentage and honour, that you show yourself worthy of your place and kindred'.[74]

On his nephew's return to England, Huntingdon looked about to provide him with a wife and discovered an ideal candidate in Sarah Harington, daughter of Sir James Harington to whom he already owed considerable debts. A marriage between the families could stave off, if not cancel, demands for their speedy repayment and, after seeing the 'good liking' between the young people, Huntingdon brought about a settlement in 1585.[75] The parents duly named the eldest son of this marriage after his great-uncle and at a tender age sent him to his household for his schooling. Huntingdon called Nathaniel Gilby (the son of Anthony Gilby), away from Cambridge where he held a fellowship at Emmanuel College, to be his tutor in 1595, and there the ten-year-old boy found himself stranded on Huntingdon's death in December. 'The child hath been well educated and taught', the secretary of the Council in the North reported to Burghley in January 1596, 'for one year and a half at York, by a learned and godly schoolmaster, appointed by his late noble and religious deceased uncle, who took special care for the education of this child being in expectation the heir of the house. He is something low of stature, but of comely countenance and lineaments, his wit sharp and ready.'[76]

Huntingdon supervised the upbringing of his other nephews less closely though he was very ready to advise when consulted as when he tried to persuade the Earl of Lincoln to place his grandson and Huntingdon's eldest sister's son at Cambridge. He concerned himself also over Henry, another of Sir George Hastings's sons, and arranged his marriage as well as his brother's. Huntingdon wished to draw Sir Francis Willoughby of Wollaton, a comparatively near neighbour from Ashby across the Leicestershire border, into the family circle and in 1587 won his consent for a marriage between his daughter, Dorothy, and Henry Hastings. Huntingdon had the young couple to live with him at York until after the birth of their first child when he at length succeeded in getting Willoughby to settle the estate of Woodlands in Dorset upon them.[77]

Outside the immediate family, Huntingdon early assumed responsibility for the orphaned children of the first Earl of Essex. He and Huntingdon were first cousins since Dorothy Hastings, his mother, was Huntingdon's aunt, but he seems to have remembered Huntingdon for his godliness as much as for ties of kinship as he lay dying in Ireland in September 1576. He felt confident that the Earl and Countess of Huntingdon would not refuse his daughters and his younger son, Wat, and he chose wisely, for not only did Huntingdon take complete charge of these children until they married but also became a supernumerary guardian of Robert, the new Earl of Essex. In November 1580, Huntingdon hoped Essex might be allowed to leave Cambridge to come north to spend Christmas with his brother Walter in his household. By 1582 Essex had run up such debts that his guardians resolved upon the drastic step of removing him from the university altogether and obtained the queen's consent 'that the said Earl of Essex should be resident at York under the oversight of the Earl of Huntingdon' where his excessive spending might be curbed. Essex went north soon after 20 February 1582 and stayed with Huntingdon for a year and a half: in spite of the unpropitious circumstances he did succeed in winning Essex's goodwill, though scarcely in instilling in him the virtues of economy. After his death Essex voluntarily spoke of him as one 'whose name without sorrow I shall never mention'.[78]

The younger children of the first Earl of Essex depended upon Huntingdon entirely for their promotion. Lady Penelope Devereux attained her place in society first; while in Newcastle on the queen's service in 1581, Huntingdon found time to suggest to Burghley a match between her and young Lord Rich. Materially the marriage was a brilliant one for Rich's wealth exceeded that of many earls, but the parties proved quite unsuited and even by 1588 Lady Penelope had given all her affection to Sir Charles Blount, later Lord Mountjoy. Perhaps taking heed of her sister's unhappiness, Dorothy Devereux took the arrangement of her marriage into her own hands and clandestinely married Sir Thomas Perrot without her guardian's consent: Huntingdon forgave the erring pair and later stood surety for the discharge of Perrot's debts.[79]

In this age of arranged marriages, Walter Devereux found his wife within Huntingdon's own household. In the 1580's Arthur

Dakins, a Yorkshire gentleman and his wife confided the up-bringing of their only child, Margaret, to the Earl and Countess of Huntingdon: several sought the young heiress in marriage but Huntingdon reserved it for his 'cousin Wat', and socially the Dakins cannot have been displeased to see their daughter wedded to the younger son of an earl. For their marriage settlement the young couple acquired an estate at Hackness in Yorkshire, Arthur Dakins paying £3,000 of the purchase money, the Earl of Essex another £3,000 and Huntingdon himself £500. Again husband and wife had some difficulties in adjusting to each other: Walter Devereux, high spirited like his brother, seems to have thought Margaret rather dull and Huntingdon had to chide him for not spending more of his time with her. Gently he entreated him 'that your good wife, for so I may rightly term her, may receive that comfort of your coming to her, as in right, and by her desert is due unto her', adding, in a passing reference to Margaret's parents 'this will be no small comfort to the old grey-headed man and his good wife'. Yet little time remained for reformation: Margaret Dakins was suddenly widowed when a stray cannon ball struck Walter as he was fighting for the Pro-testant cause with his brother in the Low Countries and back the young lady returned to Huntingdon's household to be again sought by impecunious gentlemen.[80]

Among his wife's relations, Huntingdon undoubtedly loved the Sidney children best. Even in 1574 little Thomas Sidney accom-panied his aunt to court to act as her page and the queen rewarded him with a cap embellished with hearts and roses in gold and enamel.[81] Huntingdon, no less than the courtiers about the queen succumbed to the charm of Thomas's eldest brother, Sir Philip Sidney, that ideal Protestant courtier of the new generation, who when he died from wounds received at the battle of Zutphen against Spain became a heroic legend. The news of his death in 1586 came to Huntingdon as 'a most great loss' and he felt compelled to console Walsingham, Sidney's father-in-law, com-mitting him to God 'who only is the sole comforter of those that be his, and so you must think, though good Philip be gone, whom I did love as well as you could ever do'. Since he was detained on the queen's business in the north, Huntingdon at once sent a servant to London to comfort his countess, 'who I am sure is most full of grief and melancholy for the loss of her noble nephew'.[82] Sir Philip's death following so closely on that of his father brought Robert Sidney to the head of his family: Thomas, the youngest boy, was still under age and Huntingdon took his care upon himself, doing all in his power to help both brothers. After Leicester's death Robert Sidney, as the oldest son of his eldest sister, had a claim upon his inheritance: Huntingdon lent him his own counsel to draw up a legal case but both he and the queen herself had long been dead before Sidney made good his title to the Earldom of Leicester. During the long period of waiting Lady Huntingdon remained his constant advocate, often intervening on his behalf with the queen: on Sidney's frequent sojourns abroad on business of state some of his little daughters stayed behind with their great aunt much to her pleasure who in 1618 could still make the proud boast that 'I think there will none make question but I know how to breed and govern young gentlewomen.'[83]

After his father's death, Thomas Sidney went to live with Huntingdon at York to continue his training as a gentleman: just before the coming of the Armada he began to take a part in northern government and reviewed the York musters for his uncle; by 1591 he was of an age to be married.[84] Once the news of Walter Devereux's death was known in England fresh suitors appeared for his widow's hand and the redoubtable Lady Russell in particular determined to gain her for her younger son, Sir Thomas Hoby (called 'Posthumus' by his erudite mother since he had been born after the death of his father, Sir Thomas Hoby, the translator of Castiglione's *Courtier*). Spurred on by his mother, seconded with letters of recommendation from Burghley he pleaded his cause, but in vain: Huntingdon decided his nephew should have Margaret Dakins. As soon as Walter Devereux's body had been given burial in his native soil the second marriage was quietly performed and Thomas Sidney became the new Lord of Hackness and the most cherished of Margaret's husbands. Huntingdon paid some of his debts and settled the manor house of Hull on him and his wife for their further advancement while still keeping a lodging for his nephew and his Meg in his own house at York.[85]

Margaret Dakins learnt the lesson of the transience of human life early for her second marriage lasted less than four years before Thomas Sidney died in his turn. The Countess of Huntingdon heard of her nephew's death with great grief, 'her rest in the night . . . very unquiet and frightful'. Once more Margaret came back into the marriage market, once more Sir Thomas Posthumus Hoby tried his luck. Understandably Margaret Dakins showed little eagerness for yet another venture into matrimony but no rebuffs from the lady could quell Hoby's ardour.[86] Huntingdon, on his death-bed, hesitated to force a marriage on his ward yet he believed the match might advance Protestantism in a backward part of Yorkshire; in the furtherance of true religion personal inclinations must give way:

Mistress Margaret. Bear with me whatsoever I write, for I was not in a greater pain since my last journey then I even now am in. . . . For God's cause have care of all our credits, and so handle the matter as his [Hoby's] coming again may be neither offensive to you nor displeasing to himself.

To one as devout as Margaret Dakins such an appeal was irresistible; in the summer of 1596 she and Sir Thomas married and Huntingdon's desire was abundantly realised. At Hackness, despite the opposition of obstreperous local Catholic gentlemen, Lady Margaret and her husband together created a model settlement of evangelical piety.[87]

Even when ties of blood were remote, or nonexistent, the godly household of the Earl and Countess of Huntingdon attracted the children of like-minded contemporaries. The sister of the Earl of Rutland spent a time there before moving on to the Earl of

Pembroke: Huntingdon always acted in the most friendly way towards the Manners family, rejoicing greatly when he heard the news in 1573 that the third Earl of Rutland's own choice of a wife had fallen on one who 'fears God, loves the gospel and hates popery'.[88] Men saw in Huntingdon one who would perform what he had promised, though it might be to his own hurt. Sir Thomas Barrington, the second husband of Huntingdon's aunt, Lady Winifred Pole, made him a trustee of his two younger children, Henry and Katherine: Huntingdon guarded their interests, seeing that they received the lands and payments intended for them by their father when they reached their majorities. About 1588 Katherine Barrington married William Bourchier, eldest son of Ralph Bourchier, an important Yorkshire gentleman and since Huntingdon was living at York at this time and witnessed the settlement he may well have arranged the match.[89] From the time the Earl of Warwick had married the first Earl of Bedford's daughter, Huntingdon, through his wife, had been connected with the Russell family. In the 1560's William Russell appointed him a trustee for his daughter, Katherine, and the Court of Chancery confirmed his responsibility for her education. For a time he cared for the second Earl of Bedford's heir, Edward Russell, who, in the summer of 1585, had gone to the Border with his father who was there accidentally killed in an affray with the Scots. Huntingdon immediately took the boy under his protection and he remained with him until later in the year when, on the death of his grandfather, he became the third Earl of Bedford.[90] In 1588 Sir Christopher Hatton sent his nephew north and it seemed obvious to him to confide him to Huntingdon.[91] Philip, Lord Wharton felt beholden to Huntingdon for his kindness to his son while another Yorkshire gentleman, Sir John Biron, told Huntingdon he would be very thankful if he thought his grandson, young Jack Atherton, worthy to marry a cousin or friend of his.[92] In his will proved in March 1581 another northerner, Thomas Boynton earnestly requested Huntingdon, 'that man of God', to assume the guardianship of his only son, Francis.[93] Martin

Birkhead, a lawyer and official member of the Council in the
North from 1574 until he died in 1594 left a large family of six
young sons and seven daughters: on his death-bed he asked
Huntingdon to take all the boys, or at least one of them, into his
service.[94]

Elizabethan gentlemen were well aware of the benefits which
accrued to their children from a training in a noble household,
prospects of careers for their younger sons, of good matches for
their daughters, a scholarly education for them all. Huntingdon's
household, in common with many others fulfilled this socially
useful function, but, with its emphasis on godliness as well as
learning it did far more. The importance of recusant households
in preserving Catholicism in England and providing missionary
centres for the fresh enthusiasm of the Counter-Reformation has
long been recognised: these Puritan households acted in a
similar way in spreading the knowledge of informed Protestantism
over the country. A large number of children passed through
Huntingdon's hands: some of them, like two of his own brothers,
Sir George and Walter Hastings, may well have been quite
unaffected by his godly indoctrination but others, Margaret
Dakins, Sir Francis Hastings, young Henry Hastings, later the
fifth Earl of Huntingdon, were permanently influenced by their
experiences in his household. They, when their turn came, set up
Puritan establishments and so perpetuated for the next generation,
and the generation after that, the Protestant practices they had
learnt from the Earl and Countess of Huntingdon.

CHAPTER THREE

Noble Poverty

THE HASTINGS ESTATES AND
THEIR MANAGEMENT

MOST Elizabethans had little sympathy with the medieval idealisation of poverty. They lived in a materialistic age which saw in prosperity evidence of God's favour, in poverty a mark of his disapprobation. Consequently when the religious Earl of Huntingdon died and left his lands in ruin his apologists faced a moral dilemma: if God had accepted his zealous life surely he would not have visited his estates in this way? Sir Francis Hastings meditated upon the problem, grieving that it kept the fickle multitude from remembering his brother's heroical qualities, his devotion to religion, love to his family and loyalty to his queen.

All the speech now amongst some is to lay blame upon him for wasting his patrimony, and leaving his heir in so weak terms of ability to maintain himself according to the dignity of his place [he complained]. And herein I would easily give my consent to conclude him worthy to be blamed, if by his own riot or want of care he had wasted the same, but all the world will free him from the first as being never found worthy to be touched with proud prodigality or licentious consuming, and myself and divers others can witness with him for the latter, that such was his care and so great as he did mightily toil and even tire both his body and mind with labouring about those matters, and if the Lord had pleased to give him leave to see London again his state had been left in far greater quiet then now it is, he had both devised the way how to do it and had settled down a resolution in himself to perform it. But

as it becometh me not to meddle with God's secret determination
herein, so will I spare to enter into innumerations of things outward
that may seem to be causes of this his decay. It shall suffice me in both
these to set down this only truth: that the means were such to bring
him hereunto as he could not possibly avoid, and therein his posterity
must yield to the providence of the almighty who if it please him can,
and in his good time (I hope) will raise up some good means to repair[?]
the ruins and decays of our honourable house.[1]

It is significant that Hastings did not try to veil the disaster
which had come upon the family, it would have been futile for
him to have done so, for the large-scale sale of lands, the ever
increasing debts and the expedients to which his brother had
resorted in order to raise money all gave positive proof of his
insolvency. He only argued that forces quite beyond his control
had brought about his failure. Perhaps Sir Francis here spoke a
little less than candidly: why Huntingdon should have failed
so dismally in matching his income with his expenditure was
certainly a complex matter but he did not live alone in an
age of inflation and some of his fellow peers, like the ninth
Earl of Northumberland, contrived much more realistically
to adapt the management of their estates to the necessity of the
times.

The economic history of this period yawns with pitfalls and
few can hope to circumvent all of them. In Elizabethan accounting
little is what it seems to be and in particular financial valuations
must be accepted with more than the average caution and never
apart from their context. To quote a most obvious instance, the
figure placed upon an estate for the purposes of death duty
would be a mere fraction of its contemporary market value.
Elizabethans readily adjusted the valuation to the occasion but
the modern observer cannot pretend to do this with anything
approaching accuracy; he can only bear in mind that in the
sixteenth century two and two can rarely be added to make four.
Again almost invariably estate records have not survived in their
entirety and their very incompleteness leads to distortion. Never-

theless, in spite of these major qualifications and in spite of the inevitable imprecision, a reconstruction of Huntingdon's financial affairs is worth attempting because money, or the lack of it, dominated all sides of his life. A biography must be concerned with a man's economic resources, although in the past many biographers succeeded in ignoring them.[2]

The lands to which Huntingdon succeeded in 1560 compared not unfavourably with the inheritance of an average member of the nobility of the time.[3] Ever since the rise of William, Lord Hastings exactly a century earlier the little town of Ashby de la Zouch in Leicestershire, controlled by the great castle he had built, had formed the centre of the Hastings estates and around Ashby the manors of Bagworth, Barrow-on-Soar, Kirby Muxloe, Wistow and Newton Harcourt, Kilby, Lubbesthorpe and Enderby made a fairly compact block of lands particularly in the north west of the county. Outside Leicestershire the estates were more scattered. In Yorkshire with the manor of Slingsby only a fragment of the oldest ancestral property remained but Huntingdon still held the important manor of Stoke Poges with its surrounding lands in Buckinghamshire which had come into the family on the marriage of William, Lord Hastings's son, Edward, to Mary, Lady Hungerford. The same marriage had also enriched the family with extensive estates around Aller and North Cadbury in Somerset and many smaller manors in Devon and Cornwall. Very recently Huntingdon's own mother had had restored to her in her own right as one of the heirs of Margaret, Countess of Salisbury the manor of Stokenham and other lands in Devonshire and Christchurch and Ringwood in Hampshire. In addition to these lands which passed to Huntingdon either in possession or reversion he also inherited manors or smaller estates in Wiltshire, Sussex, Oxfordshire, Northampton, Nottinghamshire and Rutland. The very dispersed nature of the estates presented administrative problems but if these could be overcome they contained rich potentialities. Their nominal yearly value set out in the fine Huntingdon paid to the crown for permission to take possession

F

of his lands on the death of his father was a little over £1,360.[4]
This figure cannot be seen as anything approaching his actual
income but it provides a useful means of comparison with other
noble estates. The livery fines of the Earls of Derby and Pembroke
at £3,040 and £2,691 very considerably exceeded Huntingdon's,
those of the Earls of Cumberland, at £1,821, and Shrewsbury, at
£1,730, stood at a higher, though not very much higher rate,
while that of the Earl of Bedford fell short of his by £100.[5] The
fate of these last three noble families which contemporaries
roughly equated with the Hastings family in wealth about 1560
illustrates the difficulty of generalising about the fortunes of the
nobility. The Cliffords, like the Hastings soon fell on evil days and
partly through extravagance, and partly through lack of male
heirs their estates were broken up in the seventeenth century. The
Talbots, however, more than held their own while the Russells
went from strength to strength to become one of the most
affluent of English noble houses.

In 1560 Huntingdon was the ultimate heir to extensive estates
yet within less than a year of entering into his inheritance he
found himself being driven to encroach upon his main asset, land.
In January 1561 he sold his first manor, that of Morecloses in
Bramshaw in Wiltshire for £220 and in the next five years the sale
of manors and lands in Wiltshire, Cornwall, Somerset, Devon,
Yorkshire and Nottingham followed in rapid succession. Many
of these can only have been small estates, purchased for a few
hundred pounds or less but the Somerset manor of Newton St.
Loe fetched £2,600, that of Pensford and Publow £1,600,
Wootton Courtney in Somerset £2,000 and Huntingdon hoped to
get £1,600 for the manor of Slingsby in Yorkshire. This frantic
selling of lands to meet present commitments did not prove a
mere temporary measure, for throughout the rest of Huntingdon's
life the sales continued. From the time of his accession until his
death in 1595 records exist of his having alienated some 170
parcels of land and these included at least sixty-five manors: the
total amount known to have been raised by these sales was well

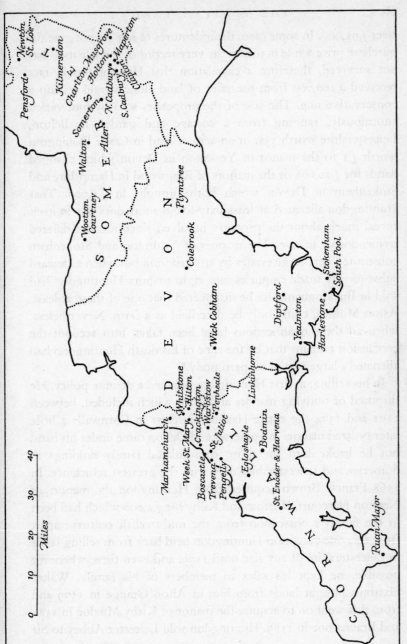

Hastings Land in Cornwall, Devon and Somerset

over £91,000. In some cases the indentures of sale do not give the purchase price while in others the very record of the sale itself has not survived, therefore a calculation that Huntingdon in fact received £100,000 from the sales of land alone would remain a conservative one. The size of the properties sold by him varied enormously, ranging from a cottage and garden in Belton, Leicestershire worth 53s. or an acre of land in Castle Donington worth £1 to the manor of Yealmton in Devon which changed hands for £10,666 or the manors of Ringwood in Hampshire and Stokenham in Devon which both brought in £5,000. That Huntingdon alienated at least sixty-five manors does not in itself reveal much about the property involved since manors differed tremendously in size. The manors of Yealmton and Stokenham constituted very large estates by any criterion but when a steward subsequently made enquiries into eight manors Huntingdon had sold in Buckinghamshire he discovered that one of these at least, Aston Mollins, could only be described as a farm. Nevertheless, when all these qualifications have been taken into account the conclusion remains that by the time of his death Huntingdon had alienated a large part of his patrimony.[6]

In his selling, at first Huntingdon pursued a definite policy. He disposed of outlying manors and lands which included, between 1562 and 1574 the entire Hastings interest in Cornwall: a little later isolated manors in Somerset and Devon came under his hand but he broke into the more consolidated family holdings in Somerset and Leicestershire only with the greatest reluctance. In 1568 Francis Brown acquired from Huntingdon the manors of Newton Harcourt, Wistow and Kilby for £2,000 which had been in the family's possession from the mid-twelfth century: apart from this one exception Huntingdon held back from selling lands in Leicestershire of any size until 1579, and even then, whenever possible, he kept his sales to members of his family. Walter Hastings bought lands from him in Alton Grange in 1579 and from this went on to acquire the manor of Kirby Muxloe in 1582 and Braunstone in 1589. Huntingdon sold Leicester Abbey to Sir

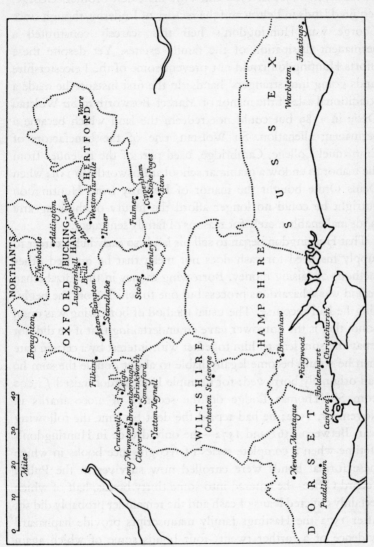

Hastings Land in Central England

Edward Hastings in 1580 and the great house in the High Street, Leicester, in 1590. In 1586 and 1591 his eldest brother, George, acquired lands in Belton and the rectory of Enderby, though since George was Huntingdon's heir this scarcely constituted a permanent dissipation of the family estates. Yet despite these efforts Huntingdon could not prevent some of the Leicestershire lands going into strangers' hands: in the first instance he made a conditional sale of the manor of Market Bosworth to Sir Wolstan Dixie in 1589 but could not redeem the land which became a permanent alienation. Sir Wolstan, one of the benefactors of Emmanuel College, Cambridge, used part of the revenues from the manor to endow a grammar school at Bosworth. In 1594 when Denis Orme bought the manor of Enderby from Huntingdon outright he could no longer afford the luxury of thinking any lands inalienable merely for reasons of family sentiment.

That Huntingdon began to sell his lands so early in his career to supply his need for cash does not mean that he ignored other methods of raising money. Borrowing money in the Elizabethan period was a hazardous process but one to which from the beginning he had recourse. The usual method of borrowing was upon bond, that is the borrower gave an undertaking that if he did not repay the sum lent to him together with interest by a certain date then he would become legally liable to about double the sum he had originally borrowed: for example Huntingdon raised £1,000 from Sir Thomas Lodge on the security of 2,000 marks in November, 1562; he had repaid the debt by June the following year. Between 1562 and 1572—the only decade in Huntingdon's lifetime when a complete series of recognisance books in which these formal bonds were enrolled now survives in the Public Record Office—he entered into some thirty bonds, half of which certainly covered loans of cash and the remainder probably did so. After 1572 the Hastings family manuscripts provide haphazard evidence of a further twenty-four bonds some of which again definitely secured loans while the remainder were presumably for the same purpose since they involved recognised money-lenders: Huntingdon almost certainly borrowed more money on bond than these surviving bonds indicate. Throughout the latter half of the sixteenth century, cash was in short supply and this type of borrowing had the great disadvantage in that both parties anticipated a quick repayment: £500 Huntingdon borrowed on the security of 1,000 marks in April 1564 he repaid the next November; £1,200 he raised on the security of £2,000 in November 1570 he returned exactly within the year of the loan. Huntingdon borrowed wherever money could be had and while he patronised some of the best-known London merchants, Sir Thomas Lodge, Sir Roger Martin, Thomas Sutton, Sir John Spencer, Sir Thomas Gresham and his brother John, he in no way

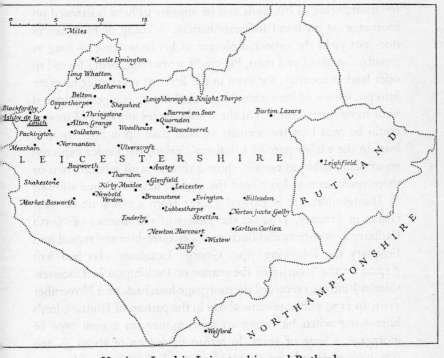

Hastings Land in Leicestershire and Rutland

confined himself to the professional money-lenders. He turned his attentions also to the more affluent members of the nobility and gentry and at different times the Earls of Sussex and Worcester, Sir Francis Willoughby and Sir James Harington came to his aid. From the case of the Earl of Sussex who lent 1,000 marks in 1565, not repaid until 1572, it would seem that borrowing from friends had a distinct advantage in that they did not demand so prompt repayment as the merchants. On the whole, at least up to 1572, the money Huntingdon borrowed on bond he very quickly repaid, yet already in the earlier part of his life he found himself continually being driven to borrow more money to repay what he owed, a trend which, after he entered the queen's service, became even more pronounced.[7]

Huntingdon discovered an alternative form of borrowing in the mortgaging of his lands and he appears to have borrowed on mortgage or on bond indiscriminately. A study of his finances does not yield the expected picture of his borrowing as long as possible on bond and then, his credit worsening, being forced to offer land as security, for even in the first ten years after he came into possession of his estates he granted ten mortgages compared with some thirty bonds. On the whole, larger amounts of money could be raised on the security of land than upon bond but, at least in the earlier part of Elizabeth's reign, the lender expected repayment within as equally short a time as with a bond: two or three years seem to have been the general length of time allowed to Huntingdon. He borrowed £2,525 from a syndicate of merchants in January, 1562 on the pledge of the manors of North Cadbury in Somerset and Barrow in Leicestershire and repaid it in February the following year. George Langham who had lent £2,000 on the security of the manor of Packington in Leicestershire in June 1563 received the mortgage loan back on 2 November 1565. In 1579 a change came about in the pattern of Huntingdon's borrowing when he began to raise money on a new type of mortgage, a lease of years. In return for a loan of about £1,500 (the recognisance is for £3,000) he 'leased' the manor of Cippenham, Buckinghamshire, to Sir Wolstan Dixie for two hundred years apparently reserving to himself the right to redeem the lease at any time during this period: in fact, Huntingdon liquidated this debt also in two years but slowly he recognised that the repayment of a loan could be delayed longer on this form of mortgage. He did not pay back £400 borrowed on a twenty-one years' 'lease' of the Rape of Hastings until 1591. The modern idea of a mortgage as a security for a loan made for an indefinite period did not become generally current until the next century but this type of mortgage by way of lease marked an important development in this direction. It freed the mortgagor from the danger of forfeiting his property through failing to repay his loan on the stipulated day.[8]

Any Elizabethan mortgagor had seriously to face the threat that if he mortgaged his lands he might never be able to recover them. Between 1579 and his death Huntingdon took up seven mortgages by way of lease while continuing to raise mortgages of the old, short-term type and among these borrowed £7,000 on 26 October 1591, from Richard Branthwaite on the security of the manors of Stoke Poges, Cippenham, Fulmer and Eton in Buckinghamshire. Branthwaite, Huntingdon's lawyer, covenanted to release the property if Huntingdon was alive on 20 July 1597 and if he had repaid the £7,000 by that date but Huntingdon died in December 1595 having repaid only half of the loan. The executors of Branthwaite foreclosed upon the property, and in spite of the efforts of the fourth and fifth Earls of Huntingdon which included a suit in the Court of Chancery in 1598 and an appeal to the Privy Council in the reign of James I, the forfeiture became absolute. Branthwaite's executors sold Stoke Poges to Sir Edward Coke who paid £4,000 to the Dowager Countess of Huntingdon for the release of her right of dower in the manor. Several generations passed before Huntingdon's heirs could reconcile themselves to the loss of Stoke Poges and the sixth earl even considered re-opening a suit for it in the same month as Charles I was executed.[9]

The lands Huntingdon mortgaged, the money he borrowed on bond, the estates he sold, do not in themselves automatically indicate economic disaster for he could have been borrowing money and selling lands in order to buy fresh property. At least at the beginning of his career he seems to have had some plan of selling outlying lands to consolidate his estates in other areas, particularly in Leicestershire. In 1562, for example, he acquired the manor of Market Bosworth from his uncle, Edward, Lord Hastings of Loughborough for £2,625 giving him the option of redeeming the purchase which he never took up. Since Lord Hastings had no legitimate children and Huntingdon could hope to be his heir this can be seen as a prudent move to safeguard his possible inheritance. In the next fifteen years he bought further lands in Leicestershire, a small estate at Belton, the site of Leicester Abbey and, far outweighing these smaller purchases, the reversion of the manor of Newbold Verdon from Walter, Earl of Essex and his trustees for £3,000. Outside Leicestershire, Huntingdon bought relatively little, but his investment in the manor of Puddletown in Dorset and the other Mountjoy manor of Canford where copperas mines lay in 1570 cost him over £4,000 for the title alone in addition to the subsequent legal expenses. Apart from this, Huntingdon purchased little new property, some houses and gardens in East and West Lilling in Sheriff Hutton, Yorkshire, and others on his manor of Christchurch in Hampshire: he does not seem to have spent much more than £13,500 on all these lands, that is about a seventh of the money he obtained from the sale of ancestral lands he used to buy new estates. Of the seven manors he acquired in this way he sold two almost immediately and by the time of his death he had overburdened the remaining five with mortgages. The greater part of his sales cannot be balanced by the new lands he bought.[10]

The special expedients to which Huntingdon increasingly turned never give the impression of his realising assets for the sake of new investments: he needed more money to live. He knew only too well the high rates of interest demanded by the professional money-lenders in return for little security, 'a most viperous generation', Sir Francis Hastings thought them, 'whose humour is to insult over both honourable, and other their betters far, and to tyrannise over their equals and inferiors and yet will they not be satisfied without use upon use'.[11] To try to confine at least some of his borrowing to his own aristocratic circle had obvious advantages, not the least of which was the expectation that gentlemen would concern themselves less with the date of repayment. Huntingdon first borrowed in 1572 £2,000 from a near neighbour, Sir James Harington of Exton in Rutland on the mortgage of the manor of Lee in the same county and eventually, in 1581, sold him the manor unconditionally together with his rights as forester in the forest of Leefield for £7,000. He recognised in Harington, who remained prosperous through husbanding his estates well and through living a retired life in the country, a useful man to be tied more closely to his interest. When in the spring of 1585 Harington agreed to the marriage of his daughter Sarah to Francis, son of Sir George Hastings and Huntingdon's oldest nephew and presumptive heir, Huntingdon confided to his brother that now he hoped to dispatch his money causes well and trusted soon to get £2,000 from Sir James to pay his present debts. The marriage certainly made it easier for him to go on borrowing from 'the little knight' as he called him; in 1589 he raised £5,200 by mortgaging Bagworth and Thornton to Harington's trustees, and as late as 1594 he relied on his connection with the family for financial support.[12]

Elizabethan noblemen, and indeed noblemen for generations after them, treated marriage as a form of property arrangement. In applying a young bride's dowry to stave off the present debts of her new family, Huntingdon in the eyes of his contemporaries was indulging in no reprehensible practice. Since she in time might well, as a widow, become chargeable to the estate and entitled by the marriage settlement to be provided with certain lands as her dower, therefore it was considered only equitable that her money should help the family in its necessity.[13] Some families, however, did object when an impoverished peer attempted to gain more than the bride's agreed dowry. Another marriage Huntingdon arranged for another of his nephews definitely had a financial motive behind it. Sir Francis Willoughby, from whom Huntingdon had borrowed considerable sums in the 1570's, had, by the next decade, amassed sufficient money from his Nottinghamshire coal mines to begin building his grandiose Flemish castle at Wollaton: his family was also well worth bringing into the Hastings circle and Huntingdon procured his daughter for Sir George Hastings's second son. Before the marriage had been effected an unknown well-wisher had warned Willoughby what its consequences might be:

The earl is about £20,000 in debt, which may greatly charge his land, and that much of this money must have come by the credit of bonds of others. . . . When you have paid two thousand pounds with your daughter, that is not their satisfaction: they shoot at another mark, for though you pay your money, yet at the marriage there shall be a key to your land, and their desire they think to bring to pass with the maintenance of their honour.[14]

Despite these insinuations, Willoughby allowed the match to proceed but was much too shrewd a man to open his estates to Huntingdon who had difficulty even in getting him to set aside land to maintain his daughter and son-in-law. Willoughby money, tied up in the building of Wollaton, can have done little to buttress the Hastings family fortunes.

In voluntarily undertaking debts to the crown, Huntingdon early discovered another way in which he could borrow money and yet be sheltered from the rigour of the money-lenders. The queen, even more than an aristocratic creditor, could be trusted not to foreclose upon land or other security immediately the day for the redemption of the loan had passed and she apparently charged no interest on the debt owing to her; certainly a debt overdue from a subject did not increase by leaps and bounds for every year left unpaid as with the ordinary money-lender.

Huntingdon first undertook a debt to the queen in 1565.[15] In February, 1564 she had lent £4,000 to the London merchant, Sir Thomas Lodge, to be repaid at certain stipulated times. Huntingdon had already had dealings with Lodge when he borrowed £2,100 from him on a mortgage in 1562 but this had been cancelled within the year: in 1564 he became bound to him on the security of 2,000 marks, probably for a further loan. Either partly for the repayment of this debt or for an entirely new loan, Huntingdon made a private agreement with Lodge to take upon himself the responsibility of the redemption of Lodge's debt to the queen and in an indenture of 28 May 1565 Elizabeth accepted the manors of North Cadbury, Evington and Market Bosworth as security for Huntingdon's repayment of the £4,000 in two separate payments in 1570. When 1570 came, however, Huntingdon had not the money to repay the debt and the queen agreed that it should be stalled for a further period. Huntingdon entered into a new indenture, in Hilary Term 1571, in which he assured the manors of South Cadbury, Holton, Kirby, Packington and Henley-on-Thames for the repayment of the sum in ten years' time: if he failed to fulfil the covenant the manors would be forfeited. In 1580 Huntingdon owed the whole of the £4,000 to the queen and still had no cash to repay it. Panic reigned in the family. Huntingdon himself could not leave his service in the north so he sent first his brother Francis, and then his wife to solicit his cause at court: for three months Hastings tirelessly lobbied Burghley and Walsingham, Leicester and Mildmay on Huntingdon's behalf but for a time it seemed there was no way out for him apart from selling more lands to repay the crown.[16] Finally the queen capitulated and very reluctantly consented to a further stalling of the debt and for the time being the threat of forfeiture was averted. The crown cancelled the old indenture and accepted from Huntingdon the pledge of his rich manor of Lubbesthorpe in place of the four manors he had offered in 1570. In the end he did succeed in paying, retardedly, part of this debt, but in 1597 his executors still owed £2,800 charged on the manor of Lubbesthorpe. Had this debt been owed to a private individual the accumulation of interest between 1565 and 1595 would have been alarming—even if the lender could have been brought to agree to the day of repayment being delayed for so long.

Another debt Huntingdon owed the crown in 1572 remained unpaid equally long. Christopher Hatton acquired from the queen early in 1572 Little Park, Leicester and other parkland formerly belonging to the Abbey of St. Mary for £1,149. 13s. 4d. which he promised to pay in six annual instalments of £199. 12s. 2¼d. beginning the following All Saints' Day: Hatton re-conveyed the property to Huntingdon, who then became responsible for the six annual payments to the queen. Huntingdon immediately raised £1,000 on the land by way of a mortgage in the form of a 500 years' lease to Edward Waterhouse; the repayment of the debt to the queen, to whom he had pledged the park of Ware, again fell into second place. In fact Huntingdon paid the first instalment of the purchase price in November 1572, but in the schedule of Huntingdon's debts to the crown in 1582 there appeared the sum of £958. 11¾d., the total of the annual instalments never paid between 1573 and 1577. The queen's accountants then merged this relatively small sum with Huntingdon's cumulative debt to the crown which he promised to repay at the rate of £383. 13s. 4d. a year.[17]

Financially, Huntingdon arranged his most important debt to the crown in 1585. Lord Lumley owed the queen £11,400 for the debts of the late Earl of Arundel and Huntingdon began negotiating with him, and, in return for a series of payments from Lumley, he shouldered his whole debt. The queen approved the transaction provided that Huntingdon would assure her lands worth £600 a year which he did, in the form of the manors of Ashby de la Zouch, Alton Grange, Packington, Knightthorpe and Braunstone, the hundred of Framland, the site of Leicester Abbey and a rent charge out of the manor of Kirby. Huntingdon promised to repay the debt at the rate of £600 a year for the next nineteen years and duly paid the first instalment at Michaelmas

1585. After that year, however, he paid nothing at all. When he died he owed the queen £5,400 on these Leicestershire manors, the instalments due for the past nine years and in addition he had arranged that £600 should be paid each year for the next nine years, which meant that his executors owed £10,800 on the manor of Ashby alone. Yet though this undertaking of Lord Lumley's debt imposed a crippling burden on his successors, Huntingdon himself derived real benefits from it. In May 1584 he wrote to his brother that he expected a payment of £1,000 any time from Lumley and that he proposed to put another of Lumley's statutes into a money-lender's hands to raise a further £1,000 which would have become payable the following November: as late as February 1588 Huntingdon still received payments from Lumley.[18] More than any other single source Lumley's money must have helped Huntingdon to reduce his debts to private money-lenders which fell due in the 'jubilee' year of 1584 and amounted to a minimum of £12,000.[19] Through this scheme of undertaking debts to the crown, Huntingdon could at least substitute a more forbearing sovereign for his host of professional creditors.

Nevertheless extensions of time could only put off the day when Huntingdon or his successor had to face the final settlement of his debts; they could not solve the problem. The queen, after much persuasion, did eventually offer Huntingdon one chance to try to clear these debts through an exchange of lands, a favour she had refused to the second Earl of Cumberland and to James, Lord Mountjoy though both had loaded their estates with heavy debts.[20] Huntingdon sent his first plea to Burghley for relief in August 1587:

thus it standeth with me [he complained], that in November next the utter ruin of my poor state will begin, and every week or fortnight until towards the end of February will increase, and by the end of that month I may say, *consummatum est*, except it please her majesty in the meantime of her gracious bounty to relieve me.

The idea behind the type of exchange Huntingdon sought was simple: he wished to offer the queen a compact estate and to receive in return many scattered parcels of crown land of a nominally equivalent value. In theory the transaction would benefit both parties, for the queen gained a consolidated block of lands in place of many possessions dispersed over a wide area while Huntingdon had many small, under-rented properties which he could exploit either by increasing the rents over the years or by re-selling immediately at a profit. The queen's reluctance to allow these exchanges between herself and her subjects on any scale indicates she knew on whose side the real advantage lay in such an undertaking and Huntingdon made several suggestions before she agreed upon the procedure. First he proposed to Burghley a scheme for exchanging some of his lands worth £450 a year for crown lands of a similar rental, £200 of which lands being charged with accustomed rents to the crown but the remaining £250 unencumbered.[21] When his petition actually reached the queen in October 1587 he aimed at a greater prize: he promised that if the queen would grant him lands worth £600 a year, £400 in fee farm, that is charged with customary rents, and £200 in fee simple, unburdened with any charges, he would guarantee to the crown land worth £1,000 for ever. Realising that this might appear too ambitious a proposal, he made the alternative suggestion that if the queen would make over to him lands worth £500 a year, £300 being in fee farm, £200 in fee simple, he would then grant her in exchange lands of the annual value of £800. He did not fail to point out that (on paper) the queen stood to gain by £400 a year from the first proposal, and by £300 from the second, revealing incidentally the extent contemporaries believed the crown lands were under-rented.[22] The exchange of lands to which the parties finally agreed more nearly resembled Huntingdon's more modest suggestion to Burghley than either of the plans he had laid before the queen. The royal warrant, dated November 1587, authorised the lord treasurer to grant to Huntingdon so much of the queen's lands as would produce a rental of £400 a year, one half of the lands in fee farm, the remainder in fee simple, on the understanding that Huntingdon

Sir George Hastings (later fourth Earl of Huntingdon) and his son, Francis

should first assure to the queen, lands of his own worth a clear £400 annually, all in fee simple.[23]

In practice much intervened to blur the clear outline of the original scheme; the first complication was that Huntingdon did not in fact exchange his ancestral lands with the queen. Some time after he had been appointed President of the Council in the North Huntingdon entangled himself with the Bowes family who had suffered much in the rebellion of 1569 for their loyalty to the crown. He lent money probably to Sir George Bowes and certainly to Robert Bowes, the treasurer of the queen's forces stationed at Berwick.[24] The Bowes could not meet their debts and in January 1587, Sir William Bowes granted to Huntingdon on the payment of £2,000 the manor of Hilton in county Durham to hold in perpetuity: the following month the mortgagees of Sir William Bowes, Sir George Bowes and Robert Bowes conveyed the manor of Bradbury, also in county Durham, to Huntingdon though in this case no purchase price was recorded. These two manors produced a combined annual rental of £451. 17s. 6d. and Huntingdon, in collaboration with Sir William Bowes, chose to alienate them to the crown in March 1588.

Further complications arose over the second stage of the exchange since the whole of the queen's grant did not pass at one time, but in three separate assignments, and since it named not Huntingdon but his agents as the recipients of the lands. On 8 June 1588, 11 February and 4 April 1589 the queen 'at the petition of Henry, Earl of Huntingdon' made three different conveyances of one hundred and one parcels of lands and rents, in fee farm and fee simple, scattered widely over England and Wales to Richard Branthwaite and Roger Bromley. Almost certainly Huntingdon had the exchange lands made over directly to Branthwaite and Bromley for reasons of convenience as the administration of the exchange involved a vast amount of work. Branthwaite, who took the lead in the business, was a London lawyer of some eminence, (he had become a serjeant-at-law by 1594) and in 1582 Huntingdon had granted him an annuity out of the manor of Kirby.[25] He acted

G

for Huntingdon in several lawsuits and after 1589 advanced loans to his master.[26] Roger Bromley of Bagworth Park, Leicestershire, had made out conveyances of land for Huntingdon from at least 1579 and he also held an annuity from him. Consequently the possibility arises that Branthwaite and Bromley may not have been acting solely as agents, but themselves were among the creditors Huntingdon intended to reimburse out of the profits from the exchange.

The fate of the exchange lands makes it abundantly clear that Huntingdon did not want these lands to extend his estates or to augment his revenues by the raising of rents: he acquired them for immediate resale and did not even retain the manors in Leicestershire. In each of the three assignments Branthwaite and Bromley had sold two-thirds of the properties within a month of the issue of the queen's letters patent. The last recorded sale took place in July 1591, but with very minor exceptions the whole of the exchange lands had been sold by the middle of 1590. Branthwaite and Bromley may have been allowed to choose those crown lands which they knew would find ready purchasers, at all events they were not left long with land on their hands. About half the lands appear to have been bought by local landowners and perhaps as many as thirty different lots went to London merchants, themselves counting upon a quick resale. Herein lay the advantage of the extremely varied nature of the grants for some small men eagerly bought their own cottage or a few acres of land when offered the opportunity while merchants considered scattered lands in a defined area a good investment. A grant of a few large manors might have been much less easy to sell, at least for cash and in addition every individual sale enlarged the chances of potential profit.[27]

Disappointingly little evidence now remains about the profits which came to Huntingdon through the exchange. Perhaps because he left the whole of the administration to Branthwaite and Bromley and because they worked in London, none of the indentures of sale found their way into the Hastings family papers.

The Close Rolls record the sale of virtually every parcel of the exchange lands but very rarely give the sale price. It is known that the manor of Framfield in Sussex (which was valued at over £93 a year and was apparently the most substantial of the manors included in the exchange) sold for £8,400, and the manor of Queniborough in Leicestershire, valued at over £25 a year, for nearly £2,000.[28] Both these manors formed part of the lands granted in fee simple but the rapidity of the sales makes it evident that Huntingdon's agents had no more difficulty in selling the lands charged with accustomed rents. The presumption must be that Huntingdon received lands very considerably undervalued and that the exchange of lands, to a certain extent, masked a free gift from the queen.

The profits Huntingdon obtained from the exchange of lands he almost certainly applied to lessening his outstanding debts but however substantial these profits may have been they did not solve the problem of his insolvency. As quickly as old debts were cleared new ones accumulated and his financial difficulties remained, to all appearances, unabated. In 1592 Sir Francis Hastings even suggested that Huntingdon might approach the queen for another grant, but for that he had not the temerity to try and by 1594 he found himself in the all too familiar position of needing to raise £5,000 in cash to pay present debts.[29] Had the queen never consented to the exchange of lands the chaos which would have resulted on Huntingdon's death defies the imagination. Matters proved desperate enough as things were for when the fourth Earl of Huntingdon at last consented to take up the administration of his late brother's estate, an obligation he had done all in his power to avoid, it emerged that the third earl owed more than £18,000 to the queen alone.[30] His debts to private individuals which had come about through his more orthodox forms of borrowing, on mortgage and on bond, were thought to have amounted to a further £17,000 excluding annuities.[31] Ultimately some of the few remaining uncharged estates had to be sold to satisfy the debts: by 1615 the manors of Canford, Newbold

Verdon and Lubbesthorpe which Huntingdon had refused to sell at the height of his extremity had gone, and in 1623 the greater part of the manor of Aller seems to have been alienated.[32] Other creditors were disposed of by the conversion of some of the mortages Huntingdon had raised into absolute sales; in this way the family lost Henley-on-Thames in 1599, as well as the rich manor of Stoke Poges.[33] Huntingdon's debt to the crown, a very heavy one when the resources he left to resolve it are remembered, had been caused almost entirely by the expedients he had used to get ready money in emergencies. He still owed £2,800 on the manor of Lubbesthorpe which he had pledged to the crown in 1582 as security for debts of £10,685 which included the debts of Sir Thomas Lodge and Sir Christopher Hatton which he had voluntarily undertaken, while of Lord Lumley's debt charged on the manor of Ashby, £5,400 was in arrears, and £600 due to be paid for each of the next nine years. In effect more than £13,500 of the £18,000 Huntingdon owed to the queen consisted of debts he had undertaken.[34]

For two generations the consequences of Huntingdon's debts to the crown remained to burden the heads of the Hastings family. Immediately on his death the crown seized under a writ of extent all his unpledged land to secure repayment. The queen allowed the fourth Earl of Huntingdon to lease back the Leicestershire lands on certain conditions: he held the manor of Lubbesthorpe for the next twenty-one years for an annual payment of £383. 13s. 8d., the manors of Ashby, Belton, Evington and other lands for an unlimited time for an annual rent of £147. 16s. 11¼d.[35] Still in 1636 acquittances among the family papers show that the fifth Earl of Huntingdon was making payments into the Exchequer for lands extended to the crown for the debts of his great uncle.[36] Almost no information survives about the repayments made to private money-lenders, or the time their debts took to be cleared, but they are hardly likely to have been less pertinacious than the crown in trying to recover their own. Huntingdon had died on the brink of bankruptcy and in the sight of the world this apparent neglect of his family proved his greatest dishonour.

* * *

In his apology for his brother's life, Sir Francis refused to discuss the precise reasons for his financial failure: while he lived Huntingdon was less reticent, at different times giving different explanations for the causes of his indebtedness, and varying the emphasis he placed on the factors he thought had contributed to his insolvency. He listed the debts he had inherited from his ancestors and the burdens of providing for his relatives: later came the undoubtedly heavy costs of acquiring the manor of Canford, the decade of litigation, and of working the mines. He made much of the expense to him personally of his service of the queen, and told Burghley in the summer of 1587, when his debts had reached a dangerously high level,

since I went into the service of the north I have spent more than her majesty's allowance above 20,000 li. But I do not set this down, that I count it among the causes of my hindrance. For I hold both my life and living to no other end but that I may therewith serve God and her majesty.[37]

Some contemporaries saw his undoing in his alleged lavish support of Puritan ministers, while a later earl bewailed his carelessness of his posterity. Underlying all seems to have been the fact that with the incoherent management of his estates Huntingdon had not the resources sufficient to withstand the increasing demands made upon them.

When Huntingdon succeeded his father the gross annual income from the family estates should have approached £6,000, for later he sold lands worth nearly £100,000 which were not likely to have produced an annual income of less than £5,000 and still some lands remained to his heir at his death. Huntingdon, however, actually received a mere fraction of this income: he had possession of less than a third of the estate, his mother held the remainder, part as her dower but the greater part as one of the heirs of Margaret, Countess of Salisbury, and the Dowager Countess of

Huntingdon outlived her husband for sixteen years.[38] For a man of his station throughout this period Huntingdon had indeed little to live upon and his wife cast about for stratagems for making ends meet. In 1561 she sought the help of her brother, the future Earl of Leicester, in a scheme for economy: she knew her husband could not avoid attending court to pay his respects to the queen but begged Dudley to see he did not stay long, and to get permission for her not to come at all:

I assure you when he shall go he shall not be hable to carry forty pounds in his purse to bear his charges the whole journey, but if he spend more I am sure he must borrow it there, and that he needeth not, for I trow he oweth five or six thousand pounds at the least, and may not spend a year past five or six hundred. Good brother, consider his state and help that he may not spend more then he hath.[39]

Just when his resources were at their lowest, Huntingdon had to meet heavy calls upon his estate in order to resolve his father's debts and to provide for his brothers and sisters. The sums the second Earl of Huntingdon owed to the crown do not seem to have been considerable, perhaps under £1,000, and certainly they fell far short of those Huntingdon himself left, but his obligations to private money-lenders amounted to much more. Huntingdon later said that his father's debts, his legacies and the expenses of his funeral came to £11,000. 'My lands were charged also with sundry annuities', he wrote in 1587, looking back to the beginning of his troubles, 'which do continue to this day, which at first pinched me greatly, because I had then so little to live on.'[40] The greater part of these annuities originated in the second earl's desire to create a sufficient maintenance for all of his younger children. While his mother yet lived and held a large part of the family lands away from Huntingdon he paid the yearly stipends to Edward, Francis and Walter as laid down in his father's will and made over to each of them lands worth £60 a year when they reached their twenty-first birthday: his four sisters also received their allowances of £20, and for two of them, Frances and Elizabeth who married before 1572, he had to raise dowries of

£2,000 each. Huntingdon found it necessary to set aside lands worth £480 a year to pay these annuities and to begin to pay off his father's debts. It seems that the younger Hastings children benefited from an unusually generous father (the Earl of Worcester who died in 1549 only left estates worth £20 a year for his younger sons while his daughters received dowries of about £500) and their brother, instead of begrudging them their portions, in some cases doubled them.[41] These family responsibilities in the 1560's and 1570's go far to explain why Huntingdon had to sell lands and borrow extensively on bond from first entering into his inheritance.

The Dowager Countess of Huntingdon did something to help her son in his difficulties. The lease which she made to him in 1562 of all her lands (except the manor of Lubbesthorpe) for an annuity of £960 and the undertaking by Huntingdon to double his sisters' dowries did not stand long, since it was cancelled in 1564 but in exchange for it the countess granted her son a lease of the manor of Stokenham in Devon and permission to sell certain of her Cornish lands.[42] Ten years later she renounced further rights in other Devon and Cornish manors to enable Huntingdon to carry out further sales and received in compensation three Somerset manors for life.[43] Similarly, she assigned the park of Ware in Hertfordshire to him so he might pledge it for his debts to the crown, in return for an annuity of £33. 6s. 8d., yet, as the fine Huntingdon paid on inheriting his mother's estates shows, she kept the greater part of her estates in her own possession until her death in 1576 and her own separate household at Lubbesthorpe.[44] Huntingdon never freed himself from the debts he incurred while his mother lived and held so large a part of the family lands: ironically his own wife outlived him by twenty-five years and most of this time detained the manors of Loughborough, Barrow, Aller and Canford away from the head of the family, by far the major part of the inheritance Huntingdon had saved for his heirs. Longevity of dowager countesses could prove a serious encumbrance to a noble estate.

Huntingdon can scarcely be blamed for helping his brothers and sisters since it was so evidently in accord with his father's wishes, yet there remains something in the charge of the seventh earl, the friend of Dugdale, that he neglected to think of his heirs.[45] Certainly he did not pass on intact the estates he had inherited yet he cannot be accused of indulging in riotous living, even when he first tasted independence. The third Earl of Cumberland in the late 1570's quickly ran up large debts in London, while the Earl of Northumberland later reproached himself for his youthful profligacy, but until the queen sent him into the north, Huntingdon spent his days soberly in Leicestershire.[46] Social convention required him to provide for a household in accordance with his rank, but again his household seems to have been a relatively modest one. At Michaelmas 1564, he had seventy-seven servants at his castle of Ashby de la Zouch: Richard Bertie and Katherine, Duchess of Suffolk had eighty persons in their household at almost exactly the same time. The Earl of Northumberland retained many more servants, and in 1568 his check-roll numbered one hundred and twenty. While Huntingdon's household included four gentlewomen, ten gentlemen and twenty-six yeomen, in 1578 Lord North kept twenty-four gentlemen and seventy yeomen in his service. For the half year in 1568 Huntingdon's wages bill came to over £60, and this total is incomplete so that a reasonable estimate of his annual expenditure on servants, before he held office, would be about £150 quite apart from the cost of feeding so large an assembly. Labour may have been cheap but to keep up such a household together with his family dependants, especially in his early years, must have absorbed most of Huntingdon's unassigned revenues.[47]

The style of living which Huntingdon could not avoid maintaining although costly, was still in itself not enough to bring disaster upon the house and Huntingdon never pretended that it was the one or even the chief cause of his failure. The debts he subsequently regretted came not from ostentatious living but from his 'causeless contention' with Lord Mountjoy. Legal cases, especially over the possession of land, tended to take years to settle in Tudor England and bring heavy costs in their wake. Even in this context Huntingdon's suit with Mountjoy over the manor of Canford in Dorset stands out since it concerned not only the possession of land but also of mineral workings established upon the lands. Members of the Elizabethan aristocracy quite frequently involved themselves in industrial projects. The Earls of Devon, Cumberland and Shrewsbury and Lord Paget all worked the coal mines on their estates and Sir Francis Willoughby for a time waxed wealthy from Nottinghamshire coal until his building programme ate into his capital. The Earl of Shrewsbury also had lead smelting works at Rievaulx. Leicester, Pembroke, Warwick and Burghley all consciously interested themselves in new ventures but Huntingdon, to all appearances by accident, found himself a minor industrialist *malgré lui*.[48]

Since the break with Rome, the English government had felt uneasy over the knowledge that the chief source of the supply of alum, an essential ingredient in the dyeing industry, lay in the Papal States and encouraged prospectors to seek for an alternative centre of production, preferably in England.[49] Sir Thomas Chaloner first seriously tried to mine for alum, making his essay in Ireland and when in 1557 James Blount, Lord Mountjoy married his step-daughter he drew him also into the enterprise. Mountjoy owned two-thirds of the extensive manor of Canford in Dorset which stretched as far south as the English Channel and included much of what later became the towns of Poole and Bournemouth and on the discovery of copperas ore there he had high hopes of producing alum. In 1564 he took a Fleming, Cornelius de Vos, into his service, obtained a patent of monopoly from the crown for the digging of alum and copperas and at his own expense brought over Italian workmen to begin mining at Canford Cliffs. Mountjoy himself took up residence at Canford to supervise the mines but in spite of this precaution de Vos soon tired of the experiment and returned to Flanders forcing Mountjoy, if he wished to continue, into acquiring the monopoly in his own

name.[50] There can be little doubt that at this stage Mountjoy
would have untertaken any risk which showed any possibility of
making profits: his debts which were substantial even before his
marriage had been further increased by de Vos's abortive
attempts so he determined to invest his remaining capital in the
mines. In fact the prospect of producing alum commercially at
Canford never materialised, although by 1566 copperas, an equally
essential compound in dyeing, was being manufactured there in
considerable quantities.[51] The profits, however, came too late to
save Mountjoy's estates: in 1567 he and his wife mortgaged their
part of the manor of Canford to John Browne, Lady Mountjoy's
uncle, and the following year Mountjoy leased the alum and
copperas workings to George Carleton and John Hastings and at
the same time assigned to them a mortgage on the manor of
Puddletown in Dorset.[52] Carleton was a kinsman of Lady
Mountjoy while John Hastings, who had probably been an exile
for the sake of religion in Mary's reign and whom the Elizabethan
government employed in 1575 as an envoy to William of Orange,
was distantly related to Huntingdon.[53]

A decade later, Mountjoy's counsel alleged that Huntingdon
had recommended Carleton and Hastings to the late Lord Mountjoy
as men suitable to help him in his difficulties with the sole
intention of gaining the lands for himself. Carleton and Hastings
always strenuously denied this, maintaining they had become
Mountjoy's mortgagees long before Huntingdon knew what they
were doing. At all events they had not the resources to withstand
the demands being made on Mountjoy's overburdened estates and
soon set to work to get help from Huntingdon. In 1570 they
persuaded him to buy the manor of Puddletown from them for
£2,500 and at the same time John Browne conveyed to him for a
further £2,100 his title in the manor of Canford.[54] Subsequently
Huntingdon said that Browne had been trying to dispose of the
land for the previous three years without success as the bonds and
statutes, amounting to £30,000, charged by Mountjoy on the
property had made it virtually impossible to sell.[55] His defenders

claimed that Lady Mountjoy had welcomed the transaction and had been thankful that Canford had come to such an honourable man as the earl and hoped that through him perhaps something might yet be salvaged from the mass of debts for herself and her sons.[56]

So in 1570 through these complicated manœuvres, which may well have arisen from nothing more sinister than Huntingdon's desire to help a relative in difficulty, he found himself in possession of the manor on which the alum mines stood, but he did not own the works themselves. Lord Mountjoy, who asserted that the whole transaction had been carried out without his knowledge determined to prosecute his claim to the end and reserved to himself the right to manufacture alum and copperas. Huntingdon cannot have entertained any high hopes for a quick return on his outlay and in fact had to spend the next decade in gaining a surer title to what he had already bought. In 1576 Sir Lionel Duckett, a London alderman, released to him his rights in Canford and Puddletown for £450 and in 1579 George Montague surrendered any claim he still had in Canford. Mountjoy, in the meanwhile, continued raising mortgages on the mines, borrowing £400 from Henry Smith on the security of a twelve years' lease to manufacture 200 tons of copperas a year.[57] When Lady Mountjoy died in 1577 the uneasy calm ended and the title in the mines which Mountjoy had vested in her and her children passed to her sons, William and Charles Blount. They looked upon Huntingdon's intrusion with far less favourable eyes than their mother had done, and not even waiting for their father's death opened legal proceedings. Huntingdon, on his side, thought the time opportune for asserting his control over the mines which he had so far refrained from doing out of consideration for Lady Mountjoy.

Huntingdon's six years of litigation with the Blount family began when William and Charles Blount tried to grant a lease of Oakman's mining house at Canford to Edward Meade which Huntingdon considered an encroachment upon his manorial rights: he wrote in April 1581 from Newcastle, where the queen's business detained him, to protest to Leicester and Walsingham.[58] In the autumn of 1581 James, Lord Mountjoy died and his lands, including Canford and Puddletown, were seized by the crown for his debts. Legally Huntingdon gained from this action since it enabled him to bring a case in the Exchequer which formally recognised his title to two-thirds of the manor of Canford and to the manor of Puddletown, and ordered their restoration to him.[59] Yet his ownership of Canford without possession of the mines gave him an empty victory: realising that the mines were his only bargaining counter the new Lord Mountjoy rejected all Huntingdon's proposals for compensation if he would surrender his claim.[60] At this impasse the dispute came before the Privy Council who consigned its hearing to the two Chief Justices and the Master of the Rolls. To add to the legal uncertainties, Mountjoy and his brother chose this time to set about acquiring the third part of the manor of Canford which their father had never held and consequently which had never passed to Huntingdon. In the spring of 1582 the Privy Council issued interim orders: for the time being the working of the mines was to remain with those lessees who had held them before the disputes arose, all local suits were to be stayed and a commission set up of the sheriff and local justices to examine all those who at any time had participated in the management of the alum and copperas works.[61] Throughout May and June both parties got their lawyers to draw up voluminous interrogatories and the queen gave Huntingdon permission to come south for the summer to safeguard his interests. He confided to Walsingham that he thought Mountjoy and his lewd counsel 'will leave nothing unattempted by which they may think most to harm me' and in spite of the sums of money he had undertaken to pay Mountjoy, did not venture to dispose of the copperas at Canford from the sequestered mines without explicit permission. The case dragged on all through 1582, and still Huntingdon could not bring Mountjoy to produce the documents which would enable his lawyers to examine his rights to the mines.[62]

Nothing could have been more illusory than Huntingdon's hope for a speedy end of the case: not until August 1583 did it again come before the judges and then he could not get leave to come south to attend the Dorset assizes. On his prompting, the queen commanded the judges 'to do upright and indifferent justice' that his cause might not suffer in his absence, while Huntingdon persuaded Sir Francis Hastings to represent him in Dorset and send him reports of the proceedings.[63] Huntingdon had all the more need of a member of the family at Canford since Lord Mountjoy was quite openly building up his faction there, starting rumours that he would have re-established himself at Canford house by Christmas. The situation became more and more explosive; the tenants divided themselves into factions, Mountjoy's men against Huntingdon's men, until riots seemed inevitable. Hastings's overseer thought the carrying of turves for use in Oakman's mine might well provide the occasion for fighting to break out and Huntingdon dared not dispense with his brother's presence even for a short visit to Leicestershire.[64] Hostilities intensified between the tenants and as Huntingdon's men built up a ditch, Mountjoy's people cast it down again. Hastings moved into Canford house and soon realised there could be no peace in the locality while the principal antagonists, Mountjoy and Huntingdon, remained unreconciled. He composed letters to Walsingham and Hatton explaining the 'reasonableness' of his brother's demands and did his best to compensate Huntingdon for Mountjoy's ease of access to the queen.[65] Hastings rallied all Huntingdon's friends at court, turning especially to his brother-in-law, but Leicester, to Huntingdon's annoyance, favoured a compromise:

If my title to the land be good, and my dealing in the purchasing of it have been honest [Huntingdon protested to his brother], then I hope they that have laboured to slander both shall in the end gain little against me thereby. But I that have been forced (to my great charges) to defend myself in both, shall I am sure by arbitrament obtain little. But I may by yielding of this request easily become subject to more reproach then by anything that they can do or say. . . . And therefore to conclude this matter I say once again I will never compromit my title to this land to the arbitrament of any.[66]

However much Huntingdon might declare in righteous indignation 'this opinion is firm in me and never to be altered' the passage of time forced a more compliant attitude upon him. In 1585 Francis Hastings came down to Canford for a three years' stay, with authority from Huntingdon to determine all matters at issue between him and his tenants. He succeeded in getting the case between Huntingdon and Mountjoy transferred from the brawls in Dorset to the Privy Council to whom at last in May 1585 Mountjoy submitted his formal plea for the restoring of Canford and Puddletown.[67] Leicester's imminent departure for the Low Countries added urgency to the proceedings, for Huntingdon's solicitor feared that if no agreement was reached before he left, Mountjoy would use the long interim to his advantage: Leicester again urged Huntingdon to compromise.[68] Still in April 1586 the solicitors for both parties continued to plead their clients' cases before the judges assigned by the Privy Council, but at last a settlement seemed possible. On 29 May 1586 the Lord Chancellor and the Lord Treasurer called Huntingdon and Mountjoy before them to signify the queen's pleasure concerning the final end of the controversy: the law recognised Huntingdon as the undisputed owner both of Canford and the mines but required him to pay Mountjoy £6,000 for the renunciation of all his claims. Meditating on this relatively satisfactory outcome, Huntingdon gave all the credit to his brother: nothing now remained for him except to submit to Mountjoy's professions of friendship, 'of whose good will I shall be more willing to accept then his bad dealing towards me hath deserved, because if I can not forgive him, I may fear a worse matter to befall me, then by him or any other can come to pass against me'.[69]

Subsequently Huntingdon had good reason to reflect whether the years of litigation to secure his title to Canford had been worth the expense; quite apart from the compensation to be paid to

Mountjoy the legal costs in themselves must have been very
heavy. He complained to Burghley in 1587 that 'the suit with
Lord Mountjoy hath cost me, I might rightly term it, a *nemo scit*':
when Huntingdon himself would not name a figure it is impossible
today with the bills of the lawyers' fees lost to make an exact
estimate but Huntingdon's total costs may well have been in the
region of £10,000.[70] He entered into a considerable amount of
litigation throughout his life, chiefly to secure his absolute
possession of certain manors he had inherited or his rights against
his tenants but in regard to expense this one case over Canford
exceeded them all.[71]

   Huntingdon's debts had been increased by the cost of the manor
and the long law suit, and Canford, when assured to him by all the
majesty of the law, still continued to drain him of capital.
Huntingdon would have wasted all his labour if he had not kept
the mines in operation, yet to work them profitably apparently
required a larger investment than he could make. Particularly in
the 1580's after the law suit had ended he faced seemingly endless
costs. First the leases of Mountjoy's erstwhile tenants had to be
bought out; Huntingdon claimed to have paid between £8,000
and £9,000 to obtain a lease which had originally been granted to
Lecolt by James, Lord Mountjoy, and by 1588 he acknowledged
himself to be in debt to his tenants at Canford to the extent of
almost £13,636.[72] Even when these leases had been acquired
Huntingdon had yet one more obstacle to encounter before his
mines had a chance of operating profitably. The whole success of
the commercial undertaking depended upon the monopoly of
mining alum and copperas confirmed to Mountjoy by an act of
parliament of 1567 which expired in 1591. If it were not renewed,
Huntingdon feared competition from other copperas workings
would cause him to lose his tenant, Philip Smith, to whom he had
recently assigned the venture, so that his rents would fall drastic-
ally, and the works erected at such a charge would become
redundant. 'What I should lose by the decay of my mines,' he
confessed to Burghley in an attempt to enlist his support, 'your

honour doth partly know, for the buying of Lecolt's lease, besides
my charge by her majesty's commandment to the Lord Mountjoy
has made the same to be most extreme dear to me.'[73] Going on to
petition the queen and parliament for the monopoly's renewal
Huntingdon asserted he had spent the round sum of £20,000 on
the mines and manor of Canford. No act of parliament was passed
to confirm the continuance of the monopoly, but since copperas
went on being produced at Canford with apparently no abatement
years after the expiry date it may be assumed that the queen
sanctioned its renewal.[74]

Although in the last years of his life Huntingdon had constantly
to meet the threat of financial ruin, whatever other lands he sold,
he never contemplated the alienation of the Canford mines, and,
indeed, the manor of Canford and the mines was one of the few
parts of the estate to pass relatively unencumbered to his wife on
his death. Huntingdon seems to have hoped in these last days that
the mines might yet justify the capital he had poured into them.
The failure of the attempt to produce alum at Canford has over-
shadowed the fact that copperas was mined there very profitably
from early in Elizabeth's reign. A tenant valued a lease of the
mines which Lord Mountjoy had granted to him in 1579 for £100
at £1,500 in 1585, and he did not exaggerate unduly, for Huntingdon accepted Smith's offer of £1,300 for the lease in 1588.[75] This
thirteenfold rise in the declared worth of a lease in less than a
decade is some indication of the profits obtainable in the manufacture of copperas. Throughout the 1580's and 1590's, indeed,
Huntingdon relied on the sale of copperas to meet some of his
debts: in the spring of 1584 he expected Francis Hastings to be
able to set aside £100 a month coming in from the mines to pay
off a debt of £500. Later in the year he heard the news that Hastings
had one hundred tons of copperas or more at Poole with a buyer in
London offering cash: he anticipated that this would satisfy his
debt of £413 to Fisher, £100 to Blunt and Culliner, £100 to Philip
Smith, Mr. Spencer and other similar rents paid out of the mines,
and £133 due to Mr. Milward, besides £500 he owed to Sir James

Sir Edward Hastings

Harington—a combined total of well over £1,200. In 1587 Huntingdon allowed a tenant to dispose of thirty-nine tons of copperas at £9 a ton, a valuation probably under the market price. He went on allocating profits from the mines in this haphazard fashion to repay particular debts until 1587, when he made a deliberate attempt to place the management of the mines on a more regular basis, and granted a lease of the mines to Philip Smith at an annual rent of £1,300. At the same time all Huntingdon's debts outstanding to the various undertakers at Canford were collected together and found to amount to a little over £13,635. In order to liquidate this debt Huntingdon decided that Smith should pay the whole of the annual rent directly to his creditors, and if all had gone according to plan the debt would have been paid off within ten years. In 1600 the fourth Earl of Huntingdon alleged that £500 of the debt remained unpaid through the negligence of the lessee, yet even so the major part of the debt had disappeared. To a limited extent Huntingdon succeeded in using the rents from the mines to resolve the debts incurred in their purchase.[76]

At Huntingdon's death the mines, like all his other lands sequestered by the crown, were neither providing a source of new revenue nor draining the estate of capital any further. His heirs clung just as desperately as Huntingdon to the hope that great profits might yet be made by the mines. So long as Philip Smith's lease ran (it was not due to expire until 1608) the fourth Earl of Huntingdon could not intervene directly in their management but he did bring a case in the Exchequer for arrears of the £1,300 annual rent which he claimed Smith had ingeniously avoided paying by betaking himself to prison with the intention of spending the rest of his life there.[77] When Smith's lease expired, the fifth Earl of Huntingdon made a final attempt to recover the arrears of rent and began proceedings in the court of Chancery but patently by 1608 the mines no longer functioned on a basis profitable to anyone. The Chancery judges awarded the fifth earl £800 which they considered to be the profits of the mines in 1602 and 1603 together with £1,050 compensation for the destruction of the

H

mining works by the tenant, a meagre recompense for 'the great mass of money' the third earl had 'spent therein to the great hurt of himself and maim to his house and posterity'.[78] Nevertheless the fifth earl could still recoup some considerable sums from the wreckage. Having acquired the elusive third part of the manor of Canford which his great uncle had always intended to buy but had never bought, in February 1612 he sold the reunited manor, the manor house and the mines for a total apparently approaching £13,000 to Sir John Webb.[79]

With the advantage of hindsight it is all too easy to condemn Huntingdon for ever allowing himself to become entangled with Canford and the mining enterprise. He did not know, when he first became a security for Mountjoy that the queen would require him to reside at the opposite end of England: if Mountjoy could not make income balance expenditure watching over the mines from Canford manor house Huntingdon had little chance of being more efficient from York. Yet copperas and alum mining, though risky, was not an undertaking doomed from the start, it did temporarily produce large profits and some of these reached Huntingdon. The history of his dealing with the mines shows, what might have been obvious to a man more experienced in the financial world, that he did not hold sufficient capital to carry a speculative venture to a stable and profitable conclusion.

Apart from the Canford mines, Huntingdon scarcely indulged in examples of conspicuous spending common among his contemporaries. Elizabethan aristocrats loved to build great houses, Lord Burghley at Theobalds, the Countess of Shrewsbury at Hardwick Hall, Sir Francis Willoughby at Wollaton, to mention only a few, but Huntingdon imitated them to a very limited extent. Ashby castle remained virtually in its fortress state as planned by William Lord Hastings in the uncertain times of Edward IV and had now become quite old-fashioned when compared with the new mansions in the neighbourhood. Huntingdon did undertake some building of his own at Stoke Poges and between 1583 and 1587 (the only years for which accounts exist) the building costs fluctuated from £64 to approaching £200 a year, sums which were easily met out of the revenues of the manor.[80] The fourth and fifth Earls of Huntingdon claimed that over £10,000 had been spent on the house at Stoke Poges but their statements are suspect since they made them when they were trying to regain the forfeited manor from Coke. Huntingdon carried out other reconstructions at the King's Manor at York, the administrative centre of the Council in the North but he may well have paid for them out of the fines taken in the council as his predecessor, Sussex, is thought to have done.[81]

The fifth Earl of Huntingdon, who explicitly criticised his great uncle for ruining his inheritance, and who ultimately suffered most because of the debts he had left, complained not of his extravagant consumption, but of his generosity to his servants, claiming that he had too freely sold them lands at less than the market value, and granted them annuities.[82] As his difficulties increased, Huntingdon certainly sold or mortgaged lands to his lawyers and surveyors. Edward Ameredith, the surveyor of Huntingdon's Devonshire manors as early as 1562, ended his career in possession of the manor of Harlestone, an interest in the manor of Langford Leicester, the manor of Stokenham and the hundred of Colridge, all in Devon, and lands in Aller in Somerset but he paid his lord at least £7,000 for them. Serjeant Branthwaite bought, between 1581 and 1595, the manor of Cippenham for £3,000 and (with Thomas Spencer) that of Ringwood for £5,000 and accepted mortgages upon Christchurch and Stoke Poges for a total loan of £12,000. Other men, servants in a more technical sense than these two prosperous lawyers, received grants of leases. Stephen Harvey, who progressed from the office of Huntingdon's surveyor to being his deputy-auditor and then full auditor took a 99 years' lease of a farm in Maperton in Somerset in 1582. Robert Baynbridge, bailiff of Ashby de la Zouch in succession to his father, Thomas, had a lease of watermills at Ashby in 1590, paying £200 as an entry fine in addition to the annual rent. Other servants obtained annuities. Huntingdon gave Roger Bromley and his prospective bride an annuity of £50 in 1580, and Richard Branthwaite and Christopher Southouse conjointly one of £20 two years later.[83] Clearly Huntingdon's servants could have exploited their master's resources, for they knew more accurately than he the value of any particular estate on the open market, yet there is no irrefutable evidence that they abused their positions of trust, and the charges that they bought lands for less than their true worth may be little more than the irrational protests of a man who believed himself wrongfully deprived of his estates. The fifth Earl of Huntingdon, indeed, felt himself so injuriously treated that he contemplated virtually any lengths, including employing a lawyer who specialised in overturning lawful conveyances, to recover some of the lost family lands.[84] Others less personally interested could have argued that the annuities to Branthwaite, Bromley and Southouse, to name but a few instances, constituted a just reward in return for a lifetime's service.

Camden first published the rumour that Huntingdon, 'a man of a mild disposition, but inflamed with a zeal to the purer religion, wasted his patrimony much by relieving (at his great cost) the hotter spirited ministers'.[85] As time went on the legend grew, and Dugdale after the Restoration confessed to the seventh Earl of Huntingdon, a good Anglican with no leanings towards Non-conformity, that he had no doubt that the Puritans had proved so chargeable guests to Huntingdon that they consumed him.[86] Huntingdon's devotion to the cause of advancing the gospel cannot be questioned. The Elizabethan clergy, like other sections of the community, suffered from the rapid rise in prices, and consequently one issue which concerned them closely was over impropriations, ecclesiastical livings which had come into lay hands at the dissolution of the monasteries whose revenues were now diverted from the Church.[87] A pamphleteer at the time of the Civil War remembered the tradition that 'it was once voted in parliament in Queen Elizabeth's time that an act might pass to make it lawful for them that would be willing to restore impropriations to the Church . . . and that the religious Earl of

Huntingdon offered to restore all the impropriations of his estate which then was great and might have many in it.'[88] He did not in fact restore his impropriations, as he did not make good his alleged proposals to sell his lands to go to the aid of the French Protestants in 1569; his actual religious benefactions took a much more modest form.[89] He certainly presented his four most valuable livings to Emmanuel College soon after its foundation, while the rent charges he made over to Wyggeston's Hospital in Leicester (chiefly designed to increase the salary of the headmaster of the Free School and provide scholarships for promising boys who intended entering the Church) could not have fetched £1,000 at twenty years' purchase. He gave the Ashby Grammar School land valued at about £200 and, at the time he offered the living of Ashby to Arthur Hildersham, declared that when his plans had been accomplished it would be a sufficient place for any learned preacher.[90] Most probably those who dedicated religious books to Huntingdon received some taste of his bounty, those whom he maintained at the university sang his praises abroad and his household chaplains, Browne, Andrewes, Nathaniel Gilby among others obviously lived at their lord's expense. The cost of this patronage to Huntingdon cannot be estimated with any accuracy, yet unless his generosity was far in excess of what it seems to have been his estates in normal times should have been able to withstand these gifts with ease. The surviving evidence is far too scanty to support the opinion that his indebtedness was primarily caused by his patronage of Puritans.

Speaking in confidence to his friends, Huntingdon himself attributed his mounting insolvency to quite different causes: he blamed his debts partly on the family responsibilities he had inherited, partly on his suit with Lord Mountjoy and expenses over the mines, but partly also on his service of the queen. From 1572 onwards as President of the Council in the North he received the annual sum of £1,000 for the council's diet, a fee which had been set down in the reign of Henry VIII and which Elizabeth made no attempt to adjust to the rapidly rising cost of living. As the queen's representative, Huntingdon had to maintain a vice-regal state, yet even at the beginning of the 1570's men could see his stipend fell below what he required. In 1574 Grindal worried that the Lord President 'surcharged' himself in the zealous performance of his duties.[91] Ten years later Huntingdon took stock of the expenses of his office: he hoped that now his brother Francis had taken over much of the management of his estates, and his own wife the supervision of his household, matters would be so eased that his charge at York would prove a far lighter burden that he had hitherto found it.[92] The chance survival of the expenditure-book for the York household for the year from Michaelmas 1584 shows that Huntingdon's scheme of retrenchment had brought at least a temporary improvement: the cost of provisions for the whole year exceeded the £1,000 allowance by only £20.[93] Throughout his presidency, Huntingdon had trouble obtaining cash to pay for the upkeep of his household: in May 1584 he said he had had to borrow £400 at York for household provisions since Lady Day. A year later he owed £200 for provisions at York, while in 1587 he spent practically the whole of the £400 he had raised on bond on provisions because his rents came in so slowly.[94] Despite any obvious success Huntingdon went on practising economy. In 1595 the old Countess of Shrewsbury could not understand why he had not bought some lordships from Mr. Adderton when he had the opportunity. Her servant suggested that the multitude of his debts might have prevented him from doing so: 'she replied, she feared he had a great store of money, because he had sold much land and lived but at a small rate. . . .'[95]

Since housekeeping more than absorbed his official allowance, Huntingdon had to make direct application to the queen from one emergency to another for the cost of administration in the north. On its legal side the Council in the North certainly partly financed itself: the fees of the legal councillors bound to continual attendance upon the court came half from the receiver in Yorkshire, half from fines imposed in the council, and apart from this they naturally received fees from their clients.[96] For the specifically administrative work of the council, however, the queen made no regular provision. So long as the north remained quiet and Huntingdon could live at York for long periods she had some reason for expecting him to live off his allowance, but years of unrest considerably increased the cost of government. In a year like 1575, when the queen appointed Huntingdon as her chief negotiator with the Scots over a Border raid, expenses must have risen steeply: from July to September Huntingdon and his advisers made Newcastle their headquarters and from there went to the Border to confer with the Regent of Scotland, the Earl of Morton, leaving the remainder of the council to continue its normal functions at York. Scottish politics again drew Huntingdon to the Borders in 1581 when he levied troops in a vain attempt to save Morton's life: he had to bear the first charge of raising the troops himself and only three months later received £3,000 from Walsingham in London to pay the soldiers.[97] When he complained to Burghley the following April of the weight of his personal debts, Huntingdon begged for nothing apart from the speedy payment of his allowance as lord lieutenant: he claimed to have spent almost £1,000 of his own money since he had come to Newcastle in January; he could not spare a penny of this, yet without horses and men it would have been impossible for him to have served there.[98] At the time of the Armada, Huntingdon found himself in the same predicament: he exposed a great deficiency of arms and munition in the north and sent to London for new supplies only to discover a similar shortage there, and so had to dispatch a merchant to eastern Europe to buy the requisite powder and shot, promising to pay him the current market price on his return.[99]

This continual anticipation of payments to be sent down from London placed another strain on Huntingdon's already over-burdened finances. The Armada crisis forced him to have recourse to desperate measures. Finding repayment from London too lengthy a procedure in his necessity, he reimbursed himself out of the money intended by the queen for the King of Scots. This unofficial appropriation did not come to light till 1593 when Burghley asked him to account for sums of £5,000 and £6,000 sent for Scottish causes, and particularly wanted details of the spending of the second sum. Huntingdon acknowledged receiving £6,000 in August 1588: Sir William Reed had deducted £40 for the carriage of the money north, he explained, and he had no difficulty in showing how £3,960 of the remaining £5,960 had been allocated. £3,000 had indeed gone to the King of Scots, Lord Scrope had received £100 and £860 had been left at Newcastle to buy victuals for the queen's service, but for the £2,000 still outstanding Huntingdon sought the queen's mercy. £600 of it, he maintained, he had spent directly in her service but confessed to Burghley 'for the £1,400 which remained I am loath to write the truth; I pray your favour until I may give good satisfaction for my whole debt yet unpaid, and I hope sometime next term to say that to you which you will not mislike.'[100]

Not only did his office involve Huntingdon in debts which more properly belonged to the central government, it also gave him, or he felt it gave him, responsibility for the debts of other government officials in the north. From his first appointment he sympathised with the Bowes family and it seems in his private capacity lent them money for which he was eventually compensated by the conveyance of Bradbury and Hilton, the manors he exchanged with the queen. In the 1590's he became entangled again in Bowes affairs. Robert Bowes, the treasurer of Berwick, held part of the monopoly for the manufacture of salt in the north and tried to set up salt pans. The venture failed in 1591 leaving Bowes with debts of £7,000 to the garrison of Berwick, £3,000 to Berwick corporation and £1,500 to Sir Thomas Smith, and in his subsequent bankruptcy Huntingdon shared.[101] The fourth Earl of Huntingdon alleged in an Exchequer case that his brother had lent Bowes sums totalling £4,487 most of which he had either made over to him directly or paid to his creditors. He maintained that £270 of this debt had been entrusted to Bowes by certain Durham justices to buy armour: Bowes had misappropriated the funds and Huntingdon had had to buy the armour out of his own purse. The fourth earl hoped to persuade the court to compel Robert Bowes's executors to repay these debts, especially because 'the same several sums of money were disbursed by the late earl in her majesty's service and for the furtherance thereof.'[102]

To some Elizabethans, office-holding in itself proved to be an avenue to enrichment; Burghley elevated his family into the aristocracy in one generation from the profits of royal offices. The contrary happened to Huntingdon, his office seems to have drained him further of what he had. The presidency of the Council in the North, being newly created, apparently did not have the substantial perquisites attached to it as an office of similar standing in the south, or if it did, Huntingdon was not the man to take advantage of it. He and his countess regularly received gifts in the north, of wine and of sweetmeats, but they never seem to have accepted *douceurs* of a more permanent value.[103] Sir Francis Hastings most emphatically stated his brother refused to profit from his office, that he loathed and detested to seek gain from public causes: it may well have been so.[104]

Huntingdon consequently with some justification complained of the cost to himself of serving the queen in the north on an inadequate official allowance; nevertheless, he tended to forget the recompense the queen gave to him indirectly for his service. Admittedly she did not make numerous grants to Huntingdon, and three of these came before he attained high office: in 1561 she presented him with the office of the Master of the Hart Hounds with the fee of 12d. a day which his father had held before him; in 1564 the next presentation of Terrington church in Norfolk; and in 1569 the wardship of Henry Kendall together with the management of his lands in Leicestershire and Derbyshire.[105] In addition, through the mediation of Leicester, Huntingdon held other offices under the crown of which the formal record no longer survives: he became warden of the Great Park at Windsor and accounts still existing for the manor of Stoke Poges show that sums varying from £11 to £144 a year came from this post. He also apparently held another office in Pickering Leigh, and his steward feared he might forfeit both on Leicester's death unless Essex or Walsingham could obtain a reconfirmation for him.[106] After he had become President of the Council in the North he received seven grants from the queen: in 1574 a twenty-one years' lease of woods in Deighton and Riccall in Yorkshire, in 1579 a lease of the rectory of Enderby, Leicestershire, for a similar time, at an annual rent of £9. 6s. 8d., and two twenty-one-year leases in 1583 of lands in Sheriff Hutton, Yorkshire, at an entry fine of £60 and an annual rent of £35. 15s. and of mills at Christchurch, in Hampshire, at a fine of £14 and an annual rent of the same amount. None of these leases offered opportunities of any considerable profit and Huntingdon only held three of them for a few years before he alienated them. Lastly, the queen granted Huntingdon the wardship of Thomas Waterton together with his lands in Yorkshire: no evidence now remains about how Huntingdon dealt with young Waterton, or with Henry Kendall, his other official ward, but neither of their estates was sufficiently large for Huntingdon to have benefited much from them.[107] On their own these grants from the queen cannot be seen as adequate reward for Huntingdon's years of service.

The remaining two grants the queen made to him, however, fall into quite a different category. He first petitioned for relief from his debts in 1576 when he wrote to Burghley that unless the queen could give him some assistance so he could take order for his debts, he did not see how he could return to his charge in the north.[108] In August, the queen granted him the monopoly of exporting 8,000 broadcloths for four years. (On the expiry of this monopoly Bedford had an identical grant in 1580.) Since 1564 the Merchant Adventurers Company had held the right of exporting 30,000 undressed cloths a year but the continental market could absorb twice this number and it had become the practice for the queen to license individuals, often noblemen, to export cloths in excess of the Merchant Adventurers' limit: by purchasing these licences from the recipients, in practice the Merchants retained their monopoly. Leicester, Walsingham and the Lord Admiral Howard all received licences to export broadcloths: Walsingham had permission to export a total of 200,000 cloths, Howard 100,000 which he assigned to Sir Edward Stafford. Compared with these figures, Huntingdon had a small grant. The Merchant Adventurers paid Stafford 2s. 4d. for every cloth exported and, taking this as a guide, Huntingdon may well have gained in the region of £1,000 profit from the transaction: all that definitely emerges is that he owed the crown over £3,400 for customs duties in 1582.[109] Even less is known now about the profit which came to Huntingdon from the queen's most signal act of favour, the exchange of lands to which she agreed in 1588: this could hardly have fallen below several thousand pounds but the sequel showed it was not enough to resolve all his debts. Measured against the twenty-three years Huntingdon represented Elizabeth in the north, even these concealed grants seem a not over-generous reward. His debts may not have been caused primarily by his service of the queen, nevertheless he had good reason for complaining that his presidency only added to his insolvency.

In another way, intangible but no less real, Huntingdon's financial position deteriorated through the fact of his holding office. From the autumn of 1572 until his death, of necessity he spent by far the greater part of his time in the north, far away from the Midlands and the West Country where all his estates lay. Usually the queen did not permit him to come south for any length of time more than once a year and, if the political situation was threatening, not as frequently as that. He had no choice but to be an absentee landlord. Elizabethan tenants appreciated this type of landlord for under him their rents remained fixed while through the great rise of prices their profits increased. People saw Huntingdon's forbearance as a deliberate act of policy:

> His tenants that daily repaired to his house,
> Was fed with his bacon, his beef and his souse;
> Their rents were not raised, their fines were but small
> And many poor tenants paid nothing at all.

> Such landlords in England we seldom shall find,
> That to their poor tenants will bear the like mind.
> Lord Hastings therefore is joyfully crowned,
> With angels in heaven where peace doth abound.[110]

Huntingdon, however, gained this crown largely by accident. He did indeed concern himself over the state of the poor but there is no evidence at all that he deliberately refrained from exploiting his estates. On the contrary he groped towards managing his estates more scientifically: that these plans never reached fruition made the financial debacle on his death inevitable.

Since Huntingdon never had any uninterrupted length of time after 1572 in which to think out the reorganisation of his estates he had to rely on the efforts of others and increasingly he depended on the advice of his brother Francis. From the early 1570's Francis Hastings had interested himself in some of the more minor aspects of estate business; he attended the holding of some of his brother's manorial courts, yet he does not appear to have begun to contemplate Huntingdon's finances as a whole until 1580.[111] The autumn of that year certainly brought home to him the extent of his brother's debts and only through his unwearying efforts at court was the forfeiture to the crown of Huntingdon's manors of South Cadbury, Holton, Kirby, Packington and Henley, for the non-payment of Lodge's debt, averted and a six years' respite gained.[112] This near disaster seems to have made Huntingdon and Sir Francis determined to try to force the under-rented family estates to produce a greater annual income. Huntingdon had sold all his Cornish lands, but large estates remained to him in Somerset and Devon which were rarely visited by the family since they lay far from his accustomed route between York and London. Francis Hastings resolved to make good this lack of knowledge and probably in 1583 set out to inspect the lands in the south-west himself, with characteristic thoroughness making notes on all he saw.[113] He pounced upon all derelictions of duty with relish: Huntingdon's officers at Stokenham had not exercised his right to ships wrecked off Start

Point; his brother had been entitled to the profits of the May Fair at Wellow but these had been withheld while the market at Somerton had been completely discontinued. Hastings considered Somerton a town ripe for redevelopment and thought that if the assizes and sessions could be brought back there it would prove again a 'pretty town'. He discovered that enclosure was being extensively carried out on Huntingdon's lands, but with little reference to the lord. His tenant at Hardington had behaved particularly badly: he had enclosed the whole village and converted all to pasture, leaving no house but his own and then had refused Huntingdon's officers right of entry to take strays and also to come himself to Huntingdon's court. Enclosure had also taken place at Hatherley, Maperton and Clapton. Hastings had no objection to enclosure on principle, indeed he himself suggested that if a down of 200 acres should be enclosed at Kilmersdon 'it were more commodious both to the lord and the tenant': he complained because so far the benefits from unsupervised enclosure had accrued to the tenants only and none had reached their lord.

The survey pointed to an obvious conclusion: Huntingdon's interests would continue to be disregarded unless he had a personal representative at hand to safeguard his right. Step-by-step Hastings took the responsibility upon himself. At first he went to Canford to maintain his brother's rights only so long as the dispute with Lord Mountjoy lasted and he had no intention of abandoning Leicestershire to live permanently in the south-west. In 1583 Huntingdon seized the opportunity of handing over the day-to-day running of his western estates to Hastings: he wanted nothing more, he wrote from York, than to settle his estate problems that he might 'with better quietness more diligently follow my vocation here than this few years past I have done, or could do'. Consequently he asked Hastings to take this care upon him 'that you see to the order of my whole lands, for setting, letting, sale of woods and receipt of rents etc.' He promised to appoint others to help his brother, but none were to act without his authorisation.[114]

Huntingdon exchanged Hastings's Leicestershire manor of Market Bosworth for the family manor of North Cadbury in Somerset and Sir Francis took up residence to oversee the Hastings estates in the south-west for the remainder of Huntingdon's life.

The time for long-term improvements had passed: these would have had to have been made a generation earlier to have been of any assistance to Huntingdon in his present troubles and Hastings had to find a way quickly to increase the revenues from the western lands in order to satisfy some of his brother's most pressing debts. He could not avoid turning to a common expedient of hard-pressed landlords in the Elizabethan period, the granting of very long leases for high entry fines.[115] On the manor of Stokenham, for example, from 1581 onwards Huntingdon leased land for terms ranging from 1,000 to 3,000 years for large fines and very small reserved rents and in three years he obtained almost £5,000 from this one lordship in the knowledge, however, that these fines once levied could never be repeated. In essence, as Huntingdon realised, little distinguished a lease of 3,000 years at a token reserved rent from an outright sale and he went on later, for further payments, to release his tenants from these rents and to grant them the fee simple of their properties. Long leasing reached its logical conclusion at Stokenham with the sale of the manor in 1586.

The fate of Stokenham illustrates how the insistent pressure of Huntingdon's debts caused the attempt at coherent estate planning to fail before it could even be put in force. Not only did Huntingdon need Francis Hastings in the West Country to supervise the raising of his revenues there, he required him at the same time to be in London to see to the actual repayment of his debts as they fell due. Constantly he anticipated estate revenue to ward off his creditors. The series of hectic letters which passed between Huntingdon and his brother between 1580 and 1595 conveys with far more realism than any formal indentures of alienation, mortgage or list of bonds the sense of crisis in the family.

Huntingdon all the time was asking his brother to do the impossible. In May 1584, when something like £6,000 had to be found to redeem debts for that month alone, Huntingdon wanted him to try to put off the claims of two creditors until they could be paid out of the next survey of the manor of Aller, to get credit for the payment of others from Mr. Ewens and Mr. Hext on the fines which had already been taken: he considered the manor of South Pool could be mortgaged to Billingsley for £2,000. Huntingdon obviously placed his hopes on fines which could be raised in the west but the letters make it clear that the greater part of the debts could only be satisfied by further borrowings which would ultimately have to be settled in their turn. Still in the same month of May 1584 he expected to borrow an additional £1,000 from one Freak, £200 each from Mr. Watson, John Alford and Francis Beaumont, he looked forward to the next £1,000 due to come from Lord Lumley whose debt he had just undertaken and thought that Christopher Southouse might lend an extra £1,000 on the security of Lumley's future payments. If he could get £600 from Playfair, persuade Francis Beaumont to pay £400 which did not become due till the next term and borrow £1,000 from Sir James Harington, then Huntingdon thought he could clear his debts for the month.[116]

With reason, this incessant borrowing worried Hastings and he believed it to be quite essential that the number of bonds issued by Huntingdon should be lessened as soon as possible. He described to his brother how the merchants took note of the bonds passed under his seal and the defaults made on some of them, yet the only way he could suggest of curtailing them was by passing them on to others for payment.[117] All the time these debts accumulated, Huntingdon continued to dissipate his resources by granting long leases, mortgaging further lands, selling others: under these circumstances the yearly revenues from the estates were bound to fall. When on occasions Hastings could not keep himself from reproaching his brother for failing to concentrate on his financial affairs and pursue a systematic course, Huntingdon somewhat naïvely assured him that his good intentions would eventually bring him that quietness for which he longed.

Let me tell you that me think you conceive my lack of constant resolution to be some great cause of the continuance of my chargeable troubles [he replied in answer to Hastings's remonstrances in 1587]: if I knew that fault in myself, I hope I should soon amend it. Indeed I do know that I have been subject to many changes and alterations of my purposes. But how those have grown, I do best know: my resolution is constant in this, as time shall show, that I will pay every man his own, how bare so ever I do leave myself. Live I, die I, this shall be done, God willing.[118]

Apparently the profits from the exchange of lands with the crown did enable Huntingdon to repay some of these creditors and for the next four years the letters on financial matters passing between the brothers decrease alike in number and urgency though Huntingdon could still not afford to neglect any rents or fines which could serve him for his 'ordinary needful charges'.[119] By 1592 the complicated machinery of the exchange had been carried through: Huntingdon admitted that 'her majesty's grant will not clear me by far.'[120] Once again debts began to mount while less and less land remained for exploitation and sale. Sir Francis felt compelled to make one last great protest.

Can you establish the house of Ashby with a strong maintenance by land in Leicestershire [he asked Huntingdon]? Bagworth and Thornton is gone, Bosworth is gone, and Lubbesthorpe is in the queen's hands, if these shall be brought back to the house they must cost money, and that in no small sum. This money must be had either by a suit from her majesty or by sale of land: suits be lingering and uncertain and your land so far spent already as . . . I know not where it will be had.

He went on to stress that if Ringwood went to settle Atherton's debt that only left Christchurch and Canford to be sold in the west, for he hoped Huntingdon would never consider alienating Aller. Quite apart from this his brother needed money to redeem Bosworth, Lubbesthorpe, Bagworth and Thornton and to reserve Newbold Verdon to the house. Begging Huntingdon to make some settlement before it was too late, he reminded him of the speeches made when the Earls of Bedford and Leicester died, that their goods were on sale and their estates in such confusion, yet both left land enough behind them:

But if the now Earl of Huntingdon die (which I pray God I never live to see) and dying leave his heir great sums to pay, and little land to enjoy, the weak state of his heir shall be wholly imputed unto him, and he and his profession shall *male audire* of all men for it, and indeed being thus left how shall his heir be able to show his head in the countenance of an earl, wanting ability every way to maintain it?[121]

In the circumstances, Hastings's advice to concentrate on laying a strong foundation of land in Leicestershire was the only possible course, but Huntingdon had not even the resources to achieve this. The debts he had contracted through his obligations to his own family, his law suits and his mining venture, his service of the queen and his unsystematic estate management combined to render him virtually powerless. In the autumn of 1595 he had every intention of going down to London that winter to make a new settlement of his lands and had devised a new scheme; all he forgot was his brother's admonition, 'time is precious and passeth fast away, the life of man is but a weak thread which standeth subject to breaking by many casualties.' Death caught him at York, unawares, before anything could be accomplished and his estates descended in chaos to his heir.[122]

PART TWO

The Public Figure

CHAPTER FOUR

The Apostle of Leicestershire

PURITAN GUARDIAN OF MARY, QUEEN OF SCOTS

As soon as Lord Hastings succeeded his father as third Earl of Huntingdon in June 1560 he ceased to be a private man, for his rank inevitably imposed upon him public obligations which he realised he owed first to his own locality. Now that he had become an earl, and the leading nobleman in Leicestershire, the queen and her councillors held him responsible for the quiet government of the county. The town of Leicester, the justices for the shire, in their turn looked to him to protect their interests against outsiders, to advance their local schemes at court, generally to act as their 'good lord'. Huntingdon had been prepared for these duties from his birth, he had already served an apprenticeship under his father and knew exactly what men expected from a nobleman in his locality. But he was more than a conventional nobleman; from the first he saw that his rank brought him power to bring not only good but also godly government to the county. His father, content to keep Leicestershire loyal to the crown, had apparently not troubled himself about the state of the souls of men under his rule: Huntingdon cared intensely about their religious beliefs. Already in 1560 he conceived of his work in Leicestershire in specifically religious terms as the punishment of superstition and error and the encouragement of true religion wherever it had begun to show its face.

Much of Huntingdon's authority came from his personal standing; men obeyed him because he was the Earl of Huntingdon, yet in addition to this intangible influence the government conferred upon him certain definable powers. From his accession until his death it placed him on the commission of the peace and included him among the quorum of those justices, without whose presence important cases of breach of the peace could not be tried. In military as well as in judicial matters the queen considered him her chief official in the county: in normal times he headed the commission of musters responsible for the military defence of the county. At the beginning of the reign, lords lieutenant were still only appointed in times of emergency and their powers withdrawn once the danger had receded: the government required no lords lieutenant after 1560 until 1569 when the rising in the north threatened the whole of England with civil strife, then it placed a lord lieutenant over every county while the unrest lasted and Huntingdon became the Lord Lieutenant of Leicestershire. Later in the reign the ever present danger of a Spanish invasion forced the government to change its attitude towards lords lieutenant: there was no peaceful interval when they could be released from their duties and gradually from about the 1580's the office came to be considered a permanent one. Although by this date Huntingdon had been entrusted with a multitude of duties in the north of England which required his personal supervision, from at least 1587 until he died he held the Lord Lieutenancy of Leicestershire. With the Elizabethan respect for degree it would scarcely have been possible to have passed over such a loyal supporter of the government in his own locality, however great his responsibilities elsewhere.[1]

Obviously Huntingdon could not perform all his various local offices himself, he had to employ deputies: for the central government it was sufficient to know he carried the ultimate responsibility. Delegating authority might have meant abandoning it, but because of his numerous relations, Huntingdon's absence actually brought about an increase in his control over the county for he always had some of his younger brothers at hand to give him their help. Sir George Hastings, Huntingdon's eldest brother and ultimate heir, settled first at Loughborough and then at Castle Donington and he saw to the family's interest in the north-western part of Leicestershire where the bulk of the Hastings estates lay. Once he had retired from his military life Sir Edward Hastings, the third brother, represented Huntingdon in Leicester itself. About 1580, Sir Edward acquired Leicester Abbey and for the remainder of his life intervened frequently, though not always successfully, in civic affairs. He increased his authority in the town in 1591 when Huntingdon made over to him the stewardship of the Prince's Fee in Leicester together with the Receivership of the Honour of Leicester which the crown had granted Huntingdon in 1572.[2] Until he moved to Somerset in the 1580's, Sir Francis Hastings from his house at Market Bosworth immersed himself in Leicestershire government, and even twenty years after he had left the county he still felt confident of persuading the town corporation to carry out his wishes.[3] Walter, the youngest of the Hastings brothers, never lived outside Leicestershire: he made his home at Kirby Muxloe and since he also held the manor of Braunstone, it fell to him to maintain the family within Leicester forest. Particularly after 1572 when he took up residence at York these brothers acted as Huntingdon's official deputies. In their own right Sir George, Sir Edward and Sir Francis all became Justices of the Peace and the Privy Council soon recognised them as suitable substitutes for their brother. In the commission which called for the routine exercising of the Leicestershire militia in 1577, the government authorised Sir George Hastings to carry out Huntingdon's duties: in 1580 Sir Francis had the same task and in the commission of 1587 which appointed Huntingdon Lord Lieutenant, both brothers were named as his deputies.[4]

Yet in spite of these opportunities for delegation the central government expected Huntingdon to undertake a surprising amount of work in person. Essentially they saw him as the chief maintainer of public order in Leicestershire who could be relied upon to ensure that the laws were observed and disturbances prevented, no light responsibility at a time when no salaried guardians of the peace existed. In the day-to-day running of the county he had to be on the outlook for occasions which might lead to disorder. Tudor governments always feared widespread popular discontent, and rightly so, for they had not the resources at their disposal to control it; only through these local administrators working throughout the county could the state of popular opinion be known. Zealously Huntingdon watched his people. He happened to follow his father just when the central government was trying to revalue the currency and replace the old coinage, greatly debased in the reign of Edward VI, with a new coinage whose value would correspond with its silver content. The Privy Council required Huntingdon to see that no disturbances occurred while the old currency was withdrawn and the new brought in: he did his best, punishing those who would not receive testons at the official valuation of $2\frac{1}{4}$d. but he worried because in the interval before the arrival of the new currency few goods were being offered for sale in the local markets and he felt the poor were suffering.[5] Prices, particularly the prices of food, had always to be his concern, for when food was dear the poor were likely to riot. After the bad harvests of the 1590's, in 1595 the Privy Council pressed him to see that the price of corn was kept down in Leicestershire and the local graziers and farmers persuaded not to feed pease to their stock but sell it instead to the poor at a reasonable price.[6]

The poor were not the only section of the community liable to become discontented over money matters. As Elizabeth's reign progressed, parliaments were summoned at ever decreasing intervals to vote the crown subsidies to meet the rising cost of government. A majority in the House of Commons might be inspired by a spirit of ardent nationalism but when individuals came to be assessed for the subsidy in their own localities they showed themselves no more willing than in times past to loosen their purse strings. The government assigned to Huntingdon the ultimate responsibility for the collection of the subsidy in Leicestershire and time and again his name headed the list of commissioners. He rarely attended the meetings at which the commissioners decided on the method of collection, as his many duties elsewhere prevented him, nevertheless he still remained accountable for slow payments or open defaults. The queen's scheme for raising a temporary loan to defray some of her most immediate war debts just after the Armada involved Huntingdon in even more unpopular financial activities on the government's behalf. Through Sir George Hastings, his deputy lieutenant for Leicestershire, local gentlemen received royal warrants, known as privy seals, asking them to lend the queen cash in sums of £100, £50 or £25 as their means might allow so that a total of £1,500 might be sent from the county. The proposal provoked widespread resistance and Huntingdon in a letter to the Privy Council wrote that recent losses from the cattle plague prevented local gentlemen from lending such large sums, and suggested that several gentlemen might join to make up the sum specified in one privy seal, to which the councillors agreed. In this instance he showed he could temper the demands of the government to local difficulties and still fulfil the needs of both parties.[7]

Poverty, interference with an individual's property and goods could both cause unrest within the county: Huntingdon had also to deal with fermenters of disorder who might come in from outside. At the time of the rebellion in the north, Leicestershire remained completely loyal yet even in this Protestant county some conservative sympathisers continued to exist who, if they were provided with a leader, might welcome a forcible change of sovereign and change of religion. So in 1571 Huntingdon had good reason to take seriously the news that a Scottish schoolmaster had been discovered at the village of Prestwold who had spoken against Elizabeth's treatment of Mary, Queen of Scots and against the state of religion as established in England, and to confer with the Privy Council about his punishment. The Catholic priests, dispatched on the mission to reconvert England, constituted a far greater danger, in the eyes of the government, to the general peace than any wandering Scot. From 1582 Huntingdon and other local gentlemen received commissions to search for seminary priests in the county and, during Huntingdon's absence in the north, Sir Francis, the most zealous of the brothers, provided the Privy Council with the fullest information of the gentlemen's houses in the county where priests might gain protection. Huntingdon's authority was such that when any suspicious characters were apprehended, news went first to him rather than to the central government as happened in May 1582 when books (presumably Catholic books) written against the Book of Common Prayer were seized at the house of a Leicester carrier who had brought them from London. Not until Huntingdon had given his advice did the mayor venture to send details of the incident to Walsingham in London.[8]

The government's chief concern, however, was that Huntingdon should supervise the military defence of Leicestershire and safeguard the county both against local unrest and attacks from without. He received his first letter from the Privy Council about the mustering of the local militia only a month after his father's death and this proved to be the first in a regular stream of communications giving directions when the musters were to be held, the number of men to be trained, the weapons they might use, even the coats they might wear. Huntingdon by no means discharged all these tasks by deputies. In August 1569 he and his fellow commissioners tried hard, by upgrading the gentlemen and towns charged with contributions for defence, to provide the county with the arms and the armour the government had called for but their reorganisation caused delays and the certificates of the number of men who actually appeared at the musters consequently arrived late in London. These preparations were timely, for two months later when parts of the north rebelled, Leicestershire remained in quietness. Huntingdon's move to the north caused no slackening in his interest in the Leicestershire musters: in 1576 he actually bought the coats for the Leicestershire men himself and when he was in Leicester in 1590 he made time to watch the training of forty militia men. Towards the end of his life he had the extra burden of seeing that the county dispatched regular contingents of trained men to fight for the queen in Ireland. The Elizabethan state expected much from its local administrators, unloading on to them in this way some of its most onerous undertakings, and it was not often disappointed even though it extended no prospects of any visible reward. For the days Huntingdon spent ordering the local markets, distributing the demands for loans, reviewing the musters or sitting on the bench all at the government's behest, he received nothing apart from a little guarded praise: he was merely performing the work expected of a nobleman. Yet it is inconceivable, if he had been offered the choice, that he would have refused these services and allowed them to have been performed by another in his stead: the loss of status would have been so great that the most menial tasks imposed by the state seemed infinitely preferable. No nobleman would willingly be lowered in the eyes of his own fellow countrymen.[9]

As the leading nobleman in Leicestershire, Huntingdon was not only by virtue of his rank the servant of the state he was also in a very real sense the servant of his locality: the county as well as the national government expected much of its earl. Automatically the citizens of Leicester and the gentlemen of the county assumed he would advance local men and local causes and again he fulfilled the part demanded of him. From the very first he patronised local men. His household in itself offered considerable chances of employment and most of his servants in his early years came from Leicestershire: obviously his estates in the county could be served best by the appointment of local stewards but even when he chose professional retainers Huntingdon seems to have preferred his fellow countrymen. Roger Bromley, one of the lawyers who frequently acted for him in the later part of his life and who with Richard Branthwaite carried through the complicated exchange of lands with the queen, lived at Bagworth Park in the county.

Local scholars invariably gained Huntingdon's sympathy: only a month after his father's death he wrote to the Archbishop of Canterbury and to the Bishop of London urging upon them the qualifications of Christopher Johnson, a young man from across the Derbyshire border who had 'spent all his time in study and learning', for the post of master of Winchester College. During his ten years there, Johnson proved an admirable headmaster and also achieved a reputation as a Latin poet before he retired to embark upon a second, equally successful career as a physician in the city of London. After his generous gift of livings to Emmanuel College in 1586 Huntingdon gained considerable influence among its fellows, and the young men from Leicestershire the college rewarded on his recommendation included Nathaniel Gilby, son of Anthony Gilby, and Joseph Hall, the seventeenth-century Bishop of Norwich: Hall matriculated at Cambridge from Emmanuel College in 1589 where Nathaniel Gilby acted as his tutor. By 1595, Hall in his turn had advanced sufficiently in learning to be considered for election to a fellowship but the college statutes which prevented two men from one county holding office at any one time precluded him. Much later, when he assembled his *Works* for publication he gratefully recalled Huntingdon's intervention which procured him a fellowship at the college:

It fell out that the father of my loving chamberfellow, Mr. Cholmley, a gentleman that had likewise dependence upon the most noble Henry, Earl of Huntingdon, having occasion to go to York, unto that noble lord, fell into some mention of me. That good earl, who well esteemed my father's services [he was bailiff at Ashby], having belikely heard some better words of me than I could deserve, made earnest enquiry after me, what were my courses, what my hopes: and hearing of the likelihood of my removal, professed much dislike of it, not without some vehemence, demanding why I was not chosen fellow of that college, wherein by report I received such approbation. Answer was returned that my country debarred me, which being filled by my tutor, whom his lordship well knew, could not by statute admit a second. The earl presently replied that, if that were the hindrance, he would soon take order to remove it. Whereupon his lordship presently sends for my tutor, Mr. Gilby unto York, and, with proffer of large conditions of the chaplainship in his house, and assured promises of better provisions, drew him to relinquish his place in the college to a free election.[10]

Huntingdon's support of local causes usually involved him in undertakings more onerous than the writing of letters to smooth the paths of promising scholars. Undoubtedly his assistance in the 1580's when the Corporation of Leicester sought a charter of incorporation from the queen and a grant of the fee farm of crown property within the town, materially helped the corporation in its progress towards independence. In 1585 Richard Archer, the town's solicitor, reported to the corporation that he had found Huntingdon 'their very good lord' in the matter: while he had been in London he had also consulted Sir Francis Hastings, then in the city about his brother's financial affairs, on the form the town's petition to the crown should take. For the next three years the corporation repeatedly applied to Huntingdon for advice: in February 1587, Archer set out to speak with him at Greenwich where Huntingdon had kept Christmas at court, the next month he hired more horses to take him letters, in April he had to make an expedition to York to see the earl, while June found him waiting on Huntingdon at Theobalds. As a result of this activity the queen authorised a survey of crown property in Leicester to be taken in the summer of 1587 and named Francis Hastings as one of the commissioners. In April 1588 Archer made yet another journey to Huntingdon at York and at last in 1589 the queen conceived both to incorporate the town and to make over the fee farm of crown property at a fixed annual rent: the main purpose of the grant as the corporation, and in all probability Huntingdon, conceived it 'was that a preacher should be maintained and a clothier for the benefit of the poor in the said town'. The corporation, having achieved its object, tended to forget its obligations: Huntingdon refused to rest until Archer, who had been so diligent in prosecuting the town's suit, received his promised reward.[11]

Because of Huntingdon's paternal concern for his own locality, Leicestershire lacked none of those charitable schemes which recently have been shown to be so noticeable a feature of Elizabethan and Jacobean England.[12] Through his intervention two schools were founded or refounded, an old people's hospital reformed, a library to increase the literacy of the clergy set up and several schemes intended to relieve the poor begun. Unquestionably Huntingdon's chief interest lay in the education of the young. With his uncle, Lord Hastings of Loughborough, Huntingdon obtained from the queen a grant of certain lands and houses in Ashby de la Zouch which had been given to the parish church for the perpetual celebration of masses for the dead and in 1567 he enfeoffed Anthony Gilby with the lands for the maintenance of a schoolmaster. This marks the beginning of a flourishing school at Ashby whose most eminent student in Huntingdon's lifetime was probably Joseph Hall and whose series of radical Protestant masters culminated in Huntingdon's choice of John Brinsley, the author of *Ludus Literarius: or, the Grammar School*.[13]

At exactly the same time as he was establishing his school at Ashby, Huntingdon turned his attention to education in the town of Leicester but here he had to work for ten years before he had created a school in accord with his religious views. Before he died in 1537 Thomas Wigston, the clerical brother of the wealthy Leicester wool-merchant, William Wigston, had left money to maintain a schoolmaster and in the reign of Mary the right of appointing this master became vested in the Hospital of St. Ursula founded by his brother. Huntingdon regarded this hospital for twelve old people with great suspicion, for to him it appeared the one centre of conservatism in a Protestant town: first he obtained a commission of enquiry into the management of the hospital and during the time of the inspection the Marian master conveniently died. The queen consented to Thomas Sampson being appointed the new master who had been dismissed from his deanery at Christchurch for his Nonconformity two years previously, in spite of Huntingdon's representations to Archbishop Parker. Now

Huntingdon had an ally within the hospital as eager as he was to banish all traces of Catholicism and through their combined action a reformed hospital emerged, no longer bearing 'the name of any fancied saint or other superstitious name', and provided with a master bound to constant preaching. Unable to face this hostile tribunal John Potts, the schoolmaster, who had obtained his post under the old regulations, fled the town and confirmed the worst fears of the radicals by taking one of his former pupils with him to the Jesuit college at Louvain.[14] From the coming of Sampson, Huntingdon felt confident that the charitable purposes which the hospital existed to promote would be carried out and he proceeded to add to its endowments. In 1576 not only to improve the estate of the chaplains and poor 'but also for the good and diligent instruction of the inhabitants of the town and county of Leicester in the true knowledge of God and the Christian religion' he gave to the hospital rent-charges of the total annual value of £66.13s.4d. a year. Out of this sum the master of the hospital undertook to pay £10 annually to the master of the Free School to augment his salary, £30 to the brother (or confrater) so long as he preached in St. Martin's, the civic church of Leicester, on Sundays, Wednesdays and Fridays, £10 to scholars of the school who intended to become preachers of the gospel and £6. 13s. 4d. to the poor of the hospital. Huntingdon allowed the master to keep the remaining £10 to augment his salary. The stipulations concerning the distribution of the £10 set aside for scholarships are interesting since they show that as early as 1576, Huntingdon had devised a scheme to help gifted local boys advance from the school to the university and from there to preferment within the Elizabethan Church. He wished one scholar from the school studying at Oxford and another at Cambridge to receive £3 yearly for the maximum of five years, and in addition that two poor boys who intended to go to the university and then enter the Church might also have 40s. a year for five years to enable them to stay at the school. He reserved the nomination of these scholars for himself so long as he lived. The school statutes in which Huntingdon

again took the greatest personal interest date from about this time
and they made it abundantly clear that the chief purpose of the
school was the production of godly Protestants. To crown his
efforts in furthering religion and good learning in Leicestershire,
Huntingdon gave 'many books' to St. Martin's church for the
benefit of ministers and scholars. These books were in the library in
St. Martin's belfry by 1587 and in the next century were transferred
to the new library at the Guildhall which still exists on its original
site.[15]

Huntingdon's benefactions to his native county did not end
with the founding of schools and the reorganisation of the hospital.
In the 1570's he initiated a scheme to provide cheap coal for the
poor of Leicester: he gave £42 to be spent at the rate of £6 a year
for seven years to buy coal and the services of his tenants to carry
the coal to Leicester which the corporation then sold at low prices
to the poor. He also tried to deal with unemployment in the town
by introducing a clothing industry. He brought over a clothier
from Gloucester, Thomas Bradgate, who undertook in 1573 to
provide work for the local poor and at Huntingdon's special
request the corporation lent him 100 marks and followed that
with a further loan the next year. By 1584 Bradgate had given up
the struggle; nevertheless, Huntingdon determined that the
scheme should continue and the corporation submitted to him the
name of another clothier who promised to bring men over from
Norwich to begin the manufacture of Bays in the town. This
attempt also failed. By 1592, however, a considerable amount of
money had accrued to the corporation from selling coal to the
poor and on Huntingdon's insistence the corporation reluctantly
lent it to yet another clothier, John Clarke.[16]

There can be no doubt that Huntingdon considered his religious
duty lay in helping those who could not help themselves, particularly the poor of his own locality. Any deeper probing of his
motives would be profitless, yet it is equally undeniable that his
generosity greatly added to his influence. His reward was not
delayed until the next world, for his good works brought him the

affection of the populace and made him a very powerful man in Leicestershire. Local opinion constantly waited upon his judgment. At the least sign of any untoward happening in Leicester the mayor applied to 'their good earl'. It fell to Huntingdon, not the mayor, to raise the hue and cry when a prisoner, a tall man with red hair and red beard and little holes like smallpox round his nose, escaped from Leicester's gaol. He again had the task of delivering a complicated arbitration between Leicester parents and their daughter and son-in-law even though these matters lay well within the provenance of the mayor. When one Agnes Bowker purported to have given birth to a monster cat at Market Harborough, a copy of her statement was dispatched straight off to Huntingdon.[17]

Especially after Huntingdon became President of the Council in the North, Leicester corporation's habit of consulting him at every turn meant that local news took an unnecessarily long time to reach London. In 1576, for example, the local justices took the grave step of imprisoning the mayor, William Norreys, on a charge of falsifying the coinage, and immediately sent to inform Huntingdon of what they had done: from Huntingdon a week later the Privy Council came to hear of the matter and only then could take action. In times of distress, nothing less than his personal intervention could satisfy the locality. He was in the north when a bad epidemic of the plague caused the town of Leicester to be sealed off from the county in 1593: the corporation appealed to him to use his influence to persuade the county justices to levy a contribution to relieve those who had become destitute in Leicester through lack of work. Sometimes, a latter day Solomon, he found himself having to hear rival claims from the town and county as happened in 1594 when the traders of Mountsorrel petitioned Huntingdon against their exclusion from Leicester market at the same time as the Leicester corporation expressed its indignation at the idea that they should be admitted. The Privy Council cut through this knot by advising Huntingdon and Sir Edward Hastings and others to see that the ordinance

K

against 'foreigners' buying and selling in Leicester market should be upheld.[18]

Because he had done so much for Leicestershire, Huntingdon assumed his wishes would be respected locally, and they practically always were. As of right he took it upon himself to make nominations to several offices in Leicester as they became vacant and to suggest recipients for leases of corporation property. In 1594 he decided that the head usher, Thomas Jesson, should be removed from the Free School: without even enquiring into Jesson's deficiencies the corporation obediently complied and appointed Huntingdon's new candidate, Robert Aston, in his place. In relation to the school, as its new founder, Huntingdon enjoyed an especially privileged position; in the government of the town he did not always have matters his own way. In 1592 he heard the rumour that Parkyns, the then recorder, contemplated resigning, and wrote from York recommending that Humphrey Purfrey, a member of the Council in the North, should succeed him. The mayor replied that as far as he knew, Parkyns had no intention of giving up his office, 'although he hath some mislike to see us disjoined [by] the popular faction of one or two, and that some of us have been so unthankful to your lordship and others, that be deserved so greatly to the benefit of our town if we could so use it': he hoped Huntingdon would agree to Parkyns remaining in office, and the recorder himself tried unsuccessfully to catch Huntingdon as he was travelling from London to York to explain the misunderstanding.[19]

The one sphere in which Huntingdon did not have a predominating voice was in the political representation of the town of Leicester and even here he had to face not an incipient desire on the town's side for more independence but a stronger patron in the person of the Chancellor of the Duchy of Lancaster. Leicester formed part of the duchy and traditionally the chancellor had the nomination of one if not both of the burgesses. At least in 1586, Huntingdon tried to challenge the accepted order of things and wrote asking for the nomination of one burgess. The mayor replied that the town had already received the names of two burgesses in the council's letters (this was the parliament when the Privy Council asked for the return of members who had sat in the 1584 parliament), but he offered eagerly to make a substitution if Huntingdon would do them the honour of allowing Francis Hastings to represent the borough. The mayor presumed too far: Hastings who had been the first Knight of the Shire in the last parliament and hoped to sit for the county again was not the candidate Huntingdon had in mind. In the end the corporation returned Henry Skipwith and Thomas Johnson, who had represented the town in 1584. In the county, in contrast, no faction ever contested the paramount influence of the Hastings family so long as Huntingdon lived. In five parliaments between 1571 and 1597 Sir Francis Hastings sat for the county: in 1584 and 1585, Sir George Hastings joined his younger brother and Sir Edward shared the representation with him in 1597.[20]

The check Huntingdon received over the nomination of burgesses in Leicester was exceptional and in general his prestige remained high until he died: unlike his brother and great nephew he encountered no stolid opposition within the town. Subsequently, the town fathers looked back to his rule as to a golden age and twenty-eight years after his death they commissioned the painting of his posthumous portrait. It still hangs in the Mayor's Chamber in the Guildhall, reminding succeeding generations that

This noble peer gave an hundred marks a year forever to sundry godly uses. As thirteen pounds to a public preacher for the whole town of Leicester, ten pounds to the chief schoolmaster there, ten pounds to four poor scholars and twenty nobles a year to the poor of Wyggeston Hospital in Leicester, besides many books for a library and a stock of twenty pounds to provide coals at the best hand for the general good of the poor, and sundry other great favours which he did for this corporation.[21]

The corporation of Leicester listed first among Huntingdon's good works his encouragement of public preaching and it may be they realised that in this their good lord differed most significantly from many other Elizabethan noblemen. Other lords served the central government with equal zeal in their localities, established as many and as varied local charities, exercised as much influence within their counties, but few can be compared with Huntingdon in the fervour he showed from the very beginning for the propagation of the gospel in the land. On his accession, Huntingdon's first thoughts turned to the state of the Church in Leicestershire and as soon as he had the patronage he began at once to befriend those Protestant clerics who had spent Mary's reign in exile on the Continent. He extended his protection not so much to the moderate Protestants, who in any case had little difficulty in obtaining benefices in the Elizabethan Church, but to the uncompromising Calvinists who found a stumbling block even in the truncated ceremonies of the new English Church. Anthony Gilby and William Whittingham, who had taken a prominent part in the quarrel among the English exiles in Frankfurt in 1555 over the use of the Edwardian Prayer Book and had retired with Knox to Geneva so that there they might enjoy an undefiled Calvinist service, were the first of the radical clergy Huntingdon attracted to Leicestershire.

In the first years of the reign when a majority of the clergy had had no training for preaching, many bishops favoured schemes for taking collections from the beneficed clergy in order to maintain a few itinerant preachers in every diocese. Huntingdon strongly supported the idea and in 1561 appointed John Londe, a prebendary of St. Margaret's, Leicester, as collector for the itinerant preachers in the county: he did not, however, receive a very heartening report from Londe on the success of his labours. He had been able to collect less than £18 from the Leicestershire clergy, he wrote, not enough to pay the stipend of even one of the preachers. Among these itinerant preachers was William Whittingham and Londe's letter makes it virtually certain that Huntingdon had persuaded him to work in Leicestershire for he goes on to remark that Whittingham would have been greatly discouraged if Huntingdon had not already been good to him, and speaks of him as a stranger in the county, 'having no friends but only your honour'.[22]

In 1562 an attempt was made to have Whittingham permanently settled in Leicestershire. John Willock, the Scottish Protestant, occupied the living of Loughborough where Edward, Lord Hastings, Huntingdon's Catholic uncle owned the presentation: as Willock combined the benefice with a chaplaincy to Thomas Randolph, then English ambassador to Scotland, he had not been able to be resident. To further the spread of Protestantism he agreed to resign his living in favour of Whittingham, but Lord Hastings, despite the arguments of the Earl of Bedford and the future Earl of Leicester would not consider any candidate apart from Adams, his papist chaplain. So Whittingham left Leicestershire, and Willock retained the living: in the long run the Protestant cause in Loughborough did not suffer for by the 1570's Willock had become resident there. Warwick, in the meantime, appointed Whittingham as chaplain to his troops at the siege of Le Havre and on his return to England induced the queen to grant him the deanery of Durham. When he went into the north, Huntingdon again encountered Whittingham and again extended to him his protection there.[23]

Historians have tried to trace the origins of Leicestershire Nonconformity back to Wycliffe's parsonage at Lutterworth: the little town of Ashby de la Zouch seems a much less disputable source for the spreading of radical Protestantism in the county. At about the same time as Whittingham appeared as an itinerant preacher, Anthony Gilby took up residence there, though he was probably never vicar. It seems more than likely that his scruples over the ceremonies and vestments yet remaining in the Church prevented him from accepting preferment as they did Coverdale and Fox, Cole and Philpot and that he deliberately chose the lectureship offered by Huntingdon since it would leave him free to teach and preach. So Father Gilby began his reign at Ashby from where he exercised an influence as great as any bishop's.[24] He kept in close touch with his friends of the Marian exile: those who had accepted office in the Church received reminders from him about how they should undertake their duties. Bentham, the Bishop of Coventry and Lichfield, heard from Gilby that he considered he had not dealt sufficiently firmly with the backsliding ministers in his diocese. When his office of Master of Trinity College and Vice-Chancellor of the University of Cambridge compelled Robert Beaumont, a former exile in Geneva, to enforce the wearing of the surplice in the university, Gilby sent him a 'mild' rebuke for returning 'to the toys of popery and pulls of superstition for the pleasure of men'. In 1570 he wrote an open letter of exhortation, 'godly and zealous', to his brethren in Christ, Coverdale, Turner, Whittingham, Sampson, Humphrey, Lever, Crowley and others that 'labour to root out the weeds of popery'. Gilby, always eager himself to encourage the preaching of the word in Leicestershire by fasts and exercises as well as by Sunday sermons, did not urge upon his fellow ministers tasks which he had not already first attempted himself at home.[25]

While Gilby planted Protestantism in the county, Huntingdon turned his attention to the town of Leicester where the soil was already prepared for the seed: in Mary's reign twenty-eight persons from St. Martin's parish alone had been indicted for displaying scorn toward the sacrament of the altar. Huntingdon's hand can clearly be discerned under the formal enactments of the town council which ordained in February 1562 that one member of every household should attend the sermons given every Wednesday and Friday on the pain of 4d. fine. The following year Huntingdon had his own pew set up in St. Martin's where these lectures were delivered. In 1566 when the Common Hall agreed that the weekday lectures should begin at seven in the morning and end at eight they disclosed that the original decree instituting the lectures had been made 'by the advice and consent of the right honourable Henry, Earl of Huntingdon, in the mayoralty of Mr. Thomas Fowler'. The corporation showed active sympathy but there can be little doubt that the prime mover behind this scheme of Protestant indoctrination was Huntingdon himself.[26] With the coming of Thomas Sampson to Wyggeston Hospital he had a minister abundantly qualified to undertake the lecturing. The townspeople of Leicester had no escape, from their earliest schooldays to their declining years they were shepherded to attend this continuous round of sermons. By the 1570's the adherence of the corporation to the reformed religion was unquestionable, and the aldermen's devotion extended even to their purses. In the surviving deacons' book for the French Church in London for the year 1572–3 which records the gifts of English gentlemen to the Church, the mayor and aldermen of Leicester are one of the very few civic corporations to be listed: they contributed, doubtless on the prompting of Sir Francis Hastings, the considerable sum of £13. 6s. 8d. to help French Protestant refugees.[27]

The changes Huntingdon had enthusiastically urged in the 1560's went on without serious hindrance when he no longer lived in the county and the years after 1572 mark the flowering and fruition of the young plants of Protestantism he had so carefully nurtured during his first years as an earl. Anthony Gilby continued to dominate the Church in Leicestershire: in 1571 Archbishop Parker tried to discipline him, for all men knew he sought an alteration in the established order of the Church in England, but he remained in Ashby until his death in 1585 secure and undisturbed.[28] The young zealots of the next generation looked upon Gilby as their 'loving and reverend father in God'. John Field, the energetic organiser of the revolutionary movement to make the Church of England Presbyterian from within, venerated Gilby as the leader of those exiles who on their return to their own country had refrained from sullying their consciences by conforming to the Anglican ceremonies. He was most eager to win Gilby's approval, and again and again wrote to him bewailing his deprivation from his ministry which prevented him from preaching and had forced him to turn to the mere teaching of children. When the ecclesiastical authorities in London took the logical step and imprisoned Field and his associates for their divisive activities he appealed to Gilby, by way of conference, or otherwise, to think of some way how to let and hinder this great mischief, for otherwise it cannot but come to pass that our churches by mutual dissensions shall be quite overthrown, the truth be oppressed, God's saints persecuted and religion itself so forsaken that instead thereof a certain kind of religion framed out of man's own brain and fantasy far worse then that of popery (if worse may be) patched and pieced out of theirs and ours together shall be erected and established.

Lawrence Tomson got Mr. Hastings (almost certainly Francis Hastings) to carry down to Gilby an *Admonition*, following on *The Admonition to the Parliament* which Field and Wilcocks together had drawn up towards the end of the 1572 session of parliament when it seemed the Commons would have no success in bringing in drastic alterations in Church government. Gilby, however, when he had read it, felt perturbed by the young men's haste and shared Lawrence Humphrey's concern lest the enthusiasts should go to too great extremes. Their duty, he counselled, lay in praying to God to open the queen's ears that she might be willing to hear of a reformation which 'many brethren and nobles also wish. . . . Openly to publish such admonitions as are abroad, I like not, for that in some points and terms they are too broad and overshoot themselves.'[29]

Humphrey, Sampson and Gilby, the old exiles, advised waiting until the magistrates took the initiative in reforming the Church further; Field and his associates called for immediate action; nevertheless, the new generation did not entirely break away from the old. Between 1573 and 1575, Gilby continued to receive detailed descriptions of the sufferings of the godly in London prisons from Thomas Wilcocks. Together with a copy of Beza's epistles for which Gilby had written, Wilcocks sent word that the London ecclesiastical commissioners were going on with their 'naughty' proceedings and forcing ministers to conform or be deprived: their brother Cartwright had escaped from England and found a refuge in Heidelberg. Gilby, who in the 1550's had been among the most outspoken of the radicals, had mellowed and now exercised a moderating influence from the provinces. He never developed into a thorough-going Presbyterian like Cartwright or Field, he saw nothing inherently wrong in a system of Church government through bishops, provided godly men were chosen to be bishops. The effect upon the Church in Leicestershire of having in Gilby a leader of national as well as local repute was of lasting importance. Through him news from London reached the Leicestershire ministers, and although they might no longer be in sympathy with the van of the Puritan advance they could still retain their close connection with the main body of more moderate reformers.[30]

These Leicestershire clergy who in the 1570's thought of Gilby as their bishop appear as a clearly defined Nonconformist group among a generally conformist clergy. Having brought Gilby to Ashby, Huntingdon had gone on, as far as he could, to establish and retain other convinced Protestants in the county. He owned at least eight presentations in Leicestershire and while five of these livings were very poor, being worth on the Henrician valuation less than £10 a year, the rectory of Loughborough valued at over £40 and that of Market Bosworth at more than £55 a year were among the richest livings in the county. Huntingdon took his obligations as a patron very seriously and whenever possible chose graduates or men who had studied for a time at the university. Learning and a virtuous life were the two requirements he sought before he nominated any to a benefice and, later in his life, he condemned sternly 'the preferment of such as are not so qualified which hath been occasioned either by the unlawful policies of some patrons in presenting or by the ungodly abuses of incumbents in entering (if there be no default in admitting)'.[31] By the 1570's a decade of conscientious appointments had begun to take effect. John Willock, B.D., now resided at Loughborough: before he had come to England he had co-operated with John Knox in the production of the First Book of Discipline and the Bishop of Lincoln had good reason for his suspicions that he continued to conduct communions within the English Church according to the Scottish pattern. His successor as rector of

Loughborough testified in 1605 that kneeling at communion, the sign of the cross in baptism and the wearing of the surplice had not been used in the church there all through Elizabeth's reign.[32] The bishop associated Robert Spark, M.A., with Willock in his censures. Spark seems to have remained Huntingdon's chaplain throughout the rest of his life and he also obtained the Leicestershire livings of Burbage, Broughton Astley and Aston Flamville, although they did not form part of Huntingdon's patronage. At Market Bosworth another scholar had been appointed in the person of Adam Squire and (whatever his private delinquencies) he collaborated willingly with his 'brother' Gilby.[33]

The episcopal visitation of 1576 shows that even on his poor cures, Huntingdon's candidates managed to perform their duties at least adequately at a time when the general ability of the country clergy was low. John Bares (or Burrowes), vicar of Belton, though ignorant of Latin showed himself to be 'moderately versed in sacred learning, a teacher in his benefice'. The vicars of Markfield and Packington also had no Latin but the episcopal visitors found them 'better entered in the scriptures'. The living of Castle Donington, like Markfield and Packington was valued at less than £10 a year, nevertheless they discovered Peter Wood ministering there, 'a preacher in his own cure, understanding the Latin tongue and competently learned in the scriptures'. In 1604 Peter Wood, still in the same benefice, appeared before the bishop for not wearing the surplice; he conformed and his case was dismissed. Already in 1576 another of Huntingdon's ministers, Peter Eglesall, who held his donative cure of Measham, had suffered for not wearing the surplice. Thomas Wood, the godly layman of Groby, and also one of Huntingdon's annuitants, described with enthusiasm the transformation Eglesall had wrought in the eighteen months of his ministry at Measham. By his continual diligence he had brought it to pass 'that there is not one in his parish of lawful years but are able by heart to make a good and godly confession of their faith which they use to do before the receipt of communion'. At Ashby itself, nominally not worth £15 a year, the visitors examined Thomas Wydowes, then in possession of the living: they reported he was 'a preacher, licensed by the said Bishop of Lichfield, not graduate, brought up in Cambridge at St. John's College'. His mighty father-in-law, Gilby, appears in the survey merely as the lecturer.[34]

This little band of zealots led by Gilby assisted by other like-minded ministers changed the religious climate of the county within a generation. From before 1570, exercises for increasing the knowledge of the clergy were held at Ashby under regulations approved by Thomas Cooper, Bishop of Lincoln. When the queen in 1576 commanded the suppression of the exercises in the province of Canterbury the 'poor ministers' of Ashby addressed a vigorous protest to Cooper. They argued they had never acted in any way contrary to civil or ecclesiastical laws:

We did assemble none neither by commandment nor by persuasion, but first we, the ministers coming together ourselves by the law of them that were in office, the bishop your predecessor and his officers, and since your entry, by you and your officers: we would do nothing nor say anything in secret corners, lest we might have been misjudged; but leaving open the church doors as was convenient, the people of themselves, knowing that it is always lawful to hear God's word holy day and working day by many preachers, or by few, did of themselves quietly come to pray with us, and to learn some good lessons in God's schoolhouse.[35]

Cooper found this type of argument convincing and, basing his opinions on a report submitted by Spark and Willock he told Grindal in July 1576 that he thought on the whole the exercises had been very profitable in educating the clergy. He had taken pains to see novel opinions had not been aired at these clerical gatherings, though he admitted that in the town of Leicester things had got rather out of control:

The worst place, and that which I have always most suspected, is Leicester town, where indeed I understand that a layman, but a graduate and very handsomely learned, both in philosophy and the scriptures, hath once or twice spoken, and one Johnson that is a moderator there, and a reader appointed before my time, and maintained by a stipend of my Lord of Huntingdon, is somewhat a rash man, and so much as he dare, inclined to novelties, and so be one or two more in the shire.

Nevertheless, Cooper made it clear that on balance he believed the beneficial results of the exercises outweighed their defects and when he had been translated to the bishopric of Winchester he forgot all about these occasional excesses and remembered Leicestershire only as a model evangelical county. He attributed the winning of the county to Protestantism to the activities of John Aylmer, who had first come to Leicestershire as a tutor to Lady Jane Grey, and to 'the noble Earl of Huntingdon': 'by their two means', he wrote in 1589 in his *Admonition to the people of England*, 'that shire, God be blessed, was converted and brought to that state that it is now in, which in true religion is above any other place, because they retain the Gospel without contention which few other places do.'[36]

Huntingdon's fellow apostle, however, looked back upon his early labours with far less satisfaction. In 1576, the year before he became Bishop of London, Aylmer was still Archdeacon of Stowe and held in plurality the Leicestershire livings of Market Bosworth and Cossington and so must have experienced the county's Protestantism at first hand. He disagreed violently with his bishop about its uncontentious nature and from Cossington wrote to Grindal himself to protest against the disruptive effect the local exercises were having upon the religious settlement.

Since my coming into Leicestershire I have observed the course of this course . . . and I assure your grace I have found greater boldness in the meaner sort which will ere it be long, bring great confusion in the Church if it be not speedily prevented. There is of late a rank of rangers and posting apostles that go from shire to shire, from exercise to exercise, namely Patchet, Standon etc. accompanied, countenanced and backed with Sir R. Knightly, Mr. Carlell and others out of Warwickshire, Northamptonshire and other shires to Ashby where Gilby is bishop, to Leicestershire where Johnson is superintendent, to another place where the monk Anderson reigneth, to Coventry etc. And there are bishops railed at, metropolitans wondered at for their visitations, for their officers, their pomp, their not visiting and what not. . . . I have myself some parishioners, that refusing my communion because we kneel, resort to a walking communion at Leicester ministered by an ignorant man. Your grace's inquisition was by my Lord of Lincoln committed to one Spark and Willock who themselves never minister the communion because they will wear no surplices, and use standing communions, with other disorders: therefore your grace had need take heed how you credit the certificates.[37]

Reports such as this one by Aylmer only confirmed the queen in her view that the prophesyings potentially endangered the state, if they did not actually do so, and despite Grindal's brave remonstrance, she ordered the ban on the exercises to be enforced. Nothing daunted, the Leicestershire enthusiasts cast round for some alternative where their exhortations to the clergy and the laity could continue and they discovered a suitable substitute in the solemn fasts held before communions. In 1579 Archdeacon Squire and James Gosnell, a Leicestershire minister who by 1584 had migrated to Bolton, both approached Gilby to assist in the preaching at fasts they intended to conduct. The Catholic priest, William Weston, has left a graphic description of this form of Puritan gathering which he watched from his cell in Wisbech Castle. The people flocked in from the surrounding countryside to participate and for the first few hours they heard three or four sermons interspersed with devotions. The ceremony reached its culmination in their receiving communion from the minister when they walked about, and did not kneel, that it might resemble the Passover in very deed. At the same assembly the ministers set up a tribunal where they castigated their brethren for their misdoings. The people all came with their bibles in which they sedulously looked up the texts cited by the preachers, and argued points among themselves: after a day spent in prayer and study they went off to a feast.[38] The Leicestershire assemblies in 1579 may not have reached the elaboration of the Wisbech fasts of about fifteen years later but they certainly already gave much scope to preaching. The results of Gilby's pastoral work in Leicestershire became apparent in 1584 when over three hundred Leicestershire ministers, so it was claimed, would only make a limited subscription to Whitgift's Three Articles by which he hoped to enforce conformity: they added the reservation 'that if it shall hereafter appear upon mature deliberation that any part of the Book [of Common Prayer] doth contain anything contrary to God's word, we mind not by this our subscription to approve of it'. . . .[39]

Besides Ashby, Cooper and Aylmer both picked on the town of Leicester as a centre of Protestant radicalism. Huntingdon had nominated Geoffrey Johnson, whose influence as a moderator at the exercises had alarmed Cooper, as vicar of St. Martin's, the principal church in the town, in 1570 but he never entered into possession of the living, presumably preferring like Gilby the greater freedom of a lectureship.[40] Leicester corporation gave further proof of its commitment to Protestantism in April, 1586 when it petitioned Huntingdon to appoint 'the godly preacher, Mr. Travers, a man, as we are credibly informed, of singular goodness and approved learning' as town preacher in place of Johnson who had recently died. Since his death, the corporation added, they had been 'destitute of the blessed benefit of a resident preacher faithfully to divide unto us the bread of our salvation'. Travers, who had been the minister to the Presbyterian church of the English Merchant Adventurers in Antwerp and, until his inhibition the previous month, Hooker's adversary in the Temple, was too distinguished for even Huntingdon to secure: he chose to remain at the heart of the Presbyterian organisation in London.[41] Huntingdon appears to have recommended William Pelsant B.D. instead, who was presented to the living of Market Bosworth in 1588 where he succeeded in avoiding wearing the surplice until 1604: in April 1589 the corporation wrote anxiously to Huntingdon about 'the detaining of Mr. Pelsant, our preacher'.[42] The next preacher Huntingdon found for the town was Thomas Sacheverell, and he persuaded the corporation to pay him £30 a year, an increase of £10 on the previous minister's stipend: the town councillors, however, subsequently decided Sacheverell's services did not warrant the increase and forbore to pay him altogether and so drew down upon themselves the wrath of their lord. 'When your town had any need of the help of me, and other friends, then they could promise and offer to deal both liberally and lovingly towards their preacher', Huntingdon reminded them, yet now when they had a man who well deserved their ungrudging support their promises went unfulfilled. He told them roundly that he had long hoped that Leicester people were men who loved the gospel but their recent action gave him little reason to believe it was true.[43]

In Huntingdon himself this love of the gospel never grew dim. When the vicarage of Ashby fell vacant in 1593 on the death of Thomas Wydowes, he decided that Arthur Hildersham, a distant kinsman whose father had disinherited him when he had been converted to Protestantism at Cambridge, should have the living.

Since that it hath pleased the Lord to call Thomas Wydowes to his mercy [he wrote to Hildersham], who was (in my opinion) both faithful, careful and diligent in his function, according to his talent, I do wish with all my heart the supply of that place to be such as that which good father Gilby and he, by the good providence and mercy of God, have planted in and about Ashby may be continued and increased. Therefore I choose to present you unto that pastoral charge of Ashby, which, I trust, by that time that I have finished my long intended purpose, shall be a sufficient place for any learned preacher. . . . Yet let this be your care, to advance the glory of God by exercise of your ministry which you shall do best when you are in your pastoral charge.

Hildersham had given an earnest of his ability during the previous five years when he had been the lecturer at Ashby and he had already appeared before the High Commission for preaching without a licence. He did indeed amply perform Huntingdon's charge to continue the tradition of personal evangelism begun by Gilby, though after Huntingdon's death he discovered that the toleration his predecessor had enjoyed would no longer be extended to him. One of the most active managers of the Millenary Petition whereby the radicals hoped to win from James I a greater freedom for themselves within the Church, Hildersham was silenced by the Bishop of Lincoln in 1605 for his Nonconformity and deprived from his benefice. Subsequently he regained his lectureship at Ashby but had to face another prosecution before the high commission as a schismatic in 1614. In 1625 he resumed his work at Ashby, in 1630 he was again silenced for not wearing the surplice: he was finally restored to his ministry just before his death in 1632. He published his chief literary work, *CVIII lectures on the Fourth of John*, in 1629 and dedicated it to the fifth Earl of Huntingdon, Huntingdon's great nephew,

to give public testimony unto the world of my duty and thankfulness unto your honour, and unto your noble house: unto whom (next under God) I do owe whatsoever poor abilities he hath pleased to give unto me for the service of his Church. For as that noble uncle of yours (whom his wisdom and serviceableness to his prince and country, even with the great neglect of his own estate and family, and specially his zealous care to promote the Gospel of Christ, did make much more honourable, then the nobleness of his great birth could possibly do) did first maintain me in the university, and after brought me to the exercise of my ministry in this place: so have I been by the favour and bounty of your noble grandfather, and of your honour continued here, now more then forty years.

So long as Hildersham lived, Ashby remained the centre of Protestant piety which Huntingdon had caused it to become when he had established Anthony Gilby there more than seventy years earlier.[44]

*   *   *

In 1557 Thomas Paulfreyman had confidently predicted not only that Huntingdon would rise to prominence in his own locality but that he would be called to high office in the state. History proved him to have been far too optimistic: Huntingdon had to wait nine years before the queen entrusted him with any national office, twelve years before he received permanent responsibility commensurate with his rank. No lack of eagerness on Huntingdon's part caused the delay, his dearest wish was to follow in the footsteps of his ancestors and serve his country: from the beginning of the reign he regularly attended court, and, like other courtiers, presented New Year's gifts to the queen—

which generally were silk purses containing £15 in gold. From the beginning, also, he possessed in his brother-in-law an ally with unique influence with the queen, and in fairly frequent letters from himself or his wife he did his best to win Leicester's favour. All was to no avail. In the face of Huntingdon's main stumbling block, his birth, even Leicester had to admit defeat.[45]

So long as Elizabeth continued unmarried there remained the unhappy prospect of a disputed succession to the throne. To the modern observer the obvious candidate in the event of her dying without a direct heir may seem to be Mary, Queen of Scots, the granddaughter of Henry VIII's eldest sister, but Mary was both a Catholic (and England had only just emerged from the rule of one Catholic queen) and a foreigner and was, moreover, precisely excluded under the will of Henry VIII. An alternative choice lay in the granddaughters of Henry's younger sister, Mary, through her marriage to the Duke of Suffolk: Lady Jane Grey had already been put to death because of the claims made on her behalf but her sisters, Lady Katherine and Lady Mary survived. Rumour had it that in religion Lady Katherine inclined towards Catholicism, in any event her chances of being officially recognised disappeared on her surreptitious marriage to the Earl of Hertford in 1561. Elizabeth had the marriage (which no witnesses dared attest) declared null and void and Lady Katherine confined to the Tower. The diminutive Lady Mary Grey received a similar punishment when she had the audacity to marry the queen's serjeant keeper. Her fall meant the eclipse of all the candidates in the direct Tudor line. The Tudors, however, had not yet ruled England for a century, other pretenders could trace their ancestry back to Yorkist or Lancastrian kings and among these was the Earl of Huntingdon directly descended through his mother from Richard, Duke of York, father of Edward IV. He happened to be both male and a Protestant and these circumstances combined to give his claim more weight than perhaps intrinsically it deserved.

Any account of the succession intrigues must almost inevitably

L

be biased and confused since most of the information comes from the correspondence of the Spanish ambassador: there is virtually nothing to place against it on the Protestant side. Certainly speculation began very soon after Elizabeth ascended the throne: in January 1560, de Quadra had heard the rumour that the opponents of Lady Katherine Grey, and Cecil was one of these, had declared no woman should succeed; they had spoken for Lord Hastings, Robert Dudley's brother-in-law. In March, de Quadra believed the queen might go so far as to name him as her successor, though Hastings himself thought otherwise and went in dread of being sent to the Tower. As Dudley's friendship with the queen grew, so support for Huntingdon's claim increased. De Quadra next reported to Spain that Cecil had said Huntingdon was the real heir of England and that all the heretics wanted him: he believed that because he was the greatest heretic in the realm even Dudley's enemies would favour him. All these speculations had little immediacy until Elizabeth suddenly fell ill of smallpox in October 1562: then they took on a frightening urgency. For a day or two, until the smallpox eruption developed, the queen's life was in danger: on 16 October, the day of crisis, de Quadra sent word to the Duchess of Parma that if Elizabeth died it would be soon; Lord Robert had a large armed force under his control and would probably pronounce for his brother-in-law. The next day the queen seemed a little better, the next week she had become convalescent, but men now found it difficult to forget that the tranquillity of England depended upon the life of one woman.[46]

In the weeks that followed, different rumours circulated about what the council had actually discussed when the queen seemed to be on the point of death. De Quadra heard that the council had deliberated upon the succession twice, and that three different opinions had been put forward. Some wanted Henry VIII's will to be observed and Lady Katherine declared the next heir. Others, who found flaws in the will, favoured the Earl of Huntingdon: Lord Robert, the Earl of Bedford, the Earl of Pembroke, and the

Duke of Norfolk together with others of lower rank supported his claim. Only a few councillors would consider a Catholic candidate. At the beginning of the new year as the government made plans for calling parliament, speculation over the succession increased; gentlemen held meetings to discuss the succession under the pretext of dining together and a new party grew up around the son of Lady Margaret Lennox, cousin of Mary, Queen of Scots who had had the advantage of being born an Englishman. The only rumour which can be substantiated is that the queen herself had resolved not to name anyone and insisted on her right to bequeath the succession.[47]

In February 1563 the English government, suspecting de Quadra of fermenting the intrigues he so avidly related to the King of Spain, demanded his recall, and the detailed commentary on the state of the support for Huntingdon's claim ceases. Rumours, however, continued to pass and in France Challoner heard that during her illness the queen nominated Huntingdon as her successor in her testament.[48] Huntingdon, pointedly ignored by the queen though he himself appears never to have canvassed his own claims, found his position too galling to be endured in silence. When the Countess of Huntingdon attended court Elizabeth publicly snubbed her on account of her husband's pretensions, or the pretensions his supporters were forcing upon him, and he used this occasion to write to Leicester a letter patently designed for a general audience.

My honourable good Lord. I am sorry that my present disease is such that there are left me but these two remedies, either to swallow up those bitter pills lately received, or to make you a partner of my griefs, thereby something to ease a wounded heart. At my wife's last being at court to do her duty as became her, it pleased her Majesty to give her a privy nip, especially concerning myself, whereby I perceive she hath some jealous conceit of me, and, as I can imagine, of late digested. How far I have been always from conceiting any greatness of myself, nay, how ready I have been always to shun applauses both by my continual low sail and my carriage I do assure myself is best known to your lordship, and the rest of my nearest friends; if not, mine own conscience shall best clear me from any such folly. Alas! What could I hope to effect in the greatest hopes I might imagine to have in the obtaining the least likelihood of that height? Will a whole commonwealth deprive themselves of so many blessings presently enjoyed, for a future uncertain? Inferior to many others both in degree, and any princely quality fit for a prince, for a prince both for excellent qualities and rare virtues of nature; of great hopes of an inestimable blessing by her princely issue in reason of her youth, for a poor subject in years, and without any great hope of issue? No, no: I cannot be persuaded they would, if I should be so foolishly wicked to desire it, or that my mind were so ambitiously inclined. I hope her Majesty will be persuaded of better things in me, and cast this conceit behind her, and that a foolish book, foolishly written, shall not be able to possess her princely inclination with so bad a conceit of her faithful servant, who desires not to live but see her happy. What grief it hath congealed within my poor heart (but ever true) let your lordship judge, whose prince's favour was always more dear unto me than all other worldly felicities whatsoever. This I am bold to make known to your lordship, humbly desiring the same when you see your opportunity to frame a new heart in her Majesty's princely breast, whose power I know is not little in effecting of far greater matters than this, for never shall there be a truer heart in any subject than I will carry to her Majesty so long as I breathe.[49]

The queen, however, needed more than mere words to allay her suspicions of Huntingdon's pretensions to the succession. He never again referred to his birth in writing and certainly never openly encouraged his supporters but the very fact that he continued to be a celebrated patron of Protestants inevitably drew the radicals to his cause. Occasionally after 1563 men still discussed his title: in 1566 the new Spanish ambassador anticipated that the forthcoming parliament would debate the succession and considered the Protestants were divided between Lady Katherine Grey and 'the Earl of Huntingdon, who is the man to suit them best'. After the marriage of Mary, Queen of Scots to Darnley and especially after the birth of James and his subsequent Protestant upbringing the numbers of those who supported Huntingdon's claims seem rapidly to have declined. Yet the queen could not be brought to abandon her distrust so quickly and until 1569, when the northern emergency forced her hand, she refused to consider him for any office in national life. She did not exclude him from the court; he took part in several ceremonial occasions, assisting at the creation of Dudley as Earl of Leicester in September 1564, attending the memorial service for the emperor in London in the same autumn and accompanying the queen on her progresses in the summers of 1565 and 1566. When parliament met in 1563 and 1566 Huntingdon followed the proceedings in the House of Lords most assiduously but in some respects he still remained his own worst enemy.[50]

Huntingdon knew that in the queen's eyes his two great disabilities were his birth and his Protestant enthusiasm: the first he did his best to minimise, yet his religion he never made any attempt to disguise. The 1560's proved an anxious decade for English Protestants: after some hopes of a compromise the religious wars began again in France. The sympathies of English zealots went out to the Huguenot garrison of La Rochelle and some gentlemen, under the leadership of Sir Henry Champernoun, Sir Walter Raleigh and other West Country men volunteered to fight with Coligny. Huntingdon could not contain his emotions: the story reached Spain that at the very time these gentlemen petitioned the queen for leave to serve in France he asked her for a licence to sell his lands and join the Huguenot army with 10,000 men.[51] Probably the tale was exaggerated in the telling, certainly the queen would never have entertained so wild a scheme: Huntingdon seemed to stand as far distant from the queen's confidence as he had ever been. Then suddenly the rapid deterioration in English internal politics transformed his chief disabilities into assets. Ever since Mary, Queen of Scots had fled from Scotland into England in the spring of 1568, Elizabeth had feared she would become a rallying point for all those discontented with the established government. In 1569, plans to marry Mary to the Duke of Norfolk, the highest ranking nobleman in England, came to light, together with the even more serious news that they had the backing of many members of the nobility hostile to Cecil. Armed rebellion seemed more and more likely and Elizabeth had to find an absolutely reliable guardian for the Catholic queen then in the custody of the invalid Earl of Shrewsbury in his house near Sheffield. Huntingdon's rival pretensions and his Protestant zeal assured his immunity in advance to Mary's blandishments and in September 1569, Elizabeth appointed him one of her new custodians.

Before she had ever met him, Mary revealed her strong dislike of Huntingdon. On her first entry into England she had been lodged at Bolton Castle, but the government soon realised the danger of exposing northern gentlemen to her intrigues and arranged to transfer her to the Earl of Shrewsbury at Tutbury. Before she left Bolton, one of Cecil's emissaries had an interview with her and 'learnt how loth the queen was to leave Bolton Castle, not sparing to give forth in speech that the secretary [Cecil] was her enemy, and that she mistrusted by this removing he would cause her to be made away: that her danger was so much the more because there was one dwelling near Tutbury who pretended title in succession to the crown [meaning the Earl of Huntingdon]'. Despite her protests, Mary had no choice but to come south to the Earl of Shrewsbury in Derbyshire, and she had been living under his care for nearly nine months when Elizabeth instructed Huntingdon and his cousin, Hereford, on 12 September to assist Shrewsbury in all the measures he was taking to resist Mary's escape. Tormented by gout, Shrewsbury willingly accepted these reinforcements and went so far as to ask Cecil to gain his complete release from his charge: in the meanwhile he co-operated in moving Mary from Wingfield to the greater security of his house at Tutbury.[52]

From the moment the party reached Tutbury Huntingdon's troubles began, for Cecil took Shrewsbury's plea to be relieved of his charge at its face value and on 22 September Elizabeth commanded Huntingdon to assume sole responsibility for Mary and her train, although to do so 'in another's house may seem somewhat sudden and strange'. To Shrewsbury the order seemed not only strange but a signal reflection on his honour: the guarding of Mary may have been burdensome but it seemed as nothing compared with the loss of prestige involved in resigning her to another. Huntingdon arrived at Tutbury only to find that, instead of Shrewsbury's household being at his disposal as the queen had promised, Shrewsbury would only offer lodging for himself and two of his men. He concluded Shrewsbury could manage equally well without him and wrote for leave to return to his own house at Ashby, only eight miles away. The next day he explained his difficulties to Cecil, how he was obstructed on the one hand by Shrewsbury and on the other he had to endure the hostility of the Scottish queen:

First, I find my lord not very willing to be rid of his charge: the same mind I guess to be in my lady, though both have said they be glad of the looked for discharge. The contrary may be collected from his letters. He hath sent one up with all speed which he never told me till he was gone, yet neither my messenger nor his message did I keep from him, for I read my letter to him. . . . The Queen of Scots also I perceive is not willing to change her keeper, and especially for me.

Already Huntingdon and Shrewsbury had disagreed over Mary's treatment: Shrewsbury would have allowed her to write to Elizabeth which Huntingdon would not countenance: in anger Shrewsbury had broken out, 'I can do nothing without my Lord of Huntingdon, till my man come again from the court.'

I perceive also [Huntingdon continued], *non facile patitur aequalem*. Therefore I heartily require you, if my discharge may not take place, let me be *solus* or have some other match. And to Ashby I would carry her, if I should have her, where by the grace of God I would make a true account of her. Still, if with favour I may be discharged, so be it.[53]

In the letters to Cecil and the queen which, with reason, he had kept from Huntingdon, Shrewsbury had written that since his health had improved, there no longer remained any cause why the sole responsibility for Mary should not be restored to him, without Huntingdon or any other being joined to him: 'which would be as great a discredit and dishonour as could chance him'. Until they could receive further communications from London the two noblemen had no choice but to join their forces in readiness to resist any attempt to 'recover' Mary. Elizabeth's latest instructions, that since Shrewbury's servants had probably been corrupted by Mary they were to be replaced by Huntingdon's men, only further lacerated Shrewsbury's pride. Mary, for her part, seized the opportunity of adding to the disputes among her guardians; her servant, the Bishop of Ross, spread the rumour that on his first visit to Mary at Wingfield, Huntingdon had spoken of his title to the succession and, for good measure, he accused Hereford of uttering 'unfit' speeches concerning Norfolk and Leicester. In great agitation Huntingdon penned a refutation to Cecil:

As to what he [the Bishop of Ross] said of me for pretence of title, I trust neither word nor act of mine is cause of his speech. If he say either is, I am ready to answer it. As for my Lord of Hereford there never passed any such speech from him.[54]

Further letters came down to Tutbury from court but none contained the decision over Mary's custody for which Huntingdon and Shrewsbury impatiently waited. In unwilling alliance they made a search of Mary's chamber and, since it now seemed that the threat of a northern rising had diminished they obeyed instructions and reduced the number of the men they had raised to guard Mary. Elizabeth's next request, in which she asked them to try to find letters Mary had received from Pembroke and Leicester the previous Easter, caused another scene with their royal prisoner. Mary complained so vociferously to Elizabeth that men armed with pistolets had broken into her chamber that Shrewsbury and Huntingdon hurriedly sent up their version of what had happened in the search. Within three days Elizabeth signified she was well pleased with their conduct and desired them to make this known to Mary. Against this turbulent background of rivalry between the two principal gaolers and with their prisoner attempting to outwit them both, Huntingdon had some justification in exclaiming to Cecil, 'I pray God assist the queen and you her councillors in the spirit of wisdom and fortitude, considering the causes, the time and persons you have to deal with.'[55]

At last on 15 October the queen made known her decision concerning the custody of Mary, but in a way pleasing neither to Shrewsbury nor Huntingdon: she wished Mary to remain under their joint care. Elizabeth told Shrewsbury she had heard that Huntingdon had no lodging in Tutbury Castle meet for his health, and that at mealtimes his servants had had to go into the town, far distant: she required him to remedy those matters, to cut down Mary's servants and to look to his own who had probably become corrupted by Mary's people without his knowledge. The greatest blow to his self-esteem came in her postscript: she could not believe his desire to have sole control of Mary was his own idea, but thought it must have come from some about him 'too much affectionated' to her. Shrewsbury rushed to make a categorical denial: no one had prompted him to ask for the sole control of Mary, Huntingdon did have an adequate lodging, his servants could eat at the castle; and by the same post he begged Cecil to regain the queen's favour towards him. News of the royal rebuke penetrated to Huntingdon who in the hope of avoiding further quarrels told Cecil he would not have his lodging altered,

but as one ignorant what her Majesty hath written, pass it over and do as I have done: I know it will please him, and be my best mean to quench that as is kindled. I am sure also (under correction) this to do will prove best for her Majesty's service and my quiet.[56]

Towards the end of October more details of the intended marriage between Mary, Queen of Scots and Norfolk were uncovered and the queen ordered fresh precautions to be observed against her escape: she feared the extra cares might have caused Shrewsbury's health to worsen and asked for particulars of his welfare. In a private letter of the same date Cecil explained to Huntingdon the meaning behind these manœuvres. Various opinions had been aired in the council with the queen that day: some thought Huntingdon should have charge of the Queen of

Scots at Ashby, others that the Chancellor of the Duchy of Lancaster should come to Tutbury and both Huntingdon and Shrewsbury be discharged, yet others that the chancellor should be joined with Huntingdon at Ashby. Cecil took pains to make it clear there was nothing personal in this mistrust of Huntingdon 'but to excuse the challenge which the Queen of Scots maketh to you'. These deliberations merely resulted in Henry Skipwith's being sent as a messenger from the Privy Council to Tutbury to see conditions for himself. In a revealing aside, Cecil thanked Huntingdon for his good opinion of him and hoped it would continue: he begged him, nevertheless, not to utter it openly as he perceived he did lest, perhaps through some misliking, Cecil found himself hindered from doing what he would. To Cecil by return of post and to Skipwith in person, Huntingdon renewed his plea to be permitted to leave Tutbury.[57]

The fresh enquiries into his state of health alarmed Shrewsbury anew and he again denied to Cecil that his wife had ever been too friendly to Mary, or that she had persuaded him to petition to have the sole charge of Mary restored to him: he hoped Elizabeth would not so discredit him as to give her over to Huntingdon. This time his representations produced an effect. On 4 November the queen informed Shrewsbury that Mary might remain in his custody, having never doubted his loyalty, only that of his servants: since he had recovered his health she would license Huntingdon to depart to Ashby on the understanding Shrewsbury would recall him immediately if he became ill again. 'And so we wish you to allow of him as of a very true and loving neighbour or friend', she admonished him, 'for so surely he hath showed himself to be, in all this time of his continuance upon you.' The very afternoon the queen's letter arrived Huntingdon left for Ashby.[58]

His respite proved to be only of a few days' duration for the government had not, as it hoped, forestalled a rising in the north. In fulfilment of his promise Shrewsbury sent to tell Huntingdon on 11 November that he had had news from the secretary of the

Council in the North that Northumberland and Westmorland had so far refused to obey the queen's command to return to the court. Very quickly after this the earls raised the north in revolt; on 15 November they and their followers entered Durham and heard mass there, by 21 November Shrewsbury had news they had reached Tadcaster, eight miles south of York and he summoned Huntingdon and Hereford to be with him the next day. Shrewsbury realised Tutbury could never withstand a pitched battle and he had no alternative but to move Mary further south. Elizabeth ordered that she should be taken to Coventry. On 25 November, Shrewsbury and Huntingdon together reported that they had reached Coventry that night with Mary under the guard of four hundred soldiers: their next problem lay in finding suitable accommodation for the Scottish queen which complied with the Privy Council's directions, that she must not be kept where she could be seen by the common people or where she might have access to speak with any.[59]

The chaos created by Mary's eruption into Coventry prompted Huntingdon to resume his correspondence with Cecil. In direct contravention of the Privy Council's wishes, he told him, Mary had been lodged at an inn where there was not even room for Huntingdon himself to sleep: her servants lived in the town and they had no control over them at all. He had succeeded in finding another house, but they could not move there because Shrewsbury had not brought any furnishings with him and he thought they desperately needed further instructions from the queen. The next day Huntingdon felt so strongly about the situation that he dispatched two private letters to Cecil besides the formal one he wrote with Shrewsbury. With a divided command no decisions could be kept for more than four days and however explicit the directions from court he believed there could be no improvement: 'quod natura dedit, nemo tollere potest'. He had again, without success, urged Shrewsbury to move Mary, for in the inn she got news of all that was happening. He acted like one at his wits' end: 'I have many times said that to do and say nothing were the best, but I can but speak and give advice, to others the order belongeth.' As the day progressed Shrewsbury's plans emerged: he wanted to take Mary to Nottingham and gave no sign of moving her to the private house in Coventry which the local magistrates had now made ready. Huntingdon wrote angrily that if he were expected to remain long in Coventry he felt he should be given the sole charge of Mary, not for his own sake but so that the duty could be properly discharged. When the queen's orders arrived they fully justified him in some of his representations: Elizabeth had been horrified to learn Mary had been lodged in an inn when it was known positively that the Friars House, or one of the merchants' houses, could accommodate both the queen and her train. She wished the double charge to continue and Huntingdon as well as Shrewsbury to reside in the same house as Mary. From the north came the heartening news of the rebels' retreat and the government considered that the guard around Mary could be reduced to its former numbers.[60]

Only after receiving the royal instructions did Shrewsbury agree to move Mary to a private house and he was so far from abandoning his former plans that he persuaded Huntingdon to sign a letter suggesting that Nottingham Castle would be the safest prison for her. The two noblemen seemed not to be able to make the simplest decision together and they found it necessary to write to London for advice over exactly which servants should be excluded from Mary's retinue. Huntingdon continued to send his private letters to Cecil, with the request that he would burn them after he had read them, but Cecil could offer him little encouragement. 'Being informed as I am by your letters I am able to see the dangers, but not able to remedy them as I would. It is a common device to render advices of surety for our lady to be suspected with opinion of evil will to the other'.[61]

During the first two weeks in December, the government forces in the north turned the rebels' retreat into a rout, the likelihood of an attempt being made to release Mary progressively decreased and Huntingdon began to hope he might even be home for Christmas. In a more realistic mood, knowing that 'her Majesty is not hasty in resolving', he prudently reserved a house in Coventry for his family for the season. Still he could not prevent himself worrying over the divided command, pointing out that 'all offices may be satisfied here with a good keeper, without which no place will serve', and suggesting his own position might improve if he were allowed to bear half the cost of maintaining Mary's guard which the queen had laid upon Shrewsbury alone. By this time, however, it must have been clear that the emergency had ended and at last on Christmas Eve the queen sent orders to Shrewsbury and Huntingdon to conduct Mary back to Tutbury. Immediately after Christmas they took matters in hand, Mary was taken to Derbyshire on 2 January and Huntingdon had permission to go home. With obvious relief Shrewsbury regained the sole custody of Mary which he retained for the next fourteen years until political necessity once more demanded more exacting and more Puritanical keepers.[62]

So ended Huntingdon's first taste of public employment. It had been a curious episode in which neither Huntingdon nor Shrewsbury, each vying with the other to obtain his companion's displacement, appeared in a particularly creditable manner. On the other hand, the guardianship of Mary, Queen of Scots was an occupation which it probably was not given to any human being to perform successfully, while Elizabeth herself by her vacillation put both men into a thoroughly difficult position. Yet, in spite of his reluctance, Huntingdon certainly benefited from the experience he gained and particularly from the growing intimacy with Cecil which these months of service fostered. Before he had always looked to Leicester, now he turned first to Cecil. Without Leicester's patronage he still could not hope to advance far at court but he undoubtedly gained from having in Cecil an additional friend at court, both more reliable and more stable. Cecil, moreover, approved Huntingdon's intense application to duty which characterised all he did, and he naturally appreciated Huntingdon's constant deference to his wishes. Subsequently,

Huntingdon was to pour out his thoughts more freely to such councillors as Walsingham or Mildmay whose religious indiscretion equalled his own and even in 1569 he confided to Mildmay his belief that 'the time doth await every honest faithful Christian to be vigilant in these dangerous tempests.' He could not contemplate without horror the restoration of Catholicism in England to which he believed support for Mary might well lead and this explains his strictness towards the Scottish queen. Mary symbolised Jezebel, and with her the sons of light could have no dealings.[63]

Once he had escorted Mary back to Tutbury in January 1570, Huntingdon retired to private life and his election as a Knight of the Garter on St. George's Day, 1570 seemed to be the only recognition of his service.[64] Again he had the leisure to pursue his religious interests and indeed early in 1571 he found himself called in to arbitrate in a theological dispute between the ministers of the Spanish and French Protestant congregations in London. Antonio de Corro, a Protestant convert from a Spanish ascetic order had sought refuge in England with his family upon Alva's arrival in Flanders and through the help of the Duchess of Suffolk, Cecil and Leicester he became pastor of the Spanish members of the Strangers' church. His impetuosity soon involved him in a quarrel with his fellow pastor of the Italian congregation who accused him of leanings towards Pelagianism. De Corro himself appealed to Beza who referred him to Grindal in his capacity as superintendent of the Strangers' church and for a time in 1570, on the recommendation of Cousin, the French pastor, he was suspended for slander. Unfortunately at the height of these bickerings de Corro chose to publish his *Tables of the Christian Religion* which his enemies pronounced to be theologically unsound though he had in fact written it some years previously and had had it approved by the Archbishop of Canterbury. Besides appealing to English and German scholars, de Corro also dispatched his offending *Tables* to Huntingdon, explaining that he would indeed have presented it in person if the Bishop of

Chichester had not been calling him to his proper work. Cousin, the French minister, felt much aggrieved that this disturber of the Church of God should trouble one of the godly nobility with so frivolous an appeal and at once sent an Italian, one Captain Franciotto, to make clear to Huntingdon why the French ministers had found it necessary to condemn certain points in the *Tables*. No information remains to show how the controversy ended; de Corro, for his part, weathered the storm and became a prebendary of St. Paul's though suspicions of his orthodoxy on matters of predestination were never entirely forgotten. This evidence of Huntingdon's otherwise unknown connections with the foreign Protestant congregations in London emphasises anew his concern for the reformed Church throughout Europe, not merely his local Church in England, which became increasingly apparent as his career progressed.[65]

His lack of employment left Huntingdon free in other ways in 1571 to try to advance the Protestant cause. Parliament sat for two months that year and Huntingdon attended committee after committee, often alone among the temporal lords apart from his fellow enthusiast, Bedford. Very early in the session, the Commons in conference with the Lords tried to remodel the whole body of canon law on Protestant lines, as had been suggested during the reign of Edward VI. If it had been successful the attempt would have fundamentally altered the whole administration of the Established Church but only the blindest optimist could have supposed that it would be. The bill got no further than the committee. The Puritan lords had no better luck with a whole series of Protestant bills, bills against priests disguising themselves in strange apparel, against fugitives overseas, other bills for certain offences to be made treason, for compelling men to come to church and receive communion, for ministers of the Church to be sound in religion and against corrupt presentations and simony. Huntingdon sat on the committees for all these bills. The only evidence to survive is of lists of attendance but it is difficult not to see him as one of the leaders of a small group in the Lords as eager for the reformation and regulation of the English Church by parliament as any in the Commons.[66]

After parliament had been dissolved, Huntingdon as usual accompanied the queen on her summer progress and again in 1572 he joined the royal cavalcade on its way to princely festivities at Leicester's house at Kenilworth. As the illustrious company passed through the borough of Warwick the town clerk thought fit to list the queen's train in the Warwick Black Book:

> The Lord Burghley, lately made Lord Treasurer of England, the Earl of Sussex, lately made Lord Chamberlain to her Majesty, the Lord Howard of Effingham, lately made Lord Privy Seal, the Earl of Oxford, the Lord Great Chamberlain of England, the Earl of Rutland, the Earl of Huntingdon, lately made President of the North, the Earl of Warwick, the Earl of Leicester, Master of the Horse, and many other lords, bishops, ladies, and great estates. . . .

So casually did a contemporary record Huntingdon's promotion to an important and permanent office under the crown. Sussex, whose policy of leniency in a wayward region had ended disastrously in the Northern Rebellion had been recalled to the court: accident can have played little part in Elizabeth's decision to replace him with one among her nobility renowned for his devotion to the new religion.[67]

CHAPTER FIVE

The Queen's Viceroy in the North

ON 28 November 1572 the corporation of York received the
news that 'the right honourable the Earl of Huntingdon, now
Lord President of the queen's majesty's honourable council
established in these north parts, will be here at this city
tomorrow', and made haste to celebrate the occasion with suitable
solemnity. The corporation decided that 'he shall be met at
Micklegate bar by my lord mayor and his brethren, the aldermen
in scarlet, the sheriffs in their best apparel, and the twenty-four in
crimson, and certain other of the most honest and substantial
citizens in their best apparel, and welcome his lordship to this
city'. To honour yet further the queen's chief representative in the
north, the city chamberlains presented him with a tun of Gascony
wine, with maynbread (a kind of cake-bread peculiar to York),
with sugar loaves weighing twenty pounds and with two gallons
of Hippocras. The magnificence of the reception shows the kind
of respect the corporation felt should be given to the most
powerful royal official in the north of England who had now
come to reside in their city.[1]

Huntingdon's sudden promotion to a position of such authority
surprised many of his contemporaries. The presidency of the
north became vacant for a noble outsider on the general exchange
of offices which followed the death of the aged Lord Treasurer,
the Marquis of Winchester, in March 1572: the queen then

M

ennobled William Cecil as Lord Burghley and appointed him Lord Treasurer, and gave Sir Thomas Smith his place of Principal Secretary; at this same time she created Lord Howard of Effingham Lord Privy Seal and Sussex (who had been a virtually non-resident Lord President in the north ever since Hunsdon had cast reflections on his competence during the Rebellion of the Earls) succeeded to his office of Lord Chamberlain. Some jumped to the conclusion Huntingdon had gained power through the Earl of Leicester; the seventeenth-century historian, Heylyn, always ready to attribute evil motives to the radical Protestants, believed Leicester had purposely obtained the post from the queen for his brother-in-law so that in the event of her death, Huntingdon could have the disposing of the north while he took control at court.[2] Sinister rumours current at the time provide a little substance for this allegation: Christopher Rokeby, an unconcealed adherent of the house of Northumberland, dwelt on his fears of Huntingdon's increasing authority. As the representative of the queen, the Lord President would be dutifully obeyed, he reported to Burghley, 'yet some will have it he has an ill-meaning: if he should attempt what many fear, I and my friends may be a block in his way, as he has been in mine, yet I cannot think he will take any enterprise in hand, so long as her majesty reigns over us; but I feel greatly afraid if he continue long in this office, he will grow stronger in this country.' These aspersions upon Huntingdon's motives for seeking office can neither be proved nor disproved: history never provided an opportunity for the unfolding of this supposed plot concerning the succession and when the queen came to die in 1603, both Leicester and Huntingdon had long since been dead.[3]

While Leicester may have taken the initiative in advancing Huntingdon to the office of President in the north, Burghley certainly supported him in his ambition to be given permanent office. When he had acted as a temporary guardian of Mary, Queen of Scots, Huntingdon had proved to Cecil that he could be relied upon to send him detailed information of all happenings, and that he would be his man: Cecil realised the value of sending

a convinced Protestant with no northern connections to rule over
a region where pockets of conservatism and Catholicism had so
recently been uncovered. Huntingdon himself thought he owed
his office to Burghley:

And where it seemeth that some should mislike your lordship's haste
in preferring me to this place [he told him in 1573], I am sorry for it
with all my heart, yet I trust, I have not done anything to the offence
of any, but if I have ... they might tell me of my fault. I think I have
committed many errors, but this I dare boldly affirm, in the fear of God,
that since my coming hither I have in all causes had a mind to do that
which might most advance the glory of God, best further the good
service of her majesty and be most fit for the common good and quiet
of this people.[4]

As President of the Council in the North, Huntingdon was both
an administrator and a judge. The queen considered him immediately responsible for the orderly government of the five
counties north of the Trent: Yorkshire, Durham, Northumberland, Cumberland and Westmorland. (Lancashire, since it was
part of the duchy of Lancaster, never lay within the jurisdiction of
the Council in the North.) He had the task of seeing that the
central government's policies for the north were carried out in the
localities. In addition he presided over the court of the Council in
the North which took cognisance of practically all offences,
criminal and civil, committed within the region: frequently the
Privy Council referred back to it for final determination northern
cases originally heard in London. The business transacted before
the court increased all through the latter part of Elizabeth's reign
largely because of the court's relatively swift procedure and
convenient location for northern suitors.

Even at the beginning of his presidency when the number of
reliable northern gentlemen was limited, the central government
deliberately assigned the Council in the North a wide membership.
It named twenty-nine men as members of the council in the
instructions sent to Huntingdon in May 1574, but only appointed
the great majority of these, northern gentlemen and leading

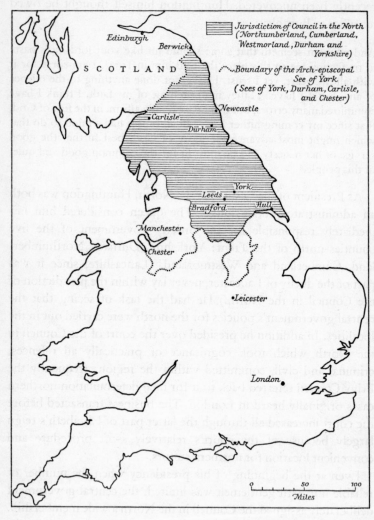

Administration in the North of England

northern ecclesiastics, in an advisory capacity. The nucleus of the council lay in its legal members bound to continual attendance. The government required the salaried members, Sir Thomas Gargrave, Lawrence Meeres, Ralph Rokeby, Francis Rodes and Thomas Eynns, to live permanently in York and paid them annual fees ranging from 100 marks, for Gargrave, to £6. 13s. 4d. for the council's pursuivant.[5] For the council to re-establish its authority over the north these resident members of the council had to be completely trustworthy. In 1572, Ralph Rokeby had replaced William Tankard, whom Gargrave had classed as a neuter in religion, and as Huntingdon's local knowledge grew he intervened more and more to get the government to appoint sound men as he did in 1581 when George Blyth, the council's secretary, lay dying and Huntingdon wrote urgently to London to ask that 'an honest, wise man may succeed him'. Knowing that the competition for the post would be great he begged Burghley to see that a man should be chosen who

will be careful to understand the state and disposition of this people. . . . Yet because whiles I serve in this place, I am desirous to be matched with religious and skilful men, as at my first entry (when your lordship did tell me of the displacing of Tankard and the placing of Mr. Rokeby, men then unknown to me) I was bold to say unto you and prayed therein your continuance of your lordship's favour towards me.

Huntingdon had his way in this, as in much else, and the queen made Mr. Harry Cheke the new secretary, of whom he entirely approved. Chiefly through Huntingdon's diligence, surprisingly quickly after the disturbance of the Northern Rebellion, the professional members of the Council in the North had been wielded into a team upon which the central government could absolutely rely.[6]

Besides the professional members of the Council in the North, the only other member the government expected to attend regularly was the Lord President himself: no court could be held in Huntingdon's absence, or the absence of his deputy whom he could nominate at pleasure. Some idea of the seriousness with which he undertook his duties can be gained from a list which still survives of those who attended the opening and closing meetings of every session of the court of the Council in the North: during the twenty-three years of his tenure of office, Huntingdon was present at two-thirds of these meetings. By the date of his appointment the court had already become a formal institution which sat four times a year, each sitting lasting a month. According to Huntingdon's first instructions the government intended that the court should be held three times a year at York and that the fourth session should be equally divided between Newcastle, or some other place in Northumberland, and Carlisle, or another town in Cumberland or Westmorland. In 1574 the court did sit at Carlisle at the beginning of August and at Newcastle later in the month but subsequently Huntingdon only moved away from York with the court on rare occasions. The 1580 commission gave him power to choose where the sessions of the court should be, and he obviously preferred York where the council chamber in the King's Manor provided a suitable setting for the majesty of the law. Huntingdon had his statute books and other reference books conveniently to hand there and the splendour of the scene, the chairs upholstered in cloth of gold, the cushions, some embroidered with coats of arms, others of crimson and tawny velvet worked with silver, the green carpets and the turkey carpet on the cupboards could scarcely have failed to impress even the most hardened litigants.[7]

This is not the place for a detailed discussion of the constitutional importance of the Council in the North, particularly as Dr. Reid has dealt with the subject exhaustively in her book. Since she wrote, relatively little new material has been uncovered relating to the council: while in the last fifty years the minute books of the northern High Commission have reappeared, the official records of the Council in the North seem to be lost irretrievably. Here the Council in the North will be considered only from the personal angle: what the duties were which this office imposed upon Huntingdon, how he carried them out and how he himself affected the working of the council at a time when, it had been argued, it reached its maximum usefulness. In turn, his dealings first with the nobility and gentry, then with the towns, and then with the administration of justice will be examined.[8]

Huntingdon arrived in York with few practical qualifications besides his experience in local government to equip him for his work. Apart from the information he had gleaned from his attendance at court and at parliament he had little direct knowledge of the greater complexities of national government and Matthew Hutton later described Huntingdon as being at this time 'very raw'. Yet in this he did not differ from other Elizabethan noblemen: when called to high office few had had any specific training for their work. The salaried under-officers existed to instruct their masters in their tasks and Huntingdon was especially fortunate in that he could draw upon the vast experience of Sir Thomas Gargrave. Ever since 1544, Gargrave had been one of the legal members of the Council in the North; he had sat for parliament many times, first for the city of York, later as a Knight of the Shire and had been the Speaker of Elizabeth's first parliament. Shrewsbury had first nominated him Vice-President of the Council in the North in 1560 and since then he had customarily directed the council in the absence of the Lord President. From the time Sussex withdrew from the north early in 1570 until Huntingdon's arrival, Gargrave had been in charge of the day-to-day administration in the north and since he was a councillor bound to continual attendance, he could advise Huntingdon from his fund of accumulated knowledge, until his death in 1579.[9]

Throughout the period of the rising in the north, Gargrave had rallied support for the crown and immediately the earls' men had been driven back, much against his will, he had been made sheriff to replace Richard Norton who had been implicated in the rebellion. When Huntingdon took up office the emergency had ended; the southern army led by Clinton and Warwick had withdrawn, and Sussex, before he had retired to the south, had presided over trials of rebels at York, Durham and Carlisle. Yet memories of the revolt had not had time to fade and as recently as August 1572 the attainted Earl of Northumberland had been executed at York. Huntingdon went north charged to re-establish and maintain a lasting peace in his region and throughout his presidency this always remained his prime consideration. In his first brief instructions issued in October 1572, before he left London, the government reminded him of the influence the great men in the north had exercised over the simple people: it particularly urged him to see that they did not retain men contrary to the laws of the land and to take pains to bring to justice rebels who had fled. Within a month of reaching York Huntingdon took action. He shared Burghley's opinion that 'popery and treason went always together' and consequently he made sure that some justices suspected of being Catholics, though not as many as he wished, had been omitted from the commission of the peace issued on the appointment of a new president. He had circularised the northern justices, he told Burghley, with articles requiring detailed reports on known and suspected papists, 'enemies of God and good order', vagabonds and those who spread false rumours, on unlawful conventicles of those who had taken part in the rebellion, of the names of all former rebels, of those who kept servants who had been rebels, together with all those who retained men contrary to the statute. Even as late as March 1574 Huntingdon examined suspected rebels before the council.[10]

Without organised leadership, no one considered these humble men particularly dangerous: the government feared the great men in the north. Undoubtedly the failure of the rebellion struck a severe blow at the lingering feudalism of the north; Huntingdon had to see the lords did not recover their former unbridled influence and he turned his attention first to the families of the three earls who had led the rebellion. As Henry Percy had remained loyal to the crown in 1569 and had not joined the Earl of Northumberland, the queen permitted him to succeed to his brother's title but within a year he compromised himself by beginning a correspondence with Mary, Queen of Scots and

offering to help her escape. For this the government sent him to
the Tower, tried him for treason and imposed a heavy fine,
although within eighteen months it permitted him to leave his
close imprisonment and live in limited freedom on his southern
estates. Not without cause Huntingdon never trusted him and in
January 1573 he heard the news that Northumberland might even
be allowed to return to the north. The mere rumour had already
raised the hopes of the discontented:

I hope it is not so as was reported, neither let it be if you can let it
[Huntingdon wrote to Leicester in alarm]; truly I wish the gentleman
to do well, and if by the law he be an earl, God make him a better earl
then his brother was. And although I doubt not but he be well warned,
yet surely, my lord, if he should come here, where the vain opinion of
his own force and credit, with such pretty persuasion as he should find
plentifully here, except he be wonderfully armed in God his grace,
because he is a man I may fear his falling and therefore these things doth
make me to think it far better to let him dwell in Sussex than in the
north.[11]

As Huntingdon wished, Northumberland continued to be
confined to his southern estates, though the government did not
act upon his radical suggestion that he be compelled to exchange
his northern lands for others in the south. He pointed out at the
same time the folly of allowing Tynemouth Castle to remain in the
care of one of Northumberland's supporters but the queen waited
until 1582 when Northumberland had been committed again to
the Tower for his complicity in Throckmorton's plot before
depriving him of the governorship of the castle: he died during
his third imprisonment in 1583. The ninth Earl of Northumberland learnt much from the fate of his uncle and of his father.
Prudently he spent most of his time in London and at first showed
more interest in military affairs abroad than in the administration
of his northern estates: he served with Leicester in the Low
Countries in 1585 and 1586 and sailed in the fleet sent against the
Armada. His marriage to Dorothy Devereux in 1595 which
linked him with the strongly Protestant party among the nobility

provided an additional security for his good behaviour. Since the first Earl of Essex had entrusted the care of his younger children to Huntingdon, he personally, as well as Burghley, may have had a hand in arranging Lady Dorothy's second marriage; at least he had the satisfaction of seeing that as long as he lived no Earl of Northumberland again troubled the peace of the north.[12]

In contrast with the subsequent history of the Earls of Northumberland, the rebellion proved to be an unqualified disaster for the Neville family. The Earl of Westmorland fled into exile, forfeiting his lands and leaving no male heir to continue the family's interest in the north: his four young daughters had to live as best they could in relative poverty. Lady Katherine and Lady Margaret Neville later considerably embarrassed the Council in the North by harbouring Catholic priests, but they never had a strong enough following to become a serious threat to the government.[13]

During the Northern Rebellion the Earl of Cumberland had behaved equivocally: he died soon afterwards leaving his son a minor. Huntingdon approved entirely of the boy's being made a ward of the Earl of Bedford who, he knew, would strive to graft him in all virtue: he warned Burghley in 1573 that some of his countrymen had begun to wait on the new earl and feared that they might gain an undesirable ascendancy over him. By his marriage to Bedford's daughter, Margaret in 1577, Cumberland, like Northumberland later, was brought into the sphere of the Protestant nobility and his career at sea gave the government no cause to suspect his loyalty. Huntingdon never forgot the influence the nobility could have in the north: those with 'minds well affected to religion and justice might be here well bestowed to the glory of God, service of the prince, and comfort of the country; but one great one of the contrary disposition may do here much more hurt than in any part of the realm that I know.' Chance, and his own advice to the central government brought it about that within ten years of his first becoming Lord President all the northern earls had lost their capacity for causing any serious hurt in his province.[14]

Yet faction which could so easily be turned to plotting against the queen had by no means died out in the north: the case of the Dacre inheritance shows the strength of feudal allegiance among northern tenants. In 1569 the young Lord Dacre, who was both the ward and stepson of the Duke of Norfolk, died and his estates were divided between his three sisters, also Norfolk's wards and betrothed to his sons. Leonard Dacre, the uncle of the heiresses, contested this legal decision, claiming that his father had entailed the estates and consequently, by the law of succession, they were rightfully his. The possession he could not obtain in the courts he achieved by force during the Northern Rebellion until Hunsdon drove out his retainers and he and his second brother, Edward Dacre, were forced to flee to the Low Countries where they both soon died. In 1578 Mary Dacre also died, leaving her sisters, Ann, married to the Earl of Arundel, and Elizabeth, married to Lord William Howard, the sole inheritors of their father's estates. The Howards did not come from the north and they were not popular there: murmurings began to be heard against them and in 1581 Huntingdon thought it necessary to inform Walsingham that some common men in Westmorland and Cumberland had great affection towards Francis Dacre, the only surviving brother of Leonard Dacre.[15]

The suspicion Huntingdon in the north felt towards Dacre had to be set against the central government's distrust of the Howards. Early in the 1580's the Earl of Arundel became a Catholic and Lord William Howard followed his example; by doing so inevitably they prejudiced their case. Francis Dacre judged that the political climate favoured his making a new attempt to regain his nieces' lands and, so Lord William Howard later alleged, Leicester supported him. In 1584 he entered into some of the Dacre lands in the north, a majority of the tenants recognised his claim and began paying their rents to Dacre instead of to one of the Howards, still their nominal lords: the Privy Council asked Huntingdon to sequester these lands on the queen's behalf to prevent serious disturbances.[16] From 1584 continuous litigation took place before the Lord President and the Council in the North and in the court of Chancery between Francis Dacre and the Earl of Arundel and Lord William Howard until 1587 when the Privy Council tried to settle the controversy and ordered both parties to stay their suits in the north and to come to London for a final determination. Lord William maintained that the majority of decisions there went against Dacre but in 1589 both he and Arundel had been imprisoned in the Tower, suspect for their religion, and the time was certainly inopportune for the recognition of their title. On the other hand, the government had as little faith in the political reliability of Francis Dacre and conceived the plan of claiming the whole inheritance for the queen. In an attempt to forestall this outcome of events, Dacre began plotting at the Scottish court; he was attainted, the government decided that the Dacre lands had been entailed (which up to that time it had officially denied), and all the lands reverted to the queen. Until 1601 she enjoyed the revenues from the Dacre lands and then, almost certainly prompted by the sympathy with which James VI had received Dacre in Scotland, she allowed the widowed Countess of Arundel and Lord William Howard to buy back their respective shares of the estates. The northern tenants had shown they were still only too eager to acknowledge a Dacre as their lord: the return of the Howards, chastened by misfortune, seemed the only way of controlling them. This long-drawn-out case proved a source of unrest in the north throughout Huntingdon's presidency.[17]

Guided by the Privy Council, Huntingdon did not think of the quietness of the north as being merely the absence of aristocratic ambitions and feudal intrigues: he worked as much to create a new political stability as to destroy the type of society in which revolts had been possible and his appointment marks the beginning of reconstruction after the Northern Rebellion. At the same time as he helped subjugate the great northern families he encouraged the lesser nobility and gentry to co-operate actively with the Council in the North. From the beginning he had been provided with a large council (the 1574 commission named twenty-nine men to be of the Council in the North). The government included some members whose loyalty was unquestioned, such were the Archbishop of York, the Bishop of Durham, the Deans of York and Durham and the two judges of assize: for others nomination to the council in itself became the reward of good behaviour. In 1574, the queen named as members of the council the Earls of Shrewsbury and Rutland, both important landowners in the north, and also added Henry, Lord Scrope, John, Lord Darcy, Cuthbert, Lord Ogle as well as representatives of the gentry families of Foster, Bowes, Gates, and Constable. As Huntingdon's presidency continued, the number of these mainly honorary members from the nobility and gentry increased significantly: the government trusted the young Earl of Cumberland sufficiently in 1580 to place him on the council, and with him Sir William and Sir Thomas Fairfax came in as new members.[18] The opinions of the Lord President and his advisers with their specialised local knowledge, carried particular weight with the Privy Council when it renewed and revised the membership of the council and of the commissions of the peace for the northern counties. They knew certain families, like the Bowes, to be pillars of the queen's authority: Sir George Bowes had suffered much at the hands of the rebels in 1569; Robert Bowes served Elizabeth both as treasurer of Berwick and ambassador to Scotland. The Gates family they recognised as equally dependable: Sir Henry Gates, a southern gentleman by birth, had only settled with his family at Seamer at the beginning of the reign but since he was a convinced Protestant he had been at once included on the council and retained his membership until he died in 1589. About this time new northern families rose to importance: the influence of the Savilles grew, although little is heard of Sir John Saville before the reign of James I; Sir Robert Stapleton seemed about to embark on a glittering career in the north and then lost all his chances by trying to blackmail Archbishop Sandys. Slowly the number of

gentlemen upon whom the Council in the North could rely to carry out its orders increased, but they never became abundant: one of the reasons why Huntingdon pressed Margaret Dakins to marry Sir Thomas Posthumus Hoby was his eagerness to have a sound, Protestant gentleman established at Hackness in a part of Yorkshire otherwise dominated by the Catholic Cholmleys. As late as 1595 the council still had to be on the watch for political discontent.

In all his striving to bring about good government in the north Huntingdon could count upon the support of the northern towns; their interests and those of the government coincided, for both wanted to have the irresponsible actions of the old nobility and gentry curbed. No town had willingly sided with the rebels in the 1569 rebellion and Halifax, which Grindal claimed had been ready to bring three or four thousand men into the field to serve the queen, had surpassed itself in displaying its loyalty. Yet Huntingdon soon discovered that the towns no less than the surrounding countryside required close supervision. Throughout his presidency he exercised an especially thorough surveillance over York itself since the Council in the North had its headquarters in the city. Poverty made York particularly susceptible to unrest, and from 1574 Huntingdon expected reports every six weeks from the corporation on the quietness of its inhabitants. In 1576 frequent disturbances drew from him a list of articles for the corporation to answer and for the better regulation of the city he decided that high constables should be appointed and asked the corporation to submit four suitable names from which he would choose two. The city did not agree to this curtailment of its liberties without protest: the lord mayor indeed supplied Huntingdon with the names of four candidates but he made it very clear which two the city favoured. Further disorders troubled York in 1578 and called forth fresh articles from the council together with a rebuke to the city justices for slackness. Even the most parochial matters occupied the Lord President's attention and he settled in person a virulent argument over whether butter, corn and eggs should be sold in the Thursday market, or on the Pavement. Not surprisingly, therefore, in times of emergency, Huntingdon appeared early on the scene to offer advice: at the dreaded times when plague broke out in the city he not only suggested precautions to prevent it spreading but also sought divine intervention. Toby Matthew, the future Bishop of Durham and Archbishop of York, gives one glimpse of Huntingdon in such a time of epidemic where he describes in his sermon diary how he preached in the minster on 24 October 1593 before Huntingdon, Shrewsbury and others, 'at the extraordinary exercise for the plague' taking as his text Galatians vi, verses 7 to 10: 'Be not deceived; God is not mocked: for whatsoever a man soweth, that shall he also reap. .... As we have therefore opportunity, let us do good unto all men, especially unto them who are of the household of faith.' Huntingdon must have commissioned very many of these official sermons but this is one of the very few details of them to survive.[19]

Though on occasions it could show itself stubborn, York realised the weight the Lord President's support could carry in its suits in London. In 1586, the corporation asked Huntingdon to stand their good lord to further their petition to Burghley for the compounding of concealed lands within the city and made constant appeals for his favour in their ship-money dispute with Hull. They would receive directions from him to which they would not submit coming from any other body; a case in 1590 illustrates how closely the city stood upon its privileges. Edward Withes, acting for Sir James Croft, comptroller of the queen's household, had demanded £16 in lieu of cattle from the Ainsty of York without first consulting the city; the corporation wrote immediately to Huntingdon protesting that the levy had been set, not by the Lord President, but by the Justices of the Peace for the West Riding, who, since they were not justices for the city, had intruded upon the liberties of York. They assured Huntingdon they would readily pay the commutation if he personally assessed the sum or if he ordered the justices of the city to be included among those who met to decide the amount of the assessment.

The respect York always showed to Huntingdon stands in marked contrast with the constant bickering between the city and Lord President Sheffield in James I's reign.[20]

In religion, York long remained one of the most conservative of the northern towns, yet despite Huntingdon's many struggles with the city he never doubted its allegiance to the established government. The spontaneous outburst of loyalty from the northern towns in general on the news of the formation in October 1584 of the Bond of Association to defend the queen's person gave him particular pleasure, coming as it did just over a decade after the rebellion. At the beginning of November, York asked Huntingdon for information about how the corporation might join the association and added that 1,300 people had already subscribed the oath there. The little town of Pontefract petitioned him to be allowed to belong a week later and from then enquiries flooded in from zealous corporations and individuals alike all anxious to show their eagerness to defend the queen. Three hundred gentlemen who had missed signing the instrument at Doncaster came to Huntingdon at York wishing to add their signatures to the list: others met together with the meaner sort of gentlemen, freeholders and clothiers with the result that around Wakefield, Halifax and Bradford, 5,300 people took the oath and the situation threatened to get quite out of hand. Huntingdon complained to Walsingham that 7,500 seals had made the instruments far too bulky to be sent up to London by post and that he had been forced to have abstracts made.[21]

Though not resident within their bounds, Huntingdon maintained a relationship with other northern towns as paternal as that he had with York. In Hull, admittedly, the mayor did challenge the Lord President over the extent of the town's jurisdiction and the corporation on one occasion withstood his attempt to interfere in a parliamentary election. Hull is the only town in the north where Huntingdon is certainly known to have asked for the nomination of burgesses to parliament: in September 1586 he wrote both requesting one of the nominations and that the election itself be delayed until he could send word of his candidate. Despite the letter, Hull returned two of its townsmen as had been its ancient custom. Nevertheless, Huntingdon had great personal influence in the town and he continued to act as its protector supporting the local people when they fell into difficulties over paying the cost of a ship for the Armada, or for repairs to the castle and blockhouses.[22] Huntingdon may well have intervened with more success in parliamentary elections in other towns: Henry Cheke, the secretary of the Council in the North, represented Boroughbridge in 1584; George Purfrey, whose elder brother was a legal member of the council, became one of the members for Beverley in 1586 and John Mansfield, Huntingdon's servant, and at one stage his lessee of the Canford mines, obtained the seat for Beverley in 1593, while another lawyer on the council, Ralph Hurlestone, sat for Aldborough in Yorkshire, again perhaps through Huntingdon's good offices. York, like Hull, kept its representation for its own citizens, yet even this city felt it politic to inform the Lord President of its actions in parliamentary matters: on 10 November 1584, the very day they had elected their burgesses for parliament the lord mayor and his brethren waited on Huntingdon to tell him of their choice.[23]

During the latter part of Huntingdon's rule, faction arose in the town governments of Beverley, Newcastle and Doncaster which the Privy Council called upon him to settle. At the beginning of 1588, the commons of Beverley complained of abuses they said had been committed by the mayor and governors of the town and Huntingdon had the matter referred back to him for his examination and decision. Some of the younger sort of the inhabitants of Newcastle, 'given to turbulence and innovation', as the mayor alleged, petitioned Huntingdon in 1592 to bring about a reformation there. They thought that if he confiscated the town's book of orders the misgovernment would become apparent, and protested that too much of the town's money had been spent without reasonable warrant, that unsuitable people had been given office, papists allowed a vote and that there had been

N

malpractices in the town's coal mines. As the petitioners hinted, religious differences had exacerbated the unrest in Newcastle: the long ministrations of the Scottish Magbray followed by those of Richard Holdsworth at St. Nicholas's church in combination with a brief course of lectures from John Udall had created a radical Protestant element in the town which clashed with the conservatism of some of the more senior aldermen who were undoubted Catholics.[24]

Relations between the President and the Council in the North and the town of Doncaster were complicated by an issue which did not apply in the cases of Hull, Newcastle or Beverley. Doncaster had in the Earl of Shrewsbury its own special lord whom the council could not risk alienating. In 1590, however, the commons of Doncaster began to agitate for more influence in the town's affairs and the council became concerned, much to Shrewsbury's annoyance. In Huntingdon's absence the council attempted to justify their intervention to Shrewsbury: they 'never meant to intermeddle with the ordering of the election of the Mayor of Doncaster for the year to come, otherwise than to see the peace preserved and tumult shunned, in which we are so far bound in duty to do, that we must do it, by direct word of her majesty's directions'. Huntingdon, at the same time, wrote to Shrewsbury from London making no claim to the appointment of the mayor in which Shrewsbury had an interest, but suggesting that the town's charters and evidences should be brought up to London the next term so that it could be decided who had been rightfully elected mayor.

My care for the peace and public quiet of the town hath moved me in this consideration [he explained], a matter which your lordship doth know, I am by the place of president bound in duty to regard, and this course can in no sort prejudice your lordship's claim whatsoever it be.

In the following year the Privy Council gave Huntingdon complete authority to investigate further tumults in the town and eventually his perseverance had its desired effect. In 1595

Stanhope, a member of the Council in the North, could inform
Huntingdon that he had visited Doncaster:

> where I was in respect of my place there to attend the next day the
> election of the [mayor], where by foresight and good means, without
> contradiction or show of faction (not usual heretofore) William Hansley,
> one in duty and service towards your lordship, was chosen their
> mayor.[25]

Many of these urban discontents were at their root economic
and at least from 1572 the government had realised that to bring
lasting peace to the north it had to ensure a minimum prosperity.
Huntingdon concentrated first upon York and not long after he
had come to live there, stirred up the corporation to make a
frontal attack on the problem of poverty in the city where there
existed only a rudimentary scheme of quasi-voluntary donations
to the poor. The corporation itself had not overlooked the benefits
to be derived from the large household of the Lord President
resident at the King's Manor and by 1576 had received guarantees
from Huntingdon and other members of the council of annual
benevolences. This private alms-giving proved quite inadequate
and in 1577 Huntingdon informed the lord mayor of a special
conference he had had with the Archbishop of York to consider
the problem: they thought the great numbers of poor people in
the city reflected discreditably on the magistrates and he and
Sandys had tried to find some redress for the evil. Soon, Huntingdon told the mayor, the city would find the archbishop very
forward, but in the meantime he asked for a certificate to be
completed within a fortnight giving details of how many of the
poor were impotent, how many could work and of the work for
which they were best fitted and he also wanted to know the
amount of money the city raised for poor relief. By October a new
scheme had been prepared: on the undertaking by the lord mayor
that the poor should not beg openly within the city the Archbishop
of York covenanted to give £20 a year in poor relief, Huntingdon
£13. 6s. 8d. and twenty-one other members of the council and

other officials amounts from £8 to five shillings. Charity alone could never satisfy Huntingdon; he went on to insist that employment should be provided for the poor and, as he had done at Leicester, particularly promoted the setting up of new cloth manufacturers. Early in 1585, he sent a man who specialised in cloth to the mayor and corporation for their consideration and certainly two years later there was at least one clothier established in the city thought to be doing much good in setting a number of the poor on work. As seems frequently to have happened to such entrepreneurs, however, he fell into financial difficulties and the Privy Council asked Huntingdon and the archbishop to protect him against his creditors until he could recover himself.[26]

Huntingdon did not only concern himself with the urban poor: with the encouragement of the Privy Council he consistently protected tenants against their landlords that they might continue farming undisturbed. The central government charged him with safeguarding the food supply in the north and early in the 1570's ordered him to enforce the ban on the illegal export of corn in strangers' vessels which it considered impoverished the country and caused excessively high prices. In years of dearth, especially in 1573 and 1587, he sponsored the import of corn from Danzig by merchants from Hull and Newcastle; he regularly warned the city of York against the malpractice of withholding corn from the markets in order to enhance its price and tried to get the law against it observed. Similarly he urged the city to keep the fish days as laid down in the queen's proclamation to stimulate the northern fishing-fleets. Yet this was no one-way interchange of commands. The northerners never hesitated to complain to Huntingdon when they considered their trading rights had been infringed. In 1584 fish was scarce and the price high and the corporation of York believed this had been brought about by the statute of 23 Elizabeth which forbade the import of herrings and salt fish into England (previously the merchants from York, Hull, Newcastle, Lynn and Boston had imported large quantities of fish from the continent and served the whole of the north at reasonable prices); they hoped Huntingdon, by approaching the central government, could gain redress.[27]

Northern industry and trade came directly under Huntingdon's oversight. When the mineral company, established with government aid by Daniel Hochstetter in Cumberland, appeared in imminent danger of collapse he began investigations and he found the miners had received no wages for so long they had threatened to withdraw their labour completely. He supported Hochstetter's petition to the queen for a further grant of £1,000 in the emergency and in the interval drew up an agreement between the company and its workmen. These mining privileges and other monopolies granted in Westminster which extended to the north constituted a particular cause of discontent in an area where trade did not seem to be expanding. Huntingdon had trouble especially over the monopoly of trading in white salt at the ports of Hull, Lynn and Boston which Elizabeth had given to Thomas Wilkes, one of the clerks of the Privy Council. Persistent complaints forced the Privy Council to authorise him to hold an enquiry and when in London in 1589 he succeeded in composing an agreement between the knights and citizens of the county and city of York, and Wilkes and his deputy. Wilkes made considerable concessions: he promised to retain the monopoly for only four years more, although the original patent had been for eighteen years, and to supply sufficient salt at fixed prices during that time. Nevertheless the monopoly even in this attenuated form still remained unpopular and the Privy Council found it necessary in the next year to instruct Huntingdon to take action against certain forward persons at Hull, York and elsewhere who had lately set themselves against the execution of Wilkes's grant.[28]

Requests for the protection and stimulation of northern industry found a ready supporter in Huntingdon. He wholeheartedly seconded the petition Newcastle corporation made to Burghley in protest against freedom being given to strangers to buy coals directly from the Durham coalfields to the neglect of coals got on the north side of the Tyne. Newcastle's foreign trade was affected in 1592 by the staying of goods at Boulogne and again the corporation appealed to the Lord President and took the extra precaution of gaining the good will of his secretary. Huntingdon forwarded the town's memorial to the Privy Council who left it to him to decide whether to hold French ships in Newcastle until redress came from France, or to allow ships to continue to come and go lest trade be further restricted. Despite these difficulties Newcastle caused Huntingdon far less concern than the port of Hull. During the protracted ship-money controversy between Hull and York he went on with his negotiations until the York merchants consented to share Hull's expenses. In 1590 he favoured measures intended to halt the falling off in Hull's trade. The Derbyshire lead trade had always been Hull's particular staple, but in recent years London merchants had established a depot at Bawtry and by-passed Hull; they had added to their offence by supplying the country along the rivers which flowed into Hull with wines and other merchandise to the exclusion of Hull merchants. Huntingdon brought this intrusion of Londoners into Hull's sphere of trade to the Privy Council's notice.[29]

The attention paid by the Council in the North to the regulation of the cloth industry has been suggested as one of the chief reasons for the hostility shown towards the council at the very end of the sixteenth century. During the years Huntingdon held office, this determined effort by the central government to control the size and quality of northern cloths had scarcely begun: the act of 1552 seems virtually to have been a dead letter and the clothiers of the West Riding lived untrammelled for the greater part of his presidency. Huntingdon expressed his intention in 1577 of executing the Privy Council's directive concerning clothiers and buyers of wool but little seems to have come of it, and the government did not renew its interference until 1590. Then, on the complaint of Randall Tenche, a Leeds clothier, over the corrupt practices of wool-gatherers, the Privy Council ordered Huntingdon to enforce the statute of 5 Edward VI and the proclamation of 21 Elizabeth restricting wool sales to certified times and places, and required him to bind over broggers and engrossers (that is, all wool jobbers and those suspected of trying to monopolise the market), to prevent abuses in future. Later in the year, when reports came in of the artifices of Yorkshire clothiers who chopped up flocks and rubbed these into their finished cloth to improve its appearance, the Privy Council moved on from wool selling to the manufacture of cloth and instructed Huntingdon to license certain clothiers, of whom Tenche was one, to go round destroying all blocks which could be used to chop up flocks. This intrusion of government officials may well have caused resentment but it amounted to little compared with the open resistance which came after his death. In 1597 parliament passed an act to prevent all stretching of cloth by tentering, a process almost universal in the West Riding: the local justices refused to observe the legislation and the bitter struggle between the Council in the North and the clothiers began which was one of the chief causes of the council's unpopularity with the northern gentry in the reign of James I.[30]

For trade merely to continue at its accustomed pace, a constant watch had to be kept by the Council in the North over the state of communications. Soon after he arrived in the north Huntingdon sent out orders about the maintenance of the bridges at Boroughbridge, Thornton, and Morton, and over the Foss near Sheriff Hutton and he had always to be on the alert to see the localities fulfilled their obligations to keep their bridges in repair. Sometimes a bridge provided a vital link in the communications of the whole of the north and did not just serve the surrounding area, then he considered the larger centres of trade also partly responsible for it. He urged the corporation of York to make a contribution to the repair of Wansford bridge in 1578, pointing out that the bridge stood on the direct route from York to London and so directly benefited the city. He thought Newcastle qualified for national aid, and supported the corporation's petition to the queen for the renewal of the grant made by Richard III of an annuity to help maintain the town's walls and its great bridge. In 1592

Huntingdon came to Newcastle to view the state of the bridge; he had himself rowed out into the centre of the Tyne so he could report on the bridge's strength at first hand.[31]

Free passage of the seas affected northern trade at least as much as good land communications, though it is doubtful whether it was ever attained in the north during Elizabeth's reign. The Privy Council first instructed Huntingdon in 1574 to put down piracy and ensure that those who had been plundered should have their goods restored to them, but the Council in the North seems to have waited until 1577 before taking any very decisive action. Then it received from London a royal commission against piracy and Huntingdon and other councillors presided over a trial at the Guildhall in Hull where the master and many of the crew of *The Elizabeth* of Chichester were indicted on a charge of piracy, found guilty and executed. Huntingdon had private doubts that this special commission might conflict with powers granted to the Lord Admiral's deputies, nevertheless, on the prompting of the Privy Council, he went on to appoint his own deputy commissioners to oversee every creek and landing-place in Yorkshire in an attempt to bring piracy under control. His commissioners certainly uncovered information which enabled Huntingdon to send a certificate to the Privy Council of the value of the goods and lands of thirty-five northerners, convicted pirates. Yorkshiremen seem to have been so generally involved in piracy that the Council in the North appears to have imposed fines almost indiscriminately, with promise of a general pardon: neither it nor the court of Admiralty had the resources to bridle the many offenders. In 1582, James VI complained to Elizabeth of the damage inflicted on Scottish trade by northern pirates and in 1586 the Privy Council still felt it necessary to ask Huntingdon to protect some Amsterdam merchants who had travelled north in search of a ship captured by George Bullen, a pirate; in spite of a commission issued by the court of Admiralty a murderous attack had already been made on these Dutch merchants by Richard Brandling, a gentleman of Newcastle.[32]

In its dealings with piracy, the Council in the North showed the flexibility of its procedure, at one moment it could be constituted a special court to try offenders, at the next act as an office of administration for the central government. So long as Huntingdon remained Lord President the council had at its head one who undertook his judicial responsibilities with the greatest seriousness. Many of his contemporaries believed that in the execution of justice a man approached most nearly the prerogative of God and the Protestant preachers continuously emphasised the high calling of magistrates. Huntingdon, a zealous frequenter as well as promoter of sermons, may well have been present when Archbishop Sandys delivered his sermon at the opening of the assizes at York, taking as his theme the obligation of a governor to those he governed:

Let the magistrate pay unto the people the debt which he oweth them. The debt of the magistrate is the just execution of lawful punishment against transgressors. The sword is delivered to him for that purpose. . . .

Such as are magistrates, to whom the deciding of causes and punishing offences is committed should be chosen out of all the people the best and fittest men for their wisdom and courage, their religion and hearty affection to the truth, and for the hatred which they bear to covetousness. For this is no office for a fool: and he that feareth not God will show partiality: he that loveth not the truth will justify the wicked, and condemn the innocent: he that hateth not covetousness will take rewards, and be corrupted with bribes, as the sons of Eli, which received gifts with the one hand, and with the other perverted judgment. The eyes even of the wise are blinded herewithal. Fear also, affection and commiseration, with desire to please men, are great hurts unto justice. . . .

The north needed a president who would be a godly man, severe in his own righteousness, unconnected with northern factions and so the more inclined towards impartiality, one who scorned to accept bribes or be diverted from a just decision, and Huntingdon was just such a man. The central government could scarcely have chosen a nobleman better fitted than he for establishing the rule of law in a region where alarming outbreaks of lawlessness were still likely to occur.[33]

The savage state of the remote parts of the north and the correspondingly savage nature of northern justice have been vividly evoked by Macaulay in a passage in his celebrated third chapter:

The judges on circuit, with the whole body of barristers, attorneys, clerks and serving men, rode on horseback from Newcastle to Carlisle, armed and escorted by a strong guard under the command of the sheriffs. It was necessary to carry provisions; for the country was a wilderness which afforded no supplies. The spot where the cavalcade halted to dine, under an immense oak, is not yet forgotten [Macaulay published his first volume of the *History* in 1848]. The irregular vigour with which criminal justice was administered shocked observers whose life had been passed in more tranquil districts. Juries, animated by hatred and by a sense of common danger, convicted housebreakers and cattle stealers with the promptitude of a court martial in a mutiny; and the convicts were hurried by scores to the gallows. Within the memory of some whom this generation has seen the sportsmen who wandered in pursuit of game to the sources of the Tyne found the heaths round Keeldar Castle peopled by a race scarcely less savage than the Indians of California, and heard with surprise the half-naked women chaunting a wild measure, while the men with brandished dirks danced a war dance.[34]

To enable it to try to subdue this lawlessness, the court of the Council in the North had a wide jurisdiction with powers to deal with both criminal and civil cases. In theory, there was a clear distinction between the quarter sessions and the assizes where the ancient, customary common law ran and the conciliar court of the north which concerned itself only with those offences for which the common law had no remedy, but in practice, as in so many aspects of the government of the north, the distinction became blurred. The central government always included Huntingdon and the professional legal members of the Council in the North on the commissions of Oyer and Terminer and Gaol Delivery and they sat with the judges of assize. In August 1573 Huntingdon, Gargrave, Rokeby and Ennys reported to the queen on a session of the court of the Council in the North they had been holding for the administration of justice between party and party which they had interrupted to join the assize judges for a hearing of Oyer and Terminer and Gaol Delivery at York Castle. At this one session sixty prisoners were brought before them and thirty-six indicted: they found thirty-two guilty and ordered twenty-five to be executed, committed two to their ordinary by reason of their clergy, had three whipped and punished for petty larceny and reprieved the remaining two. They also condemned and punished eleven rogues as the statute required. Huntingdon assisted at another gaol delivery in 1577: then only thirty-four prisoners were indicted and of these eighteen found guilty; ten of the eighteen were executed, two punished for petty larceny, two discovered to be clerks and burnt in the hand and four reprieved. Though the surviving evidence is meagre, it seems likely Huntingdon regularly joined with the judges in executing justice at the assizes. On occasions the Privy Council asked him to prepare cases in advance of the assizes, as happened in 1581 when it ordered him and other gentlemen to examine witnesses about the murder of one Richard Peacock: after Huntingdon's preliminary enquiry this case was heard at the northern assizes and then transferred to the Queen's Bench. At the assizes the judges accorded Huntingdon pride of place as the queen's representative and the common lawyers always respected his authority, in contrast with the occasion in 1600 when Serjeant Yelverton, the assize judge, started a bitter controversy by trying to exclude the Lord President, Burghley, from the bench when the writ to open the proceedings, the Nisi Prius, was read.[35]

Huntingdon's close co-operation with the assize judges on circuit in the north helped check disorder while the authority given to him by the government to try offences not fully recognised at the common law further contributed to the maintenance of peace. He had the power to assess fines for riots (though the Privy Council retained the right to have serious cases sent back to itself) and could punish seditious words by mutilation, fine or imprisonment as prescribed by law. In practice, Huntingdon

acted far more as an agent of the Privy Council than as an independent judge and a continuous stream of letters went back and
forth between the Privy Council and the Council in the North.
Usually the Privy Council referred complaints of disorders in the
north it had received to Huntingdon for him to make a preliminary
examination if he could not settle the matter entirely. The case of
Gerard Lowther, a member of the influential Westmorland family
and subsequently Sheriff of Cumberland, provides an example of
the procedure: the Privy Council informed Huntingdon of an
assault Lowther was alleged to have committed upon the servants
of Richard Cleiburne of Westmorland, since the offence had
occurred in his jurisdiction, and at the same time commanded
Lowther to appear before the Lord President. Huntingdon
examined him and sent his report of the disorder to the Privy
Council which then passed it on to the Lord Chief Justice for an
opinion. Only after this detailed scrutiny did the Privy Council
give Huntingdon permission to consider Cleiburne's petition
further and 'proceed according to law in all parts'. The same
Gerard Lowther and his elder brother Sir Richard took part in
another affray in 1577 with one Vaux of Cumberland; on this
occasion, when it remitted the case to Huntingdon, the Privy
Council allowed him full discretion, requiring him only to discover
the truth between the parties and then, if he found them guilty, to
punish them according to the law.[36]

After the rebellion, the government had become sensitive to
any rumours of unrest in the north, however trivial, since a local
quarrel could easily develop into a riot and disrupt the whole
region. The Selby–Collingwood affray showed how easily passions
could be stirred in the north: near the end of October 1586
William Selby, son of Sir John Selby, with a band of eighteen or
so of his men, laid an ambush on Morpeth Moor for Sir Cuthbert
Collingwood with whom he had a feud and attacked Collingwood
as he rode by with his wife, his three children and the Sheriff of
Northumberland, killing the sheriff's brother and wounding Sir
Cuthbert. The news reached Huntingdon at Durham and he lost

little time in going to Newcastle to look into the matter. On 6 December Selby, Strowther, the man actually responsible for the sheriff's brother's death, and the rest of the band appeared before Huntingdon and other commissioners for gaol delivery, on the charge of murder. The jury favoured the accused, and returned verdicts of manslaughter against Selby and two others, and of not guilty against Strowther, much to the indignation of Huntingdon who thought a verdict of wilful murder should have been reached against them all. Yet once the case had been tried he could do nothing except inform the Privy Council of what he considered had been a miscarriage of justice, and recommend that compensation be made to the sheriff for his brother's death. His prompt action in this and other disturbances, in itself goes far to justify the existence of a resident governor in the north: only by this routine extension of authority could pockets of northern particularism gradually be eliminated.[37]

In spite of its importance, Huntingdon's criminal jurisdiction only occupied a relatively small part of his time when compared with the amount of business transacted under his civil jurisdiction. From its foundation, the Council in the North had been considered a court of equity and from his first entry into his office the government had charged Huntingdon to redress all wrongful taking of commons, the decay of husbandry and the oppression of the poor, and of all the civil cases heard before him for which evidence now remains the greatest single number involved disputes between landlords and tenants. When the tenants could prove their grievances the Council in the North invariably protected them and even when right seemed to be on the side of the landlord it still intervened on their behalf. The dispute between the Dean and Chapter of Durham and their tenants, which began in 1574 when the Privy Council sent a petition of the Durham tenants to Huntingdon, lasted for the first ten years of his presidency. The tenants complained they were being dispossessed by the dean and chapter or made to pay unreasonably high entrance fines: an investigation proved the tenants were tenants at will, and they did

not, as they claimed, hold by tenant right, nevertheless Huntingdon and other councillors, with the approval of the Privy Council,
gave a decision safeguarding their tenancies. While they acknowledged that the tenants were merely tenants at will they stipulated
that they could not lose their tenancies except for treason,
rebellion, murder or other felony and ordered the dean and chapter
to grant reasonable rents since otherwise the tenants could not
serve the queen on the frontier or elsewhere for fifteen days
without reward, which was a condition of their tenure. The ruling
of 1577 did not end all discontents and in 1581 the Privy Council
called upon Huntingdon again to take action in a case between the
Bishop of Durham and one of his tenants.[38]

At the same time as this controversy between the dean and
chapter and their tenants, the Almoner and Brethren of Sherborne
House, Durham, brought a parallel case against their tenants who
also claimed to hold their land by tenant right. The Privy Council
again sent the matter to Huntingdon to decide, suggesting in
June 1580 that he should hear it in conjunction with the one
between the Dean and Chapter of Durham and their tenants, to
lessen the hospital's costs in the suit. In March 1582, the Privy
Council in a letter to Huntingdon set out its policy towards
dispossessed Border tenants: the Privy Councillors had been
disappointed that the act passed in the last parliament to remedy
the decay of the Borders, which had been caused by landlords
raising rents and taking excessive fines, had not yet been brought
fully into operation. Recently, they continued, tenants at Hexham
had sent in a petition and they advised Huntingdon that if Gerard
Lowther, or any other landlord or lessee should begin any suit
before him which might tend to the weakening of the Border, or
the oppression of tenants, to order the matter according to the
statute and to stay all further proceedings upon any lease which
might be pretended to the contrary. This protection of tenants
continued until the end of the reign, yet the court did not favour
tenants quite without discrimination: on one occasion, Huntingdon took steps to see that the tenants of the Earl of Northumber-

land stopped their unlawful activities in breaking up an enclosure in Yorkshire made thirty years previously.[39]

Apart from these cases of tenant right in which the central government had an interest, relatively little is known about the cases between party and party brought by private individuals before the Council in the North because of the loss of the council's minute books, yet almost certainly this type of case made up the main part of the council's civil business. At the beginning of the next century a dispute arose over the fees which could be charged in civil cases and during the course of it a list of commissions issued between 1579 and 1586 was exhibited: in those seven years sixty-one different cases between private parties were brought voluntarily before the council for a hearing and this is unlikely to be the full number of cases being tried. Sometimes a decision made by the Council in the North came to be enrolled in the Exchequer but, on the whole, detailed information on the extent to which northerners turned to the council for the settling of their quarrels no longer exists.[40]

This absence of records relating to personal suits does not extend to the northern corporations for when a corporation brought a case before the Council in the North it usually took the precaution of setting out the particulars in full in its own muniments. During the latter part of the sixteenth century, relations between northern towns were anything but harmonious and town clerks had much to record. In the 1570's a long standing trade rivalry between York and Hull grew in intensity and in 1575 the York corporation decided to bring a test case before the council, agreeing to pay the costs of some York sailors who were to sue the Mayor of Hull for having deprived them of their oars by way of distress. In the next year again the corporation paid the expenses of several of its citizens who had brought a case against an inhabitant of Hull. Both York and Hull tried to win Huntingdon's good will and, in 1578, the Mayor and Corporation of Hull wrote to him to explain why they had been forced to take certain measures which might 'annoy' York and asked him not to credit the feigned causes by which York men might try to excuse their actions. Hull corporation, in fact, had gone so far as to forbid any of its inhabitants from trading with York men, in retaliation for York's prohibition of the loading or selling of any goods from Hull. In June 1578, Huntingdon called representatives of both parties before him when he heard of the disturbances and persuaded them to resume normal trading. In 1585 the corporation of York looked towards Beverley, and supported one of its citizens who brought a suit before the council against a Beverley man: through this action the corporation hoped to gain the abolition of the tolls the townspeople of Beverley demanded from York citizens.[41]

These lesser rivalries, however, seem as nothing when compared with the great ship-money controversy between York and Hull. In the spring before the sailing of the Armada, the government had asked Hull to furnish two ships and one pinnace to serve the queen for two months at sea; since it thought the town could not afford the expense alone, it asked Huntingdon to persuade the merchants of York and the surrounding district who used the port of Hull to contribute towards the cost. York corporation immediately reacted against what it considered an infringement of its privileges. When the news reached London in the autumn that those of the 'best ability' there had refused to yield, the Privy Council told Huntingdon to assess them for their rateable contribution and, if they still refused to pay, to bind them over to appear before the Privy Council itself for their contempt. A plaintive letter from the mayor and aldermen of Hull in which they described how they had spent £900 in the last twelve years on forts at Hull, in addition to their expenses over the ships, only confirmed the Privy Council in their course of action. Nevertheless, York remained obdurate even when Huntingdon wrote again to the corporation advising them not to offend the Privy Council any longer by not paying their share of the cost of the ships. In consequence, York citizens appeared before the Privy Council: there they continued to argue that Hull gained far more

benefit from York, than York from Hull and that, having sufficient
expenses of their own, they should not be expected to bear Hull's
charges. The Privy Council gave their decision against them on
15 December: they had already authorised Huntingdon to proceed
with a scheme to levy a contribution from those best able to
afford it in York, and in 1589 worked out the details: since Hull
had paid £1,015 for the ships they thought it reasonable that York
should repay Hull £600. York made yet one more attempt to
evade payment by sending Huntingdon statistics to illustrate the
benefits Hull derived through trade with York and to prove that
Hull could not need their aid. Huntingdon was unimpressed and
by June 1589, York had paid Hull £300 and the following month
borrowed £200 in London towards paying the rest of the debt
though in the autumn he had to remind the city it still owed £100.
The corporation, humbled at last, begged him to intervene to
compel the non-freemen to contribute for they had so far refused
to give anything. Yet York soon recovered its resilience and by
the middle of 1591 felt able once again to protest to Huntingdon
against being required to give more towards the provision of a
ship than Hull: in obedience to an order from the Privy Council
the corporation had consulted with Hull, offering to pay half the
cost of a ship for service against the king of Spain, but Hull had
wanted them to pay two-thirds. York remained convinced Hull
ought to pay more than York, not vice versa, and in spite of their
former experiences looked to Huntingdon for support.[42]

Huntingdon had not only to adjudicate between rival northern
towns but also to deal with towns jealous that the court of the
council might encroach upon the freedom of their corporations.
He had barely been in the north a month when the clerk of York
recorded how one Henry Hobson had sued the sheriffs of the city
and their officers before the Lord President and the council, which
was a foreign court, contrary to his oath and against the liberties
of the city: the corporation had fined him forty shillings and
ordered him to leave off his suit upon pain of disenfranchisement.
This proved a common occurrence, and not in York alone. The

o

town of Berwick in 1573 disenfranchised one of its inhabitants who had appealed to the Lord President and council at Newcastle and six years later refused to free the same man to allow him to prosecute his suit at York, even upon the express command of Huntingdon: the Mayor of Berwick considered it his duty, he explained, to defend the privileges of the town which was exempt from all other counties in England. In 1580, Huntingdon feared that the Dean and Chapter of Durham, angered by the numerous cases brought by their tenants before the Council in the North, had begun a concerted effort to abridge the council's jurisdiction in the bishopric: this prompted him to dispatch to Burghley a defence of the court's continuing usefulness:

And by the little experience, which I have gathered in the time of my service here, both of the common people, and also of the better sort, that do inhabit these parts, for the disposition of their minds, bewrayed by words and motions, that come from them often times, assuredly if this council were not, I am persuaded that the disorders here at this time would compare for number, and greatness, with former times.[43]

Nothing came of the suspected machinations of the Dean and Chapter of Durham, but in 1590 York turned again to attack the council. A meeting of the aldermen agreed to send a bill of complaint in the name of the city to the Lord President and council asking the council to refrain from issuing letters of privilege, or of habeas corpus, to set free persons arrested to make answer in the York sheriff's court: they maintained that this procedure violated the city's liberties and that because of it some citizens and others had lost their debts. Yet these incidents should not be magnified too much to give the impression of continuous warfare between the council and the northern towns: when a corporation proved to Huntingdon's satisfaction its right of jurisdiction in any particular instance then he remitted the case from the council to the local court. The Mayor of Hull, for example, sent the town's charters to Huntingdon in 1573 to show that it had the powers to try a case of forcible entry into a house in Hull: the council recognised the town's right to hold such pleas and sent the case back for trial before the mayor and sheriffs, and in 1587 Huntingdon dealt with a similar case from Hull in the same way.[44]

Apart from these occasional conflicts between local courts and the council over conflicting jurisdictions, all the evidence attests the value and general popularity of the court of the Council in the North. After Huntingdon's death, the Archbishop of York, who had been appointed the acting president, asserted that the court heard a thousand cases in equity a year, mainly connected with tenant right where the tenants had been expelled or charged extortionate fines. With the growing amount of business, the staff of clerks and other officials associated with the court increased to such an extent that by the beginning of James I's reign it was claimed there were then

thirty families whose principal maintenance came by the drawing of those bills in their places, and about forty clerks kept for the more easy and quick dispatch of the suitors in the court most of which were enabled to live well and to pay subsidies and other duties to his majesty.

There must have been an element of exaggeration in these statements but Huntingdon's building activities attest that a considerable expansion in the work of the court did take place. The abbot's lodging of the former Abbey of St. Mary at York became quite inadequate for the accommodation of the Lord President and his household, the executive council and the officials in continual attendance, and Huntingdon had built the range of brick buildings to the north-west of the old manor house.[45]

The objections the lawyers at Westminster had begun to make by the 1590's to the court's jurisdiction give additional proof of the success of the Council in the North as a court of equity. They questioned the council's authority to stay an action in Chancery even when both the parties in the case lived in the north and could show no valid reason against it. Huntingdon held that the practice could be fully justified; he argued that it had been used ever since the court had been set up, it had been authorised by his commission and announced his intention of continuing it so long as the queen and the Privy Council did not direct to the contrary.

He had his way as long as he remained president, but in 1599 judgment was given in Chancery that the council at York had no powers to issue inhibitions to stay proceedings in Chancery or in any superior court at Westminster and that the residence of the parties in the north in no way affected the judgment. Thus the very success of the court provided reasons for its limitation, if not for its abolition. With the establishment of some order in the north the necessity for a special court diminished, and more and more after the accession of James I its value began to be questioned by common lawyers, themselves financially involved because of the local popularity of a rival system of law.[46]

During the twenty-three years of Huntingdon's presidency the Council in the North both as a court and as an administrative body reached the height of its political and social efficiency. The office of Lord President burdened Huntingdon with innumerable duties: he had the responsibility for encouraging the development of a new society in the north no longer dominated by the old nobility in which loyal, Protestant gentlemen played a growing part, for stimulating the economy of the region, for trying to secure an impartial system of justice, in effect, for bringing the north of England in line with the south and ensuring that its local particularism could never again threaten the peace of the whole country. In working for this reformation, time and again he ran into countless petty vexations, great noblemen the government could not afford to alienate who felt that their proper influence had been curtailed, towns obstinately standing upon their privileges or suicidally warring among themselves, local gentlemen whose ready anger led them all too often to take the law into their own hands. He never made claims to be an originator of policies; the queen sent him north to bring good government to the area and he carried out her wishes as far as in him lay. Huntingdon's long residence in York, far longer than that of any other Elizabethan Lord President, meant he attained to a unique knowledge of his province and slowly the queen herself arrived at a proper appreciation of his devoted service. When refusing

Huntingdon leave to go south in 1594 she sent him one of her rare letters of praise:

But now that things are as they be (whereof the issues are yet uncertain) and that the looseness of those northern parts is fit to be guided by wise and sound directions, though we know your own vigilant and watchful care is such as you would be loth to be absent in this tickle time, yet do we require you then (even seriously from ourself) to have care of your health and state of body, in such sort, as you may neither prove wearisome to yourself (which is the fruit of sickness) or be less able to continue so serviceable unto us as we have found you, and for such a one do and will esteem you. . . .[47]

CHAPTER SIX

The Hosts of Midian without

IN governing the north, Huntingdon showed himself the willing servant of the Privy Council, sympathising with its orders, eager to carry them into execution, but he never had the freedom to devote himself entirely to internal administration. All through his presidency the good government he tried to bring to the north was threatened by hostile forces from without, first by a Catholic faction in Scotland, later, and much more seriously, by the might of Catholic Spain. In complete contrast with the queen, the Protestant zealots looked at international politics in frighteningly simple terms. Together with others in the central government Huntingdon saw a conspiracy developing to deprive England of the pure light of the gospel so recently won after years of strife. In France, in the Low Countries, Protestantism had been forced on to the defensive: more and more the soldiers of Antichrist closed in upon the faithful remnant. In this all-out war Huntingdon could not remain a passive agent. He believed passionately in the need for England and Scotland to unite against Spain and, given the opportunity, he worked unremittingly for this end, even when it might involve him in exceeding his instructions. Ardent nationalism went hand in hand with his theories of religious obligation.

When Huntingdon became President of the Council in the North the government did not at the same time create him Lord Lieutenant; it still envisaged the office as that of a general in charge of the shire militia and consequently required his services only when the militia turned out to defend the county from invasion from without its boundaries. In normal times the duties of raising and exercising militia men could be entrusted to Justices of the Peace acting as commissioners of musters. In the south of England the Privy Council directly supervised the commissioners of musters and only very gradually, with the increasing fear of foreign invasion, began to realise that a permanent lieutenant could more effectively supervise the mustering of the shire levy and perform other administrative duties as well as lead in person the musters in the field. This development in the nature of the office of Lord Lieutenant, tenuous and incomplete even at the end of Elizabeth's reign for the greater part of England, was by force of circumstances anticipated in the north: there the Privy Council already did not govern directly but through its delegacy, the Council in the North; whereas in the south by its own letters it spurred on negligent commissioners of musters, in the north it acted through the president of the council. So it happened that the President of the Council in the North became for all practical purposes the Lieutenant for the north although some time elapsed before the government recognised his *de facto* position by issuing a formal, permanent commission of lieutenancy: this evolution took place during Huntingdon's period of office.

For the first eight years of his presidency, Huntingdon seems to have exercised the authority without formally holding the office of a Lord Lieutenant. His instructions issued at his first going into the north did not touch upon his military duties at all but at least by May 1573 he had received a comprehensive commission for holding musters throughout Yorkshire: while the towns of York and Hull had not been included by name, Huntingdon informed Burghley that he had decided to act as though they were and in August notified the Corporation of York that the queen had granted him a commission to hold general musters. In this commission Huntingdon still appears merely as the first among a number of commissioners for musters—Sir Thomas Gargrave, Sir George Bowes, Sir Henry Gates, Christopher

Hilliard, all incidentally members of the Council in the North—although his authority must have been far greater than that of any one commissioner in the south.[1] Whether he yet had official instructions to intervene in matters of defence in other northern counties besides Yorkshire is not at all clear, but in practice he certainly did: in September 1573 he described to Burghley how on a visit to Newcastle he had taken the opportunity of inspecting the fortifications at Tynemouth; the state of the 'old ruinous piece' there horrified him and he advised that the castle should be put in the keeping of a man of proven loyalty. By the end of this decade he had definite powers to direct military affairs outside Yorkshire and in March 1580, the government even placed him on the commission of musters for Lancashire, an area outside his jurisdiction as president of the Council in the North.[2]

His service in Leicestershire had made Huntingdon familiar with the duties expected of a commissioner of musters; on going north he found his responsibilities were of the same type, but far more extensive. The government still required him to oversee the mustering of the local militia in person and to send detailed administrative reports up to London. The defence of the north, as indeed of the rest of the country, was still organised on a county basis: theoretically all the able-bodied men of a county between sixteen and sixty (the age limits varied) rose to the defence of their districts in times of emergency. The county commissioners held general musters where they provided a little general training; increasingly at these musters they chose a certain number of men to be given more specialised training in the use of arms supplied by the county. At those times when the state had undertaken military commitments abroad, the commissioners, at these general musters, had the invidious task of selecting men to join the English army: once the men had left the country, however, their maintenance became charged to the national government and no longer to the locality. Huntingdon lost no time after he had come into the north finding out how the men under his government compared with those he had known in the Midlands.

We have here begun the musters [he reported to Burghley in the spring of 1573], and in some mo [more] places I have gone myself, for my better knowledge of the country, and setting forward of the service, then else I would have seen: where surely I found great numbers of tall men, and a people most willing and ready to serve her majesty, even in Craven, where they are most ignorant of God and of religion.[3]

In the actual organisation of the defence of the north, Huntingdon acted as a valuable intermediary between the central government and the localities: in the autumn of 1573 the Privy Council asked for 600 men armed with muskets to be raised in Yorkshire that trained men might be available in time of danger: it left the arrangements to Huntingdon. Firstly, having divided up the men required between the three Ridings he informed the commissioners of musters, and Justices of the Peace for each Riding, of his proposals: he chose St. Matthew's day and St. Bartholomew's day for the musters since an earlier date might have hindered the harvesting. He wished the men selected for the city of York and the surrounding country to assemble at York so that he might review them himself with Sir William Mallory and Sir Robert Stapleton, and ordered those for the West Riding to gather at Leeds, for the East Riding at Beverley and for the North Riding at Thirsk. All the men had to be at their stations by 10 October; two days later, Huntingdon decided to muster at York all the horsemen for the whole county together with their armour, and required the commissioners to send him their certificates immediately the musters had ended that he might forward them to the queen. He then went on to get arms for the men. He wrote to Burghley that the commissioners had agreed 1,200 shot and 800 corselets with pikes should be provided but that they could not decide whether it should be stored centrally in York, or distributed between the market towns; in the latter case he predicted a short life for the armour: 'if the country should have it, they toss it from constable to constable, and so the best stuff becometh in few years nothing worth.'[4]

The central government had particular reasons for calling for this overhaul of the system of defence in the north of England so soon after Huntingdon's appointment. Throughout the reign the north remained a frontier region: across the Borders lay the independent state of Scotland. Apart from the troubled years between 1561 and 1567 when Mary, Queen of Scots had governed her kingdom in person, Scotland had been ruled by a succession of regents ever since her accession within a week of her birth in 1542. When in July 1567, after her scandalous marriage to the Earl of Bothwell (the suspected murderer of her husband, Darnley), Mary was forced to abdicate in favour of her infant son, James, a baby in arms for the second time in the century came to the Scottish throne. Civil wars broke out afresh and the supporters of Mary fought the supporters of James for control of the country. As a recent Scottish historian has written, 'force, faction and feud still dominated Scotland as of old; and to old contentions was now added that of "the religion".' Nominally Scotland had become a Protestant country, but the Protestant lords had by no means won decisive control. Regent replaced regent with a regularity which precluded any hopes of establishing a settled government. In 1570 the Earl of Moray, Mary's half-brother, was assassinated by the Catholic Hamilton. The following year the Earl of Lennox, the young king's grandfather, who took his place, was killed by Huntly, another Catholic lord. Mar, the third regent who attempted to govern for James, died in 1572 and still, although Mary's supporters were growing weaker, no pacification seemed possible. In 1572, James VI was six years old; until he reached an age when he could rule in fact as well as in name there seemed little likelihood of any stable government in Scotland.[5]

The political anarchy in Scotland tended to increase rather than decrease the influence of Scotland in English politics. If the Scottish Protestants triumphed then a new era of co-operation between Scotland and England might be about to begin but in the winter of 1572–3 the government of the king's lords had not yet gained complete ascendancy. Although they had the assistance of the towns, the Catholic supporters of Mary, led by Kirkcaldy and

Lethington, held Edinburgh Castle and so long as that fortress remained in their hands they could hope for military reinforcements to come in from France which might transform the whole political situation. This was the critical turn of affairs which confronted Huntingdon immediately on his arrival in York in November 1572.

One of the very first dispatches Huntingdon could have received was from the Earl of Morton in which he announced his election as regent of Scotland, and his desire to continue the good understanding with England. The Protestant Morton could scarcely have found a more willing collaborator and it so happened that Huntingdon very soon was in a position to help the Scots. In February 1573 severe gales drove six Scottish ships from Dieppe en route for Aberdeen into Scarborough harbour and on board one of the vessels the Bailiff of Scarborough discovered a Monsieur Virac with money and letters intended for the defenders of Edinburgh Castle. Huntingdon ordered all the ships to be impounded until the queen signified her pleasure: the incident, as he confided to Burghley, further revealed the uncertainty of the present state of Anglo-Scottish relations. If the English government would only show itself wholeheartedly in favour of Morton, then this kind of intervention by the French could be effectively excluded: 'a little charge would prevent these practices, and save many men, and more pounds, for Edinburgh Castle could not hold out if her majesty would send in but half a foot, and that would stay many devices.'[6]

At this juncture the queen at last agreed to act, she accepted Huntingdon's offer to levy troops in the bishopric of Durham and by the beginning of April he had sent five hundred soldiers and two hundred pioneers to support the regent in the siege of Edinburgh Castle. The campaign even became something of a family affair: Sir Edward Hastings, who had joined Sussex's expedition into Scotland against Mary's supporters in 1570 and who now yearned to be in at the kill, applied to the government for the captaincy of the troops his brother had raised. At first the intervention of the English troops did little to alter the military situation and to his alarm Huntingdon heard that the queen threatened to withdraw her troops all together unless the castle speedily fell: first with Leicester, then with Burghley he argued against the folly of this step, urging rather that more ammunition should be sent to make the victory certain. He had his way, the English contingents continued with the Scots in their assaults on the castle and finally on 28 May it capitulated. It seemed that the menace of French troops on Scottish soil had ended and that a period of close alliance between England and Scotland could begin. Huntingdon pressed the government to consolidate its position: English gold, he explained to Burghley, would be the surest way to bind the Scots;

that which hath been so lately done at Edinburgh hath set a good stay, and, if it be followed, in such sort as your lordship knoweth is meet, with the bestowing of some few pensions etc. it will, I hope, in time break the neck of all popish practices.[7]

The friendship between England and Scotland under the Protestant rule of the regent, Morton, proved to be far less secure than Huntingdon hoped. For six years Morton guided Scottish policy and began gradually to reassert the powers of the central government but he never gained complete control over the lawless counties adjoining the English frontier where the inhabitants continued to pursue their ancient feuds. The lands on either side of the Border had long been divided into Marches; the Scottish West, Middle and East Marches each ruled by its own warden, which corresponded to similar Marches on the English side. In 1575 an incident on the Border brought the two countries to the verge of war. On 7 July the English warden of the Middle Marches, Sir John Forster, and John Carmichael, deputy keeper of Liddesdale, met for a day of truce at Redswire to settle the grievances of the inhabitants of both sides of the Border. For a time the administration of justice proceeded in an orderly way until Carmichael demanded the delivery of a prisoner whom Forster had condemned for default. The two leaders began to quarrel, their followers did not hesitate to join in and before they realised what had happened a pitched battle developed. Both leaders then remembered their instructions and tried to curb their men, but it was too late; on the English side Sir George Heron and five others were killed and more gentlemen and their servants injured while five Scots also died and several were hurt. Since more Scots than English had come to the day of truce, their greater numbers had forced the English to fight on their side of the Border: the Scots then proceeded to carry off the English warden, Sir Cuthbert Collingwood and other English gentlemen into Scotland to save them, as they claimed later on, from any further injury. In itself, the affray differed little from those other feuds which plagued the Border areas at this time and if nothing had occurred apart from the killings it is doubtful whether the English government would have called for more than compensation for the injured. The abduction of the English warden, however, quite altered the case: Elizabeth considered this a direct affront to her honour and determined to teach Morton he could not presume on her friendship.[8]

Huntingdon, who had gone up to Newcastle when he had first heard about the disturbance, tried from the beginning to minimise the incident. In a series of letters he pointed out to Walsingham that the government then in office in Scotland was far more congenial to England than Scottish governments had been for years back. He asked him what the alternatives were: Elizabeth surely could not want James in the custody of France or of any other foreign prince? If Elizabeth went to war, would this not give the supporters of Mary an opportunity to re-enter the country? England had good reason to fear the policies of any administration which might replace that of Morton. Apart from ordering the English wardens to see to the maintenance of quietness (Morton gave a similar order from his side of the Border) Huntingdon himself could take no action until he received instructions from London. Then on 19 July he received

a commission from the queen authorising him to begin negotiations with the regent and the news that the Scots had released the
English warden and his companions prepared the way for a
reconciliation. The queen's adamant refusal to allow her representative to cross the Border, coupled with the bad weather,
delayed the meeting of Huntingdon and Morton until 16 August;
Huntingdon used the interval to inform himself as fully as he
could from Forster about what had actually happened at Redswire
and gained the impression that the English, no less than the Scots,
had something to hide.[9]

When at last Huntingdon confronted Morton he found a Scot
he could unreservedly admire. With his inclination to over-
simplify the issue he saw the powerful, yet unpopular regent, the
very embodiment of a sixteenth-century politique, merely as a
champion of Scottish Protestantism against the gathering might
of Rome. Consequently he willingly accepted Morton's inter-
pretation of the Redswire raid as an irresponsible affray between
rival Border clans which neither country could properly control:
Huntingdon's own investigations had already in any case led him
to the same conclusion. Morton took the opportunity to emphasise
the advantage the French would gain from any breach between
Scotland and England: rather than that the matter should turn to
war he offered to seek peace on his knees. Huntingdon proved
more than sympathetic. He told Sir Thomas Smith bluntly he
thought both sides ought to share the blame:

All that was done at the Redswire was . . . an accident sudden and unlooked for, not premeditated or determined before. For surely the
ground of it was choler suddenly stirred, which might have been better
tempered with considerate discretion than it was. And herein, if I be not
deceived, both sides will be found to be in some fault.

By 21 August, both Huntingdon and the regent felt all their
differences could be amicably concluded if the queen would only
name the compensation she required for the insult given to her
warden: Morton had even privately offered to send Carmichael,
his offending warden, to the queen and Huntingdon believed that

nothing more in justice could be asked of him than that.[10]

Upon these friendly negotiations suddenly descended the weight of the queen's displeasure. While she acknowledged Huntingdon's good intentions she did not hide the fact that she thought he had erred far too much on the side of leniency: no private declaration by the regent of Scotland could atone for the slight done to her honour. For her public vindication she demanded that justice be executed upon those responsible for her subjects' deaths and that those who had imprisoned her warden should be delivered unconditionally into her hands. Huntingdon could not hide his consternation. He had never exceeded the limits of the queen's instructions, he protested to Leicester: the length of the negotiations had increased the unrest on the Borders and he still believed justice should be done on both sides *in terrorem* to curb the lawless and to diminish the likelihood of a further breach. Eventually on 13 September, Morton and Huntingdon signed the articles of agreement: the regent made an almost complete capitulation to Elizabeth's commands. Peace continued between the two nations, and both sides promised to seek redress of the Border hurts. Morton agreed that eight Scottish gentlemen, including Carmichael, should go to the English court to seek the restoration of Elizabeth's goodwill and that they should remain in England as hostages. On 23 September, the queen at last permitted Huntingdon who had been exclusively occupied with the investigation on the Borders for nearly three months, to return to York and, at his request, delegated the leadership of the new commission for the meting out of justice to those involved in the raid to Lord Hunsdon, who had been associated with him in the talks with Morton since the middle of August.[11]

A final intervention from Huntingdon brought the Redswire incident to a close: he had already incurred the queen's displeasure because of his sympathy for the Scots Protestants but not even the possibility of a second reprimand could deflect him from again urging that leniency should prevail.[12] During the negotiations he had complied with the royal commands and insisted Morton should displace Carmichael from his office but now he begged Walsingham to try to persuade the queen to release Carmichael from his custody in York, excuse him from appearing as a petitioner at the English court and to intercede with the regent for his restoration to office: before the accident Carmichael's service on the Border had been of value to England and Scotland alike and it would be hard for the regent to find another to replace him.[13]

Time vindicated Huntingdon's opinion of Morton as a 'very wise man' and one more likely 'to be kept devoted to her majesty sooner than any of his nation'; during the 1570's Anglo–Scottish relations, apart from the crisis over the Redswire raid, proved more stable than they had ever been since Elizabeth's accession or indeed were again for the rest of the reign. Within Scotland, however, Morton had many enemies among the nobles who as early as 1577 laid plots to seize the king from his custody. During that autumn the queen appointed Robert Bowes, a personal friend of Huntingdon, as ambassador to Scotland and he began to supply him with very full newsletters on the state of Scotland in addition to those his office bound him to send to London. In 1578 Bowes's reports made it plain that the nobility might at any time rise against the regent. The queen ordered Huntingdon to go to Berwick in August to consult with Hunsdon and Forster: at a warning from Bowes she authorised Hunsdon and Forster to march into Scotland with a force of 2,500 men while Huntingdon remained in Berwick to safeguard their supplies. In the event the English did not attempt another invasion; the queen instead offered to send Huntingdon, Hunsdon and others to work for a general pacification among the Scottish nobility but her proposal met with no response. Morton, for the time being, retained his office but all could see he had lost control of the country and the arrival in Scotland from France of Esmé Stuart, Earl of Aubigny, in the autumn of 1579 undermined his authority yet further. Aubigny, who though a Scot by descent and cousin of James VI had lived all his life in France, by his ingratiating manner quickly gained the favour of the thirteen-year-old king and he created

him first Earl then Duke of Lennox. The Scots ministers and the
English government both suspected Lennox of being a papal
agent sent to work for the restoration of Mary and of Catholicism
in Scotland. For the time being, however, the English could do
little to change the situation or to strengthen Morton's party,
though Huntingdon, doubtless with the connivance of the central
government, sent aid to the Scottish Hamiltons, who had fled
into England.[14]

The rapidly deteriorating situation in Scotland and England's
worsening relations with Spain caused 1580 to be something of a
turning-point in Huntingdon's government in the north. Up to
that time he had supervised northern defences and raised troops
for action in Scotland under special temporary commissions sent
up from London for the occasion. In 1580 the queen conferred
upon him the specifically military office of Lord Lieutenant: again
the reaction of the city of York mirrors the importance contemporaries attached to this new dignity. Early in 1581 the
corporation of York made preparations for a solemn reception of
the Lord President now Lord Lieutenant. At nine o'clock on the
morning of 16 January the lord mayor and his brethren in scarlet,
the sheriffs and the twenty-four in crimson, received Huntingdon
into the city and escorted him through the streets to the Guildhall
with the city's sword borne before him. There, after he had been
given the sword, and the commission of lieutenancy had been read
aloud he made 'a very wise and godly exhortation to the people
then being present, being many in number, declaring the effect of
her highness's commission of lieutenancy'. It seems likely that
Huntingdon's authority now extended to the whole of the area
governed by the Council in the North, and not to Yorkshire alone,
though it is impossible to be certain as the commission itself has
not survived. After 1586, when Huntingdon received a renewal of
his commission from the queen this was indeed the case, and then
he was named Lord Lieutenant for the counties of York, Northumberland, Cumberland, Westmorland, the bishopric of Durham,
the city of York and the towns of Kingston upon Hull and

P

Newcastle upon Tyne: this commission remained in force right up to Huntingdon's death in 1595. From 1580 the office of Lord Lieutenant became permanently annexed to the presidency of the north, so much so that in 1594 a northerner could assume that one of the authorities which naturally would be granted to the president in the north was that of lieutenant that he might supply the place of the prince 'in all temporal affairs, politic and martial'.[15]

Huntingdon had barely returned to York with his commission of lieutenancy when the crisis in Scotland broke. By the beginning of 1581 Aubigny (now Lennox) and his faction had risen so high in James's favour that even optimists recognised Morton's rule could last little longer. Elizabeth ordered Randolph, the new English ambassador to Scotland to use all his influence on behalf of Morton whenever he had conference with James and at the same time instructed Huntingdon and Hunsdon to have a force in readiness on the Border should a milder course not bring the king to discern his enemies from his friends. Huntingdon, dashing off a note to Walsingham as the bell in York was summoning him to a sermon, felt pessimistic about either course: while a substitute for Morton could probably be found he thought no one could be such a reliable ally of England; the queen must on no account give any support to Aubigny for he would utterly alienate the king and the whole realm of Scotland from the English interest. In compliance with the queen's wishes he moved from York to Newcastle to be in closer touch with Scotland and a triangular correspondence between Randolph at the Scottish court, Huntingdon on the Borders and Walsingham in London developed to give almost a day by day commentary on the situation. Circumstances linked the three zealots who all looked upon this political struggle as a contest between the forces of true religion and Antichrist. In the heat of the battle Randolph could even wish Huntingdon were with him in Scotland to hear their daily sermons in that time of fast: 'they pass any that ever I heard', he told him, 'for plainness and earnest crying out against wickedness and sin and the vices of this time.' Since the crisis prevented Huntingdon from attending parliament Walsingham also diligently kept him posted of events: in his first report he described a 'sour beginning' with the hostile reception of Paul Wentworth's resolution for a public fast and later in the session retailed the news, welcome to Walsingham and Huntingdon alike, of the passing by the two Houses of the bill against recusants which Walsingham had at one stage feared would not go through.[16]

Huntingdon, in the meanwhile, continued his campaign in the north to try to advance God's cause against the 'Guisian Romanists'. Early in January the government had allocated him £3,000 from the £5,000 sent to Hunsdon for the raising of troops and by the end of the month Huntingdon could report on the daily assembling of Border levies at Newcastle. Now that he had been created a Lord Lieutenant his power, even in military matters, equalled that of the governor of the garrison at Berwick and, had not Walsingham used all his powers of persuasion, Huntingdon would have gone on to contest Hunsdon's supreme command over the troops. This, however, was scarcely the moment for questions of honour: the central government had such little hope for the English sympathisers at the Scottish court that it even authorised Huntingdon to try to form an English party from the unpromising material of the Scottish borderers, though he soon discovered that of all the people in Scotland with whom he had to deal, the clans were the worst. Among the nobility, he thought, the greatest trust could be placed in Angus and he encouraged Randolph to build up a party of well-disposed nobles around him: subsequent events justified his opinion for in 1582 Angus and his party did overthrow Aubigny, though their triumph proved only a temporary one.[17]

In spite of the abundant intelligence received, the complexity of Scottish political intrigues early in 1581 confused even the main participants and drove Walsingham, in a letter to Huntingdon, to think of a singularly apt comparison:

the state of Scotland . . . may well be resembled to a diseased body, that one day yields hope of life, and another utter despair of recovery.

Sometimes it seems to stand on indifferent themes which minister comfort of redress, though the inward disease had much weakened it. At other times it appears most desperate and not to be cured without desperate remedies.

Certainly English policy fluctuated wildly in an attempt to cope with the rapidly changing situation: at one stage the government contemplated using force and kept Huntingdon in readiness for three months to direct operations from Newcastle. Perhaps only an invasion of Scotland by the English could have saved Morton, a course which both Walsingham and Huntingdon favoured: the Spanish ambassador sent home a dispatch that Huntingdon had bribed Morton's partisans to raid England and so give Hunsdon a pretext for entering Scotland. The ruse failed, Hunsdon's men fell back and, according to Mendoza, the queen turned her wrath upon Walsingham, exclaiming, 'You Puritan, you will never be content until you drive me into war on all sides and bring the king of Spain on to me.' The queen knew very well that the intensity of the feelings of some of her advisers against Spain made them ready to risk war: for the time being, however, her desire for peace prevailed, and, apart from this minor skirmish, the English did not cross the Scottish frontier.[18]

Abandoning these 'desperate remedies' the government next tried 'indifferent themes': while Huntingdon never felt the slightest confidence in Aubigny even he went so far as to suggest that the queen should offer to mediate between the factions and accept Aubigny's feigned professions of friendship in order to gain Morton's release. In the middle of February he thought an attempt at conciliation when the Scottish nobles met in their convention might work some good and would, in any event, be better than war, but by the beginning of March he had become convinced that nothing could be hoped for from a treaty and that some 'good stiff course' would have to be used, though he did not want an open breach if it could possibly be avoided. Nevertheless, by the end of March the English government had put aside all thoughts of invading Scotland to restore Morton, probably because it realised how little support he had in the country, and it decided that Scotland could best be pacified by a meeting of commissioners: to the dismay of Huntingdon, Walsingham and other Privy Councillors, the queen ordered the disbanding of all the companies placed on the Borders. The three months of feverish activity on the part of the English had accomplished very little, and helped Morton not at all: in June he was executed on a charge of being implicated in the murder of James VI's father, an accusation which could equally well have been brought against other Scottish lords.[19]

However much Elizabeth might protest against the inevitability of war with Spain, even she realised England could not risk having a hostile Scotland across her northern border and when Mendoza's grand design for the invasion of England through Scotland was uncovered, the government fully comprehended the gravity of its failure to prevent the establishment of a Scottish government under Aubigny sympathetic to France and Catholicism. Scotland had to be recovered, and the capture of James VI by Angus and his party, which the Spanish believed had been engineered by Huntingdon, together with the flight of Aubigny in the autumn of 1582 gave the English their opportunity. Already in 1583 the government contemplated a treaty of mutual defence between England and Scotland but the English party within Scotland had not the strength to begin negotiations before 1585. Then the queen chose Huntingdon and Lord Eure, another member of the Council in the North to act as special commissioners 'touching the treaty for common defence against the conjured enemies of the Gospel' and instructed them to be at Berwick to meet the Scots commissioners by 20 September. When at last an alliance between the two countries seemed about to be consummated hopes were again dashed by another irresponsible affray. Lord Russell, the Earl of Bedford's heir, was accidentally killed in a border incident and the English refused to consider the larger issue of a treaty until the Scots had made redress for his death. Late in September, Huntingdon sought to be released from his duties as a commissioner 'in respect of his indisposition' (he

was in the midst of a course of physic) and he apparently took no
very active part in the discussions which resulted in the signing of
the Treaty of Berwick in July 1586. Nevertheless it can still be
seen as a culmination of a policy he had always advocated and in
in its consequences he was not disappointed. The treaty introduced
a period of better relations between England and Scotland and
James VI, now at last old enough to reign in his own right,
consented to become, for most purposes, a pensioner of the
English queen.[20]

The agreement with Scotland came none too soon. Already in
1584 the English government had been compelled to consider
realistically the threat of a Spanish invasion and its attitude
towards the internal defence of the country took on an urgency
which had hitherto been absent. The change in government
thinking showed itself particularly forcibly in the north. In 1584
the Privy Council ordered Huntingdon to train 10,000 men in
Yorkshire alone, a tenfold increase in the number demanded in
1573, which it thought could easily be levied out of 42,000 men
certified at the last general musters. Huntingdon at once protested
that the county could not furnish so large a force, the whole shire
did not contain sufficient armour for a far smaller number and he
could not even be sure of providing the four hundred light
horsemen required, since only three hundred had been viewed at
the last muster. Eventually the Privy Council agreed to a compromise figure of 6,000 men, suitably armed, in place of the 10,000
for which it had originally asked. In July 1584 Huntingdon also
certified that the bishopric of Durham could raise 2,000 men; 90
light horsemen, 370 archers, 540 billmen, all armed, and 1,000
able men, unarmed. For the first time in the reign defence preparations against an external enemy placed a heavy and moreover
an increasing burden upon the localities; northerners did their
best to avoid creating precedents for themselves in the future and
only by a constant watchfulness could Huntingdon ensure that the
antiquated system functioned at all. Whenever possible, com-
munities conveniently forgot their obligations; three years of

prevarication passed before Huntingdon prevailed upon the city of York to buy two lasts of powder and 1,000 matches from a London merchant; the city returned the reply that its private citizens had a good store and asked to be excused since powder soon decayed and there was no market for it in the town: in 1587 Huntingdon repeated the order; this time York obeyed and its supplies of powder did something to relieve the general shortage in 1588. In May of the Armada year he instructed the city to retail some of its stocks to Pontefract, Leeds, Claro, Barkstone and the North Riding; very reluctantly the city complied.[21]

The gentlemen of Yorkshire shared an equal concern with the York burgesses lest the charges imposed on them in the times of emergency might become automatic for the future. The Privy Council expected them to provide 400 light horsemen, but Huntingdon never succeeded in having a view of this number at the musters: gentlemen who he knew had six good horses would scarcely show one for fear of being set down in the muster book. Before the queen's accession, he explained, it had never been the custom for the shire to provide a fixed number of horsemen, but in times of danger the gentlemen produced as many mounted men as their means could afford: now when preparations were on foot against the Armada they held back not, he considered, from disloyalty but because they suspected that the service might become fixed and be demanded against some other parts of the realm, or abroad, instead of only against Scotland as in time past. He proposed to get round the difficulty by making a private agreement with the gentlemen which would not bind them for the future.[22]

For the time being the northern gentry could still usefully engage in their ancient task of acting as watch dogs against Scotland. In spite of the Treaty of Berwick the English government could never be certain of Scotland's dependability: James VI had too assertive a nature to accept with equanimity the restraining hand of England over his foreign policy. Although the English money which flowed in to relieve his poverty and the prospect of the succession to the English throne proved to be inducements to keep him reasonably loyal to the English interest, several times in the decade after 1586 his dalliance with Spain and France caused the English government considerable anxiety. England itself was largely responsible for the first crisis. James and most of his nation had shown little love for Mary, Queen of Scots when alive but when the English actually carried out her execution in the spring of 1587 a wave of anti-English feeling swept the nation. As a precautionary measure Elizabeth ordered Huntingdon to levy men to strengthen the English Border and later in the year the rumour that the Duke of Parma hoped for an understanding with the Scots again threatened the alliance.[23]

By the autumn of 1587 the government knew that the Spanish attack could not be delayed much longer. It gave Huntingdon supreme command over the whole of the north of England, with Lord Hunsdon as his lieutenant, the Earl of Cumberland his marshal of the field, Sir Henry Lee general of the horse and Sir Robert Constable general of foot. Again he had to face the anger of Hunsdon which he had first encountered in 1581: since Hunsdon then had not in the end been forced to share the command of the army for the invasion of Scotland with Huntingdon, so now he adamantly refused to serve under him. He had just heard, he protested to Burghley, he had been made a lieutenant under Huntingdon:

I have been her majesty's lieutenant myself, when I should a gone to win Edinburgh castle, and now to be a lieutenant under one that never saw any service, nor knows in any respect what appertains to be a captain, much less to be a lieutenant, I am offered greater wrong then I did think would a been offered me by that lord: but I perceive it is a great matter to be an earl. But, my lord, knowing how ill he and I shall agree for sundry other respects, and that what good service soever shall be done shall redound to his honour and glory, and if any ill, it will be laid upon me, I pray your lordship let her majesty understand that I will serve her majesty here or anywhere else with 20 or 30 horse without pay, but to say I will take this charge upon me, her majesty must pardon me—for surely I will lie in prison rather.

Fortunately for Huntingdon, his other under officers accepted their inferior position: without protest the Earls of Shrewsbury, Derby, Pembroke and Rutland and the Lord Treasurer received the queen's instructions to hold 3,400 foot and 170 horse in the counties of Derby, Stafford, Chester, Lancaster, Shropshire, Lincoln and Nottingham in readiness to come to Huntingdon's aid if he should summon them.[24]

Within the confines of his own jurisdiction despite the wintry weather, Huntingdon took stock of his own men and felt able to send a fairly confident report to Walsingham in January 1588. He described to him how he had spent his time viewing the armour in Yorkshire and had gone through every wapentake in the three Ridings except for the one on the Westmorland border which he could not inspect because of the great fall of snow. He had found the country reasonably well furnished and thought the requisite number of 6,000 men would be forthcoming: out of each hundred men forty had weapons, and all had been divided up into bands and placed under captains. What comforted him most was 'the cheerful and willing disposition of the people to serve the queen'. Elizabeth, responding to this display of loyalty, 'willed their lordships in her name to yield to his lordship right hearty thanks, and ... signify unto them [her northern people] her majesty accepted thereof for their better encouragement to persist therein'.[25]

With the coming of spring, efforts to defend the north were intensified. Huntingdon felt anything but confident that the Scottish alliance would bear the strain and that James would remain true to the English interest yet he put his hope in the Scottish Protestants who he thought must realise a war would mean 'the overthrow of them and of the cause'. In April the queen ordered further general musters to be held: Huntingdon had never been very strong and now his health began to weaken under the tension and at the beginning of the month he was not well enough to take a view of the horsemen from Yorkshire; consequently the gentlemen produced fewer horses than they might otherwise have done. At the end of April he went over the work which had been carried out by his deputies and took a view in person. In May, in collaboration with his fellow commissioners, he devised a scheme for training the troops: from Whitsun until 22 July he decided the footmen should be drilled for three days continuously every fifteen days and that these exercises should take place throughout the north; to compensate the men for their loss of earnings he instructed the county authorities to pay them sixpence a day, and their lieutenants six shillings and eightpence. Amid the mass of his official correspondence on arms and men, Huntingdon occasionally let slip his own feelings as England's testing time approached. He could speak the most freely to Walsingham who of all the leading members of the government most nearly resembled him in religious enthusiasm. By the middle of May everyone coming north from London brought news of nothing but war and denied all hopes of peace.

And after our long happy peace [he wrote to Walsingham], which God in his mercy hath hitherto vouchsafed us, and which hath been by us so much abused, it may be the Lord will send a war somewhat to correct us. . . . [Yet he believed God would not be chiding them for ever.] Let her majesty trust in God, and in the courageous hearts of her faithful subjects: for, no doubt, by his grace and favour, they will give her enemies such a welcome whensoever they come as shall nothing please them. I trust assuredly upon it, and I mind unfeignedly to spend my life in it.[26]

It was well for the northern levies that their leaders had this certainty that God fought on their side, for their worldly equipment was anything but adequate. Once the selected men arrived to begin their three days' training at Whitsun, Huntingdon discovered the supply of ammunition and shot to be quite insufficient. Early in June he told Walsingham that the powder he could get in York and Hull would only last for three days more and unless a new supply could be found the training would have to cease: news had also come from Sir Simon Musgrave that he had no powder left in Newcastle. Huntingdon had hoped York and Hull merchants could have imported new supplies from eastern Europe but they had informed him that a certain Dale had the monopoly and so he could not do anything except dispatch Dale overseas and promise him the county would pay him the queen's price for the powder. For the next three months he made constant appeals to the government to send ammunition north with little success for the scarcity seems to have been a national and not merely a regional one: in the middle of June the queen authorised the Earl of Warwick to deliver three lasts of powder to be kept in reserve but this could do little to alleviate the overall shortage. By the same post Huntingdon received the news that the King of Spain's fleet had left harbour and that the Duke of Parma in the Netherlands had renewed his preparations for the invasion of England. The moment of decision had arrived. The queen commanded Huntingdon to go to Newcastle to defend Tynemouth Castle and the surrounding coast against foreign forces. He replied with an appeal for money, armour, munition and victuals to be sent there, '*ne forte* Scotland should prove to be a worse neighbour than I hope it will'. A week later, writing with great pain (it seems his sciatica had still not left him), he protested to Burghley that he had neither the forces nor the stores to withstand any 'sudden attempt' at Newcastle.[27]

Huntingdon had some reason for complaining about the government's delay in sending supplies and in thinking it had neglected the north as against the south of England. Yet not all southerners forgot him in his time of need and Robert Sparke, one of his chaplains, comfortably beneficed in Leicestershire, eagerly offered to leave his safe refuge to bring spiritual reinforcements to his patron. In July 'when the Spaniard was then near approaching to our coasts', and he thought 'that they would covet to make their entry in the north parts, and so their first force and fury there to be showed' Sparke wrote to ask Huntingdon for permission to join him. Just as he would 'need a strong army, and a good guard for your own person, which I wish to be of your own men, and of the trustiest of them, so I assured myself that you would have a preacher in your tents near unto you, which also I wish to be one of your own chaplains'. The two reasons which prompted Sparke to abandon his study for the field of battle reveal with extraordinary vividness how close at hand to the zealots Armageddon seemed to be:

The one, I suppose that I am the eldest or at least the oldest in continuance of your chaplains, and therefore think it my duty to be forwardest or at least with the forwardest in any service. I have found you always a good, a loving and a kind master ready always to counsel, to comfort and to succour me, and I have borne, I thank God, always a faithful and loving heart to your honour, ready to do any service unto you: but when opportunity hath hitherto wanted to yield any service of account I am now the more willing in this dangerous service to offer myself. One other cause which moveth me hereunto is that I find in myself that the Lord all this year hath settled in me a constant persuasion that he would overthrow and confound this anti-christian army, as it hath plainly appeared to all which either have heard my sermons or my private talk. God will overthrow Babylon, the time of the growing of Antichrist, and the time of his revealing no man, no power of the sword, no wisdom, learning, diligence could withstand. The time of his fall is come, man's power shall seek to uphold him, but in vain. *Nam fortis est dominus qui iudicat hanc meretricem.* But howsoever God give victory, the cause is so honourable, as I see great cause to move me to spare no labour, pains or travail, no not life itself if the Lord so appoint it. . . .

Concluding, Sparke felt no doubt that 'my prayers shall be of as great force as any double cannon, so merciful is our good God to his poor servants'.[28]

This was the sort of religious excitement in which the Protestant radicals awaited the coming of the Armada: yet while Huntingdon fully entered into his chaplain's hopes and fears he did not forget that God would be the more willing to help those who helped themselves. So much remained that he could do. When he reached Newcastle he found nothing fit for service, except a few cannons, and no powder at all, and made a last desperate appeal to the queen herself. He asked permission to send ships from Newcastle to London for supplies, including ammunition from the Tower and emphasised yet again the great folly of leaving the north defence-less: 'for though the storm appear now to be greatest in the south parts of your realm, yet how soon it may be turned hither, your majesty hath greatest cause to doubt. For sure I am, the enemy cannot be ignorant of the weakness of these parts, neither doth he doubt to find some friends here.' The following day, 4 August, a Sunday, when men hourly expected news of a Spanish landing, Huntingdon went in state to hear a sermon preached by Toby Matthew at Newcastle. The Dean of Durham took as his text 2 Chronicles xx. 20: 'Jehoshaphat stood and said, Hear me, O Judah, and ye inhabitants of Jerusalem; believe in the Lord your God, so shall ye be established; believe his prophets, so shall ye prosper.' Well might his congregation draw comfort from the miraculous deliverance God granted the Jews from the Am-monites and Moabites and the inhabitants of Mount Seir: not until 14 August, by which time all danger had passed in the south, did the Privy Council permit five lasts of powder and two thousand pikes, bills and other arms to be shipped from the queen's store to Newcastle and Berwick.[29]

The coming of the long-dreaded Armada to the north proved to be an anticlimax. The tempestuous winds and the English fire ships had broken the battle lines of the Spanish fleet in the Narrow Seas and the Armada was a spent force long before it entered northern waters. Huntingdon heard on 2 August that the Spanish fleet had passed through the Channel and had headed north with the Lord Admiral and the English navy in pursuit: the Privy Council ordered him to supply the English commander with food, powder and shot so soon as he reached northern shores. On 8 August he received a report that one Spanish ship had entered the Forth near Leith; the next day news came of the sighting of twenty great ships off Eyemouth, five miles from Berwick: no one could tell whether they were Spanish or English but it seemed possible that the Spaniards might attempt a landing after all. The Privy Council ordered the Earls of Shrewsbury, Derby, Pembroke and Lord Burghley to go with their men to whatsoever place

Huntingdon might name, and, at his request, dispatched to him 'men skilled in martial services'. Fortunately for the credit of the central government and the Lord Lieutenant alike, Spanish troops never tested the amateur defences of the north: on 19 August Huntingdon had certain word from the Lord Admiral of the scattering of the Armada; the danger was over for the year. When he passed on the joyful tidings to Elizabeth Huntingdon prayed 'the Lord Almighty always to fight, as at this time He hath pleased to do both mightily and mercifully'. Yet even in this moment of triumph he insisted on looking to the future. He believed the Spaniards would never sit down under the indignity they had sustained but that they would be bound speedily to try to revenge it; the best insurance he could see against Spanish practices was for the queen to keep Scotland her firm friend, 'so as by the grace of God, your faithful subjects of England shall hereafter enjoy your most happy government many more years to come, as we have done already many years past, in peace and all good blessings, to your highness's great honour and our most singular comfort.'[30]

The summer of 1588 had been a proving time for James VI, and he had remained true to the Anglo-Scottish alliance. From this time Huntingdon became the channel through which he received England's bounty rather than, as before, the sentinel continually on the alert against an alien government. In August 1588 the queen instructed Huntingdon to pass on £3,000 out of £6,000 which had come from London to the King of Scots, and the following year, when James set out for Denmark to bring home his bride, Huntingdon kept watch for him over his kingdom, and on the queen's orders had a force of foot and horsemen in readiness to go to the aid of James's supporters should the need arise. Yet the Scots could never be trusted implicitly and Huntingdon took pains to keep his information service functioning. In 1593 he received evidence of new intrigues by some Scots noblemen with Spain: Angus, Huntly and Erroll had all subscribed the 'Spanish blanks', draft letters which were taken to prove the existence of a new Spanish plot for the invasion of England through Scotland. Right up to his death, reports came to Huntingdon from the English ambassador in Scotland and the wardens of the English Marches: while the Protestantism of the king by this date could scarcely be questioned the Catholicism of some of the Scottish nobles which James at times seemed to condone continued to give the English government cause for concern. Nevertheless, in spite of the hindrances, England had at last achieved a working relationship with Scotland and Huntingdon, for one, could rejoice in the amity 'of all true professors of religion in both realms'.[31]

After 1588 Huntingdon did his best to overcome the great weaknesses in the defences of the north which the Armada crisis had revealed and in 1589, 1591, 1592 and 1595 held fresh general musters throughout the region. The old idea that every county should be responsible for its own defence still persisted; all he could do was to try to force life into it, as in 1590 when the Privy Council asked him to persuade the inhabitants of Durham, Northumberland, Cumberland and Westmorland to provide more arms for themselves than they had previously done. The Privy Council also took steps to make the militia a little less amateur, and sent up a professional soldier to train the northern musters, but the counties had to shoulder his expenses. Huntingdon, for his part, paid special attention to Newcastle which he had found so singularly wanting in 1588 and held a muster in the town in person in 1592: but these small improvements could be no more than palliatives: to make this antiquated system of defence efficient was a task far beyond the capacity of one man.[32]

As Lord Lieutenant answerable for the internal defences of his region Huntingdon confronted a problem sufficiently large in itself: the government, however, required from him even more and, as with the rest of England, it expected the north to contribute its quota of men for the English armies abroad. Traditionally the north had supplied men against Scotland, the old enemy, and Huntingdon had no difficulty in raising troops for the siege of Edinburgh Castle in 1573, or for the abortive invasions of

Scotland in 1578 and 1581. Northerners took far less kindly to
service overseas though, at the Privy Council's request, he succeeded in sending soldiers and light horse from the north to fight
in Ireland in 1575, 1579, 1585 and 1595 and other contingents
in 1585 and 1587 to serve under Leicester in the Netherlands.[33]

Occasionally individualists rebelled. One John Fairbarne, a
master mariner and pilot, petitioned Huntingdon in 1577 against
the Mayor of Hull, who, he alleged, had unnecessarily pressed him
for the queen's service just as he was about to sail with a cargo of
wines, the property of a merchant of York. He maintained that his
ship had been commandeered as a means of enforcing Hull's
economic blockade of York and that the mayor had used the
queen's service as a mere pretext. Another case concerning a
freeman of Hull, which reached Huntingdon in the same year
through the local magistrates' court shows that some northerners
objected nearly as strongly to the special training schemes within
Yorkshire as they did, far more understandably, to being dispatched to fight abroad. Robert Armyn asserted that out of their
ill-will towards him the commissioners of musters at Hull chose
his son as one of the ten men from the town to be trained in the
shooting of arquebuses. The mayor imprisoned Armyn for these
malicious words and he promptly appealed to Huntingdon who
ordered both parties to appear before him in York: when he
learnt of the disrespect Armyn had displayed to the mayor at the
muster he confirmed his imprisonment and ruled that it should
continue until he made a full apology.[34]

Yet the government did not remain entirely oblivious of the
disruptive consequences military service could have on local
working men: it emphasised the duty of the county to compensate
the men chosen for special training for the time they lost from
their work and ordered that those who had survived service
abroad should be received back in their former occupations. By
1591 sufficient northerners had been wounded in the wars for
their sufferings to constitute another problem for the Lord
Lieutenant: the Privy Council instructed Huntingdon to see that

James Douglas, fourth Earl of Morton. Regent of
Scotland 1572–81

the disabled received relief and the lame soldiers' book at Northallerton proves that some indeed collected small pensions. Other duties, much less obviously military, the queen placed upon Huntingdon in his capacity as Lord Lieutenant. As in Leicestershire so in the north she used him to distribute royal warrants to raise a loan after the Armada: since he was at court at the time Huntingdon wrote to his Deputy Lieutenants enclosing these privy seals and instructed them to send them to gentlemen in a position to contribute and to take bonds from any who refused to co-operate. He probably had to perform this unwelcome task at other times in the north as he certainly did in Leicestershire.[35]

However much the central government sent out instructions, however much the Lord Lieutenant strove to execute its commands, in the end all these attempts at coercion came to a halt before the barriers of northern conservatism: with the resources available, only limited reforms could be achieved. By 1595 Huntingdon had gained a fairly firm control of the defence of the southern part of his charge, Yorkshire and the bishopric of Durham, but towards the Border matters were very different. In 1595 the Privy Council called for a special survey of the Border defences: until he received these instructions Huntingdon's advisers had considered his authority did not extend into the Border regions and that these areas were the special responsibility of their particular wardens. Whatever the rights of the case the result had been that the Border strongholds had long been neglected and had fallen into decay, that disorders had increased and that raids had been made well into county Durham. The onus of this state of affairs rested with the wardens, particularly with Sir John Forster, the notorious warden of the Middle March, who by 1595 had become a nonagenarian but still refused to relinquish his office. In September the Privy Council sanctioned his dismissal, which Huntingdon had long urged, and appointed Lord Eure in his place although six weeks later Forster still had not handed over his authority. Hearing of the hindrances Forster was putting into Eure's path, and also that no muster had yet been

Q

taken of the men of Northumberland, Huntingdon resolved to go to Newcastle himself.[36]

Huntingdon intended by this visitation to impress upon the gentlemen of Northumberland their duties in the defence of their county. He had reason to doubt the trustworthiness of certificates which he had previously received so he arranged for a muster of the men of the Middle March to be taken the day before he arrived by the gentlemen of the counties of York and Durham as well as of Northumberland in the hope of getting a more accurate return. On Tuesday, 25 November Huntingdon came to Newcastle, accompanied by Lord Eure and began first an enquiry into the conduct of Sir John Forster: he requisitioned the warden court books, and heard reports from commissioners but he gained little assistance from the aged warden himself who, he confessed to his secretary, 'did wind like an eel'. Huntingdon made 27 November, the day of Eure's formal installation as the new Lord Warden, an occasion to overawe the Northumberland gentlemen: in the morning he attended a sermon, in the afternoon went with Lord Eure to the castle where his commission was read out and promulgated before a great assembly of gentlemen. He then added a speech of his own, exhorting them to settle their feuds and quarrels and to turn to the better defence of their March; the queen expressly commanded that they should leave all their wrongs to the sword of justice, and not to private revenge. Huntingdon's earlier suspicions proved to be justified: the new reports returned by the impartial commissioners revealed that there were only 115 horsemen furnished for the defence of the Middle March, far fewer than Forster had set down. After further admonitions to the gentry over reports of murders and unjust ransoms in the March, Huntingdon returned to York on 29 November meaning to go down at once to London to inform the queen and Burghley of all that had passed. He realised a completely new system of defence needed to be worked out for the north of the region and he had some plans for doing it but death cut him short with his work unfinished.[37]

It can be no accident that the only contemporary portrait of Huntingdon to survive, probably the only portrait painted in his life time, is dated 1588 in the fifty-second year of his age, and shows him armed ready to stand against the Catholic troops of Philip of Spain. Huntingdon never relaxed his vigilance after 1588, and was for ever advising the queen on further precautions necessary against Spain yet he lived long enough to look back to the Armada year and recognise it as that marvellous time when the forces of Antichrist gathered for a mighty effort against the Protestant English, and failed. Huntingdon saw himself as a defender of true religion; in the technical sphere, as Hunsdon unkindly pointed out, he had no qualifications which entitled him to be considered a military man. Throughout the period he acted as Lord Lieutenant in the north he remained a very amateur soldier and could contribute little to the reforming of the system of defence in the north. He had not the knowledge to do more than carry out the orders of the central government which he did with a zeal all the more inflamed as he knew that upon his efforts, and the efforts of men like him, the future of his religion and of his country depended. As a diplomatist, however, Huntingdon had the tenacity and the information to influence the government's policy. Even the queen, in spite of her antipathy towards the Scottish Presbyterians, realised that an alliance with Scotland was in England's interest and Huntingdon in his relationship with Morton helped prepare the way for the Treaty of Berwick. When he died the problem of defence of the north may have been far from a solution, but a lasting amity had been created with the Protestant nation of Scotland across England's northern border.

CHAPTER SEVEN

The Emissaries of Antichrist within

ALTHOUGH he armed his region to withstand the attacks of
Catholic Spain, Huntingdon could never comfort himself with
the knowledge that his countrymen had united to defend their
religion: he knew that even within the camp the spies of Antichrist
had penetrated and been made welcome. The Rebellion of 1569
had provided the government with evidence for linking Catholicism with treason, and as the fear of Spain grew stronger,
increasingly the Catholics in the north, and particularly the priests
there, came to be considered enemies of the state. The persecution
of northern Catholics originated with the central government, not
with Huntingdon, but he carried out his instructions with
enthusiasm. At first he worked chiefly through the Northern High
Commission until, with the passing of the new recusancy laws in
the 1580's he could deal more effectively with Catholics in the
civil courts, and he gained a reputation of a tireless persecutor.
Yet for him, whatever the intentions of the government, plucking
up Catholicism was but a means to an end, not an end in itself: he
believed firmly in his mission to plant Protestantism. During the
early years of his presidency he collaborated closely with Grindal
and long after the archbishop had gone south he continued with
his policy of placing Protestant preachers in northern towns: he
sponsored exercises for the better education of the clergy and
interfered over a wide area to get godly ministers appointed. By

the time of his death, he more than any other one man had brought about a marked change in religious attitudes in the north. Even today some northern towns, like Leeds, remain strongly Protestant: the influence of eighteenth-century Methodism has frequently been held responsible for this but some of the causes of northern attraction to Nonconformity must surely lie in the latter part of the sixteenth century.

From the beginning of his rule Huntingdon had been entrusted with various powers, all of which could be turned against Catholics as Richard Holtby, a Jesuit actually ministering in the north during the Elizabethan persecution, distinguished very clearly. He wrote, about 1594:

The President in this north country hath had, and hath yet, as he taketh upon him, three several and printed authorities granted unto him, of President, of Lieutenant and also of Head Commissioner, next after the supposed Archbishop of York, who is the foremost and first of that commission. By the two former he supplieth the place of the prince's majesty . . . in all temporal affairs, politic and martial; by the last he hath to deal in causes concerning religion, together with the rest joined with him in the commission; wherein, notwithstanding he maketh a show to the contrary, yet in truth all is directed, ordered and executed at his pleasure and according to his only will and appointment . . . he useth these several offices in such sort, that he maketh one of them to countenance the other, and confounding their distinct functions and places, applieth either of them to perform the office of the rest.[1]

Father Holtby's chronological account of the development of the Lord President's powers to combat recusancy has much to commend it though it could be argued that it came about more through the propensity of the government and parliament as the reign proceeded to look upon Catholicism as a civil and not solely an ecclesiastical offence than through Huntingdon's personal malevolency. Certainly in 1572 he most obviously derived his authority in matters of religion from his membership of the Ecclesiastical Commission in the north. Within two months of his arrival Grindal wrote to Burghley for the renewal of the Ecclesiastical Commission for the province of York so that the new Lord

President might be included upon it, and from this time until Grindal's translation to Canterbury late in 1575 he and Huntingdon worked together in the greatest harmony. From the beginning of the reign the High Commission in the north had functioned as an organised court with its own officials and with an established routine: it sat frequently, had no limited terms and, during Grindal's episcopate, occasionally had as many as twelve sessions a month. Because of their many other duties Huntingdon and even Grindal could not be expected to attend all the sessions of the court, and, indeed, the lesser officials of the court could cope perfectly adequately with ordinary offenders in cases of religion or morals but when cases concerning the gentry were heard, then the Lord President or the archbishop or both tended to be present to add by their personal standing to the solemnity of the proceedings: up to 1581 Huntingdon took part on the average in about six sessions of the court of high commission every year.[2]

The cases brought before the High Commission in May 1573 when Huntingdon sat with Grindal for the first time, foreshadowed the type of problems he encountered for the remainder of his life. Four men stood before the court accused of being papists: Huntingdon by his presence at their trial publicly associated himself with the process of forcing Catholics into conformity which had been gaining momentum since the queen's accession and which had been accelerated after the northern rebellion. The court customarily bound over suspected Catholics on their first appearance, giving them until a certain date to produce a certificate which would prove their recent attendance at church: in May 1573 it extended this concession to Thomas Leade of Leadhall, gentleman (one of the four accused), even though he was said never to have taken communion since 1558. The court allowed him until October 1573 to resolve his religious scruples and, according to its stipulation, he conferred with Mr. Palmer, a minister, but he could not win him from his beliefs. When October came the court granted Leade a further few days for discussions, all to no effect, and later that month it committed him to York Castle for his recusancy. In his first year on the commission Huntingdon also encountered John Towneley, already a notorious recusant whose later career showed that neither fines nor imprisonment could make him falter in his faith. At the beginning of 1573 Huntingdon had suggested to Leicester that Towneley should be offered the oath of supremacy but nothing had come of this and he had merely been required to reside in London with his brother-in-law, and fellow Lancashire man, Alexander Nowell, prebendary of St. Paul's from whose household he had returned to the north quite unconvinced. In October 1573 the High Commission committed him a prisoner to York Castle in company with Thomas Leade, Thomas Pudsey and William Lacy of Sherburn, who had also all refused to attend sermons or receive communion.[3]

Towneley, Leade and Lacy proved to be irreconcilable Catholics: the High Commission billeted those Catholic sympathisers who showed a reasonable willingness to conform upon reliable Protestant clerics to strengthen them in their resolution. Edward Standishe, in November 1573, told the commissioners that in spite of the long time already given to him he was still not satisfied in his conscience about attending church. Eventually, however, he agreed to go to church and the court ordered him to live with Mr. Hopwood of Lancashire and to appear before the Commission the following May. Similarly, in February 1575, Huntingdon and Matthew Hutton, Dean of York, gave William Ardington, who had already been fined 100 marks by the Commission for his recusancy, leave to resort to Mr. Gilpin, the preacher, in the hope of his better conformity.[4]

The government's representatives in the north particularly feared those Catholic intellectuals who could give a reasoned justification of their faith: generally they allowed them to live out their days under house arrest, but some developed too great an ascendancy over their fellow Catholics. The York physician, Dr. Vavasour, they considered particularly dangerous: Grindal explained to Burghley that he had been tolerated in his own house in York for three-quarters of a year in 1574 but he had refused to make the slightest concession to those who argued with him, and had insisted upon clinging to the literal sense of *hoc est corpus meum* (to prove the doctrine of transubstantiation).

My lord president and I [he went on], knowing his disposition to talk, thought it not good to commit the said Dr. Vavasour to the castle of York where some other like affected remain prisoners, but rather to a solitary prison in the queen's majesty's castle at Hull where he shall only talk to walls.

Tacitly the High Commission recognised that the Marian priests who had never compromised themselves since Elizabeth's accession and these rather exceptional professional men could never be reconciled: they could only hope, by placing them in custody in remote areas to minimise their influence on the Catholic laity. Grindal and Huntingdon, however, considered that by a firm policy of imprisonment the leading Catholic gentlemen could be won over in the north. Consequently, when the central government released John Feckenham, the Marian Abbot of Westminster, and Thomas Watson, the last Catholic Bishop of Lincoln, Grindal immediately protested to Burghley that this would sabotage all their carefully laid plans in the north:

The imprisoned for religion in these parts of late made supplication to be enlarged seeming, as it were, to require it of right, by the example of the enlarging of Fecknam, Watson and other papists above. We here are to think that all things done above are done upon great causes, though the same be to us unknown. But certainly my Lord President and I join in opinion, that if such a general jubilee should be put in use in these parts, a great relapse would follow soon after. . . .[5]

The central government continued to allow the Northern High Commissioners a relatively free rein, and throughout the 1570's the numbers in prison for Catholicism grew. The High Commission Act Book for January, 1577 records that ten prisoners had been sent from the York prisons to the Hull blockhouses, that eleven had been newly committed to York Castle, that one prisoner remained there and that three Catholics had been stationed out in York. Before 1576 the High Commissioners had thought of imprisonment in the Hull blockhouses as an exceptional punishment and had reserved it for such influential Catholics as Dr. Vavasour: in the interval, however, between Grindal's translation to the see of Canterbury and Sandys's elevation as Archbishop of York when Huntingdon, in virtue of his office, became the chief member of the Commission, they made a greater use of the Hull prisons and among the first gentlemen they sent there in 1576 were Leade, Lacy and Towneley. Huntingdon preferred the Hull prisons to those at York because at Hull the Catholics could be kept in far greater isolation and the recourse of sympathisers prevented: he drew up precise regulations for the treatment of the prisoners at Hull. He ordered that priests and schoolmasters should be secluded from the gentlemen prisoners, that no one should have access to any prisoners without a licence from the Lord President, that the gaoler should provide them with food so that their servants had no occasion to wander abroad: he expected esquires, gentlemen and priests to be given lodgings appropriate to their rank, and that they should pay accordingly. With Archbishop Sandys he added to the regulations in 1580 when for the first time the commissioners needed to provide for women recusants and artisans.[6]

In their dealings with northern gentlemen the High Commissioners ran into fresh difficulties for some of them proved to have friends at court willing to intervene on their behalf. Hardly had Huntingdon dispatched Towneley to close imprisonment at Hull before he received a letter from Leicester asking him to release him on account of his health and accordingly the High Commission discharged him from Hull in April 1577 for another sojourn with Alexander Nowell in London. This time the Privy Council experienced his obstinacy at first hand and in desperation turned to the same punishment as the Lord President had originally prescribed. Since further converse with Nowell had not benefited Towneley they informed Huntingdon that they had decided to imprison him in London as they did not consider he should return to answer for his bonds before the High Commission because of his great influence in the north.[7]

In the attempt to win over the recusant gentry the High Commissioners made more use of imprisonment at this time than of fines: they saw the 12d. fine which could by statute be levied for every absence from church on Sundays and holy days as a more effective weapon to compel the conformity of the humbler Catholics, and first employed it on a large scale when they applied themselves to the problem of recusancy within the city of York in 1577. Sandys, Huntingdon and other commissioners called John Dyneley, the Lord Mayor of York, together with the recorder and other aldermen to appear at Bishopthorpe in October and show what the corporation had done since January when they passed an ordinance against those who refused to come to church. The lord mayor reported that distresses had been taken of several offenders and sureties for their payment but admitted that there had been some slackness. The High Commission instructed him to fine those who were at liberty (but not those in prison) and ordered him to produce a certificate of all those who had been presented to him for not attending church: as a personal warning they fined Dyneley himself forty shillings for his own absence from church—his wife had already appeared before the High Commission for her recusancy. The conservative element within the corporation could not stand out against this direct pressure: in November the High Commission received a certificate of the York absentees from church.[8]

Yet the commissioners could not hope to banish Catholicism from York by these intermittent investigations: John Dyneley was not the last of the lord mayors to be a Catholic sympathiser. His enemies charged Robert Cripling, mayor in 1579, with utterly neglecting to put into force the city ordinance against those who refused to attend church. At the end of his year of office he caused a scene in the Minster by speaking 'opprobrious, scandalous and irreligious' words against Mr. Palmer, the chancellor, and by affirming he had preached a railing sermon. The Council in the

North summoned him to make answer for this offence and, not satisfied with his excuses, committed him to prison in January 1580. This time, however, the corporation realised he had gone too far in displaying openly his hostility towards the Established Church and passed an ordinance depriving him for ever of his office of alderman and his membership of the privy council of the city.[9]

As a member of the High Commission, Huntingdon enjoyed a considerably wider jurisdiction than that which he had in his civil sphere as president of the Council in the North for, while the Council had authority over Yorkshire, Durham, Cumberland, Northumberland and Westmorland, but not over the counties of Lancaster and Chester, the ecclesiastical Province of York included within its boundaries the diocese of Chester in the west and the county of Nottingham in the south. On the prompting of the Privy Council the Northern High Commission turned its attention in 1580 to recusancy within the see of Chester which until then had been left to the local, and largely ineffective, diocesan High Commission: even in the north, Lancashire was notorious for the scant attention it paid to the national religious settlement and the central government now demanded greater conformity. In an attempt to overawe the disobedient, the Privy Councillors required Sandys and Huntingdon to join the fourth Earl of Derby and Chaderton, the newly appointed Bishop of Chester. They ordered these itinerant commissioners to impose higher fines for recusancy, since the lower ones had been little regarded, and to imprison the most obstinate Catholics in Halton Castle: as in the diocese of York they instructed them to concentrate on the principal gentlemen in the area since they believed that once they had been brought to conformity the ordinary people would follow. This extended campaign meant an arduous summer for Huntingdon: from 18 July until 7 September he accompanied this extraordinary itinerant session of the High Commission which sat, besides York, at Beverley, Malton, Ripon, Skipton, Wakefield and Southwell. The commissioners themselves could not stay long enough in any one area to do more than gain an idea of local conditions and try to impress upon the inhabitants the government's determination to drive out Catholicism. They examined some of the most convinced recusants in person who they then bound over to appear at the Michaelmas sitting of the High Commission at York although they concentrated mainly on empanelling local juries which could then continue to enquire into recusancy in the respective deaneries and send suspected persons before the High Commission in the autumn. The Michaelmas session of the High Commission, in consequence, found itself flooded by all these cases of newly discovered recusants. The court punished these Catholics who still refused to conform by charging fines upon their lands, if they were of any social significance, and by binding over the rest, including a number of women, to attend church. It continued to follow up the cases of the recusants discovered in 1580 for some time, but the presence of the Lord President or indeed of the archbishop was not necessary for the routine functioning of the High Commission.[10]

In the decade after 1580 Huntingdon attended the court of High Commission only very infrequently, though, as his activities in other spheres proved, this does not mean that his zeal in suppressing Catholicism decreased. In normal years the court under the direction of such clerics as Matthew Hutton, and the ecclesiastical lawyers Lougher, Bennet, and Gibson could cope with all the cases before it without the need for an influential president. Then in 1592 Huntingdon's presence was required anew, and he sat on the Commission six times in that year. The Privy Council, inspired by Burghley, began a fresh campaign against recusants, particularly against the recusant wives of gentlemen who had conformed: the severer measures affected the whole of England, but they fell especially hard upon the north. A number of the recusant wives belonged to leading northern families and they refused even to make a token conformity: in April six of these ladies, Lady Constable, Mrs. Metham, Mrs. Ingleby, Mrs. Babthorpe, Mrs. Lawson and Mrs. Hungate made their appearance before the court. They had all already been placed in selected Protestant families in a vain attempt to convert them and now the commissioners decided to transfer them to strict imprisonment in Sheriff Hutton Castle: later in the same year Huntingdon witnessed the binding over of further husbands and sons for the appearance of their wives or mothers before the Commission.[11]

Yet, as had happened in the 1570's, the Privy Council had no sooner determined upon a course of action than some of its members began to waver in their support for it and to interfere to shield certain gentlewomen. In 1593, some councillors sent up to the Northern High Commission a petition they had received from Thomas Metham, William Ingleby, Henry Cholmeley, Ralf Babthorpe and Marmaduke Cholmeley on behalf of their wives who had been in prison for the last eighteen months: they pointed out that the gentlemen themselves conformed, that Katherine Radcliffe alone, one of the unmarried gentlewomen, already paid two-thirds of her living in fines and suggested all the ladies should be freed on bond. Not without some justification Huntingdon and his fellow commissioners protested against abandoning a course of action they had only half completed, arguing that much harm might result from enlarging the recusant ladies merely on the security of their husbands' conformity, and they put off freeing them until they had heard again from the Privy Council. The next letter provided further evidence of divided opinions at Westminster: some councillors maintained that they had no recollection of the former letter. Upon further consideration they approved Huntingdon's action in retaining the ladies in prison and gave him complete discretion in his dealings with them in future. Nevertheless he must have realised the practical impossibility of winning over mature and resolute Catholics for he began to take a fresh interest in the Protestant upbringing of the next generation and ordered a new enquiry into the young men who had been sent from York to study abroad in Catholic schools. When he sat again in the High Commission in November 1593 he ordered the release

of Mrs. Metham from Sheriff Hutton on her husband undertaking
to have the Book of Common Prayer read in his house and offering
a surety for her appearance before the Commission the next May.
In this one action the High Commission virtually admitted the
failure of the attempt to coerce the gentlewomen recusants into
accepting conformity.[12]

The dealings of the High Commission with recusancy, however,
constitute only one side of the attempt to crush Catholicism in the
north. Throughout Huntingdon's presidency the government
considered Catholicism as much a civil as an ecclesiastical offence
and so, to the indignation of Father Holtby, to be attacked with
civil as well as ecclesiastical powers. Because of the circumstances
of the rebellion of 1569 the central government required Huntingdon from the beginning to regard Catholicism as a political
offence and in the first commission he sent out from York, in
obedience to the queen's instructions, he associated enquiries
about papists who refused to attend church with others about
those pardoned for their part in the rebellion, those who kept
retainers and those who formed illegal conventicles or lurked in
secret places. In 1573 one William Wharton, a self-appointed spy,
offered to expose to Huntingdon politically disaffected Catholics
in the north who had been negotiating with Mary, Queen of
Scots and, after some prompting from London, he did arrange
for the examination of some suspects. Wharton with Sir John
Forster then devised a much more ambitious plan for exposing
the devices of the Queen of Scots and for revealing her secret
friends in England; the project misfired and by the end of 1574
Wharton found he was in danger of imprisonment himself. The
episode, though insignificant, reveals the uncertainties of the
government: no sources of information on possible political
defectors could be ignored.[13]

This fear of the political implications of recusancy explains why
from the moment of his appointment, Huntingdon issued commissions in the queen's name from York in his capacity as Lord
President concerned with church attendance when he might have

been expected to have grappled with this matter through the High Commission. He took action soon after his arrival in York, and in November 1574 he sent a royal commission from the King's Manor to the mayor and aldermen of York asking for the names of all those who absented themselves from church and especially those of men of wealth and not merely of the humblest citizens as hitherto: he took the occasion to reprimand the civic dignitaries for not setting a good example in this respect themselves. Little improvement followed, and in 1576 he issued a further commission together with an injunction to the corporation to observe more strictly the act for fining recusants. He confessed to Burghley at the same time he thought the 'declination in matters of religion is very great and the obstinacy of many doth shrewdly increase' and he felt that the queen, with the advice of the Privy Council, should take steps to reform matters, 'and of this opinion are both the best and wisest men in these parts with me. Yea, I hear some say, that they were not worse to be liked a little before the last rebellion, than at this present.' Towards the end of 1576 he received the certificates he wanted of the names of recusants in York, together with the reasons for their refusal to attend church and estimates of their wealth: they bore out the statement he had made to Burghley that by far the greater part of the recusants were women, possessing hardly any property of their own who had been too humble as yet to have attracted the attention of the High Commission.[14]

The necessity for harsher measures against recusants which Huntingdon urged upon the government in 1576 gradually gained acceptance: the idea of the extraordinary session of the High Commission in 1580 can be seen in this context; then in 1581 came the new law against Catholics. The 1559 Act which had prescribed a mere 12d. fine for every absence from church had, even when enforced, proved a bagatelle for substantial recusants: now parliament provided for the levy of a fine of £20 a month from proven Catholics. Immediately cognisance of the new law was taken in the north: the judges at the assizes held in York in

July 1581 convicted sixteen on a charge of recusancy. Huntingdon
had now a weapon with teeth to use against the leading Catholic
families; for the first time heavy fines could be imposed on
Catholics under the common law and this may go a long way to
explain why he so rarely attended sessions of the High Commission after this date: Catholics could be more effectively dealt
with in the common law courts. The passing of a law in Elizabethan England by no means implied that it was rigorously
enforced and it has been shown recently how even after 1587
there were never more than nineteen recusants from Yorkshire,
or more than fifteen from Lancashire recorded on the recusancy
rolls as paying all or part of the £20 monthly fine, an infinitesimal
fraction of the known Catholics in the north. The only two
northern Catholics who paid the fine with any regularity were
John Sayer of York and John Towneley of Lancashire, whose
sufferings indeed approached the heroic. Neither physical pains
nor pecuniary mulcts could make Towneley renounce his faith,
as the artist who painted his picture in 1601 recorded for the
benefit of posterity:

This John about the 6 or 7 year of her majesty that now is, for professing the apostolical Catholic Roman faith was imprisoned first at
Chester Castle, then sent to Marshalsea, then to York Castle, then to the
Blockhouses in Hull, then to the Gatehouse in Westminster, then to
Broughton in Oxfordshire, then twice to Ely in Cambridgeshire, and
so now of 73 years old and blind, is bound to appear and to keep within
five miles of Towneley, his house: who hath since the statute of 23rd
[Elizabeth] paid into the Exchequer £20 the month, and doth still, that
there is paid already above £5,000.[15]

Yet the fact that numerically few of the most prosperous
northern Catholics paid the £20 fine does not detract from the
weight the 1581 Act could have *in terrorem*: the knowledge that
the fine could legally be demanded from them at any time must
have been a continuing anxiety for many northern gentlemen.
For persisting in the Catholic faith the 1581 Act prescribed fines
and imprisonment, but for the even greater crimes of turning

John Towneley and his family, of Towneley, Lancashire, at prayer

Edwin Sandys, Archbishop of York 1576–88

from Protestantism to Catholicism, or of receiving the reconcilers, the Catholic priests, the penalty was death. The Elizabethan government reserved its full animosity for the priests themselves who by their ministrations continued to strengthen in their faith those very Catholics it had hoped to reduce to conformity. At one stage the government may have looked forward with some confidence to the time when the Marian priests would die a natural death and the problem of recusancy come to an end but the foundation of seminaries for the training of English priests on the Continent in the 1560's which rapidly produced a new generation of priests for the English mission together with the dispatch of the first Jesuits to England in 1580 dashed all these expectations. Throughout his fight with recusancy in the north Huntingdon recognised the priests as his most dangerous adversaries.

He first took action against Catholic priests in the north in 1578 when he sent a personal letter to the corporation of York together with the formal royal commission to emphasise the need for a strict watch to be kept. He exhorted the corporation to search with the utmost diligence for priests lurking in disguise, since the matter

doth so specially touch the glory of God, the surety of her majesty in her royal seat and the common quiet of this whole state that I am bold to desire you as heartily as I may to have due regard, from time to time, to the doing of your duties in this behalf, for surely there cannot be a worse people in any commonwealth then these Romish, runnagate, reconciling priests be who under the pretence of holiness seek most wickedly to steal the hearts of the simple people from their God and their lawful and undoubted prince.

After the issuing of a proclamation by the queen against Jesuits and seminary priests in January 1581 the government's pressure upon Huntingdon to secure their capture became even stronger. The first Jesuits, Edmund Campion and Robert Parsons had reached England after Easter the previous year: Campion remained at liberty for little more than twelve months before

R

being captured in Berkshire in July 1581 but during this time he had travelled widely in the north encouraging Catholics to stand firm, receiving sympathisers into the Church, preaching to eager congregations in gentlemen's houses. Once they had extorted a confession from Campion, albeit a very guarded one, the Privy Council sent Huntingdon the details of his itinerary in the north: Campion had visited Mrs. Vavasour in York, Mrs. Boulmer, Sir William Babthorpe, Mr. Grimston and Mr. Hawksworth all in Yorkshire before going on to Sir John Southworth's house in Lancashire where he met Mr. Moore and his wife. He had spent Easter 1581 at St. John's Mount, Mr. Harrington's house, and had written there a good part of his book against Protestantism, *Decem Rationes*. The Privy Council wished Huntingdon to have all these places searched and the families questioned how often they had been in the company of Campion or any other Jesuit.[16]

The government so much feared the influence these new, dedicated priests might have in the north that they made strenuous efforts to cut short their missionary activities before they had properly begun: nevertheless some priests succeeded in breaking through their guard. Huntingdon ordered the corporation of Hull, probably in September 1581, to make search between ten o'clock one Wednesday night and eight the next morning for the priests Edward Windsor, alias Digby, and John Boast, alias Harkley. In a short time he built up a spying system which not only informed him of the names priests had assumed in self-protection but also of the places they were the most likely to visit on their journeys: he had his force of searchers ready to set off at short notice, his chosen men on watch over the region. Yet so much did he feel personally involved in this struggle against the enemies of Protestantism that he could not be content with relying on his subordinates: sometimes he threw himself into the thick of the battle. With mounting excitement in October 1581 he described to Walsingham how he had joined in the hunt for Windsor. When the news came in from his spies that the priest had certainly taken refuge at Arthington house he made a surprise ride, late at night, twenty miles west of York: Windsor, he was now convinced, must have escaped the very moment they arrived. He had never seen a better house, he continued, for hiding people in and after he had taken the widow of the house and her family into custody he had intended ordering the floor boards to be taken up, since he had heard there were vaults under the ground, when his searchers found a priest. This priest confessed that Windsor had been there but asserted that he had gone to Nidder-dale; so Huntingdon at once sent some of his men there to see whether he spoke the truth: they had no success. Nevertheless he believed that Windsor must still be in Nidderdale and he told Walsingham he meant to go there himself the next day in the hopes of catching both Windsor and his protector, David Ingleby. Again Windsor eluded the Lord President and had five years of freedom before he fell at last into his hands in November 1586.[17]

This was the sort of energy that Huntingdon would expend on the taking of only one priest: the persecuted Catholics, not surprisingly, saw his organisation as an agency of the devil. Richard Holtby, at this time one of the priests in the north who went in daily fear of his life related how Huntingdon

hath his council of chosen men for the turn, his espials, his informers, his executioners, of picked companions, so ready to run, to seek, to take, to spoil and to execute whatsoever he biddeth them, with such expedition, such insolency, such cruelty, that neither fear of God, respect of law or equity, nor regard of civil honesty, taketh any place amongst them: and although he himself be of a weak constitution of body yet it is incredible what pains he taketh both day and night, in watching, in writing, in travelling, without respect of frost, snow and other importunate weather.[18]

Once a priest had been taken, the Council in the North went on to conduct a preliminary examination which could be little short of an interrogation. Alexander Rawlins, a priest who died for his faith at York in April 1595, left behind his own account of his first appearance before Huntingdon; it proved to be an encounter of two intransigents each convinced he alone possessed the truth.

The proceedings opened inauspiciously when Rawlins refused the oath Huntingdon tendered to him, arguing that a priest ought not to be sworn; next he would not agree to kneel before the Lord President on both knees, saying that he reserved both his knees for God alone and that he must be content with his kneeling on one. With these skirmishes past the examination began with Huntingdon asking the priest his age and how he had spent his time up to that date: Rawlins revealed nothing except the fact that he was about forty years old. After a break, Huntingdon pressed him again to say where he had been reconciled to the Church and where made a priest but got no reply and he disclosed that already he knew a considerable amount about him; he implied that Rawlins had been a recusant when he lived in London, that he had then gone overseas and studied at Rheims, later returned to England and had stayed at Thornley with Father Holtby. Rawlins still refused to speak and Huntingdon and the rest of the council accused him of being a traitor. Rawlins replied he had never entered into any matter of state against his queen or country, but if to be a priest constituted treason, then by their laws they might make him one. This touched Huntingdon to the quick: he insisted that being a priest were no treason, if he had kept himself out of England, but he had left his country without leave and then deliberately associated with such men as Father Holt, Father Parsons, Father Worthington, Dr. Clifford and Sir William Stanley who had lately sworn to encompass the queen's death. This connection between Catholicism and treason was then, and is now, difficult to prove; no such oath as Huntingdon described had been sworn, but Robert Parsons was in correspondence with Philip II, and Sir William Stanley, when in the service of Elizabeth, had betrayed a Dutch fortress into Spanish hands for the sake of religion. Rawlins's examination lasted several hours, with Huntingdon at one moment threatening him, at the next offering him rewards if he would speak, but Rawlins gave nothing away about the families he had visited in Northumberland, Cumberland, Richmondshire and Yorkshire. On reaching this stalemate,

Huntingdon ended the enquiry promising Rawlins his friendship if he would be an honest man; he assured him that he would never say mass again, either there or anywhere else.[19]

If, like Rawlins, a priest refused to speak, the Council in the North could do no more since it had not the power to use torture: for this reason, among others, it frequently sent priests to London for a further examination. The actual trials of priests were always held at the assizes where alone the death penalty could be imposed for the crime of withdrawing the queen's subjects from their allegiance. As Lord President, Huntingdon had the right to sit with the assize judges: he seems to have taken a significant part in the trials, on occasions putting off coming south until they had ended, and when he could not be at the assizes in the summer of 1582 the judges sent to tell him how much they had missed his presence, adding that nevertheless they had been active against traitors and recusants. The first execution of two priests took place at York in August 1582, another priest was hanged there in November and from this time, on an average, two priests were put to death every year in the north until the end of Huntingdon's presidency. Sometimes the Privy Council sent priests who had been captured in the south, or had been conveyed to London for interrogation back to the north to die. By the end of 1595 thirty priests had been executed in the north and eight lay-people, all of whom, with the exception of Margaret Clitherow, had been convicted of harbouring priests. 1586 was the peak year when two priests and three lay-people died at York: four, including one layman, were executed there in 1589 while four priests suffered death in Durham in 1590. This cannot be the full total of all the priests captured when at work in the north for some were executed in London or elsewhere in the south after having been sent there for their trial.[20]

Never during the 1580's and 1590's did the central government allow Huntingdon's attack on northern recusancy to slacken. In 1587 the Privy Council heard that certain people had been appointed to come into the realm to work mischief and treachery, and warned him to have a watch kept at all ports and towns of passage. Again in 1592 they urged him to seek for certain priests secretly concealed in houses within his jurisdiction, and, if he discovered them, to punish them as they deserved for having 'cast off all subjectly obedience'. Since the councillors at Westminster attributed the backwardness of the north to overmuch lenience they instructed him to see that the principal recusants who at the time of the Armada had been imprisoned at Broughton and Ely but had since then been allowed to return home should again be committed to places of strength. Huntingdon responded to the government's demands for the taking of yet stricter precautions against the entry of priests: he at last took the priest, John Boast, in 1593 after many unsuccessful searches, and the next year he captured two leading Catholics, Henry Walpole, a Jesuit, and Lingen, a soldier who had served under Sir William Stanley, very soon after they had landed. [21]

The discovery of John Boast implicated Lady Margaret Neville, the daughter of the late Earl of Westmorland, as he had been seized in her house. A contemporary description happens to have been kept of her trial giving a vivid account of the procedure in recusancy cases which is all the more more valuable since the official records of the northern assizes and quarter sessions no longer survive. This gaol delivery took place before the Lord President, the Dean of Durham, Mr. Purfrey, one of the councillors at York, Calverley, the Chancellor at York and other justices. First they heard a sermon by the dean which contained 'a long amplification of the commandments of the president, in respect of his rare labour and diligence to establish their new gospel and supplant those of contrary religion': after this in the Sessions House their commission was read, the justices, coroners and bailiffs called and the grand inquest empanelled. Mr. Purfrey made the opening speech and fell into a bitter invective against the pope who, he claimed, challenged spiritual jurisdiction over the realm: he maintained that the queen showed no cruelty to any for matters of religion. On the first day only felons and burglars were tried:

the next day Lady Margaret made her appearance, 'and, as some say, the president let fall a few tears when he saw her'. The court advised her to plead guilty and seek the queen's mercy and she confessed her treason in having received a seminary priest contrary to the queen's laws: Grace Claxton was similarly convicted for having sheltered Boast, but both these ladies were respited. Next Thomas Trollope, arraigned for having conveyed a priest called Paterson, pleaded that he had been pardoned five years previously in parliament, and his case was dropped so that John Spede alone, found guilty of arranging places of refuge for a priest called Metcalf, was hanged for an offence concerning religion: in comparison nine felons died.[22]

In the face of this unceasing pressure, occasionally the courage of some committed Catholics broke. Huntingdon won over a somewhat unstable priest, Thomas Bell, in 1593 and he went on to preach in the north against his former faith. The Elizabethan priests, by the very fact of their ordination, had put their allegiance to the Church above that to the state and even lay Catholics discovered that they could not always avoid this dilemma of conflicting loyalties: again a few gave first place to the state. One R. H., a northern gentleman who had been in prison for his Catholicism, volunteered to inform Huntingdon in 1594 about the intentions of Catholic exiles on the Continent and prepared an elaborate code to give news of any proposed invasion, whether through Scotland or directly in the north: he apparently meant to spy and yet remain a Catholic. Some of those Catholics who had succeeded in reconciling their membership of an international Church with their national allegiance might not have regarded his behaviour as dishonourable: increasingly, the government played upon this division of loyalties.[23]

Both at the trials of recusants and at their execution Huntingdon did his best to see that the government's propaganda that no man suffered merely for his religious beliefs received wide dissemination. He no more than Burghley would admit that the cruelty lay in preventing men from worshipping as they thought right: the northern Catholics could not exist as Catholics without the ministrations of their priests, yet to harbour priests had become treason. As the officer most immediately concerned with the implementation of these harsh laws most Catholics regarded Huntingdon as some inhuman monster, but the more discerning of them recognised he was the agent, not the originator of the government's policy, directed especially by Burghley, 'the old practising treasurer'. Huntingdon's death brought no end to the persecution of Catholics in the north which continued to fluctuate according to the efficiency and enthusiasm of the president of the council and to the political manœuvres of the central government. These twenty years of oppression certainly did not solve the problem of recusancy: many Catholic sympathisers conformed; under Huntingdon's strict surveillance, a considerable change took place in the religious attitude of town corporations but in country districts, especially in Lancashire, the dedication of the priests protected by the local gentry won many back to the Catholic faith. The region still reflects the religious divisions of Elizabethan times: north Lancashire remains strongly Catholic and Preston has the largest number of Catholics in proportion to its population of any town in England. Within the province of the Council in the North Huntingdon seems to have held the line: the extent of Catholicism when he came to office and when he died probably did not change greatly, though its distribution altered. The type of Catholicism, however, which emerged during the persecution changed very much: those Catholics who faced fines, imprisonment and death for their faith were very different people from some of the conservative supporters of the old religion Huntingdon first met in the High Commission court. As these waverers fell away a type of Catholic filled their places prepared, even eager for martyrdom, and of these new confessors Margaret Clitherow stands as the epitome: in 1586 she was pressed to death in York for refusing to stand trial on a charge of sheltering priests. There were probably more better informed Catholics in the north in 1595, as there were more convinced Protestants: the labours of the missionary priests, the zeal of Huntingdon and his Protestant ministers had caused the shrinking of the indifferent mass where perhaps the majority of northerners still belonged.[24]

* * *

The queen with certain members of her Privy Council professed herself satisfied with a formal acceptance of the Established Church, but Huntingdon, actually working in the north, strove for a more exhilarating ideal than this. He cast down Catholicism not so much out of a love of destruction (though most Protestants then enjoyed helping to overthrow the outward symbols of Antichrist) as to build anew. He took it upon himself to establish in the void created by the breakdown of the old Catholic system a purified Protestant Church. On his arrival in York he could scarcely have found a more sympathetic helper than he did in Edmund Grindal, who had been archbishop since 1570: both men, so alike in their missionary zeal, drew comfort from their three years of partnership. Grindal who never seems to have written to Burghley without including some tribute to the Lord President began his praise only two months after Huntingdon had reached the north: 'my lord president's good government here among us daily more and more discovereth the rare gifts and virtues which afore were in him, but in private life were hid from the eyes of a great number. The old proverb is well verified in him, *Magistratus probat virum*.' Huntingdon at once reacted equally favourably to Grindal and never changed his opinion: 'severity in justice', he told Burghley, 'next to the preaching of the gospel, which truly does greatly want in these parts, will prove the best bridle for this people . . . the archbishop certifies in all matters ecclesiastical and is both diligent and severe, so far as his commission will suffer.'[25]

From this time onwards, Grindal rarely expressed an opinion on any matter affecting the north without prefacing it with a preliminary, 'my lord president and I'. He worried, as he confided to Burghley in 1574, that Huntingdon through his diligence in the queen's service might be seriously overstraining his own resources, a development none of his other friends seems to have noticed at this early stage.

Of my Lord President's good government here I need not to write: your lordship hath daily experience of it by his advertisements from hence. We are in good quietness (God be thanked), both for civil and ecclesiastical state. My lord president serveth here very honourably and chargeably, as I have heretofore signified to your lordship. I fear he surchargeth himself: I know not, but if it be otherwise, I may say, *Amice timui*. Surely I trust God hath prepared him to be a special good instrument for this commonwealth.[26]

Towards the end of 1575 the queen agreed to Grindal's translation from York to the see of Canterbury, left vacant by the death of Archbishop Parker. Huntingdon, in a letter to Burghley, rejoiced at his promotion, 'of whom I must say without offence to others, that I know none worthy to be preferred before him to that place for many respects'. Yet he lamented the great loss to the north:

And yet whiles I serve here I am as loath he should be changed, but that place requireth such a sufficient man, and therefore I shall be glad if her majesty appoint him to the place, but I beseech your lordship of your help that such one succeed him as will be comfortable to the godly and a terror to the adversary.

For Grindal and Huntingdon alike it would have proved happier if the archbishop had been allowed to remain in the north for there he had been free to encourage a higher standard of learning among the clergy and had given his blessing to the setting up of monthly exercises where the clergy catechised themselves on biblical themes to the edification of their weaker brethren, and some of the interested laity. Grindal boasted that in the six years he worked in the north he had procured forty learned preachers and graduates to come into the diocese.[27]

The queen had no such love for abundant preaching or for clerical colloquies, particularly those where lay people might intrude themselves which she regarded as possible centres for political subversion. In his first year at Canterbury the queen ordered Grindal to suppress the exercises in his province. The command ran counter to all his cherished theories; in the north he had believed that preaching and the better education of the clergy were the only ways to obtain a purified, confessing church and now the queen wished him to abandon what he saw as one of the chief instruments to bring about this end. In a letter of great power and of great courage he refused to obey the queen's commands, offering rather to resign his see than act against his conscience. The queen replied by sequestering the archbishop from his episcopal jurisdiction although she did not deprive him of his office. All Huntingdon's sympathies lay with Grindal, and he waited anxiously at York for news of his fate. In May 1578, he passed on the information to Matthew Hutton, Dean of York, that Grindal was on the point of being released, through the intervention of Hatton, when the queen heard from the Bishop of Durham, and Sandys, the new Archbishop of York, of the amount of Puritanism in their diocese and stayed her hand. Huntingdon at once taxed Sandys with sending a report so prejudicial to Grindal but he denied having written about the spread of Puritanism in general and maintained he had rather stressed the amount of Catholicism still prevalent in the north. In further argument Huntingdon even won an admission from Sandys that his diocese harboured no Puritanism. The damage, however, was done and all Huntingdon's efforts to help his friend had no success: Grindal died in 1583 still suspended from exercising the duties of his office.[28]

Huntingdon's partisan support of Grindal from the first impaired his relations with his successor. Sandys in theology shared Grindal's opinions, like him he had gone into exile in Mary's reign, but he was far more of a disciplinarian, intent upon exacting compliance to the religious settlement from Protestants as well as Catholics, and in this respect he was not the type of godly bishop, of 'a sound judgment and zeal in religion', 'wise and stout' (against Catholics) for whom Huntingdon had hoped. By enquiring too nicely into Protestant deviations from the Prayer Book, Huntingdon must have considered that Sandys might well undermine the Protestantism he and Grindal had laboured to plant: on his side Sandys, always incensed by any attempts by laymen to spoil the Church yet further of its possessions, felt bitter about Huntingdon's attempt to gain a lease of the episcopal manor of Bishopthorpe while the see was vacant. The underlying hostility between the two men came to the surface in October 1578. During the interregnum between Grindal's translation to Canterbury and Sandys's elevation to York, the centuries-old quarrel over the conflicting jurisdictions of the archbishopric of York and the bishopric of Durham had broken out afresh when, on the death of the Bishop of Durham, the Dean and Chapter of Durham had prevented representatives of the archbishopric by force from entering the cathedral. Late in 1576 the dispute had been submitted to Huntingdon who brought the two parties to agree to a compromise for the time being but Sandys arrived in York before a final agreement had been made. A hasty-tempered man, Sandys consequently had reason for his animosity towards William Whittingham, the Dean of Durham, who had led the attack on what he considered to be the rights of his see. The Lord President, on the other hand, had already acted as Whittingham's protector when he had been an itinerant preacher in Leicestershire. Whittingham had gone up to Durham in 1563, and with James Pilkington as bishop, his brothers Leonard and John Pilkington, Thomas and Ralph Lever, Adam Halliday, Thomas Horton and John Fox all holding prebends there, the diocese of Durham soon became known as a centre of extreme Protestantism. For some time the Privy Council had received petitions from Durham tenants against the harsh dealings of the dean and chapter: their alleged economic grievances, the recent controversy between York and Durham together with the rumours of radical Protestant practices caused the government to decide upon a visitation.[29]

The commission authorising the visitation of Durham Cathedral reached the Bishops of York and Durham, the Lord President and others probably early in 1578: only after a censure from the Privy Council which accused some of favouritism towards the Dean of Durham did they proceed upon it in October. The first question the commission considered when it sat in the cathedral on 23 October was whether Whittingham had been admitted a deacon or priest according to the ecclesiastical laws of England or whether he was a mere layman. In the subsequent examination, the Dean of York, Hutton, took Whittingham's part while the archbishop violently attacked him: the examination soon degenerated into a quarrel between Sandys and Hutton and the archbishop lost control of his temper altogether when the dean glanced at his own ordination in the Church of Rome. The commissioners forgot Whittingham in the hurly burly and it fell to Huntingdon to try to keep the peace between them. The archbishop then accused him of favouring Hutton for his pains and the whole sitting had to be suspended: to explain their signal lack of progress the commissioners sent a sworn account of their proceedings to London.[30]

In the interval before they resumed their visitation, Huntingdon wrote to Burghley to let him know of his personal views on the examination of Whittingham, making it clear that he, no less than Grindal, would make a stand on a matter of conscience. So far, he told him, the commissioners had not enquired at all into the general abuses at Durham, as they had been instructed to do, but had concerned themselves only with the dean:

Against the dean this matter is first articulated and most specially urged, viz., that he was not made minister according to the laws of this realm, but is mere *laicus*; and so to be deprived. . . . How in other matters alleged against him there may fall out good cause of deprivation, I know not yet; but if it be the mark, as it is indeed, if the *vox populi* be true, I wish it should be hit some other way, rather then once touched by this that concerned his ministry.

Whittingham had said he could prove his vocation to be such as all ministers used to have which led Huntingdon on to protest,

Your lordship can judge what flame this spark is like to breed, if it should kindle; for it cannot but be evil taken of all the godly learned both at home, and in all the reformed Churches abroad, that we should allow of the popish massing priests in our ministry and disallow of the minister made in a Church reformed.

Already there had been open disagreements between the Archbishop and the Dean of York on the matter: 'And for myself, I must confess to your lordship plainly, that I think in conscience I may not agree to the sentence of deprivation for this cause only.'[31]

In spite of his sympathy for Whittingham, Huntingdon still tried to appear as an impartial arbitrator when the commissioners resumed their sitting on 25 November at York. After Whittingham had provided proof of his calling at Geneva the archbishop pressed the other commissioners to give their opinions whether they thought he should be deprived or not before they had gone on to consider his other offences. Only the Bishop of Durham and Dr. Lougher, the canon lawyer, unequivocally agreed with Sandys that Whittingham should be deprived: the other seven commissioners objected strongly to this procedure, maintaining that sentence should not be given until all his alleged offences had been examined. Huntingdon moved that the whole matter be laid before the Privy Council, and put forward the cogent (and convenient) argument that since the queen had appointed Whittingham by letters patent in the first place she, with the Privy Council, constituted the best qualified body to interpret the letters patent. The sitting again broke down on this point of procedure. Huntingdon, Hutton and their five fellow commissioners sent in their majority report in which they said they thought all the charges against Whittingham should be heard before they went on to give sentence: Sandys, Barnes, and Lougher wrote directly to the queen stating that they considered Whittingham should be deprived forthwith. Before the commission could be reconvened the next spring Whittingham died, still Dean of Durham, and Huntingdon had not to make the ultimate choice between obedience to the queen's wishes and the dictates of his own conscience. In his will which was dated 18 April 1579, Whittingham left a book, with a cover silver-gilt, to the Countess of Huntingdon among others.[32]

For some time after Whittingham's death Sandys rejected all attempts by Burghley and Leicester to reconcile him to Huntingdon: hinting that the Lord President had fallen into disgrace with the queen because of his defence of the Dean of Durham, he said he would not prejudice himself by associating with him. Hutton, also, came to feel the strength of his resentment. Sandys tried to get him appointed Bishop of Lichfield to be rid of him at York, alleging that 'as long as these two [Huntingdon and Hutton] band together I shall never do good there'. A new quarrel flared up between Sandys and Hutton in 1585 when the archbishop tried to prohibit all transactions containing any element of usury. Hutton flew to the opposite extreme and acted as the spokesman of the York money-lenders: he argued that the taking of interest could be justified on theological grounds and said the High Commission had exceeded its authority by attacking a practice allowed by the state. Sandys's stratagem to secure Hutton's removal failed: he remained at York throughout Sandys's life and, after a period as Bishop of Durham, succeeded him eventually as Archbishop of York.[33]

This acrimonious dispute between Huntingdon and Sandys broke for a time but did not permanently impair the close relations which usually existed between the chief officers in the State and in the Church in the north in the last quarter of the sixteenth century. Generally, the Lord President and his councillors were at one with the churchmen in their desire to encourage evangelical Protestantism. Sir Francis Hastings scarcely exaggerated Huntingdon's industry when he described how his brother

never set a straying foot in any place, where he did not labour at the least to settle the preaching of the word to the people. And in many places I know he brought it to pass to the comfort of many consciences, and the knitting of their hearts in all loyalty and obedience to their sovereign and queen: and in whomsoever he found either backwardness or blind ignorance, he would seek lovingly to have them instructed, or else by just severity to correct and reform them.

Huntingdon and Grindal in their preoccupation with the problems which lay ahead tended at times to give the impression that they thought the north was universally Catholic in sympathy, yet in their more reflective moments they knew that this was not true. Durham had become a centre of Protestantism early in the reign. In 1561, Archbishop Parker had appointed Richard Midgley to Rochdale and first as vicar, then as itinerant preacher he had a great influence in disseminating Protestantism in Lancashire throughout the remainder of the century: even in that conservative county in the 1560's he did not labour alone. To the east, in Yorkshire, Hull had been one of the first of the northern towns to welcome Protestant ideas from the Continent. Grindal himself attributed the loyalty of the inhabitants of Halifax which at the time of the rebellion had been ready 'to bring 3 or 4,000 able men into the field to serve your majesty' to the plentifulness of preaching there. These, however, only formed pockets of advanced Protestantism; the prevailing mood in 1572 was one of apathy if not declared hostility to the Elizabethan religious settlement. Huntingdon believed he had been called to transform this indifference into enthusiasm and thought that this change could most effectively be brought about through constant preaching.[34]

Huntingdon began his long struggle with the undoubtedly backward city of York in 1579 when he suggested to a reluctant corporation that it ought to have its own preacher. The mayor, Robert Cripling (whose subsequent behaviour showed him to be no lover of sermons), informed Huntingdon that, in compliance with his suggestion, the corporation had written to every company and fellowship in the city to find out what each would give to maintain a preacher. The companies had replied that they thought York differed greatly from Newcastle or Hull which had no cathedral or bishop, or even preachers unless they made provision for them: York, they argued, already had a bishop, and he divers chaplains, besides the dean, the chancellor, two archdeacons and many prebendaries. They declared they would go to the Minster to hear sermons but did not see that they should tax themselves to provide yet another preacher — only the Fellowship of Merchants and the Fellowship of Drapers agreed to make any contribution.

This ingenious argument convinced neither Huntingdon nor the rest of the council: later in the year the city promised to appoint a preacher if enough money could be raised to support him. Huntingdon made sure that the money was forthcoming and by 1582 the corporation had collected sufficient funds to admit Mr. Middop as their preacher at a salary of £30. He did not hold the office long; at the beginning of 1585 several York aldermen obediently applied to Henry Cheek, the secretary of the Council in the North, to find another learned preacher for them, and he supplied them with Richard Harwood. A generation worked a remarkable change in the sympathies of the corporation of York: in 1607 the city fathers took the initiative in exhorting the local ministers to see that their congregations attended one of the three sermons being given in York on Sunday afternoons at two o'clock; the next year, on the petition of eighty-nine citizens, the corporation gave a willing sanction to the proposal that three additional lectureships should be created to supplement the work of the town preacher so that there might be simultaneous sermons in each of the four wards of the city.[35]

The York aldermen admitted that the towns of Hull and Newcastle already had their town preachers by 1579, but the mere institution of the office alone could not satisfy Huntingdon, he had to go on to ensure that the preachers were of a suitably evangelising temper. On his prompting, the inhabitants of Newcastle invited John Udall to be their preacher immediately after he had been deprived of his living of Kingston upon Thames for his unrestrained preaching. While still at Kingston, Udall had dedicated his book, *The combat betwixt Christ and the Devil*, to Huntingdon in gratitude for the favours he had already received from him and in the confidence that the doctrine he had expressed would be acceptable. During the year he ministered in Newcastle the rumour spread that Udall had helped in the production of the Marprelate Tracts in which the leading English bishops were cruelly lampooned: the Privy Council summoned him to London in 1590 and later in the year he was tried as an alleged accomplice of Martin Marprelate and condemned to death though the sentence was subsequently commuted.[36] Huntingdon next recommended a somewhat less revolutionary preacher to the corporation, though again he proved to be a Nonconformist. In 1584 Richard Holdsworth had lost his living in Lincolnshire because of his doubts about 'divers weighty matters and points in the Book of Common Prayer': the following year Huntingdon had made him one of his household chaplains in the north and he obviously considered him a worthy successor to Udall. In 1592 the Newcastle chamberlains found it necessary to negotiate with Huntingdon about Holdsworth's stipend and in the end they agreed to pay him £20 a year and £80 arrears.[37]

John Favour was another of Huntingdon's chaplains who became established in the north. Huntingdon, who during the latter part of his presidency used Favour to argue with obstinate Catholics, thought highly of him and in 1593 gave him his presentation copy of the Geneva Bible, as he proudly recorded on the title page: 'sum Joannis Favoris ex dono honoratissimi et religiosissimi Domini mei Comitis Hu[n]tingdoniae.' He obtained the living of Halifax in 1594 and during the thirty years of his incumbency the town developed into a notable centre of Protestantism. Favour proved to be that type of godly minister, learned and zealous, careful as well for the material as the spiritual needs of his flock that Huntingdon particularly admired. Besides writing a learned work to show the primitive simplicity of the early Church, *Antiquity triumphing over novelty*, Favour occupied his time 'preaching every Sabbath day, lecturing every day in the week, exercising justice in the commonwealth, practising of physic and surgery in the great penury and necessity thereof in the country where I live, and that only for God's sake.'[38]

Another clothing town in the West Riding enjoyed Huntingdon's special support in its strivings to obtain a plentiful supply of preaching. By 1588 Alexander Faucet, the Vicar of Leeds, had become incapacitated by age and infirmities; in the eyes of his more eager parishioners he had anyway never been well qualified to fulfil the duties of his office. To make sure that an honest, learned and able minister should succeed him, some of the leading members of the parish decided to purchase the advowson for themselves. They applied to Oliver Darnelye, the holder of the presentation, 'who demanded for the same 150 li. but understanding the godly design of the parishioners and being well affected thereunto, he abated 20 li. in the price, by the mediation of the right honourable Henry, Earl of Huntingdon, then Lord President of the north. Whereupon Robert Cooke a famous and learned man . . . was presented by the purchasers who had the monies refunded to them by a voluntary contribution of such of the parochians as were able and willing.' As a further earnest of his good will to the town, Huntingdon sent in 1589 'certain books to the schoolmaster to be taught in the school at Leeds'. For a learned curate of the parish church of Leeds, John Lyster, Huntingdon found the living of Thorp Arch in Yorkshire, and in gratitude for the fact 'that by your lordship's good means I obtained the benefice whereof I am now resident' Lyster dedicated to him his book, *A rule how to bring up children*.[39]

Neither the bounds of the see of York nor the confines of the Council in the North limited Huntingdon's field of action: the whole of the north of England became his province when the future of Protestantism was at stake. He turned his attention early to the diocese of Chester, which never came under the jurisdiction of the Council of the North, since he realised that the appointment of William Chadderton as Bishop of Chester in 1579 gave him an opportunity of winning over the largely Catholic county of Lancashire. He wrote at once to applaud the new bishop's decision to reside in Manchester, not in Chester as had previously been the custom, and as soon as he had established himself there Huntingdon, doubtless with his own successes with the town of Leicester in mind, urged upon him a scheme of public preaching:

And surely, by the grace of God, the well planting of the gospel in Manchester, and the parishes near to it, shall in time effect much good in other places: if in Manchester there were an hour spent every

morning from six to seven, or from seven to eight in prayer and a
lecture, as *brevis oratio*, as it is said, *penetraret coelus*, so short lessons,
often taught, it is like, no doubt, but the grace will pierce many hearts.
The prayer and the lecture might begin and end with the clock.

In his many struggles Chadderton never lacked Huntingdon's
support, urging him 'not to faint but go forward with good
courage, *pie et prudente*'. Huntingdon, who considered that
Chadderton as an act of policy should first plant the market towns
with good preachers, concerned himself with other towns in
Lancashire besides Manchester. 'Good my lord, be careful to
Preston and other places in your silly country. Surely the want of
diligent and faithful preaching doth wonderfully hinder the
building of our church, and in these north parts it is most apparent.' Once he had procured a good preacher not even then
could Huntingdon turn his attention to other matters. In
December 1582 conservatives in Richmond (then in the diocese
of Chester) rioted against Mr. Sothebie, 'their preaching pastor':
he recommended the bishop to act firmly and then had 'no doubt
but the Lord in time will have a pretty flock there'.[40]

Huntingdon's persistence had its reward, and in the Lancashire
towns, particularly in the hundreds of Salford and Rochdale, a
radical type of Protestantism flourished. By 1590 there were
seventeen preachers in the county who felt compelled to draw up
a condemnation of the 'manifold enormities of the ecclesiastical
state in the most parts of the county'. They abhorred most the
recourse of Jesuit and seminary priests to the county, the bad
behaviour of recusants in church and the popish ceremonies
which still continued at weddings, baptisms and funerals, and
spoke of the difficulties preachers had in keeping their congregations attentive to sermons. It is significant, that out of these
seventeen who protested, eight, together with a further three who
had not signed the condemnation, were presented before the
Archbishop of York at his visitation of 1590 for not wearing the
surplice. For these warriors against popery the emerging Anglican
ideal of the middle way had few attractions.[41]

Because of the length of the struggle with Catholicism in the north the central government and the northern prelates in particular usually overlooked a certain amount of Nonconformity there which they would not have tolerated in the south and the exercises for improving the learning of the clergy which Grindal had defended so ardently on his translation to Canterbury were never prohibited in the province of York. In Manchester the exercises, which Bishop Chadderton patronised, had a continuous history from 1585 and the leading incumbents of the area, William Langley of Prestwich, Peter Shaw of Bury, Richard Midgley of Rochdale and Oliver Carter of Manchester all acted as moderators while preachers from the Manchester exercises occasionally went across to the West Riding exercises which flourished around Leeds, Pudsey and Halifax early in the seventeenth century. The seeds for these Yorkshire exercises were sown, if they did not actually come into being, during Huntingdon's presidency: his chaplain, John Favour of Halifax, energetically helped in their organisation and a former Leicestershire minister and friend of Anthony Gilby, James Gosnell, came over from Bolton as a visiting preacher. Further exercises probably developed later, in the seventeenth century, in the East Riding in the neighbourhood of Rowley, and also in Sheffield.[42] Some details of the sermons preached at the West Riding exercises have survived but generally these seem to have been the sort of gatherings which left few records behind. The active part the Lord President took in the promotion of the exercises is indicated by a stray letter of 1595 which Francis Kaye, who had been headmaster of Durham school and vicar of Heighington before he accepted the living of Northallerton in 1593, wrote to Huntingdon in reply to his enquiry about the recommencing of the Wednesday exercises at Northallerton. When they had broken off for the winter, he explained to Huntingdon, all the preachers present had agreed that the exercise should begin again on Easter Wednesday but, since Easter fell late in 1595, he promised to do all he could to persuade his fellow ministers to accept Huntingdon's suggestion that it should start again on the first Wednesday in March as it had done in previous years:

> Yet so small hath been our encouragement and the audience so slender the last year that except your honour's countenance and other good means procure a better auditory I fear the exercise will not long continue: and the rather for that Mr. Scotte and others are like to be drawn from us to Richmond, unless your lordship be a mean to the contrary.

If towns like Northallerton and Richmond, where only ten years earlier Huntingdon had been contending with the townspeople's dislike of their preaching pastor, could support exercises it seems probable that similar gatherings grew up in the vicinity of larger towns such as York, Durham and Hull. For the two other north-eastern towns of importance, Newcastle and Berwick, a little more substantial evidence exists: in Newcastle a later vicar of St. Nicholas's asserted that prophesyings began during the incumbency of the Scottish Protestant, John Magbray (or Mackbury), who held the living for fifteen years before his death in 1584, and he also said that exercises had been established early in Berwick through the influence of John Knox.[43]

Huntingdon fostered these exercises because he believed strongly that a deeper theological education could not fail to confirm the ministers in their Protestant opinions and so make them in their turn more enthusiastic and more able instructors of their own congregations. While he lived in the north he did not confine himself to projects designed to benefit only his own region but remained a generous patron of religious scholarship whatever its origin. As a ballad writer proclaimed

> He built up no palace, nor purchased no town,
> But gave it to scholars to get him renown;
> As Oxford and Cambridge can rightly declare,
> How many poor scholars maintainèd are there.[44]

Before he went into the north his good name for rewarding works of godly scholarship preceded him. In 1572 John Stockwood, in his translation of Bullinger's *Commonplaces of the Christian religion* paid tribute to 'that natural clemency and loving mind, that hath always been found in you towards such as have yielded up their labours for the furtherance of Christ his congregation, under your honourable protection'. As the reign progressed Huntingdon lent his aid to the production of original theological works in addition to the numerous translations of these works of Continental divines. John Marbecke, the theologian and musician, who in 1550 had been the first to make a complete concordance of the Bible in English, enjoyed Huntingdon's protection: still in 1580 his great work had not appeared in print and he anxiously solicited his assistance in *A book of notes and commonplaces with their exposition collected and gathered out of the works of divers singular writers and brought alphabetically into order*:

And now, right honourable, having as yet no help for the publishing of my Concordance, which without special help is like to lie not only helpless, but also fruitless, inclosed in a huge volume of mine own writing, wherein I have spent many years, in purpose thereby to profit the studies of the godly affected, in the English tongue, so that I am not able, as my meaning was, to exhibit the same unto you: I shall most humbly beseech your honour to accept and take in good part my simple travails in this other work which God of his goodness, in these mine old years, hath now brought forth in me: that I may not seem altogether unfruitful to the Church of God, nor unthankful unto you mine especial good lord, but at the least a testification of my faithful heart to God's people, and of my goodwill to your honour, may somewhat therein appear.[45]

Hugh Broughton was another highly learned (though rather eccentric) biblical scholar consciously working to enlarge the knowledge of the godly affected and he also broadcast to the world the munificent help Huntingdon had given him. In 1580, Huntingdon intervened with Burghley that Broughton might be dispensed from residing on his prebend in Durham and allowed to stay on in Cambridge. Fourteen years later he published *A Seder Olam*, a register of biblical chronology from the creation of Adam to the ascension of Christ, which he dedicated to his patron, adding a somewhat invidious list of those others who had aided his labours but whose generosity had fallen far short of that of his good lord:

Of your lordship I may say out of Homer (*Odyssey* I), that you have been unto me as a father to the son, and I will never forget that tendering. I found many honourable patrons, but your lordship's charges were the greatest. The Archbishop of Canterbury's grace was the means, soon after my coming to Cambridge in my young years, to procure me a continual profession of Homer's tongue; whereupon with all speed the rest of my success proceeded, until Sir Walter Mildmay's lecture in Greek, with the gift of six scholarships as I would, and his fatherlike favour better encouraged my pains. And I should injure all the governors of Cambridge if I would not acknowledge continual singular cherishing, and one point in offering whether lecture I would of Japeth and Shems chief tongues. But there to me your lordship's charges were five and twenty times more then the private Greek profession, and about ten times the value of a fellowship by year. The greatest allowance any nobleman granted any scholar. So great a desire you had that my painful and chargeful race of study, which you judged by your experience able to go through the pikes against the common errors, should there have practice and trial.[46]

Huntingdon countenanced Broughton's non-residence at Durham because he believed that through his scholarship he would eventually enrich the whole of the Church. On balance, however, he must have introduced far more educated clergy into the north than the one or two from the north his generosity permitted to remain studying in the south. He opened his household to foreigners who had gone into exile for the sake of religion and foreign scholars, no less than English, had reason to be grateful for his patronage. Beza, when he dedicated his Latin version of the Psalms to Huntingdon in 1580 referred generally to the French exiles for the sake of the gospel whom he had befriended. Peter Loselerius Villerius was one of these; minister to the French congregation in London he was incorporated doctor of civil law and of divinity in Oxford in 1576 and later went on to become chaplain and adviser to William the Silent. For himself and also in the name of his fellow exiles who owed so much to him, Villerius offered Huntingdon the first fruits of his labours, a Latin translation of Beza's *Commentary on the New Testament*. One of these exiles, François de Civille, certainly found his way to York and spent some time there as a member of Huntingdon's household from which he conducted a learned correspondence with his friend, Anthony Gilby. In 1582 he went on a visit to Rouen where he fell ill, and for a time could not return to Huntingdon 'in whose service I hold nothing so dear, whether goods or life, that I would not employ it with my whole heart'. The presence of these foreign exiles in aristocratic households with their books and their learning and their stories of persecution must have had the effect of making English noblemen more European in their outlook. As Dr. Collinson has recently shown, the growth of English Sabbatarianism was largely brought about by the surprisingly wide reading of Continental authors by English Protestants.[47]

Only the households of the Archbishop of York and his three fellow bishops can have equalled the influence of Huntingdon's household upon the development of Protestantism in the north. Like them Huntingdon called learned preachers to be his chaplains and though some of these enthusiastic young men only worked in the north for a time, others, like Holdsworth and Favour ultimately settled there. Lancelot Andrewes and Thomas Morton at the beginning of their careers which later led to great eminence in the Church acted as chaplains to Huntingdon and became celebrated for their skill in disputing with Catholics.[48] Mr. Browne, late a student of Christchurch, was another of his chaplains very active as a preacher in the north: during a vacancy he temporarily filled the office of city preacher at York and Robert Sparke wanted very much to come north to join him at Huntingdon's side when the invasion by the Spaniards seemed imminent. Nathaniel Gilby, son of Anthony Gilby, and Huntingdon's last chaplain, entered his household at York only a few months before his master died. He had been one of the first students of Emmanuel College, Cambridge, and held a fellowship there: while still at Cambridge he translated Sohn's *A brief and learned treatise . . . of the Antichrist*, in which he had proclaimed the favours of the Countess of Huntingdon, and of the earl himself, his good lord, which had been 'comfortable to many of God's children, and especially vouchsafed to my father, my self and other friends'.[49]

Apart from these offices within his household Huntingdon owned no livings in the north of England yet this did not prevent him from trying to influence the choice of northern gentlemen and often he succeeded in establishing his own candidates. Robert Moore (who as rector of Guiseley from 1581 until the time of the Civil War did so much to make the southern part of Craven a Protestant area) described in his will how Huntingdon helped to bring him to his benefice. He had left Cambridge at the age of twenty-three and gone to Skipton castle at the request of the Earl of Cumberland and his wife, the daughter of the second Earl of Bedford, and there he remained a year and a half,

preaching in Craven and once or twice at Guiseley upon intreaty. It pleased God thereby to work such an earnest desire and constant resolution in my predecessor, Mr. Bateman, to resign and give over his charge of his people, by reason of his own disability, that the noble earl of Huntingdon, understanding thereof, did acquaint my lord of Cumberland and his lady therewith, and moved them to make known to that most worthy earl of Bedford.

Bedford spoke with Warwick (another son-in-law), with Lord Peregrine Bertie, Lord Willoughby, the Earl of Oxford and Sir Francis Walsingham who all happened to be at court and had heard Moore preach with such an effect that they bought the advowson of Guiseley between them and presented Moore to it. At the time of the circulation of the Marprelate Tracts, Moore was accused of having received a copy from Giles Wigginton, once minister of Sedbergh: Moore escaped punishment, but Wigginton lost his living in 1586. Huntingdon and Warwick both joined in a petition for his restoration, in this instance in vain. Wigginton must have been a remarkable and courageous man: doubtless under Huntingdon's protection, he appeared as a minister in York at the time of the trial of the Catholic Margaret Clitherow and he was brave enough to plead on her behalf.[50]

Other northern landowners encountered the president's determination to get adequate ministers settled in the north. His own aunt, Lady Winifred Hastings, held the parsonage of Rowley in Yorkshire: in 1582 he urged her to make over the next presentation to Sir Henry Gates as he felt confident he would choose an honest, learned minister. Since Rowley subsequently became a centre for the East Riding exercises it seems she granted his request. Huntingdon had less success with the Earls of Shrewsbury. He tried to persuade George, sixth Earl of Shrewsbury to present Edward Clayton to his living of Tasley, in Shropshire, in 1584 since it was sufficient to maintain a preacher: Shrewsbury replied he had already sent to Cambridge for another candidate, though he promised to appoint a preacher. Not discouraged, Huntingdon in 1592 recommended another minister to his son Gilbert for the parsonage of Drax in the West Riding 'where for many respects I wish a better incumbent were placed then for many years past hath possessed the place'.[51]

Since Huntingdon showed an interest in the filling of these obscure livings he could scarcely fail to concern himself over the appointment of bishops to vacant sees in the north. When the queen summoned Grindal to Canterbury Huntingdon merely listed the qualities he thought necessary in a man chosen to succeed him at York, but as the years passed his diffidence decreased and he began to nominate specific candidates. Hunsdon thought Huntingdon wanted Toby Matthew to be made Bishop of Durham in 1587. In fact Matthew Hutton became bishop there in 1589 but this can hardly have displeased Huntingdon as they had worked in close co-operation ever since Huntingdon had come to the north and Hutton had been one of the chief defenders of Whittingham in 1578. Toby Matthew's turn came later when the see of Durham became vacant again in 1596. In 1594 Richard Howland, then Bishop of Peterborough, thought he had Huntingdon's nomination for York: he misjudged the signs, for in that year Hutton returned to York as archbishop and Huntingdon regained 'a man skilful to govern and guide others by his counsel etc. *in rebus politicis*'. On Hutton's death Matthew again came into his office: both archbishops were noted for their tolerance of the more moderate Protestant Nonconformists.[52]

Huntingdon found it easier to manipulate the disposing of Protestant clergy in the north, bringing in a preacher here, advancing another there, than to influence the religion of the northern gentry. Nevertheless, he persevered and did his best to encourage Protestant gentlemen. The Protestant stalwarts, such as the Bowes family, or the Gates, could rely on his friendship, but the north did not boast many such families and there were indeed few which did not harbour some Catholic or conservative members. When he considered his personal example might win over the waverers Huntingdon always led the way: he rarely missed attending sermons in state, and Toby Matthew, as Bishop of Durham, recorded how he preached before the Lord President no fewer than twenty-three times. Matthew Hutton published one sermon he preached before Huntingdon and other noblemen and gentlemen at a general communion at York in September 1576: he used the occasion to try to convince his congregation by erudition rather than acerbity, that the practices of the English Church agreed more perfectly with those of the primitive Church than did those of the Church of Rome, and that Romish ceremonies, far from being ancient as his adversaries argued, were mere innovations. Huntingdon placed great faith in these general communions held, for example, in York in 1576, in Richmond in 1580 and in Durham in 1592 and apparently thought that once gentlemen had in this way publicly shown their adherence to Protestantism they were less likely to regress. Yet still in 1595 many gentlemen remained apathetic if not worse, and Huntingdon seized with alacrity the chance of marrying his ward to the Protestant Sir Thomas Hoby and so of planting one more godly household in a backward area of Yorkshire.[53]

Huntingdon's extraordinary zeal for propagating Protestantism did not pass unnoticed in his own life time. A Catholic priest converted to Protestantism owed his living at Thirsk to Huntingdon's intervention: John Bell told Burghley he thought the Lord President 'a man very zealous in Christian religion, so forward in the service of his prince, so vigilant in his charge, and very favourable to all labourers in Christ's vineyard, as he may justly be thought appointed by God himself for that only end and purpose.' The more disinterested appreciation of other northern clergy can be seen in the books they dedicated to Huntingdon, and three native-born ministers in particular waxed lyrical about the benefits of his presidency: their testimony is the more valuable in view of the sparseness of other evidence. Edmund and Francis Bunny were two famous Protestant brothers from Wakefield and both prolific writers. Edmund had been disinherited by his father on his determination to enter the Church; he persisted, however, in his vocation and gained Grindal's patronage. The archbishop appointed him Subdean of York and rector of Bolton Percy, but after holding these livings for twenty-five years he resigned them to devote himself to itinerant preaching. In his *Coronation of David*, published in the year of the Armada, he compared 'the late unnatural practices' against their queen with the attempts upon the life of David, the Lord's anointed: yet, as David, at the last, had attained to his kingdom so he believed their queen would be confirmed in the possession of her country.

Now, such as it is, if it please your honour to accept in good part, I thought it my duty for to offer the same unto you, for being of this mind that as I wish the benefit thereof unto all, so notwithstanding I speciall[y] wish it to the people here, such as belong to your honour's lieutenancy (to whom I also, in divers good respects, am most bounden), in all these parts I was not able to find anyone that was more exercised in these affairs: or to whom myself (in all humble duty) was more beholding, or under whose protection I could rather wish the same to come forth.[54]

Francis Bunny, rector of Ryton in Durham from 1578, felt a similar sense of obligation and published his *Survey of the Pope's supremacy*,

under the defence of your honour's name, to whom I acknowledge myself especially bound in many respects. Which to do I am the rather moved, that to that inward witness of a good conscience, whereby I know your lordship is incited with a continual care and vigilant eye, to prevent the perilous practices of those busy brokers for that Catholic King (as they call him) and other enemies to this Commonwealth, might also be added the outward testimony of truth, confirmed by proof and practice of the purer times, to encourage you with a constant increase in godly zeal to discharge still the duty that God (who hath called you to that honour) hath laid upon you, and requireth of you, to the service of her majesty and the safety of her subjects.[55]

Christopher Fetherstone, who described in his dedication how he had been 'trained up in the city of Carlisle' and how even in his tender years Huntingdon had not refused to accept his exercises, wrote most specifically of the nature of those benefits Huntingdon's rule had conferred upon the north:

Your deserts of God's church, your singular zeal, your unfeigned faith, your sincere profession, your especial care to advance God's glory and to root out papistry, your faithfulness towards your prince have been such that this realm generally, but my countrymen in the north parts, my native soil specially, have and shall have great cause to praise God for you in the day of their visitation, even when it shall please God of his great mercy to behold them with favourable countenance, and to take from them in greater measure that blindness and superstition, wherein they had long time been nousled, and being fast bred by the bone, is not yet (through want of means) gotten out of the flesh.[56]

So the north gave its verdict. The Protestants saw Huntingdon as a ruler sent from God, the Catholics as an instrument of Satan; both, however, agreed on the energy with which he promoted what he believed to be true religion. In his persecution of the 'busy brokers of that Catholic King' he did no more than carry out the orders of the central government for as England's relations with Spain worsened, so more and more all Catholics, laymen as well as priests, were regarded as potential enemy agents. He had no alternative but to try to root them out. The patronage he extended to Protestants came from himself alone: here he made his most original and lasting contribution to the age in which he lived. By fostering educated ministers absolutely convinced in their Protestantism, and by advancing Protestant biblical scholarship he provided conforming Catholics in the north for the first time on a large scale with an alternative faith; some rejected it, and became the zealous Catholics of the new dispensation, others accepted it equally avidly. He did not work alone but his long tenure of office during which he saw the appointment of no fewer than four Archbishops of York brought him an overriding influence. Whether by repulsion or attraction, Huntingdon must be held in no small way responsible for the religious development of the north in the latter part of the sixteenth century.

CHAPTER EIGHT

A Holy Death-bed

HUNTINGDON's health, never very good, had not seemed much worse than usual in the autumn of 1595: he had been ill in October for ten days at York but recovered quickly and resumed his customary command over northern politics. Towards the end of November he faced the hardship of a journey to Newcastle at that time of the year in order to make an enquiry in person into the decay of government in the Border Marches. Once there he attempted to examine the delinquent Sir John Forster, he attended the installation of the new Lord Warden, and tried to impress upon the gentlemen of Northumberland their duties to the crown. For one day his strength gave out, and he had to keep to his chamber, but he publicly received the Northumberland gentlemen again on 29 November and heard their proposals for reforming the administration of the Marches before he set out wearily on his return journey to York. He intended, after a short rest there, to go down to London almost immediately to inform the queen and Burghley of all that had passed at Newcastle and to explain his own ideas about the reorganisation of the Border defences.[1]

Early in December the Countess of Huntingdon, who had remained at court and had not come north with Huntingdon that autumn, received permission from the queen for her husband to come south. Ever since his return from Newcastle Huntingdon had suffered from a chill and had kept to his room: none of his servants had thought it was serious, and he himself had asked them not to tell his wife about it, since she also was sickly. He went on with his plans to set out for court on the second Thursday in December and the whole household packed their belongings in readiness to go. When 11 December arrived, however, Hunting-don was patently too ill to leave the King's Manor and that evening his personal servant realised that his health had declined fast. Something like panic seized the Council in the North. On 12 December the secretary wrote to Robert Cecil about the grave turn Huntingdon's illness had unexpectedly taken and as soon as the news reached London the queen sent Essex posting to his bedside, at the same time commanding her courtiers not to tell the countess of his danger. Even at this extremity, Huntingdon's mind never left the queen's service. He began a letter describing all that had happened at Newcastle and his grief that the number of men for the defence of the Middle March proved so inferior to the number shown on the certificates he had received and, in all good faith, passed on to the Privy Council: he had not the energy to finish it. The resident members of the Council in the North seeing that Huntingdon was dying summoned Hutton, the new Arch-bishop of York, who had been his friend since the time he had first come into the north. He advised Huntingdon to prepare himself for death, 'which he did, not using many words but such as did give good assurance he died a good Christian': he also tried to bring him to consider the disposal of his estate (he had made no will), but this 'by no means he would harken unto, and said little to it, only that it was a wild world, which he would not think upon'. He died at dawn on Sunday, 14 December. 'Often times a little before his death,' Hutton told Burghley, 'he held up his hands and said, God bless Queen Elizabeth, God save Queen Elizabeth.'[2]

The certain news of Huntingdon's death came to London the following Wednesday morning and the queen's thoughts turned at once to his widow who had not even known of her husband's illness. Elizabeth decided that she would go to Whitehall and comfort her herself: first she sent the Lord Keeper to tell the

T

countess that Huntingdon lay sick, and she promised that if he
had not already settled his estate to her satisfaction she would see
that it was done; in the afternoon he went to the countess again,
this time to report that Huntingdon had become worse and so she
prepared the way to let her know the truth. Rowland White
described to Sir Robert Sidney, the countess's only surviving
nephew, his aunt's 'unheard of sorrows'.

Upon Thursday night (having before heard by my lord keeper of her
husband's being but ill, suspecting more) she caused all the men and
women in the house to come before her, and by their very countenances,
who could not choose but lament, she apprehended the grief that so
much afflicts her. Upon Friday morning, my lady Puckering came to
see her, and finding her so disquieted, she told her by circumstances
that his danger was great, and small hope of recovery; but being
desired by my lady to tell her the very truth of it, she then told her, that
indeed assured word was come he was dead. I am not able to deliver
unto you the passions she fell into, and which yet she continues in. . . .
The queen, herself, in a litter, went to visit her about four o'clock this
evening.[3]

Others besides White found the Countess of Huntingdon
prostrate with grief. Roger Bromley, Huntingdon's old servant,
and now servant to the fourth Earl of Huntingdon, told his new
master that he had not been able to come into her presence to
discuss the business of the estate: 'my lady continueth in such
sorrow and heaviness as greater cannot be in any creature living,
certainly it is such that except the Lord in short time work some
alteration, I fear it will endanger her life.' Walter Hastings, her
brother-in-law, had spoken to her once, but she begged Bromley
and another of Huntingdon's former servants, Edward Goodman,
not to trouble her with any causes for a time; nevertheless,
Bromley continued, 'we are abouts to get her into another
lodging for in this she doth almost neither eat nor sleep, hoping
thereby her worried spirits will be refreshed.' Before Christmas
the queen gave Sir Robert Sidney leave to return from the
Netherlands to comfort his aunt and to take charge of her financial
affairs: White urged him to put to sea, even if the winds were

against him, lest he come too late to see her in this world. His fears, however, proved to be groundless, the dowager countess did not die from grieving over her 'noble, dear lord', and in fact she survived him for twenty-five years until 1620 to die a very old lady in Chelsea where her tomb may still be seen in the parish church. During the last years of Elizabeth's life, the intimacy between her and the dowager countess increased, the queen spent many hours privately in her company and White even hinted she governed the queen. Once Elizabeth also had died, Lady Huntingdon concentrated her affection upon her nephew and his family and, much to her contentment, Sir Robert Sidney frequently left some of his small daughters with their great aunt when he and his wife went on royal service to the Netherlands: right up until her death she prided herself upon the godly ordering of her household which she had first set up with Huntingdon in 1560.[4]

The Countess of Huntingdon held no monopoly of grief in Huntingdon's death, other members of the family mourned with as deep a sorrow. Probably none of his brothers had been so close to Huntingdon as Sir Francis Hastings: he had served him to the utmost of his ability in his life time and he had been admitted to the most confidential of his affairs. The suddenness of his death came as a great shock, and he, no more than his sister-in-law, had been with him when he died. Within a day or two of Huntingdon's death being known in Leicestershire Richard Saunders, who had been Hastings's servant when he lived at Market Bosworth, wrote to try to console him: he begged him not to oppress himself with overmuch grief;

If the Lord [he argued], (to show his love to your dear friend) would take him from this wicked world because he should not taste of those punishments which the Lord would send upon the world for the sins thereof, why should you grieve at all? And you have the less cause to grieve because your lordship knoweth the Lord doth all things for the best to those that love him, and that he did love the Lord those that never did see him will say, that his deeds did declare the same, for he was faithful and loving to the Church of God, his sovereign lady, the queen, and his country.[5]

Sir Edward Hastings shared with Sir Francis the 'heavy cross' they believed God had seen fit to lay upon them 'as to take away our sweet and most dear brother'. Yet he had news from Leicestershire which he felt sure would bring his brother some practical comfort. Sir George, their eldest brother and the new Earl of Huntingdon, who had previously lent towards Catholicism and certainly displayed no enthusiasm for Protestantism seemed to have undergone a conversion.

He hath begun [Sir Edward recounted to Sir Francis] at the very entry in such godly manner as not only myself but all the godly preachers and others are of my mind for he is very desirous to hear the Word preached and to that end doth most earnestly entreat the preachers to come into him, and such as already hath been with his lordship he hath used most honourably and in all kind manner, and for himself I am this far a witness; his lordship in my hearing did deliver with tears, that except the Lord in mercy would look upon him and send the grace of his Holy Spirit to guide him he was altogether unable to perform those duties that would be expected of him, and truly in my conscience I think he did speak it from the bottom of his heart, and hitherto he doth continue most comfortably to us all that wish well to the Church.[6]

The fourth Earl of Huntingdon, 'with sorrow oppressed', himself wrote to Sir Francis Hastings to bewail his 'grievous discomforts', and indeed, suddenly elevated to the head of a virtually bankrupt family, he deserved commiseration. Three days after he had succeeded his brother yet another sorrow came upon him; his eldest son also died. This was the nephew whom the third earl had carefully nurtured as his probable heir and sent to Geneva to complete his education. In the face of these calamities, the fourth Earl of Huntingdon besought his brother to pray for him, and Sir Francis responded magnificently.

My good lord [he replied], I see your sorrows by your letter, and I know your sorrows by your losses, I will pray for your lordship as you require me by your letter and I must be partaker of your sorrows, because I have an interest in your losses. And truly, my lord, though I cannot yet easily persuade myself to mitigate sorrow (which I acknowledge a fault) yet I do humbly beseech you to moderate sorrow in your self so much as may be, and labour to raise up your spirits, that you may gather strength to attend and look unto your many and weighty occasions. The staff of Ashby house is put into your hand and what strength and weakness so ever is in it, your lordship must hold it and your lordship must use all good means to uphold it, and if every good member of the house will not add his best strength therein he is to blame . . . in the meantime, I beseech your lordship, rest assured of my true love and unfeigned readiness to do anything that you shall think fit and reasonable to command me.[7]

Huntingdon had lived a public servant and mourning for his death could not be confined to his widow and his brothers; from the periphery of the family, and from outside, condolences poured in. One of the first letters of sympathy Sir Francis Hastings received came from the second Earl of Pembroke, who had married Mary Sidney, Sir Philip's sister, and so acquired a connection with the Hastings family.

Might it have pleased the giver and taker of souls to have ransomed one life with a thousand [he declared], no doubt there are no fewer in England that would have stood betwixt him and the arrow: since whose death I may truly write thus much of myself, I dream of nothing but death, I hear of little but death, and (were it not for others farther good) I desire nothing but death. The departure of Sir Roger Williams did much trouble me, more the irrecoverable sickness of Sir Thomas Morgan, but never any more, or so much, as the wanting of him for this little time of my pilgrimage, with whom I hope to live ever, I mean your most honourable deceased brother, whom now we want, but hereafter shall want indeed.

With less hyperbole Sir John Popham, Hastings's fellow Justice of the Peace in Somerset, assured him,

I can hardly withhold myself from tears to enter into the consideration of the loss of so true a servant of God, so loyal and faithful a subject and servant to our most gracious queen and so careful a man of his country's good and his sovereign's service as your brother hath ever showed himself to have been. I would to God that God in his goodness would yet raise unto her majesty many such.[8]

Popham voiced the feelings of many when he stressed the commonwealth's loss by Huntingdon's death and northern

Protestants especially missed their godly Lord President. John King, later Bishop of London had, on the prompting of Huntingdon and Archbishop Piers, in 1594 delivered forty-eight lectures on the book of Jonah to the citizens of York and had then come south intending to publish his labours and to dedicate them, as was fitting, to their 'chief founders and procurers'. By the time the lectures appeared in print in 1597, however, both Huntingdon and Piers had died, yet King still felt compelled to pay tribute to his former patrons, and, he continued,

by making some little mention of their happy memories, both to testify mine ancient duty towards them, and deliver them, what I might, from the night of forgetfulness, who were the shining lamps of the north in their life time. Such a Moses and such an Aaron, such a Josuah to lead the people, and such a priest to bear the Ark, such a Zorobabel, and such a Jehozadack, such a Centurion in Capernaum to rule the country, and such a Jairus to govern the Synagogue: when the Lord shall send together again, I will then say he hath restored his blessing amongst them. . . .[9]

King was not alone in fearing that the north could never again be blessed with such another Moses and indeed some of his contemporaries went further and saw in Huntingdon's death a judgment of God upon backsliding Englishmen. The clerk of the Privy Council, Robert Beale, believed the deaths of Huntingdon, Dr. Wittacre and Sir Roger Williams, 'all three worthy men in their calling, and hardly to be seconded again, portend some scourge upon us, for the multitude of our sins and transgressions'. Bishop Matthew, in the privacy of his diary, epitomised all these lamentations: against 14 December 1595, he noted down Huntingdon's death and then, his emotion breaking through this dry record of texts of sermons and preaching engagements, he added a saying of St. Bernard, 'Eheu, Vae nobis boni deficiunt, mali preficiunt.'[10]

At York in his bedchamber at the King's Manor, Huntingdon's body lay in state, embalmed, closed in a shroud and sealed in lead, and guarded nightly by four servants. His death, as the Council in the North reported to Burghley, had left the seventy-five or so ancient and poor servants who had attended him, without a master. The council felt even more concern over the failure of the Hastings family to give directions for the funeral. Prominent members of the council, now led by the Archbishop of York until the appointment of a new president, wished the body of their former master to be laid to rest at York and while no one at first dared to approach the Dowager Countess of Huntingdon to ask her what she wanted to be done, in January, she too gave her support to the idea of having the funeral at York, saying that her husband during his life 'desired often and earnestly that his body might be buried at York, where he hath served the queen and the realm many years very honourably'. The fourth Earl of Huntingdon would have none of this; he insisted that the burial should be in the family vault at Ashby: 'I have heard my lord (my dear brother) when he lived say that he hoped wheresoever he should end his life, his friends would cause him to be brought thither there to be laid with his ancestors.' The Council in the North, he maintained, knew nothing of Huntingdon's wish to be buried there.[11]

More was at stake than the entombment of the dead body for whoever took up the administration of Huntingdon's estate and the ordering of his funeral on him would fall the responsibility for his debts. On the advice of her friends the dowager countess refused to act, the fourth Earl of Huntingdon, protesting that he was 'the poorest earl that her majesty hath this day in her kingdom', would do nothing, and towards the end of February Burghley had to intervene. The queen had particularly noticed the delay and he called for a speedy decision: since the dowager countess would not undertake the funeral, he thought the duty clearly devolved on Huntingdon's brother and successor and suggested that to avoid the burden of his debts the fourth earl should obtain a partial administration of his goods from the Archbishop of Canterbury to satisfy the costs of the funeral. Debts or no debts, the queen required that Huntingdon should receive a funeral as befitted his rank and his service of the state, though she was not prepared to pay for it herself. Burghley considered the new earl should be the principal mourner, together with the Earls of Worcester and Lincoln who had both married into the family, and should be accompanied by Lords Clinton and Compton, Huntingdon's nephews, and that the rest of the ceremony should be performed by his brothers. To these proposals the fourth earl replied that he was a 'fatherless child, possessing nothing that was my father's' and that this alone prevented him from showing his 'dear and natural love' to his noble brother. He promised to submit himself to the queen's will, yet still he took no immediate action. From York, Hutton wrote the following month to Burghley of the grief there 'that, my lady refusing to take administration, so noble a man and so worthy a governor should be forsaken of friends, of brethren, of wife whom he so tenderly loved: it giveth occasion to the papists to speak many things.' At last, in April, to the queen's very good liking, the family agreed to have the funeral at Ashby. Humphrey Purfrey and Edward Stanhope came south as representatives of the Council in the North to perform their last duty of love while most of Huntingdon's poor servants, who had watched with the body so long, followed it south to the grave. On 26 April 1596, Henry, third Earl of Huntingdon and his nephew, Francis, Lord Hastings were buried in St. Helen's church at Ashby de la Zouch.[12]

No stately monument ever marked Huntingdon's grave in the chancel of Ashby church; his successor, rather than indulging in further expense, spent the rest of his days salvaging the ravaged fortunes of the house. Bitterly, the fourth Earl of Huntingdon complained of the 'unreasonable' demands of his 'unkind' sister-in-law and tried to enlist the aid of both Burghley and Essex in gaining the queen's indulgence for the slow rate at which the late earl's debts were being repaid. As best he could, Sir Francis Hastings remedied this failure of brotherly affection by composing a short treatise in appreciation of their dead brother which he addressed to Sir Edward Hastings and their godly friends. In it he remembered with pride how Huntingdon had openly avowed Protestantism, loyally served the queen and always concerned himself over his country's good: how he had behaved with tenderness towards his own family and with pity towards the poor, showing himself an honest man to all men. He grieved especially that now Huntingdon was dead few reflected upon his many virtues but instead spoke of him disparagingly because of the heavy debts which burdened his successor, yet Sir Francis knew that these debts had not been brought about by any faults in his brother's character. The causes of his decay had been unavoidable, but God might even yet restore their house to its former glory. With scorn he repudiated the insinuations of the irreligious that Huntingdon's debts had somehow been linked with his devotion to religion:

He confirmed his religious profession in his life time with a religious conclusion at his end, religiously he lived and religiously he died and hath received not the reward of sin which is eternal death due by desert, but hath received as a free gift from God that eternal and everlasting inheritance which was promised by the Father, purchased by the Son, and is sealed up in the hearts of all God his chosen by the Spirit of Sanctification.[13]

Sir Francis Hastings believed that men ought to dwell upon the great amount of good Huntingdon had been enabled to accomplish in his life time, not upon his failings. In his life they had an example how to live, in his death how to die and from his all-embracing Christianity they also could learn

what death is to the regenerate man, even the way of life guiding mortal men to immortality, and dust, earth and ashes to the kingdom of glory where we shall reign and remain with Abraham, Isaac and Jacob, with the Angels and Archangels, yea with God the Father, God the Son, and God the Holy Ghost, three persons and one eternal and everliving God for ever, unto the which kingdom he that bought us, bring us, Jesus Christ the righteous to whom with the Father and the Holy Ghost be all honour, glory, praise, power and dominion world without end, Amen.[14]

The popular ballad monger could not equal the inspired language of Sir Francis Hastings yet his simple rhymes no less than Hastings's studied prose reveal the love in which his contemporaries held this upright nobleman.

> To poor and to needy, to high and to low,
> Lord Hastings was friendly, all people doth know:
> His gates were still open the stranger to feed,
> And comfort the succourless, always in need.

> His wisdom so pleased the queen of this land,
> The sword of true justice she put in his hand:
> Of York he was president, made by her grace,
> Her laws to maintain, and rule in her place.

> Such merciful pity remained in his breast,
> That all men had justice, and none were oppressed:
> His office in virtue, so godly he spent,
> That prince and his country his loss may lament.
> Then wail we, then weep we, then mourn we each one,
> The good Earl of Huntingdon from us is gone.[15]

His deeds declare the man. Huntingdon's life has perforce been considered in a fragmented way, but he lived it as a whole. So long as he held no high public office he could give his mind to the running of his household, the management of his estates, the directing of his native county in matters spiritual and temporal. Yet when the queen made him President of the Council in the North she took away all his chances of leisure and Huntingdon never again contrived to bring order into his life. When he should have been in London striving to reduce his debts, the revolt of the Scots against the regent Morton kept him with English troops on the Border; when he succeeded in snatching time from northern government to write to his brother about the disposing of some of his southern lands, the church bells of York summoned him away to a sermon. Private business in the south, royal administration in the north, family interests, matters of state, Huntingdon had to accommodate them all simultaneously in his mind. Sometimes he could reconcile the one with the other. His nephew, Thomas Sidney, gained useful experience and a temporary occupation, and the state an apprentice administrator when Huntingdon used him to review the York militia on the eve of the Armada: he fulfilled his duties as a guardian of the young Earl of Essex and at the same time introduced him to the problems of governing the north when he took him into his household at York to teach him the virtues of sobriety. When he happened to be at court on his private occasions, Huntingdon furthered the civic business of the corporation of Leicester, tried to appease turbulent factions in the town of Doncaster, put before the Privy Council the case of the inhabitants of Hull against the citizens of York. Fighting Catholicism, encouraging the spread of Protestantism in the north, he still maintained his links with the international Protestant Church; Beza wrote to him from Switzerland to praise his labours for the Protestant refugees; Huntingdon's own French servant sent him news from Rouen to York; the English ambassador in Scotland could wish he were in Edinburgh to hear the Scots ministers preach. Rarely after 1572 was there a time when he could concentrate exclusively on the matter in hand.

This unceasing busyness must be the chief justification for this attempt to deliver Huntingdon from 'the night of forgetfulness'. He deserves to be remembered because he was both a typical and an exceptional member of the Elizabethan ruling class: typical in his devotion to his queen and country in carrying out routine and often tedious administration—Elizabeth inspired a similar obedience in countless English gentlemen—exceptional in his absolute commitment to radical Protestantism. Much of Huntingdon's work another nobleman could have performed equally well: another could have ruled the county of Leicester, supervised the government of the north of England, presided over the court of the Council in the North; another could have negotiated with the Scots, another might well have had more success in reorganising the military resources of the north but surely only he could have devised and executed his self-imposed task of planting Protestantism in whatsoever places he found himself to be.

In secular government, the second half of the sixteenth century produced perhaps more than its share of godly ascetics, men fired

with a love of religion and of their country, ready to sacrifice
themselves in the work for which they felt they had been called. In
spite of what to modern observers might seem an element of
harshness in their characters their stern dedication to duty evoked
admiration and even love from their contemporaries. Philip II,
who in his austere retreat at el Escorial, half monastery, half
palace, strove unremittingly to serve his God and his country,
represents the type at its most exalted. Young though they both
were when they met at the court of Queen Mary, Philip had
already accepted his vocation to act as the protector of the
Catholic Church, the future Earl of Huntingdon had become
equally convinced of his responsibility for advancing Protestantism in his own land. Their beliefs so early had pulled them to
opposite poles and there could be little communication between
them yet a spirit very similar to that of Philip burned in Huntingdon. Later, in their different spheres, regal or vice-regal, both men
worked to further their ideals to the limits of their bodily capacity,
and beyond. Philip, in his last agonising illness, drove himself to
deal with business of state until the end: the manner of Huntingdon's death also revealed the extent of his devotion to his religion
and his country. The Edwardian preachers had called time and
again for a godly magistracy; in Huntingdon they achieved their
desire.

NOTES

INTRODUCTION

(Pages xiii–xviii)

1. L. Stone, 'The Anatomy of the Elizabethan Aristocracy', *Economic History Review* (1948), xviii. 1.

2. F. Blomefield, *An Essay towards a Topographical History of the County of Norfolk* (1806), iii. 279–80.

3. Hunt. Lib., H.A. 5369.

4. M. St. Clare Byrne and G. Scott Tomson, 'My Lord's Books', *Review of English Studies* (Oct. 1931), vii. 385–405.

5. I owe this information to Mr. C. Blair of the Victoria and Albert Museum, who has questioned the traditional attribution of this armour to the Earl of Leicester, pointing out that the bears and ragged staves are not charged with the crescent cadency mark which Leicester used and has suggested the armour originally was made for Warwick in the 1560's.

CHAPTER ONE

(Pages 3–21)

1. Hunt. Lib., H.A. 5099.

2. *Sermons of Master John Calvin upon the Booke of Job*, trans. A. Golding (1574), dedication.

3. The exact date of his birth is not known. In the inquisition *post mortem* taken on 22 June 1560 following his father's death he was said to be 23 years old and more. P.R.O. E 150/1158/12.

4. English Catholics in particular feared Huntingdon might eventually resort to arms to defend the Protestant cause in England. [R. Parsons,] *Leycester's Commonwealth* (1641), 40, 53, 56. J. Morris, *Troubles of our Catholic Forefathers*, (1877), iii. 100.

5. W. Shakespeare, *Richard III* (Arden, ed. A. Hamilton Thompson, 1907), Act III, sc. iv, ll. 39–41. R. S. Sylvester, *Complete works of St. Thomas More* (Yale, 1963), ii. 52.

6. *C.L. & P. Hen. VIII*, xiii, pt. ii, nos. 804, 1280 (p. 538).

7. Op. cit. vi, no. 601; xii, pt. ii. nos. 911, 1060.

8. *A.P.C.* ii. 344, 356, 425; iii. 117.

9. *C.P.R. Ed. VI*, iii. 137; v. 228. *A.P.C.* iii. 322.

10. J. G. Nichols, *Literary Remains of Edward VI* (1857), lvii–lxviii.

11. C. Ocland, Εἰρηναρχία *sive Elizabetha. De pacatissimo Angliae statu, imperante Elizabetha, compendiosa narratio* . . . (1582), no pag.

12. J. G. Nichols, op. cit. clix. J. Strype, *Life of Sir John Cheke* (1705), 115.

13. T. W. Baldwin, *William Shakspere's small Latine and lesse Greeke* (Urbana, Ill., 1944), i, esp. chs. x and xi. M. C. Cross, *Free Grammar School of Leicester* (Leicester University Occasional Papers, 4, 1953), 15–20.

14. J. and J. A. Venn, *Alumni Cantabrigienses* (Cambridge, 1922), i, pt. ii. 328.

15. *H.M.C. Rutland*, i. 93. P.R.O. SP 11/7/1.

16. B. Castiglione, *The Courtyer, Done into Englyshe by T. Hoby* (1561), dedication, which is dated 1556.

17. W. Baldwin, *A Treatise of morall phylosophie . . . Newlye sette forth by T. Paulfreyman* (1557), dedication.

18. *H.M.C. VII, Molyneux*, 608.

19. *H.M.C. Finch*, i. 1.

20. *C.S.P. Span. 1553*, 107, 112, 119.

21. *A.P.C.* iv. 330, 356. P.R.O. C 54/499. Hunt. Lib., H.A. 'Special Seals', 194.

22. B.M. Harl. MSS. 3881, 45. *C.P.R. 1553–4*, 147, 186. P.R.O. SP 12/1/64.

23. *C.P.R. 1553–4*, 56, 85, 408. *C.P.R. 1555–7*, 113. *C.P.R. 1557–8*, 65, 177.

24. *C.S.P. Span. 1553*, 444.

25. Bodl. Carte MSS. 78, 239.

26. *C.S.P. Span. 1554–8*, 77. *C.S.P. For. 1553–8*, 135, 138.

27. Hunt. Lib., H.A. 10338. *H.M.C. Hastings*, ii. 7.

28. Hunt. Lib., H.A. 10341. *H.M.C. Hastings*, ii. 6–7.

29. John Gerard, *Autobiography of an Elizabethan*, trans. P. Caraman (1951), 193, 215.

30. Hunt. Lib., H.A. 10332. *H.M.C. Hastings*, ii. 3. Bodl. Carte MSS. 78, 249. *C.S.P. Ven. 1555–6*, 173.

31. Bodl. Carte MSS. 78, 251. H. Osorius, *De Rebus Emmanuelis, regis Lusitaniae* . . . (Cologne, 1574), * 3.

32. *C.S.P. Span. 1554*, 297. *C.P.R. 1557–8*, 147.

33. *C.S.P. Span. 1554–8*, 22–24.

34. P.R.O. SP 11/6/72. SP 11/7/1. SP 11/8/82.

35. Hunt. Lib., H.A. 10337. *H.M.C. Hastings*, ii. 5.

36. J. Nichols, *Progresses . . . of Queen Elizabeth* (1823), i. 37. *Journal of the House of Lords*, i. 541. Hunt. Lib., H.A. 'Seals', 216.

37. *C.P.R. 1558–60*, 91, 294.

38. *H.M.C. Rutland*, i. 69.

39. Hunt. Lib., H.A. Uncatalogued Leicestershire deeds. B.M. Harl. MSS. 3881, 48.

40. Longleat, Dudley Papers, I/86, I/147.

CHAPTER TWO

(*Pages 22–60*)

1. List of wages of servants in the household for the half-year ending Michaelmas 1564. Hunt. Lib., H.A. Unindexed Accounts and Inventories.

2. Baldwin, *Shakspere's small Latine . . .* , i. 254–5.

3. E. Carleton Williams, *Bess of Hardwick* (1959), 126–94. G. C. Williamson, *George, Third Earl of Cumberland* (Cambridge, 1920), 263–71, 285–9.

4. D. M. Meads, *Diary of Lady Margaret Hoby* (1930), 62 ff.

5. T. Beza, *The Psalmes of David truely opened and explaned*, trans. A. Gilbie (1581), dedication.

6. T. Beza, *A booke of christian questions and answers*, trans. A. Golding (1572), dedication.

7. H. Bullinger, *Commonplaces of christian religion*, trans. J. Stockwood (1572), dedication.

8. L. Daneau, *A fruitfull commentarie upon the twelve small prophets*, trans. J. Stockwood (Cambridge, 1594), dedication. J. Stockwood, *A very fruiteful sermon: preched at Paules Cross the tenth of May last* (1579), dedication.

9. T. Brasbridge, *Abdias the prophet* (1574), dedication.

10. *Foure sermons of Maister John Calvin, with a briefe exposition of the lxxxvii psalme. Translated out of Frenche into Englishe by John Fielde* (1579), dedication. P. Collinson, 'John Field and Elizabethan Puritanism' in *Elizabethan Government and Society: Essays presented to Sir John Neale*, ed. S. T. Bindoff, J. Hurstfield, and C. H. Williams (1961), 127 ff.

11. R. G. Usher, *The Presbyterian Movement in the reign of Elizabeth as illustrated by the Minute Book of the Dedham Classis, 1582–1589* (1904), Camden Soc., ser. 3, vol. viii. 26.

12. *Correspondence of Matthew Hutton*, Surtees Soc. (1843), 56, 71.

13. P.R.O. SP 12/225/18. M. Maclure, *The Paul's Cross Sermons, 1534–1642* (Toronto, 1958), 200, 202, 204, 205.

14. *The workes ... of ... M. Richard Greenham, published by Henry Holland* (1599), dedication.

15. Hunt. Lib., H.A. 5099.

16. Hunt. Lib., H.A. 10339. *H.M.C. Hastings*, ii. 5.

17. P.R.O. E 150/1158/12. Hunt. Lib., H.A. 'Seals', 220.

18. Hunt. Lib., H.A. Family Papers, and unnumbered deeds, Cornwall. G. E. C[ockayne], *Complete Peerage*, 1910–59, ix. 677; xii. 856.

19. J. Horsey, 'Observations in seventeene yeeres travels and experience in Russia' in *S. Purchas his Pilgrimage* (1626), 980–2. E. A. Bond, *Russia at the close of the Sixteenth Century* (1856), xlviii–liii. By 1589 a case had been begun in Chancery over a bequest in Lady Mary's will. P.R.O. C 2 Eliz./H 14/27 and C 33/77.

20. W. Camden, *Annales* (Oxford, 1717), 76.

21. P. Caraman, *John Gerard ...*, 213–15. P.R.O. SP 12/193/50. B.M. Lans. MSS. 99. 92. Hunt. Lib., H.A. 4714.

22. P.R.O. E 150/1158/12. Hunt. Lib., H.A. Unnumbered deeds, Leicestershire.

23. H. A. C. Sturgess, *Register of Admissions to the Middle Temple* (1949), i. 27. J. C. Roberts, 'Parliamentary representation of Dorset and Devon, 1559–1601', unpublished University of London M.A. thesis (1958). Appendix.

24. H. C. Porter, *Reformation and Reaction in Tudor Cambridge* (Cambridge, 1958), 101, 106, 147. *D.N.B.* iii. 673, 'John Caius'.

25. I owe this information to the kindness of Mr. N. R. Ker. S. L. Greenslade, *The English Reformers and the Fathers of the Church* (Oxford, 1960), 13–14.

26. C.U.L. Mm. 1. 43 (Baker MSS. 32), 438. J. Nichols, *Progresses of Queen Elizabeth*, i. 206. This was the time when Edmund Campion, still nominally a Protestant, made such a favourable impression on the queen and Cecil. E. Waugh, *Edmund Campion* (Penguin ed., 1954), 14–16.

27. M. Bateson, *Leicester Borough Records, 1504–1603* (Cambridge, 1905), 131. W. A. Shaw, *Knights of England* (1906), ii. 74. *H.M.C. Foljambe*, 9. *C. Scot. P. 1571–4*, 494. *C. Scot. P. 1581–3*, 6. P.R.O. SP 12/238/126. P.R.O. SP 12/241/23. Hunt. Lib., H.A. 5092. *H.M.C. Hastings*, ii. 39–40.

28. R. Challoner, *Memoirs of Missionary Priests* (1924), 221. *H.M.C. Cecil*, xvii. 523. R. Parsons, *Leycester's Commonwealth* (1641), 154.

29. Hunt. Lib., H.A. 5097.

30. J. Foster, *Register of Admissions to Gray's Inn* (1889), 46.

31. C.U.L. Mm. 1. 43 (Baker MSS. 32), 442. T. Sampson, *A briefe collection of the Church* (1581), dedication.

32. French Church, Soho. Deacons' Account Book, 1572–3, f. 30.

33. P. Collinson, 'Letters of Thomas Wood, Puritan, 1566–1577', *Bulletin of the Institute of Historical Research*. Special Supplement 5. (Nov. 1960), vii–viii, 2.

34. Hunt. Lib., H.A. 13766.

35. S. D'Ewes, *A compleat journal of the votes, speeches and debates, both of the House of Lords and Commons throughout the whole reign of Queen Elizabeth* (1693), 682.

36. Hunt. Lib., H.A. 5079. Space forbids the printing of the whole of this eloquent letter, but I hope shortly to publish an edition of all Sir Francis Hastings's letters.

37. *A.P.C.* ix. 23, 133. P.R.O. SP 12/106/21.

38. Bateson, *Leicester Borough Records*, iii. 139. J. Strype, *Annals of the Reformation* (Oxford), ii, pt. i. (1824), 567.

39. P.R.O. SP 12/117/19. *A.P.C.* x, 400.

40. Hunt. Lib., H.A. 5086. *H.M.C. Hastings*, ii. 36.

41. C. W. Foster, *Lincoln episcopal records in the time of Thomas Cooper* (1913), 39. C.U.L. Mm. 1.43. (Baker MSS. 32) 436–7. J. Strype, *Historical Collections of the life and acts of J. Aylmer* (Oxford, 1821), 124–5.

42. Hunt. Lib., H.A. 5103.

43. Hunt. Lib., H.A. 1265. *H.M.C. Hastings*, ii, 37. A. F. Scott Pearson, *Thomas Cartwright and Elizabethan Puritanism, 1535–1603* (Cambridge, 1925), 25–46.

44. Samuel Clarke, *A martyrologie . . . with the lives of ten of our English divines*, 1652, i. supplement, 93–97. B. Brook, *Thomas Cartwright* (1845), 434.

45. Hunt. Lib., H.A. 5092. *H.M.C. Hastings*, ii. 39–40.

46. Emmanuel College, Cambridge, Treasury, Box 25, A 10, Box 1, A 2.

47. Hunt. Lib., H.A. 5087. A. L. Rowse, *Sir Richard Grenville of the 'Revenge'* (1937), 300–20.

48. F. W. Weaver, *Somerset Incumbents* (Bristol, 1889), 278. Hunt. Lib., H.A. 5093.

49. Weaver, op. cit. 4, 40, 41, 104.

50. Hunt. Lib., H.A. 2380.

51. P.R.O. C 66/1464. Hunt. Lib., H.A. 5100.

52. *H.M.C. Cecil*, ix. 207. P.R.O. C 66/1495. *C.S.P. Dom. 1598–1601*, 392. *H.M.C. Cecil*, x, 26.

53. S. Clarke, *A martyrologie . . .* i, supplement, 109.

54. Hunt. Lib., H.A. 5085.

55. Hunt. Lib., H.A. 5090. *H.M.C. Hastings*, ii. 38.

56. Hunt. Lib., H.A. Religious Papers, unindexed. R. Parsons, *A temperate ward-word to the turbulent wach-word* [sic] *of Sir F. Hastings* [Antwerp ?], (1599), 27, 78.

57. M. Sutcliffe, *A briefe replie to a certaine odious libel, lately published by a Jesuit* (1600), preface, no pag. R. Parsons, *The warn-word to Sir F. Hastinges wast-word* [Antwerp ?], (1602), 6, 82.

58. *Journals of the House of Commons*, i. 88, 91, 92. D'Ewes, op. cit. 181, 188.

59. D'Ewes, op. cit. 333, 337, 343. J. E. Neale, *Elizabeth and her parliaments* (1957), ii. 154, quoting B.M. Harl. MSS. 7188, 93–94.

60. D'Ewes, op. cit. 413, 441, 640, 633, 624–6, 642, 682, 661, 394–406. *Commons Journals*, i. 230, 258, 277, 347, 350, 400, 269, 427, 434, 257–9, 432, 436, 441, 446. H. Townshend, *Historical Collections: or, an exact account of the proceedings of the four last Parliaments of Queen Elizabeth* (1680), 191, 268, 254.

61. D'Ewes, op. cit. 499, 553, 555, 561, 626. *H.M.C. Cecil*, xi. 506.

62. D'Ewes, op. cit. 335, 672. Townshend, op. cit. 277.

63. *Commons Journals*, i. 141.

64. *H.M.C. Cecil*, xvi. 132. *Commons Journals*, i. 246–7.

65. B.M. Sloane MSS. 271, 33–34. Add. MSS. 28571, 205. Add. MSS. 38492. Add. MSS. 8978, 116–17. Harl. MSS. 677, 44. P.R.O. SP 14/10/62, 81. SP 14/12/68. *H.M.C. Cecil*, xvii. 7, 26, 38, 56. And see R. G. Usher, *Reconstruction of the English Church* (New York, 1910), i. 412 n. 1.

66. P.R.O. SP 14/12/69, 73, 74.

67. P.R.O. SP 14/12/74, 94, 95. *H.M.C. Montagu of Beaulieu*, 45–47. *H.M.C. Cecil*, xvii. 134, 501, 530. xviii. 366.

68. *Commons Journals*, i. 274, 279, 284, 290, 375, 384–5, 420–1. D. H. Willson, *Parliamentary diary of Robert Bowyer* (Minneapolis, 1937), 55–56.

69. *Notes and Queries for Somerset and Dorset* (Sherborne, 1891), ii, pt. xiii, 184.

70. Hunt. Lib., H.A. Family Papers. Unindexed wills of Francis Hastings of Bosworth [*c.* 1580], and Francis Hastings of North Cadbury [before 1596].

71. Hunt. Lib., H.A. 5101.

72. T. Beza, *Psalmorum Davidis et aliorum prophetarum, libri quinque latine expressi* (1580), dedication.

73. *Catholic Record Society, Miscellanea* (1906), ii. 198.

74. A. F. Scott Pearson, *Thomas Cartwright and Elizabethan Puritanism*, 135. I. Gentillet, *A discourse upon the meanes of wel governing, . . . against N. Macchiavell*, trans. S. Patericke (1602), dedication, which is a joint one to Francis Hastings and his kinsman, Edward Bacon, dated 1577.

75. Hunt. Lib., H.A. 5373. B.M. Harl. MSS. 3881, 57.

76. J. Hall, Works . . . (1714), iii. P.R.O. SP 12/256/25.

77. *H.M.C. Cecil*, ii. 319–20. *H.M.C. Middleton*, 585–8.

78. *Devereux Papers, Camden Miscellany XIII* (1923), 5, 21. Longleat, Devereux papers, V/55. B.M. Harl. MSS. 6995, 114.

79. B.M. Lans. MSS. 31, 40. W. A. Ringler, *Poems of Sir Philip Sidney* (Oxford, 1962), 44–52. J. Strype, *Aylmer*, 217. B.M. Lans. MSS. 39, 172. Harl. MSS. 3881, 55.

80. D. M. Meads, *Diary of Lady Margaret Hoby*, 9 ff. Bodl. Add. MSS. (Fortescue), D. 109. 81.

81. P.R.O. C 115/L 2/6697. I owe this reference to the kindness of Miss N. Fuidge.

82. Hunt. Lib., H.A. 5398. P.R.O. SP 15/29/154.

83. *H.M.C. De L'Isle and Dudley*, ii. 241, 310–11, 410, 417, 454, 462. B.M. Lans. MSS. 162, 132.

84. York City Library. Housebook, 1588–92. 23.

85. S. R. Gardiner, *Fortescue Papers*, Camden Soc. (1871), vii–ix. Bodl. Add. MSS. (Fortescue), D 109. 83, 95, 97, 99. Hunt. Lib., H.A. 1305 and unnumbered deeds, Wilts. 17 Jan. 34 Eliz.

86. *H.M.C. De L'Isle and Dudley*, ii. 165. *H.M.C. Cecil*, v. 302. Gardiner, *Fortescue Papers*, xii–xiv.

87. Bodl. Add. MSS. (Fortescue) D 109. 124. D. M. Meads, *Diary of Lady Margaret Hoby*, 40–43.

88. *H.M.C. Rutland*, i. 90, 95, 99.

89. P.R.O. C 54/1104. C 54/1217. C54/1270. And History of Parliament Trust. MS. biographies, Ralph Bourchier.

90. P.R.O. C 33/31/238. C 3/93/56. *C. Bord. P. 1560–1595*. 199, 208, 214.

91. Hunt. Lib., H.A. 6226. *H.M.C. Hastings*, ii. 38.

92. Hunt. Lib., H.A. 13225. H.A. 1166.

93. J. Foster, *Yorkshire Pedigrees*, ii. (1874), no pag.

94. History of Parliament Trust. MS. biographies, Martin Birkhead.

CHAPTER THREE

(*Pages 61–111*)

1. Hunt. Lib., H.A. 5099.

2. For a discussion of the difficulties of estimating landed income see L. Stone, *The Crisis of the Aristocracy, 1558–1641* (Oxford, 1965), 129–138, 279–85.

3. This survey of the Hastings estates *c.* 1560 is based on the

inquisition *post mortem* of Francis, second Earl of Huntingdon, P.R.O. E 150/1158/12 and the receiver's accounts of 1569, B.M. Harl. MSS. 3881, 53.

4. B.M. Harl. MSS. 3881, 51.

5. B.M. Lans. MSS. 75, 29.

6. See Appendix, table of lands alienated by Huntingdon. Bodl. Carte MSS. 289, 48.

7. See Appendix, table of Huntingdon's borrowing on bond.

8. See Appendix, table of lands mortgaged by Huntingdon. M. E. Finch, *Wealth of Five Northamptonshire Families* (Northampton Record Soc., 1956), 168.

9. Bodl. Carte MSS. 289. 95, 107. P.R.O. C 2 Eliz., H 1/60. C. W. James, *Chief Justice Coke: His Family and Descendants at Holkham* (1929), 305. Hunt. Lib., H.A. 5566, 5742.

10. See Appendix, table of lands acquired by Huntingdon.

11. Hunt. Lib., H.A. 5099.

12. Hunt. Lib., H.A. 5381, 5369. Family Papers, 27 Jan. 1593–4.

13. L. Stone, 'Marriage among the English nobility in the 16th and 17th centuries', *Comparative studies in Society and History* (1961), iii. 192.

14. *H.M.C. Middleton*, 587.

15. See Appendix, Huntingdon's bonds and mortgages to the crown. On interest-free loans granted by the queen, see L. Stone, *Crisis of the Aristocracy*, 479, 541.

16. Hunt. Lib., H.A. 5081, 5083, 5084.

17. P.R.O. E 159/383. This sum was still being repaid in 1604. Hunt. Lib. Manorial documents, miscellaneous, Leicestershire.

18. Hunt. Lib., H.A. 5369, 5409.

19. This figure is based upon letters, Hunt. Lib., H.A. 5368, 5380, 5369, 5370, 5374, 5375.

20. R. T. Spence, 'The Cliffords, Earls of Cumberland, 1579–1646', unpublished University of London Ph.D. thesis (1959), 12. R. B. Turton, *The Alum Farm* (Whitby, 1938), 44. P.R.O. SP 13/H 2 Eliz.

21. *H.M.C. Cecil*, iii. 274.

22. B.M. Lans. MSS. 53, 61.

23. P.R.O. Signet Office. Doquets I. Ind. 6800.

24. Hunt. Lib., H.A. 925. P.R.O. SP 59/22/80. In acknowledgement of Robert Bowes's service the queen allowed him to exchange lands worth a little over £100 for crown lands valued at £80 p.a. P.R.O. Ind. 6743.

25. See Appendix, table of annuities granted by Huntingdon.

26. Hunt. Lib., H.A. 5367. P.R.O. C 33/81. C 33/83. See Appendix, table of mortgages granted by Huntingdon.

27. Tables of some of the lands involved in the exchange are printed

in my note in the *Bulletin of the Institute of Historical Research* (Nov. 1961), xxxiv. 178.

28. Hunt. Lib. Egerton 1264 (c). P.R.O. C 54/1308, C 54/1285, C 54/1310.

29. Hunt. Lib., H.A. 5094. Family Papers, Jan. 1593/4.

30. Hunt. Lib., H.A. 1304. P.R.O. E 368/486. The total of Huntingdon's debt to the crown is given here as £12,644. 9s. 5½d., but in addition he had undertaken to pay £600 a year for the next 9 years after 1597 which gives a total of £18,044. 9s. 5½d.

31. Bodl. Carte MSS. 78. 246.

32. Hunt. Lib., H.A. Dorset, deeds. H.A. Leicestershire deeds (for Canford and Lubbesthorpe). Bodl. Carte MSS. 78. 693 (for Aller). J. Nichols, *The History and Antiquities of the County of Leicester, 1795–1815*, IV, pt. ii. 822 (for Newbold).

33. Bodl. Carte MSS. 78. 158.

34. Hunt. Lib. H.A. 'Seals' 242. P.R.O. E 368/486.

35. P.R.O. C 66/1486. C 66/1479.

36. Hunt. Lib., H.A. Miscellaneous, Repair Box.

37. *H.M.C. Cecil*, iii. 275.

38. B.M. Harl. MSS. 3881. 51.

39. Longleat. Dudley papers 1/183.

40. *H.M.C. Cecil*, iii. 275.

41. P.R.O. E 150/1158/12. Hunt. Lib., H.A. Genealogical Papers. Accounts in Huntingdon's own hand endorsed 'my dealings for my lord's will'. W. R. B. Robinson, 'The Earls of Worcester and their estates, 1526–1642', unpublished University of Oxford B.Litt. thesis (1958), 52, 68, 71, 73. The average marriage portion of a nobleman's daughter between 1530 and 1570 was £1,000. Stone, *Crisis of the Aristocracy*, 638.

42. See Appendix, table of annuities granted by Huntingdon.

43. Hunt. Lib., H.A. Devon deeds.

44. Hunt. Lib., H.A. 'Seals' 239.

45. Bodl. Carte MSS. 78. 410.

46. R. T. Spence, 'The Cliffords, Earls of Cumberland . . .', London Ph.D. thesis, 23 ff. G. R. Batho, 'Finances of an Elizabethan nobleman, Henry Percy, ninth Earl of Northumberland', *Economic History Review*, Ser. 2. vol. 9, 433 ff.

47. Hunt. Lib., H.A. Accounts and Inventories. Comparative figures for other households are taken from G. R. Batho, *Household Papers of Henry Percy, ninth Earl of Northumberland*, Camden Soc. third ser. XCIII, xii–xiii.

48. L. Stone, 'The Nobility in Business, 1540–1640', *The Entre-*

preneur: Papers presented at the Annual Conference of the Economic History Society (Apr. 1957), 14. And, Stone, *Crisis of the Aristocracy*, ch. vii. esp. 353–5. Sir Thomas Smith interested himself in an abortive scheme to try to make copper from iron, and in 1572 he and his associates for a time leased a mining house at Poole from Lady Mountjoy. M. Dewar, *Sir Thomas Smith: A Tudor Intellectual in Office* (1964), 149–55.

49. One of the very few offences not covered by the Indulgences of 1515 (against which Luther made his famous protest) apart from offering violence to the Pope or to higher ecclesiastics and falsifying papal letters, was the import of alum into western Europe from the Turks rather than from the Papal States. W. Köhler, *Dokumente zum Ablasstreit* (Tübingen and Leipzig, 1902), 85.

50. Turton, *The Alum Farm*, 14–19, 35 ff. *Statutes of the Realm*, iv. 522.

51. *Links in the History of Engineering and Technology from Tudor Times: the Collected Papers of* R. *Jenkins* (Cambridge, 1936), 193.

52. Hunt. Lib., H.A. Unnumbered deeds, Dorset.

53. *C.P.R. 1557–8*, 299. History of Parliament Trust. Unpublished Tudor biographies, John Hastings. *H.M.C. Second Report* (Neville-Holt MSS.), 97. P.R.O. SP 13/Case H Eliz 2.

54. B.M. Harl. MSS. 3881. 52. P.R.O. C 54/820. L.C. 4/191/160.

55. P.R.O. SP 12/188/23.

56. P.R.O. SP 13/Case H Eliz 3.

57. Hunt. Lib., H.A. Unnumbered deeds, Dorset and Various.

58. *A.P.C.* xii. 225. P.R.O. SP 12/148/48.

59. P.R.O. E 159/380.

60. P.R.O. SP 12/150/76.

61. *A.P.C.* xiii. 259, 339–41, 424–5.

62. P.R.O. SP 12/155/22, 26, 81.

63. Hunt. Lib., H.A. 5386, 5365. P.R.O. SP 12/162/11.

64. Hunt. Lib., H.A. 12724, 12725, 5367.

65. Hunt. Lib., H.A. 12722, 12720, 5088.

66. Hunt. Lib., H.A. 5376.

67. Hunt. Lib., H.A. 5377, 5395. P.R.O. SP 12/177/42.

68. Hunt. Lib., H.A. 1050, 2379.

69. *A.P.C.* xiv. 134. Hunt. Lib., H.A. 5398.

70. *H.M.C. Cecil*, iii. 275. P.R.O. C 54/820.

71. For example, P.R.O. C 3/88/24, C 3/96/4, St. Ch. 5/H 16/25, C 3/92/32, C 33/77, C 78/72/19.

72. P.R.O. SP 12/177/42, E 112/12/121.

73. B.M. Lans. MSS. 67. 18.

74. P.R.O. SP 12/244/109.

75. P.R.O. SP 12/177/42.
76. Hunt. Lib., H.A. 5380, 5374. P.R.O. E 112/12/121.
77. P.R.O. E 112/12/121.
78. P.R.O. C 3/276/91. C 33/113. Hunt. Lib., H.A. 'Seals', 263, 5432.
79. Hunt. Lib., H.A. Unnumbered deeds, Dorset. The lease of one-third of the manor and the mines sold for £2,000, the lease of the other two-thirds for £7,000, the release of the whole manor for £4,000. It is possible that some of these sums contain the other, especially as seisin of the manor of Canford was granted in July, 1612 for £8,600.
80. Hunt. Lib., H.A. Repair Box. Stoke Poges Accounts. Manorial, Bucks. H.A. 5369.
81. J. S. Syme, 'The King's Manor', *Yorkshire Archaeological Journal*, xxxvi. 377. R. Davies, *The Historie of the King's Mannour House at York* (York, 1883), 6–7.
82. Bodl. Carte MSS. 289. 10. In the sixteenth century it was normal to reward estate officers with advantageous leases: they were not usually paid realistic wages until the seventeenth century. Stone, *Crisis of the Aristocracy*, 292–4.
83. See Appendix, tables of lands alienated and mortgaged by Huntingdon, and also of leases and annuities granted by him.
84. Hunt. Lib., H.A. 5636.
85. W. Camden, *Annals* (1688), 529.
86. Bodl. Carte MSS. 78. 530.
87. J. E. C. Hill, *The Economic Problems of the Church, from Archbishop Whitgift to the Long Parliament* (Oxford, 1956), 54–5, 252–67.
88. Anon. *A Certificate from Northamptonshire* (1641). Houghton Library, Harvard University. Press mark, E C 65 A 100 641 c 8.
89. J. A. Froude, *History of England* (1866), iii. 464.
90. C.U.L. Mm. 1.43.426 (Baker MSS. 32).
91. B.M. Lans. MSS. 19. 2.
92. Hunt. Lib., H.A. 5366.
93. Hunt. Lib., H.A. Accounts and Inventories. Household Account Book, 1584–5.
94. Hunt. Lib., H.A. 5369, 5384, 5399.
95. *H.M.C. Cecil*, v. 253.
96. P.R.O. SP 15/21/94. B.M. Cot. MSS. Caligula C 3. 345. Leeds Central Library, Temple Newsam collection, TN/PO 1/68. This gives a list of specimen fees charged for issuing commissions, 1579–81.
97. Hunt. Lib., H.A. 13064.
98. B.M. Lans. MSS. 33. 2.
99. P.R.O. SP 59/26/608.
100. P.R.O. SP 15/32/79.

101. E. Hughes, *Studies in Administration and Finance, 1558–1825* (1934), 58.

102. P.R.O. E 112/22/87.

103. York City Lib. Housebook 1572–4, 29. This is the first of many such entries.

104. Hunt. Lib., H.A. 5099.

105. See Appendix, table of royal grants to Huntingdon.

106. Hunt. Lib., H.A. 1020. Also Repair Box, Accounts of the receiver for Stoke Poges.

107. J. Hurstfield, *The Queen's Wards: Wardship and Marriage under Elizabeth I* (1958), 96–107. There is a detailed account here of the sort of profit which could be made by a nobleman from a private wardship.

108. B.M. Lans. MSS. 22. 81.

109. Spence, 'Cliffords, Earls of Cumberland . . .', 245–57. Stone, *The Crisis of the Aristocracy*, 429–31. Hunt. Lib., H.A. 'Seals', 242.

110. *The Crie of the Poore for the death of the . . . Earle of Huntingdon.* B.M. Press mark Huth. 50. 56.

111. Hunt. Lib., H.A. Manorial. Court roll, Ashby, 1571–2.

112. Hunt. Lib., H.A. 5081, 5083, 5084.

113. Hunt. Lib., H.A. Family Papers, 1561–76. 'A note of remembrances of things on my journey' in Francis Hastings's hand.

114. Hunt. Lib., H.A. 5366.

115. See Appendix, table of leases granted by Huntingdon.

116. Hunt. Lib., H.A. 5382, 5369, 5378.

117. Hunt. Lib., H.A. 5089.

118. Hunt. Lib., H.A. 5400.

119. Hunt. Lib., H.A. 5411.

120. Hunt. Lib., H.A. 5410.

121. Hunt. Lib., H.A. 5094.

122. Hunt. Lib., H.A. 5094, 5099.

CHAPTER FOUR
(Pages 115–58)

1. *C.P.R. 1560–3*, 439, 444. P.R.O. SP 12/58/16. C 66/1320. *H.M.C. Cecil*, i. 443. G. Scott Thomson, *Lords Lieutenant in the Sixteenth Century* (1923), 43–83.

2. Leic. Mus. II.5.47. 20.D.52. Box 3A. no. 4.

3. Loc. cit. Hall Papers III, 150.

4. *H.M.C. Eighth Report*, 417. P.R.O. C 66/1320.

5. *H.M.C. Cecil*, i. 253. P.R.O. SP 12/14/49.

6. *A.P.C.* xxv. 7. Leic. Mus. II.5.52. 20.D.52.

7. Leic. Mus. Hall Book II. 353, 423. Hall Book III. 17, 35, 55, 93. *A.P.C.* xvii. 317.

8. *Scottish Papers, 1569–71*, 460–1. B.M. Harl. MSS. 3881. 54. Hunt. Lib., H.A. 'Seals', 250. P.R.O. SP 12/150/6. Leic. Mus. Hall Papers, I, 29.

9. Hunt. Lib., H.A. 4137. 1288. P.R.O. SP 12/58/16. Leic. Mus. Hall Book III, 44. Hunt. Lib., H.A. 2539, 2542, 4147.

10. Corpus Christi College, Cambridge. MS. 114, 179. *D.N.B.* xxx. 7. (Robert Johnson). J. Hall, *Works . . . (*1714), iii.

11. Leic. Mus. Hall Papers, I, 156. Hall Papers II, 320. B.R. II/10/4. Portfolio of letters 20 D 52, II 5 10, 29, 45. Hunt. Lib., H.A. Un-indexed Leicestershire papers.

12. W. K. Jordan, *Philanthropy in England 1480–1660* (1959), esp. chapters vi, vii.

13. B.M. Harl. MSS. 4774. 135. C. W. Foster, *State of the Church in the Diocese of Lincoln*, cxxvii.

14. M. C. Cross, *Free Grammar School of Leicester*, 6–9, 11–12. P.R.O. Duchy of Lancaster, Special Commissions 44. 179. *Correspondence of Matthew Parker*, Parker Soc. (1853), 245. A. H. Thompson, *Calendar of Charters . . . belonging to the Hospital of William Wyggeston* (1933), 55.

15. P.R.O. C 54/1003. Cross, op. cit. 15–20. J. Nichols, *Leicestershire*, i. II, 505. T. North, *Accounts of the churchwardens of St. Martin's, Leicester* (Leicester, 1884), 132, 136.

16. Leic. Mus. Hall Book II, 229, 331, Hall Book III, 68. Book of Acts 1488–1581, 64. Portfolio of letters 20 D 52. II 5 32, 40.

17. As early as 1562 the churchwardens of Castle Donington were referring to 'our good Lord of Huntingdon'. Churchwardens' Accounts 1550–1571. Hunt. Lib., H.A. Accounts. B.M. Eg. MSS. 2986. 16. Lans. MSS. 101. 6. Hunt. Lib., H.A. Leics. deeds, 24 Apr. 1568.

18. *A.P.C.* xi. 290. Leic. Mus. Hall Papers IV, 17. Hall Book, III, 94. *A.P.C.* xxv, 89.

19. Leic. Mus. Hall Book III, 92. Portfolio of letters 20 D 52. II 5 34, 38. Hall Papers, III, 53.

20. Leic. Mus. Portfolio of letters, 20 D 52. II 5 15, 16, 48.

21. Bateson and Stocks, *Leicester Borough Records*, iii. 435–6, iv. 5, 13. Leicester Museums and Art Gallery, *Catalogue of Local Portraits* (Leicester, 1956), 12.

22. Hunt. Lib., H.A. 8373.

23. M. A. E. Green, *Life of William Whittingham*, Camden Soc. (1871), 13 note 1.

24. Leic. Mus. I D 41. 28/132. P. Collinson, 'The Puritan Classical

Movement', unpublished University of London Ph.D. thesis (1957), 25. B.M. Add. MSS. 29546. 57.

25. C.U.L. Mm. 1.43. (Baker MSS. 32) 434, 427–30. P. Collinson, 'Letters of Thomas Wood', *Bulletin of the Institute of Historical Research*, Supplement 5, pp. 24–25. A. Peel, *The Seconde Parte of a Register* (1915), i. 30.

26. A. G. Dickens, *The English Reformation* (1964), 276. Leic. Mus. Hall Book II, 78. T. North, *Chronicle of the church of S. Martin, Leicester* (Leicester, 1866), 163–5. Leic. Mus. Book of Acts, 1488–1581, 45.

27. French Church, Soho. Deacons' Account Book, 1572–3, 7.

28. E. Grindal, *Remains*, Parker Soc. (1843), 326–7.

29. C.U.L. Mm. 1. 43 (Baker MSS. 32), 431, 442–3, 445, 447. P. Collinson, 'John Field and Elizabethan Puritanism', S. T. Bindoff and others, *Elizabethan Government and Society* (1961), 127–62.

30. C.U.L. Mm. 1. 43 (Baker MSS. 32), 433, 439, 440–1.

31. Emmanuel College, Cambridge, Treasury, Box 1, A2. Preamble of deed of 19 Jan. 1586 by which Huntingdon granted Loughborough and other livings to the College.

32. B.M. Add. MSS. 29546. 56. C. W. Foster, *State of the Church in the Diocese of Lincoln*, cxxvii.

33. P.R.O. SP 12/100/18. SP 12/76/45. C.U.L. Mm. 1. 43 (Baker MSS. 32), 436.

34. C. W. Foster, *State of the Church* . . . , 33, 34, 35, cxxii. P. Collinson, *Letters of Thomas Wood* (1960), 20.

35. P. Collinson, 'The Puritan Classical Movement', London Ph.D. thesis (1957), 190. B.M. Add. MSS. 27632. 47.

36. B.M. Add. MSS. 29546. 42. T. Cooper, *An Admonition to the People of England*, English Scholars' Library, 15 (Birmingham, 1881), 47.

37. B.M. Add. MSS. 29546. 57.

38. C.U.L. Mm. 1. 43. (Baker MSS. 32), 436–7. P. Caraman, *William Weston, Autobiography of an Elizabethan* (1955), 164.

39. P. Collinson, thesis, 430, 458, quoting John Rylands Library, English MS. 874. 39.

40. C. W. Foster, *Episcopal records in the time of Thomas Cooper*, Lincoln Record Soc. (1912), ii. 317, 36. C. D. Chalmers, 'Puritanism in Leicestershire 1558–1633', unpublished University of Leeds M.A. thesis (1962), 31.

41. Leic. Mus. Hall Papers I, 157. S. J. Knox, *Walter Travers* (1962), 78–83.

42. Venn, *Alumni Cantabrigienses*, iii. 388. C. W. Foster, *State of the Church*, lxiv. Leic. Mus. 20 D 52/53.

43. Leic. Mus. Hall Book III, 32, 44. Portfolio of letters. 20 D 52. II 5 25.

44. C.U.L. Mm. 1. 43. (Baker MSS. 32), 426. *D.N.B.* ix. 833 (Hildersham.) A. Hildersham, *CVIII Lectures on the Fourth of John* (1629), dedication.

45. W. Baldwin, *A treatise of morall phylosophie*, trans. T. Paulfreyman (1557), dedication. J. Nichols, *Progresses . . . of Queen Elizabeth* (1823), i. 109. Longleat, Dudley papers, 1/14, 1/133, 1/147, IV/23, 1/166, 1/183.

46. *C.S.P. Span. 1558–67*, 122, 174, 192, 262.

47. Op. cit. 263, 271.

48. *C.S.P. For. 1563*, 100.

49. B.M. Harl. MSS. 787. 16.—a transcript, probably made in the seventeenth century, of an original letter, now lost.

50. *C.S.P. Span. 1558–67*, 580. J. Nichols, *Progresses . . .* , 191, 197, 207. C. Read, *Mr. Secretary Cecil and Queen Elizabeth* (1955), 327. *Journal of the House of Lords*, i. 580–617, 625–665.

51. J. A. Froude, *History of England* (1866), iii. 464.

52. *H.M.C. Cecil*, i. 400.

53. Hunt. Lib., H.A. 2536. P.R.O. SP 53/4/21. *H.M.C. Cecil*, i. 423.

54. P.R.O. SP 53/4/22, 23, 28, 29. *H.M.C. Cecil*, i. 424.

55. *H.M.C. Cecil*, i. 426, 428. P.R.O. SP 53/4/35, 36. E. Lodge, *Illustrations of British History* (1838), i. 487.

56. P.R.O. SP 53/4/33, 42, 43, 44, 45.

57. P.R.O. SP 53/4/47, 50. Hunt. Lib., H.A. 1302.

58. P.R.O. SP 53/4/48, 56, 59.

59. Hunt. Lib., H.A. 12777, 2537, 4138. P.R.O. SP 53/4/64, 65, 67.

60. P.R.O. SP 53/4/70, 71, 72, 73.

61. P.R.O. SP 53/4/79. *H.M.C. Cecil*, i. 448. Hunt. Lib., H.A. 1303.

62. P.R.O. SP 53/4/82. *H.M.C. Cecil*, i. 451.

63. *H.M.C. Cecil*, i. 451. Hunt. Lib., H.A. 2375. B.M. Harl. MSS. 3881. 53.

64. W. A. Shaw, *Knights of England* (1906), i. 26.

65. J. H. Hessels, *Epistulae et Tractatus cum reformationis tum ecclesiae Londino-Batavae historiam illustrantes* (1897), III, pt. i. 129–133.

66. J. E. Neale, *Elizabeth and her Parliaments* (1953), i. 194–7. *Journals of the House of Lords*, i. 678–9, 681, 693, 683–4, 720. D'Ewes, *Journals of Parliaments . . .* , 198.

67. J. Nichols, *Progresses . . .* , i. 309.

CHAPTER FIVE

(Pages 159–95)

1. York City Lib. Housebook, 1572–4, 29.

2. P. Heylyn, *Aerius Redivivus* (1670), 272.

3. P.R.O. SP 15/27/43.

4. B.M. Harl. MSS. 6991, 30.

5. B.M. Harl. MSS. 4990. 138. P.R.O. SP 15/21/94.

6. P.R.O. SP 15/21/86. B.M. Lans. MSS. 33. 7, 8.

7. B.M. Harl. MSS. 1088. 26–39. Hunt. Lib., H.A. Unindexed Accounts and Inventories, 1596.

8. R. R. Reid, *The King's Council in the North* (1921), esp. 209–29. The newly discovered letter-book of Huntingdon, 1580–90 (sold, lot 202, at Sotheby's on 2 May 1966 to the Huntingdon Library) has proved not to be an official record of the Council in the North. It contains material relating exclusively to the military defence of the north and was kept for Huntingdon in his capacity as Lord Lieutenant.

9. P.R.O. SP 12/262/64. J. J. Cartwright, *Chapters in Yorkshire history* (Wakefield, 1872), 1–87. Reid, op. cit. 184, 208.

10. B.M. Cot. MSS. Caligula C. 3, 345. P.R.O. SP 15/21/111. SP 15/23/50, 51.

11. Longleat. Dudley papers II/121.

12. B.M. Harl. MSS. 6991. 30. H. E. Malden, *Devereux Papers, Camden Miscellany XIII* (1923), 5.

13. J. Morris, *Troubles of our Catholic forefathers* iii. 183.

14. B.M. Harl. MSS. 6991. 19.

15. Hunt. Lib., H.A. 5356.

16. G. Ornsby, *Household books of the Lord William Howard*, Surtees Soc. (1878), 365–408. P.R.O. SP 15/29/19. SP 15/30/20, 20^1.

17. *A.P.C.* xv. 94. P.R.O. SP 15/30/20.

18. B.M. Harl. MSS. 4990. 138. Cot. MSS. Caligula C. 3. 543. P.R.O. SP 15/25/27.

19. B.M. Add. MSS. 29546. 36. York City Lib. Housebooks, 1572–74, 122; 1574–77, 78, 85; 1577–80, 99, 149; 1580–85, 97. York Minster Library, Archbishop Matthew's Diary, 39.

20. York City Lib. Housebooks, 1574–77, 85; 1585–7, 108; 1587–92, 177–81. Reid, op. cit. 327–32.

21. York City Lib. Housebook, 1580–85, 167. Hunt. Lib., H.A. 'Seals', 246. P.R.O. SP 15/28/101, 108.

22. Hull. Guildhall. L 64, 94, 95.

23. History of Parliament Trust. Unpublished Tudor biographies, Yorkshire. York City Lib. Chamberlains' Account Book, C 5, 71. Hunt. Lib., H.A. 2363.

24. *A.P.C.* xv. 394. *H.M.C. Cecil*, iv. 208; vi. 447. R. Welford, *History of Newcastle and Gateshead* (1887), ii. 481; iii. 33, 258.

25. College of Arms, Talbot MSS. i. 85, 98. *A.P.C.* xxi. 128. S. R. Gardiner, *Fortescue Papers*, Camden Soc. (1871), xii–xiv.

26. York City Lib. Housebooks, 1574–77, 94; 1577–80, 40, 60; 1580–85, 174. *A.P.C.* xv, 32.

27. P.R.O. SP 15/12/112. B.M. Lans. MSS. 18. 25. Hull, Guildhall. L 78, 68. York City Lib. Housebooks, 1574–77, 102, 107; 1577–80, 69, 81; 1580–85, 186; 1592–98, 91.

28. B.M. Lans. MSS. 19. 59, 96. York City Lib. Housebook, 1587–92, 102. *A.P.C.* xiv. 395; xix. 186.

29. B.M. Harl. MSS. 6994. 85. Newcastle Chamberlains' Accounts, 1590–96, no pag. *A.P.C.* xxiii. 233. Hull. Guildhall. M 92.

30. Reid, op. cit. 220–222. P.R.O. SP 15/25/29. *A.P.C.* xix. 168; xx, 163. H. Heaton, *Yorkshire woollen and worsted industries* (Oxford, 1920), 135–144.

31. York City Lib. Housebook, 1577–80, 94. Northallerton Record Office, Bridge Accounts, f. 6. P.R.O. SP 15/25/16. Newcastle Chamberlains' Accounts, 1590–6, no pag.

32. *A.P.C.* viii. 275; xii. 362; xiv. 224. P.R.O. SP 15/25/46, 47, 75[1]. B.M. Cot. MSS. Caligula C. 7. 109.

33. E. Sandys, *Sermons*, Parker Soc. (1841), 201.

34. T. B. Macaulay, *History of England* (1864), i. 136.

35. B.M. Harl. MSS. 18. 18. P.R.O. SP 15/25/21. *A.P.C.* xiii. 17. Reid, op. cit. 351–4.

36. *A.P.C.* viii. 294–5, 344; x. 105.

37. P.R.O. SP 15/29/160–165. Professor Stone in *The Crisis of the Aristocracy 1558–1641* (Oxford, 1965), 223–34 considers in detail this problem of the lawless behaviour of certain members of the nobility and gentry in Elizabethan England.

38. *A.P.C.* viii. 318; ix; 140–2, xiii. 146. Durham. Prior's Kitchen, Allan MSS. 7. 231–2.

39. *A.P.C.* xii. 72, xiii. 349, xxii. 527.

40. Leeds Central Lib., Temple Newsam Coll. TN/PO 1/68. P.R.O. E 159/371.

41. York City Lib., Housebooks, 1574–77, 23, 101; 1580–5, 183. Hull Guildhall, L 22, Bench Book 4, 194–7.

42. *A.P.C.* xvi. 46, 282, 394–7. Hull Guildhall, L 87. York City Lib., Housebook, 1587–92, 66, 89, 111, 140, 144, 245.

43. York City Lib., Housebook, 1572–4, 45. Berwick Guildbook, 1568–76, 41; 1576–85, 61. B.M. Harl. MSS. 6992. 66.

44. York City Lib., Housebook, 1587–92, 199. Hull Guildhall, Benchbook 4, 104, L 77.

45. Leeds Central Lib., Temple Newsam Coll. TN/PO 1/58. J. S. Syme, 'The King's Manor', *Yorkshire Archaeological Journal*, xxxvi. 1944–7, 377.

46. B.M. Lans. MSS. 86. 17. Harl. MSS. 1576. 357.

47. Hunt. Lib., H.A. 2540.

CHAPTER SIX

(*Pages* 198–224)

1. B.M. Cot. MSS. Titus F 3, 136. Lans. MSS. 16. 47, 17. 12. York City Lib. Housebook, 1572–4, 89.

2. B.M. Harl. MSS. 6991. 30. J. Harland, *Lancashire Lieutenancy* (Manchester), Chetham Soc. 49 (1859), ii. 104.

3. B.M. Harl. MSS. 6991. 19.

4. B.M. Add. MSS. 41178. 120. Harl. MSS. 6991, 28.

5. W. C. Dickinson, *Scotland from the Earliest Times to 1603* (1961), 343. D. L. W. Tough, *Last Years of a Frontier* (Oxford, 1928), esp. chs. i and xii.

6. *C.S.P. For. 1572–4*, 210. P.R.O. SP 15/23/8. SP 59/18/225.

7. P.R.O. SP 59/18/242, 260. *C.S.P. Scot. 1571–4*, 494—it is not clear whether Sir Edward Hastings was ever given this command. B.M. Cot. MSS. Caligula C 3. 463. B.M. Lans. MSS. 17, 15.

8. P.R.O. SP 59/19/116.

9. P.R.O. SP 59/19/102, 104, 108, 110, 112, 114, 118. B.M. Cot. MSS. Caligula C 5. 33.

10. P.R.O. SP 59/19/123, 134.

11. B.M. Cot. MSS. Caligula C 5. 30, 43, 49, 50, 55. P.R.O. SP 59/19/152.

12. P.R.O. SP 59/19/154. B.M. Lans. MSS. 20. 65.

13. P.R.O. SP 59/19/176.

14. P.R.O. SP 59/19/134. Hunt. Lib., H.A. 925, 926, 927, 928, 929, 930, 931. *C.S.P. For. 1578–9*, 138. *C.S.P. Scot. 1574–81*, 321, 251.

15. York City Lib., Housebook, 1577–80, 265. P.R.O. C 66/1302. *H.M.C. Cecil*, v. 523. J. Morris, *Troubles . . .* , ser. 3, 152. Huntingdon's letter-book as Lord Lieutenant, 1580–90 (acquired by the Huntingdon Library in May 1966) confirms the impression that the office of Lord

Lieutenant was considered to be quite distinct administratively, from that of Lord President.

16. *C.S.P. Scot. 1574–81*, 573. B.M. Harl. MSS. 6999. 5, 18, 42. Hunt. Lib., H.A. 13055, 13057, 13062.

17. B.M. Harl. MSS. 6999. 24, 8. Hunt. Lib., H.A. 13054, 13059, 13055.

18. P.R.O. SP 52/29/15, 17. *C.S.P. Scot. 1574–81*, 688. *C.S.P. Span. 1580–6*, 85.

19. Hunt. Lib., H.A. 5350, 5352, 5354, 13067, 5358. B.M. Harl. MSS. 6999. 62.

20. *C.S.P. Span. 1580–5*, 400. *C.S.P. Scot. 1581–3*, 504. *C. Hamilton P. 1543–90*, 672, 702.

21. P.R.O. SP 15/28/70, 89, 90, 92. York City Lib., Housebook, 1585–7, 46–47, 140; 1587–92, 35.

22. P.R.O. SP 15/30/99.

23. P.R.O. SP 15/30/13. *C.S.P. Span. 1587–1603*, 174.

24. *C. Bord. P. 1560–94*, 289. P.R.O. SP 59/25/572. SP 12/206/3.

25. P.R.O. SP 15/30/77. *A.P.C.* xv. 390.

26. B.M. Harl. MSS. 6994, 63, 67. P.R.O. SP 15/30/99. *H.M.C. Various*, ii. 102. P.R.O. SP 59/26/606.

27. P.R.O. SP 59/26/608, 611, 612. *A.P.C.* xvi. 128–9. B.M. Harl. MSS. 6994. 66.

28. P.R.O. SP 12/100/18. Hunt. Lib., H.A. 12531.

29. P.R.O. SP 59/26/619. York Minster Lib., Archbishop Matthew's Diary, 16. *A.P.C.* xvi. 233, 236.

30. G. Mattingly, *The Defeat of the Spanish Armada* (Penguin ed., 1962), esp. chs. 30 and 31. *A.P.C.* xvi. 211, 231, 234. P.R.O. SP 59/26/620, 626.

31. *C.S.P. Scot. 1589–93*, 209, 344; *1593–5*, 15. Hunt. Lib., H.A. 10712. B.M. Harl. MSS. 6999. 77.

32. *A.P.C.* xviii. 364; xix. 15. York City Lib., Housebook, 1587–92, 180. Newcastle Chamberlains' Accounts, 1590–6, no pag.

33. York City Lib., Housebooks, 1572–4, 66; 1574–7, 11; 1577–80, 180; 1585–7, 84–5. B.M. Lans. MSS. 102. 119. *A.P.C.* xv. 118.

34. Hull, Guildhall M 69. Benchbook 4. 158–63.

35. *A.P.C.* xxi. 352–4. Northallerton Record Office, Lame soldiers' book, f. 8. *H.M.C. Various*, ii. 105. P.R.O. SP 12/73/13.

36. *H.M.C. Report, X*, iv. 306. *H.M.C. Cecil*, v. 340. P.R.O. SP 59/30/173.

37. P.R.O. SP 59/30/184.

CHAPTER SEVEN

(*Pages* 226–69)

1. J. Morris, *Troubles* . . . , 3rd ser., 152.

2. B.M. Lans. MSS. 16, 24. P. Tyler, 'The Administrative Character of the Ecclesiastical Commission for the Province of York, 1561–1585', unpublished University of Oxford B.Litt. thesis (1960), 9–17. My figures of Huntingdon's attendance on the High Commission are taken from the High Commission Act Books 1572–95, in the Borthwick Institute of Historical Research, York.

3. Borthwick Institute. High Commission Act Book 1572–4, 98–99, 147–52, 159. Longleat. Dudley papers. II/121.

4. Borthwick Institute. High Commission Act Books 1572–4, 178; 1574–5, 27, 47.

5. B.M. Lans. MSS. 19. 13.

6. Borthwick Institute. High Commission Act Books 1576–80, 58, 62; 1580–5, 12.

7. P. Tyler, *The Ecclesiastical Commission and Catholicism in the North* (Leeds, 1960), 114. *A.P.C.*, x, 182.

8. Borthwick Institute. High Commission Act Book 1576–80, 91, 107–8.

9. York City Lib., Housebook 1577–80, 214, 225–6.

10. *A.P.C.* xii. 77. F. Peck, *Desiderata Curiosa* (1779), 87–88. Borthwick Institute. High Commission Act Book 1580–5, 7–34, 38, 60.

11. *A.P.C.* xxiii. 182, 192. Borthwick Institute, High Commission Act Book 1592–5, 55, 68.

12. *A.P.C.* xxiv. 317, 421. York City Lib., Housebook 1592–8, 53. Borthwick Institute. High Commission Act Book 1591–5, 142.

13. York City Lib., Housebook 1572–4, 36. B.M. Cot. MSS. Caligula C 3. 440–3, 448, 476. P.R.O. SP 15/33/45, 46.

14. York City Lib., Housebooks 1572–4, 150; 1574–7, 77, 96. B.M. Harl. MSS. 6992. 26.

15. F. X. Walker, 'The Implementation of the Elizabethan Statutes against Recusancy 1581–1603', unpublished University of London Ph.D. thesis (1961), 148, 252–75, 366. T. E. Gibson, 'A Century of Recusancy', *Transactions of the Historic Society of Lancashire and Cheshire*, 3rd ser., vii. 36.

16. York City Lib., Housebook 1577–80, 114. *A.P.C.* xii. 320; xiii. 152. Hunt. Lib., H.A. 4140.

17. Hull, Guildhall, L 27. P.R.O. SP 15/27A/23. SP 15/29/154.

18. Morris, *Troubles* . . . , 3rd ser. 132.

19. English College, Rome. Archives, Scritt 21/22 ff. I am indebted to Father Hugh Aveling, O.S.B., for this transcript.

20. Hunt. Lib., H.A. 5396. P.R.O. SP 15/27A/107. *A.P.C.* xiii, 432–3. R. Challoner, *Memoirs of Missionary Priests* (1924), xix–xxii.

21. *A.P.C.* xv, 297, xxiii. 27, 111. B.M. Harl. MSS. 6996, 19, 28, 29.

22. Morris, *Troubles . . .* , 3rd ser. 183.

23. J. Strype, *Annals of the Reformation*, vii (Oxford, 1824), 210. P.R.O. SP 12/248/25.

24. Morris, *Troubles . . .* , 3rd ser. 65, 132, 333 ff. In spite of Dr. Reid's aspersions (*Council in the North*, 209–10) there seems to be no evidence which connects Huntingdon directly with the condemnation and death of Margaret Clitherow, and it is unlikely he was in York at the time. See my note in *Recusant History*, 8, no. 3. 144.

25. B.M. Lans. MSS. 16. 24, 17. 50. P.R.O. SP 15/21/103.

26. B.M. Lans. MSS. 19. 2.

27. B.M. Lans. MSS. 20. 50, 23. 12.

28. B.M. Lans. MSS. 23. 2. J. Raine, *Correspondence of Dr. Matthew Hutton*, Surtees Soc. 17 (1843), 59.

29. B.M. Lans. MSS. 20. 50. P.R.O. SP 12/111/14, 22. SP 15/25/8. Durham. Prior's Kitchen. Hunter MSS. 32. 52–5. P. Collinson, 'The Puritan Classical Movement', London University Ph.D. thesis (1957), 31.

30. *A.P.C.* x. 337. B.M. Add. MSS. 33207, 5–7.

31. B.M. Lans. MSS. 27, 6.

32. B.M. Add. MSS. 33207, 9–15. M. A. E. Green, *The Life and Death of Mr. William Whittingham*, Camden Soc. (1871), 37.

33. B.M. Lans. MSS. 24, 80. J. P. Ellis, 'Edwin Sandys and the Settlement of Religion in England, 1558–88', unpublished University of Oxford B.Litt. thesis (1962), 47.

34. Hunt. Lib., H.A. 5099. R. Halley, *Lancashire: its Puritanism and Nonconformity* (Manchester, 1869), i. 156. F. R. Raines, *Vicars of Rochdale*, Chetham Soc. (1883), i. 42. A. G. Dickens, *Lollards and Protestants in the Diocese of York* (Oxford, 1959), 24–27. B.M. Add. MSS. 29546, 36.

35. York City Lib., Housebooks 1577–80, 189, 214, 225–6, 230; 1580–5, 54, 184; 1585–7, 10. Chamberlains' Account Rolls, C 8/3, C 8/4. J. A. Newton, 'Puritanism in the Diocese of York, 1603–40', unpublished University of London Ph.D. thesis (1956), 175.

36. *D.N.B.*, xx. 4. (John Udall). J. Udall, *The Combat betwixt Christ and the Devil . . .* (1589), dedication. A. Peel, *Seconde parte of a Register . . .* (1915), i. 226.

37. C. W. Foster, *State of the Church in the Diocese of Lincoln*, xxv. Newcastle Chamberlains' Accounts 1590–5, no pag.

38. This Bible is now in C.U.L. press mark Sel. 3. 21. B. Hall, *Genevan version of the English Bible* (1957), 11. J. Favour, *Antiquity Triumphing over Novelty* (1619), epistle to the reader.

39. R. Thoresby, *Vicaria Leodiensis* . . . (1724), 51–3. D. H. Atkinson, *Old Leeds; its Byegones and Celebrities* (Leeds, 1868), 64. Atkinson gives as his authority the churchwardens' accounts in St. Peter's, Leeds, which have now disappeared. J. Lyster, *A Rule how to bring up Children* . . . (1587), dedication.

40. C.U.L. Add. MSS. 17 ff. 38, 40–41, 44. These transcripts are printed (with occasional errors) in F. Peck, *Desiderata Curiosa* (1779), 109–10, 129, 130, 151.

41. Halley, op. cit. i. 112. *Chetham Miscellany* v (1895), i. 1–48, ii. 1–22.

42. Halley, op. cit. i. 156–77. Newton thesis, 218. C.U.L. Mm. 1. 43. (Baker MSS. 32), 436–7.

43. W. K. Jordan, *The Charities of Rural England* (1961), 239 n. 6. Hunt. Lib., H.A. 8012. R. Welford, *History of Newcastle and Gateshead*, iii. 26–27.

44. B.M. press mark Huth. 50. 56.

45. J. Marbecke, *A Booke of Notes a. Commonplaces* . . . (1580), dedication.

46. P.R.O. SP 12/136/31. H. Broughton, *A seder olam, that is, order of the worlde: or yeeres from the fall to the restoring* (1594), dedication.

47. T. Beza, *Psalmorum Davidis et aliorum prophetarum* . . . (1580), dedication. P. Loselerius Villerius, translation into Latin, *T. Beza interprete Jesu Christi d. n. novum testamentum* (1574), dedication. A. C. Miller, *Sir Henry Killigrew* (Leicester, 1963), 194 and n. 4. C.U.L. Mm. 1. 43. (Baker MSS. 32) 438. P.R.O. SP 78/7/44, 70. P. Collinson, 'Beginnings of English Sabbatarianism' in C. W. Dugmore and C. Duggan, *Studies in Church History* (1964), i. 207–221.

48. H. Isaacson, *Exact Narrative of the Life and Death of Bishop Andrewes* (1650), [2] J. Barwick, *Life and Death of Thomas Lord Bishop of Duresme* (1660), 67—Morton, however, must have been Huntingdon's chaplain earlier than Barwick implies. P.R.O. SP 12/247/21.

49. Peel, op. cit. ii. 36. York City Lib., Housebook, 1580–5, 172. Hunt. Lib. H.A. 12531. G. Sohn, *A Brief and Learned Treatise* . . . *of the Antichrist*, trans. N. G[ilby], (1592), dedication. J. Hall, *Works* . . . (1714), iii.

50. R. Marchant, *Puritans and the Church Courts 1560–1642*, (1960), 212. Newton thesis, 52–55. Peel, op. cit. 245, 256. Morris, *Troubles* . . . , iii. 416.

51. B.M. Eg. MSS. 2644. 21. College of Arms. Talbot MSS. vol. G, 252; vol. I, 157.

52. P.R.O. SP 59/25/548. *H.M.C. Cecil*, v, 11. B.M. Lans. MSS. 76. 78.

53. Minster Library York. Archbishop Matthew's Diary, 1–40. M. Hutton, *A Sermon preached at York . . . 23 September, in the eighteenth year of her Majesty's reign* (1579). *Correspondence of M. Hutton*, 27. Newton thesis, 60. P.R.O. SP 15/27/14.

54. B.M. Lans. MSS. 76. 11. E. Bunny, *The Coronation of David* (1588), dedication.

55. F. Bunny, *A Survey of the Pope's Supremacy . . .* (1595), dedication.

56. C. Fetherstone, translation of Calvin, *The Commentaries on the Acts of the Apostles* (1585), dedication.

CHAPTER EIGHT
(Pages 270–80)

1. *H.M.C. Cecil*, v. 508. P.R.O. SP 59/30/184.

2. A. Collins, *Sidney Papers*, i. 374, 378–81. *H.M.C. Cecil*, v. 507, 495. P.R.O. SP 59/30/173. B.M. Lans. MSS. 79. 47.

3. Collins, op. cit. 380–3.

4. Hunt. Lib., H.A. 1021, 5720. Collins, op. cit. 382–3, 386–7. B.M. Lans. MSS. 162. 132. *H.M.C. De L'Isle and Dudley*, ii. 236, 310, 410, 418, 462, 465, 469, 472, 474.

5. Hunt. Lib., H.A. 10675.

6. Hunt. Lib., H.A. 4714.

7. Hunt. Lib., H.A. 5277, 5098.

8. Hunt. Lib., H.A. 6722, 10348.

9. John King, *Lectures upon Ionas, delivered at York in . . . 1594* (1597), dedication.

10. Collins, op. cit. 396. York Minster Library, Archbishop Matthew's Diary, 47.

11. *H.M.C. Cecil*, vi. 93–5. B.M. Harl. MSS. 3881. 59. Collins, op. cit. 386–7. Hunt. Lib., H.A. 1304.

12. Hunt. Lib., H.A. 5276, 5279, 1304. *Correspondence of Matthew Hutton* (Surtees Soc.), 17, 106. B.M. Lans. MSS. 82. 25. Register 1, St. Helen's Church, Ashby de la Zouch.

13. Hunt. Lib., H.A. 5276, 5283, 5284, 5099.

14. Hunt. Lib., H.A. 5099.

15. Some verses from *The Crie of the Poore for the Death of the Right Honourable Earle of Huntingdon* (1596). B.M. Press mark Huth. 50. 56.

APPENDIX

Lands alienated by Huntingdon

Date	Purchaser	Property	Consideration	Source
28 Jan. 1561	Thomas Dowse	*Manor of Morecloses in Bramshaw*, Wilts.	£220	H.A. Wilts. deeds
24 June 1561	Anthony Geering and Geoffrey Clerk	Messuages and lands in Brinkworth, Wilts.	£771 6s. 8d.	H.A. Wilts. deeds
1 Mar. 1562	Francis, Earl of Bedford	Messuage called West Dawnet, Cornwall	100 marks	H.A. Seals 221
14 May 1562	Leonard Carpenter	*Manors of Retyres and Kyres and moiety of manor of Rillaton Peverell, in Linkinhorne, Cornwall*	£251	H.A. Cornwall deeds
2 Nov. 1562	Digory Graynefild	*Third of manor of Hilton Woodnall, Cornwall*	£200	H.A. Cornwall deeds]
14 Nov. 1562	R. Chamberlayne, H. Stukeley, and T. Gore	*Manor of Wootton Courtney*, Somerset	£2,000	P.R.O. C 54/638
27 Nov. 1562	Nicholas Beaumont	Lands in Overton Saucy, Leics.	£1,200	H.A. Leics. deeds
.. 1562	Sir Thomas Gerrard	*Manor of Slingsby*, Yorks.	[£1,603 11s. 8d.] anticipated price	H.A. unsorted deeds
1 Jan. 1563	William Harris	*Third of Manor of Wick Cobham*, Devon	£200	H.A. Devon deeds

Date	Purchaser	Property	Consideration	Source
14 June 1563	William Bawdrick	Messuage and land in Norton iuxta Galby, Leics.	£100	H.A. Leics. deeds
25 Sept. 1563	Richard Graynefild and George Rolle	Manor of Crackington, Cornwall	£1,000	H.A. Seals 222
21 Oct. 1563	Thomas Opie	Moiety of manor of Park, Cornwall	£465	H.A. Cornwall deeds
21 Oct. 1563	John Killigrew	Moiety of manor of Harvenna, Cornwall	200 marks	H.A. deeds 1174 A
21 Oct. 1563	Bernard Penrose	Other moiety of manor of Harvenna, Cornwall	£63	H.A. Cornwall deeds
21 Oct. 1563	William Perkins	Manor of Codford Farley, Cornwall	£90	H.A. Cornwall deeds
21 Oct. 1563	John Moyle	Site of manor house of Pengelly, Cornwall	£418 18s. 8d.	H.A. Cornwall deeds
21 Oct. 1563	Thomas Bele	Land in Pengelly, Cornwall	100 marks	H.A. Cornwall deeds
21 Oct. 1563	Richard Erisey	Messuage in Ruan Major, Cornwall	£34	H.A. Cornwall deeds
21 Oct. 1563	Thomas Williams	Messuages in St. Stephens and Penheale Hungerford, Cornwall	£60	H.A. Cornwall deeds
21 Oct. 1563	John Pie	Messuages in St. Stephens and Penheale Hungerford, Cornwall	£80	H.A. Cornwall deeds
23 Oct. 1563	Henry Bronker	Messuage and lands in Orcheston St. George, Wilts.	£373 6s. 8d.	H.A. Wilts. deeds
10 Dec. 1563	R. Roscarrock, W. Carne-shaw and J. Billing	Moiety of manor of Hamatethy, Cornwall	£460 10s.	H.A. Cornwall deeds

Date	Purchaser	Property	Consideration	Source
30 Jan. 1564	Christopher Coplestone	Messuage and lands in Wolmaston, Colebrook, Devon	£260	H.A. Devon deeds
13 Mar. 1564	Robert Fletcher	Everingham Fee, Notts.	420 marks	H.A. Notts. deeds
6 Apr. 1564	Thomas Godwyn	*Manor of Plymtree, Devon*	£1,000	P.R.O. C 54/668
8 Apr. 1564	Thomas Langham	Tenements and lands in Warbstow, Cornwall	£66	H.A. Cornwall deeds
16 Sept. 1564	Thomas Benbrig	Land in Ashby de la Zouch, Leics.	..	H.A. Leics. deeds
2 Nov. 1564	Edward Nevill	*Manor of Newton St. Loe, Somerset*	£2,600	H.A. Hants, etc., deeds
2 June 1565	Henry Beacher	*Manor of Pensford and Publow, Somerset*	£1,600	H.A. Som. deeds
24 Jan. 1566	Richard King	Land in Billesdon, Leics.	£15	H.A. Leics. deeds
15 Feb. 1566	Robert Brenarne	Land in Stretton, Leics.	£75	H.A. Leics. deeds
20 June 1566	Geoffrey Ithell	Land in Billesdon, Leics.	£54	H.A. Leics. deeds
8 July 1566 16 July 1566 }	William Barford	*Manor of Shakestone, Leics.*	[In exchange for *M. of Newbottle*, Northants.]	{ H.A. Leics. deeds H.A. Middlesex deeds
25 July 1566	John Fuller	House in St. Paul's Wharf, London	£360	H.A. Middlesex deeds
1 Mar. 1568	Francis Brown	*Manors of Newton Harcourt, Wistow and Kilby*, Leics.	£2,000	H.A. Leics. deeds
14 June 1568	William Saunders	*Manor of Newbottle*, Northants.	£1,000	P.R.O. C 54/772
20 Dec. 1569	Sir George Turpin	Capital messuage in the High Street, Leicester	£100	H.A. Leics. deeds

Date	Purchaser	Property	Consideration	Source
20 Jan. 1571	Thomas Riche	Lands in Leigh, Wilts.	£220	H.A. Wilts. deeds
25 Jan. 1571	John Farwell	Manor of *Holbrooke* in Charleton Musgrave, Somerset	£600	H.A. Som. deeds
7 Apr. 1571	Robert Golding	Lands in Leigh, Wilts.	£200	H.A. Wilts. deeds
1 May 1571	Richard Poole	Lands in Long Newton, Wilts.	£140	H.A. Wilts. deeds
10 Dec. 1571	Anthony Webbe	Lands in Burton, Brokenborough and Charleton, Wilts.	£200	H.A. Wilts. deeds
10 Dec. 1571	John Girdler	Lands in Leigh, Wilts.	£88	H.A. Wilts. deeds
10 Dec. 1571	Philip Wattes als. Gibbes	Lands in Leigh and Cleaverton, Wilts.	£280	H.A. Wilts. deeds
26 Mar. 1572	Thomas Walton	Lands in Crudwell, Wilts.	£70	H.A. Wilts. deeds
28 Mar. 1572	Isaac Stanley	Lands in Yatton Keynell, Wilts.	£20	H.A. Wilts. deeds
20 May 1572	Christopher Hatton	Manor of *Somerford Maudits*, Wilts.	£1,850	H.A. Wilts. deeds
10 Sept. 1572	Henry Chyver	The Manor Place, Leigh, Wilts.	£300	H.A. Wilts. deeds
20 Nov. 1572	Edward Ameredith	Manor of *Harlestone*, Devon	£400	H.A. Devon deeds
20 Feb. 1574	Henry Ford	Messuages and lands in Crabbesdon and Diptford, Devon	£310	H.A. Devon deeds
20 Feb. 1574	John Lavers	Lands in Diptford, Devon	£133 6s. 8d.	H.A. Devon deeds
3 Mar. 1574	William Rawle	Lands in St. Juliot, Cornwall	£80	H.A. Cornwall deeds
17 Apr. 1574	John Hender	Manors of *Botreux Castle*, *Worthivale* *Trevena*, Cornwall	£1,210	H.A. Cornwall deeds
28 Apr. 1574	J. Popham, M. Smith and E. Ameredith	Manor of *Langford Leicester*, Devon	£1,000	H.A. Devon deeds

309

Date	Purchaser	Property	Consideration	Source
1 May 1574	Henry Killigrew	*Manor of Botleat*, Cornwall	£3,600	H.A. Seals 236
1 May 1574	William Swadell als. Symon	Messuages and land in Diptford, Devon	£166 13s. 4d.	H.A. Devon deeds
10 May 1574	John Symon als. Swadell	Messuage in Diptford, Devon	£100	H.A. Devon deeds
10 May 1574	Philip Sture	Messuages in Diptford, Devon	£150	H.A. Devon deeds
10 May 1574	John Lavers	Messuage in Diptford, Devon	£71	H.A. Devon deeds
10 May 1574	Henry Coyte	Cottage in Diptford, Devon	£13 6s. 8d.	H.A. Devon deeds
10 May 1574	Thomas Hele and Stephen Hele	Lands in Diptford, Devon	[recognisance for £640]	P.R.O. C 54/948
10 May 1574	Henry Luscombe	Lands in Diptford, Devon	[recognisance for £540]	P.R.O. C 54/948
7 May 1575	William Prewet	*Manor of Leigh*, Wilts.	£340	H.A. Wilts. deeds
20 June 1575	George Gale	Messuages in Diptford, Devon	£126 13s. 4d.	P.R.O. C 54/977
2 Oct. 1575	Henry More and eleven others, as individuals, not corporately	Twelve individual assignments of messuages and lands in Belton, Leics.	£262 10s. [combined total]	H.A. Leics. deeds
2 Oct. 1575	John Campion	Messuages and lands in Castle Donington, Leics.	£66 13s. 4d.	H.A. Leics. deeds
2 Dec. 1575	Ralph Cone and 2 others, as individuals not corporately	Three individual assignments of messuages and lands in Belton, Leics.	£84 [combined total]	H.A. Leics. deeds
13 Nov. 1575	George Grenville	*Manor of Penbeale*, Cornwall	£2,950	P.R.O. C 54/975

Date	Purchaser	Property	Consideration	Source
18 Jan. 1576	Philip Sture	*Manor of Diptford,* Devon	£235	P.R.O. C 54/984
1 Feb. 1576	Roger Chetyll	Messuage and lands in Long Whatton, Leics.	£33	H.A. Leics. deeds
13 Feb. 1576	John Stumpe	Lands in Brokenborough, Wilts.	20 marks	H.A. Wilts. deeds
2 Mar. 1576	John Wryght and 14 others, as individuals not corporately	Fifteen individual assignments of messuages and lands in Belton, Leics.	£115 10s. [combined total]	H.A. Leics. and 'Ireland' deeds
2 Mar. 1576	John Porter and 3 others, as individuals not corporately	Four individual assignments of messuages and lands in Long Whatton, Leics.	£131 6s. 8d. [combined total]	H.A. Leics. deeds
2 Mar. 1576	Robert Sherrard and 3 others as individuals not corporately	Four individual assignments of messuages and lands in Castle Donington, Leics.	£17 [combined total]	H.A. Leics. deeds
2 Mar. 1576	John Smythe	Messuage and lands in Osgarthorpe, Leics.	£8	H.A. Leics. deeds
2 Mar. 1576	Steven Michell	Messuages and lands in Shepshed, Leics.	£66 13s. 4d.	H.A. Leics. deeds
2 Mar. 1576	John Henson	Lands in Normanton, Leics.	£5	H.A. Misc. deeds
11 Oct. 1576	Chaplains and Poor of Wyggeston Hospital, Leicester	Rent charges in Leicester worth £66 13s. 4d. p.a.	[gift]	P.R.O. C 54/1003
2 Dec. 1576	Hamlett Tone	Messuages and land in Belton, Leics.	£54	H.A. Leics. deeds

Date	Purchaser	Property	Consideration	Source
2 Dec. 1576	William Townesend	Messuage and land in Belton, Leics.	£12	H.A. Leics. deeds
2 Dec. 1576	W. Cowper, R. Lawrence and others	Messuages and lands in Long Whatton, Leics.	£75	H.A. Leics. deeds
14 June 1577	Countess of Pembroke	Confirmation of *Manor of Finchley*, Middlesex	..	P.R.O. C 66/1153
3 Sept. 1577	William Wanton	Messuage and lands in Sheriff Hutton, Yorks.	£400	H.A. Yorks. deeds
13 Feb. 1579	Walter Hastings	Manor house and lands in Kirby Muxloe, Leics.	[In exchange for lease of Mnr, of Barrow, Leics.]	H.A. Misc. Manorial documents
23 Dec. 1579	Walter Hastings	Lands in Alton Grange, Leics.	..	P.R.O. C 66/1194
.. 1580	Thomas Fanshaw	Confirmation of *Manor of Ware*, Herts. [Release of £80 annual rent charged on original grant of 1578.]	£410	P.R.O. C 2 Eliz./F4/49
20 Aug. 1580	Sir Edward Hastings	Leicester Abbey	gift	H.A. Leics. deeds
6 June 1581	Thomas Gresley and Christopher Horton	Repton tithes, Derbyshire	£1,000	H.A. Derbys. deeds
22 June 1581	Francis Saunders	*Manor of Welford*, Northants.	£4,000	H.A. Middlesex deeds
5 July 1581	Sir James Harington	*Manor of Leighfield*, Rutland	£7,000	H.A. Rutland deeds
20 Oct. 1581	Sir George Hastings	Measham parsonage and tithes, Derbyshire	..	Bodl. Carte 289, f. 108

Date	Purchaser	Property	Consideration	Source
.. 1581	William Peache	Messuages in Hathern, Leics.	£504	H.A. Leics. deeds
2 May 1582	Francis Hastings	Manor of Newbold Verdon, Leics.	..	P.R.O. C 66/1221
23 May 1582	Walter Hastings	Manor of Kirby Muxloe, Leics.	£1,500	P.R.O. C 54/1122
1 Dec. 1582	John Fountain	Lands in Stokenham, Devon	[£666 13s. 4d.]	H.A. Manorial, Devon P.R.O. C 66/1234
c. Dec. 1582	Thomas Ameredith	Lands in Stokenham, Devon	[£133 6s. 8d.]	H.A. Manorial, Devon
2 Jan. 1583	Edward Ameredith	Stokenham Park and lands, Devon	[£500]	P.R.O. C 66/1230.
				H.A. Manorial, Devon
2 Sept. 1583	Roger Bromley and Christopher Southouse	Lands in Aller and Allermore, Somerset	..	P.R.O. C 66/1233
2 Sept. 1583	John, Thomas and Robert Hele	Manor of Yealmton, Devon	£10,666	Plymouth city Library, Heale cartulary f. 1
2 Nov. 1583	Robert Seyman	Messuages and lands in South Allington in Stokenham, Devon	£103	H.A. Devon deeds
2 Nov. 1583	Thomas Came	Messuages and lands in South Allington in Stokenham, Devon	£193 13s. 4d.	H.A. Devon deeds
c. Jan. 1584	William and Thomas Michell	Lands in Aller, Somerset	..	P.R.O. C 66/1314
15 Feb. 1584	Bennett Wilson	Reversionary interest in Ulverscroft Priory, Leics.	£400	P.R.O. C 54/1185
7 Nov. 1585	Edward Ameredith	Hundred of Colridge, Devon	..	P.R.O. C 66/1298
20 Nov. 1585	John Nele and Alexander Cryspyn	Lands in Chilston in Stokenham, Devon	£460	H.A. Devon deeds

313

Date	Purchaser	Property	Consideration	Source
20 Nov. 1585	Richard Dyer, senior and junior	Lands in Stokenham, Devon	£720	H.A. Devon deeds
19 Nov. 1585	John and Edward Fortescue	Hundred of Stanborough, Devon	..	P.R.O. C 66/1291
30 Nov. 1585	Walter Hele	Manor of South Pool, Devon	£1,545	P.R.O. C 54/1237
11 Feb. 1586	Thomas Sharpham	Lands in Stokenham, Devon	[recognisance for £500]	P.R.O. C 54/1250
2 Mar. 1586	William Kyrkham	Lands in Chilston in Stokenham, Devon	..	P.R.O. C 66/1281
2 Apr. 1586	Francis Hastings	Manors of North Cadbury, South Cadbury, Maperton and Holton, Somerset	£940	P.R.O. E 368/445 H.A. Somerset deeds
20 May 1586	Alice Gamage	Manor of Newton Montague, Dorset	[recognisance for £1,500]	P.R.O. C 54/1247
30 May 1586	Miles Wylles	Messuages and lands in Stokenham, Devon	£300	H.A. Devon deeds
15 June 1586	Sir George Hastings	Lands in Belton, Leics.	£385 12s. 6d.	H.A. Leics. deeds
1 May 1587	Edward Ameredith and John Norden	Lands in Aller, Somerset	..	P.R.O. C 66/1298
2 Sept 1587	Edward Ameredith	Manor of Stokenham, Devon	c. £5,000	P.R.O. C 66/1298. P.R.O. C 2 Eliz./G 1/59

Date	Purchaser	Property	Consideration	Source
28 Mar. 1588	The queen	Manors of Bradbury and Hilton, Durham	In exchange for grant of royal lands worth £400 p.a.	P.R.O. C 54/1300
2 Apr. 1589	Sir Wolstan Dixie	Manor of Market Bosworth, Leics.	..	P.R.O. C 66/1327
10 May 1589	Walter Hastings	Manor of Braunstone, Leics.	[recognisance for £2,000]	P.R.O. C 54/1315 C 54/1333
20 May 1589	John Spencer	Manors of Kilmersdon and Walton, Som.	£2,400	P.R.O. C 54/1314
8 Apr. 1590	Sir Edward Hastings	Messuage in the High Street, Leicester	..	P.R.O. C 54/1361
2 May 1590	Thomas Owen	Manor of Henley on Thames, Oxon.	..	P.R.O. C 66/1350
7 Feb. 1591	Thomas Stolion	Confirmation of Manor of Warbleton, Sussex	£150	P.R.O. C 54/1380
2 Apr. 1591	Thomas Pelham	Honour, Castle, Barony, Lordship etc. of Hastings, Sussex	£2,500	P.R.O. C 66/1371 C 54/1384
17 July 1591	Richard Branthwaite	Manor of Cippenham, Bucks.	£3,000	P.R.O. C 66/1367 P.R.O. C 54/1398
25 Nov. 1591	Sir George Hastings	Rectory of Enderby, Leics.	..	P.R.O. C 54/1408
10 Jan. 1592	Francis Hastings and Edward Hext	Manor of Somerton, Somerset	£4,000	P.R.O. C 54/1408
8 June 1592	Richard Branthwaite and Thomas Spencer	Manor of Ringwood, Hants	£5,000	P.R.O. C 54/1416

315

Date	Purchaser	Property	Consideration	Source
8 July 1593	William Barwell	Mill in Ravenstone, Leics.	100 marks	H.A. Leics. deeds
18 Feb. 1594	Denis Orme	Manor of Enderby, Leics.	..	P.R.O. C 66/1411
Date not known	Purchaser not known	Manors of Aston Bampton, Standlake, Broughton, Nether Filkins, Golovers and Stoke Mules, Oxon.	..	Bodl. Carte 289/48
Date not known	Purchaser not known	Manors of Begginton, Chardesley, Ludgarshall, Ilmer, Weston Turville, Birchill, Addington and Aston Molins, Bucks.	..	Bodl. Carte 289/48

TOTAL OF RECORDED SALES: £91,590 6s. 2d.

Leases granted by Huntingdon

Date	Lessee	Property	Term	Fine	Rent p.a.	Source
				Payment		
24 Jan. 1562	John Halsey	Pasture in Aller, Som.	21 years	40s.	4s.	H.A. Somerset deeds
8 Feb. 1562	John Escott, Joan Braughton and Mary Tristram	Messuages and lands in Colebrook, Devon	Three lives and life of longest liver	£70	45s. 5½d.	H.A. Devon deeds

Date	Lessee	Property	Term	Payment		Source
				Fine	Rent p.a.	
1 Oct. 1562	William Peache	Capital messuage of Knighthorpe and lands in Leics.	..	..	£16 11s. 11½d.	H.A. Devon deeds
1 Sept. 1564	William Dent	Messuage and land in Enderby, Leics.	21 years	..	24s. 1d.	H.A. Leics. deeds
1 Sept. 1564	Robert Olyve	Messuage and land in Enderby, Leics.	21 years	..	11s. 2½d.	H.A. Leics. deeds
1 Sept. 1564	Thomas Tylley	Cottage in Enderby, Leics.	21 years	..	2s.	H.A. Leics. deeds
1 Sept. 1564	William Dent	Messuages and lands in Enderby, Leics.	21 years	..	42s. 9d.	H.A. Leics. deeds
1 Sept. 1564	Robert Freer	Messuages and lands in Enderby, Leics.	21 years	..	38s. 7d.	H.A. Leics. deeds
1 Sept. 1564	William Shawe	Cottage in Enderby	21 years	..	16d.	H.A. Leics. deeds
1 Sept. 1564	Thomas More	Messuage and lands in Enderby	21 years	..	25s. 6d.	H.A. Leics. deeds
1 Sept. 1564	William Hochyns	Cottage in Enderby	21 years	..	9d.	H.A. Leics. deeds
1 Sept. 1564	Robert Eden	Cottage in Enderby	21 years	..	2s.	H.A. Leics. deeds
1 Sept. 1564	Thomas Wylmere	Messuage and lands in Enderby	21 years	..	6s. 11d.	H.A. Leics. deeds
1 Sept. 1564	Robert Frere	Cottage and land in Enderby	21 years	..	2s.	H.A. Leics. deeds

317

Date	Lessee	Property	Term	Fine	Rent p.a.	Source
1 Sept. 1564	Rowland Richardson	Cottage and land in Enderby	21 years	..	2s.	H.A. Leics. deeds
1 Sept. 1564	John Marsshe	Messuage and lands in Enderby	21 years	..	17s. 1½d.	H.A. Leics. deeds
1 Sept. 1564	Thomas Dassorne	Cottage in Enderby	21 years	..	2od.	H.A. Leics. deeds
23 May 1565	Edward Lord Hastings of Loughborough	Messuages and lands in Long Whatton, Leics.	For life	..	£9 5s. 4d.	H.A. Leics. deeds
12 Apr. 1568	William Cowper	Meadow in Barrow on Soar, Leics.	21 years	..	15 quarters of wheat	H.A. Leics. deeds
7 July 1569	Everard Digby	Farm in Brill, Bucks.	41 years	..	..	H.A. Bucks. deeds
1 Aug. 1570	Thomas Jerome	Piece of ground in Ashby, Leics.	198 years	..	8d.	H.A. Leics. deeds
1 Aug. 1570	William Smyth	Piece of ground in Ashby, Leics.	198 years	..	12d.	H.A. Leics. deeds
8 Oct. 1571	Richard Wattes	Withybeds and fishing in Allermore, Somerset	21 years	£50	33s. 4d.	H.A. Som. deeds
26 June 1572	Thomas Cawro	Lands in Shepshed, Leics.	21 years	£6 13s. 4d.	20s.	H.A. Leics. deeds

318

Date	Lessee	Property	Term	Payment Fine	Rent p.a.	Source
1 Oct. 1572	Lady Joan, widow of Edward Lord Hastings of Loughborough	Burghley Park in Loughborough, as her dower	For life	..	..	H.A. Leics. deeds
20 Jan. 1574	Gilbert Vincent	Messuage and mill in Thringston, Leics.	21 years	..	£9 10s.	H.A. Leics. deeds
8 Apr. 1574 25 May, 1574	Thomas Fanshaw	Park of Ware, Herts.	50 years	..	£191 12s. 2¼d. until debt of £1,149 13s. 2d. to Crown repaid. For remaining 20 years 100 marks p.a.	H.A. Herts. deeds
6 Apr. 1575	Nicholas Watts	Land in Allermore, Som.	21 years	£43 6s. 8d.	26s.	H.A. Leics. deeds
19 Aug. 1577	William Cater	Lands in Anstey and Glenfield, Leics.	31 years beginning 1585	..	40s. 8d.	H.A. Leics. deeds
25 Mar. 1578	John Jackson	Messuage and land in West Lilling, Yorks.	10 years	£18	24s.	H.A. Yorks. deeds
20 Oct. 1578	Agnes Deane and Hugh and William, her sons	Lands in Holdenhurst, Hants	Three lives and life of longest liver	..	58s.	H.A. Hants. deeds

Date	Lessee	Property	Term	Payment Fine	Rent p.a.	Source
1 July 1579	Ambrose Keyllwey and wife	Lands in Christchurch, Hants	Fifty years if they shall so long live	..	£3 6s. 8d. (payable only after wife's death)	H.A. Dorset deeds
10 Oct.⎫ 1581 11 Oct.⎭	Peter Wynter	Tenements and lands in Stokenham, Devon	3,000 years	£70	7s. 3d.	H.A. Manorial Papers, Devon
10 Oct.⎫ 1581 11 Oct.⎭	Thomas Sharpham	Land in Stokenham, Devon	3,000 years	£200	62s. 8d.	H.A. Manorial Papers, Devon
10 Oct.⎫ 1581 11 Oct.⎭	Thomas Bully	Land in Stokenham, Devon	3,000 years	£60	25s.	H.A. Manorial Papers, Devon
10 Oct.⎫ 1581 11 Oct.⎭	Richard Wakeman	Land in Colridge, Devon	3,000 years	£136 13s. 4d.	8s. 4d.	H.A. Manorial Papers, Devon
10 Oct.⎫ 1581 11 Oct.⎭	John Hedd	Tenements and land in Stokenham, Devon	3,000 years	£133 6s. 8d.	19s. 4d.	H.A. Manorial Papers, Devon
10 Oct.⎫ 1581 11 Oct.⎭	Thomas Ameredith	Tenements and land in Stokenham, Devon	3,000 years	£133 6s. 8d.	16s. 8½d.	H.A. Manorial Papers, Devon
10 Oct.⎫ 1581 11 Oct.⎭	Thomas Ameredith	Further lands there	3,000 years	£68 13s. 4d.	10s. 3d.	H.A. Manorial Papers, Devon

Date	Lessee	Property	Term	Payment Fine	Rent p.a.	Source
10 Oct. } 11 Oct. } 1581	Richard Crewes	Tenements and land in Stokenham	3,000 years	£66 13s. 4d.	9s. 10d.	H.A. Manorial Papers, Devon
10 Oct. } 11 Oct. } 1581	Edward Ameredith	Tenements and land in Stokenham	3,000 years	£200	29s. 1½d.	H.A. Manorial Papers, Devon
10 Oct. } 11 Oct. } 1581	John Hodge	Tenements and land in Stokenham	3,000 years	£266 13s. 4d.	38s. 10d.	H.A. Manorial Papers, Devon
10 Oct. } 11 Oct. } 1581	Edward Ameredith	Further tenements and land in Stokenham	3,000 years	£203 6s. 8d.	30s. 6d.	H.A. Manorial Papers, Devon
10 Oct. } 11 Oct. } 1581	Thomas Ameredith	Further lands and tenements in Stokenham	3,000 years	£60	5s. 4d.	H.A. Manorial Papers, Devon
10 Oct. } 11 Oct. } 1581	Edward Ameredith	Pasture land in Stokenham	3,000 years	£466 13s. 4d.	66s. 8d.	H.A. Manorial Papers, Devon
10 Oct. } 11 Oct. } 1581	Edward Ameredith	Tenement and land in Stokenham	3,000 years	£133 6s. 8d.	22s. 2d.	H.A. Manorial Papers, Devon
10 Oct. } 11 Oct. } 1581	Thomas Jeffrey	Tenement and land in Stokenham	3,000 years	£113 6s. 8d.	13s. 6d.	H.A. Manorial Papers, Devon
10 Oct. } 11 Oct. } 1581	Philip Luscombe	Tenements and land in Stokenham	3,000 years	£133 6s. 8d.	19s. 8d.	H.A. Manorial Papers, Devon
10 Oct. } 11 Oct. } 1581	Robert Tronte	Cottage in Stokenham	3,000 years	100s.	13½d.	H.A. Manorial Papers, Devon

Date	Lessee	Property	Term	Payment		Source
				Fine	Rent p.a.	
10 Oct. } 1581 11 Oct. }	Philip Luscombe	Cottage in Stokenham	3,000 years	..	13½d.	H.A. Manorial Papers, Devon
10 Oct. } 1581 11 Oct. }	Trustees for repair of church	Chapel and houses in Stokenham	3,000 years	£6 13s. 4d.	4d.	H.A. Manorial Papers, Devon
10 Oct. } 1581 11 Oct. }	William Shote	Tenement and land in Stokenham	3,000 years	£106 13s. 4d.	13s. 7d.	H.A. Manorial Papers, Devon
10 Oct. } 1581 11 Oct. }	John Standerwicke	Tenement and land in Stokenham	3,000 years	£133 6s. 8d.	16s. 3½d.	H.A. Manorial Papers, Devon
2 Apr. 1582	Richard Stone	Tenement and land in Stokenham	..	£66 13s. 4d.	9s. 2d.	H.A. Manorial Papers, Devon
2 Apr. 1582	Henry Luscombe	Tenement and land in Stokenham	..	£66 13s. 4d.	9s. 10½d.	H.A. Manorial Papers, Devon
2 Apr. 1582	Thomasine Shave	Tenement and land in Stokenham	..	£66 13s. 4d.	9s. 8d.	H.A. Manorial Papers, Devon
2 Apr. 1582	Nicholas Stone	Cottage and land in Stokenham	..	£4	8d.	H.A. Manorial Papers, Devon
2 Apr. 1582	Richard Piers	Tenement and land in Stokenham	..	£100	13s. 4d.	H.A. Manorial Papers, Devon
2 Apr. 1582	William Marche	Watermill in Stokenham	..	£66 13s. 4d.	33s. 4d.	H.A. Manorial Papers, Devon
24 July 1582	William Lyllie	Land in Long Whatton, Leics.	21 years	30s.	3s.	H.A. Leics. deeds

Date	Lessee	Property	Term	Payment Fine	Rent p.a.	Source
Sept. 1582	Richard Halse	Mill in Stokenham	2,000 years	£66 13s. 4d.	1d.	H.A. Manorial Papers, Devon
16 Feb. 1583	Stephen Harvey	Farm in Maperton, Som.	99 years if three sons so long live	..	£4 6s. 8d.	H.A. Som. deeds
6 Apr. 1583	Thomas Sharpham	Release of 62s. 8d. rent charge	For ever	£60	..	H. A. Manorial Papers, Devon
6 Apr. 1583	Richard Peers	Rent charge of 14s. 8d. p.a. in Stokenham	300 years	£14 13s. 4d.	1d.	H.A. Manorial Papers, Devon
6 Apr. 1583	Walter Goe	Cottage and rent charge of 12d. p.a. in Stokenham	300 years	£6 13s. 4d.	1d.	H.A. Manorial Papers, Devon
7 May 1583	Sir George Hastings	Manor of Loughborough, except Burley Park, and except right of presentation to church, Leics.	21 years [surrendered 19 Nov. 1591]	..	£316 6s. 8d.	H.A. Leics. deeds
2 Apr. 1590	Robert Baynbridge	Five water mills in Ashby, Leics.	99 years	£200	£10	H.A. Leics. deeds
1 May 1593	Robert Yeomans	Meadow in Allermore, Som.	99 years (conditional on three lives)	£32	19s. 4d.	H.A. Som. deeds

Mortgages incurred by Huntingdon

Date	Mortgagee	Property	Mortgage loan	Cancellation	Source
12 June 1559	[With second Earl] Julian Hyckes	Manors of Stoke Poges, Bucks., and North Cadbury, Som.	£600	28 Feb. 1562?	P.R.O. C 54/573
15 Jan. 1562	John Hare	Manor of Stoke Poges, Bucks.	£1,000	12 May 1564	P.R.O. C 54/617
24 Jan. 1562	R. Hayward, T. Kightley, R. Pype and others	Manors of North Cadbury, Som. and Barrow, Leics.	£2,525	24 Feb. 1563	P.R.O. C 54/607
14 Feb. 1562	Thomas Lodge	Manors of Aller and Wootton Courtney, Som.	£2,100	13 Nov. 1562	P.R.O. C 54/610
1 Oct. 1562	William Peache [Assigned to Nicholas Lynge als. Proctor 1570]	Manor of Knighthorpe, Leics.	£500	19 Feb. 1579	H.A. Leics. deeds P.R.O. C 54/1057
24 Feb. 1563	Thomas Ryvett and Richard Carell	Manors of North Cadbury, Som. and Bosworth, Leics.	£2,500	9 Feb. 1565	H.A. Som. deeds
24 Feb. 1563	R. Hayward, T. Kightley, R. Pype and others	Manor of Barrow, Leics.	£680	25 Jan. 1565 ?	P.R.O. C 54/638

Date	Mortgagee	Property	Mortgage loan	Cancellation	Source
5 Mar. 1563	Henry Fanshawe	Manor of Newton St. Loe, Som.	£570	6 Nov. 1564	P.R.O. C 54/659
19 June 1563	George Langham	Manors of Packington and Alton Grange, Leics.	£2,000	2 Nov. 1565	P.R.O. C 54/643
10 Jan. 1565	Thomas, Earl of Sussex	Manors of Barrow and Bagworth, Leics.	£2,333 6s. 8d.	..	P.R.O. C 54/690
[Before 1572]	Sir Roger Martin and Richard Younge	Manor of Burton Lazars, Leics.	..	2 Feb. 1572	P.R.O. C 54/883
10 Feb. 1572	Sir James Harington	Manor of Leigh, Rutland	£2,000	20 Nov. 1572	P.R.O. C 54/875
15 Nov. 1572	Edward Waterhouse	Leicester Park. 500 years' lease	£1,000	..	P.R.O. C 54/917
30 Nov. 1573	M. Calthorpe, T. Aldersaye and W. Dixey	Manors of Aller and Allermore, Som.	£3,599	15 Nov. 1575	P.R.O. C 54/957
8 July 1577	Wolstan Dixey	Manor of Cippenham, Bucks.	£1,650	15 Nov. 1578	P.R.O. C 54/1007
20 July 1578	Wolstan Dixey	Further charge on Manor of Cippenham, Bucks.	£2,000	9 Dec. 1579	P.R.O. C 54/1040
30 Jan. 1579	*R. Scudamore and Roger Bromley	Manor of Bosworth, Leics.	..	..	P.R.O. C 66/1181

Date	Mortgagee	Property	Mortgage loan	Cancellation	Source
11 Nov. 1579	Wolstan Dixey	Manor of Cippenham, Bucks. 200 years' lease	[recog. for £3,000]	17 Nov. 1581	P.R.O. C 54/1065
12 Nov. 1579	Ambrose Smithe	Manors of North Cadbury, Maperton, Clapton and Holton, Som. 100 years' lease	[recog. for £3,000]	25 Nov. 1581	P.R.O. C 54/1094
14 Nov. 1579	M. Calthorpe, T. Aldersaye	Manor of Aller, Som. 100 years' lease	[recog. for £2,000]	Cancelled, no date	P.R.O. C 54/1094
23 Dec. 1579	*R. Scudamore and Roger Bromley	Manors of Loughborough, Barrow and Lubbesthorpe, Leics.	..	..	P.R.O. C 66/1193
14 Dec. 1581	Thomas Sutton	Lordships of East and West Lillings, Yorks.	£1,430	..	P.R.O. C 54/1143
24 June 1582	John Spencer	Manors of Evington, Leics. and Kilmersdon, Som.	£5,150	..	H.A. Leics. deeds
2 Mar. 1583	Ambrose Smythe	Manors of North Cadbury, Kilmersdon and Walton, Som.	£6,000	..	H.A. Leics. deeds
10 Dec. 1584	Thomas Isted and Thomas Collen	Rape of Hastings, Sussex twenty-one years' lease	£600	11 June 1586	P.R.O. C 54/1222
2 Mar. 1585	Lancelot and Francis Alford	Manor of Henley on Thames, Oxon.	..	..	P.R.O. C 66/1262

Date	Mortgagee	Property	Mortgage loan	Cancellation	Source
2 Mar. 1586	John Alford	Manor of Henley on Thames, Oxon.	£1,400	31 Mar. 1590	P.R.O. C 66/1274 C 54/1241
20 May 1586	Thomas Isted and Thomas Collen	Rape of Hastings, Sussex twenty-one years' lease	£400	30 June 1591	P.R.O. C 54/1249
26 May 1586	John Spencer	Leicester Abbey [Concealed mortgage?]	£5,000	..	H.A. Leics. deeds
23 Aug. 1586	Wolstan Dixey	Manors of Bagworth and Thornton, Leics. 100 years' lease	..	..	P.R.O. C 54/1334
27 Dec. 1588	Samuel Ailmer	Manor of Knighthorpe, Leics. 999 years' lease	£1,000	..	P.R.O. C 54/1320
6 May 1589	Trustees of Sir James Harington	Manors of Bagworth and Thornton, Leics.	£5,200	..	P.R.O. C 54/1308
1 June 1589	Rowland Watson	Lands in Ashby and Blackfordby, Leics.	£414	Cancelled, no date	H.A. Leics. deeds
20 Mar. 1591	Richard Branthwaite	Manors of Stoke Poges, Fulmer and Eton, Bucks.	£1,030	..	P.R.O. C 54/1396
26 Oct. 1591	Richard Branthwaite	Manors of Stoke Poges, Fulmer and Eton, Bucks.	£7,000	[forfeited]	P.R.O. C 54/1419
8 June 1592	Thomas Spencer and Richard Branthwaite	Manors of Christchurch and Westover, Hants.	£4,400	14 Feb. 1595	P.R.O. C 54/1413
24 July 1595	Walter Hastings, M. Ewens, T. Staughton	Manors of Christchurch and Westover, Hants.	£1,337 10s.	..	P.R.O. C 54/1518

* This could be the grant of a commission for making leases and not a true mortgage.

Huntingdon's borrowing on bond

Date	Lender	Security	Actual loan	Cancellation	Source	Remarks
13 Nov. 1562	Thomas Lodge	2,000 marks	£1,000	28 June 1563?	P.R.O. C 54/628	
18 May 1563	W. Devereux, R. Hyll, R. Goodale & T. Radford	400 marks	200 marks	..	P.R.O. C 54/643	
27 May 1563	Richard Springham	£800	£600	..	P.R.O. C 54/649	
19 June 1563	George Langham	£2,000	£1,000	..	P.R.O. C 54/643	
3 July 1563	Sir Henry Nevill and John Gresham	1,000 marks	..	..	P.R.O. L.C. 4/189	
27 Apr. 1564	Sir Thomas Gresham	1,000 marks	£500	2 Nov. 1564	P.R.O. L.C. 4/189	
28 June 1564	Sir Thomas Lodge	£400	£224 19s.	11 Nov. 1564	P.R.O. C 54/670	
13 Oct. 1564	Martin Jones	£400	£200	13 Oct. 1565	P.R.O. L.C. 4/189	Huntingdon bound to John Gresham and Wm. Chelsam who are bound to Martin Jones
31 Oct. 1564	Sir Thomas Lodge	2,000 marks	..	..	P.R.O. L.C. 4/189	
8 Nov. 1564	Roger Martin	£400	£224 19s.	..	P.R.O. C 54/670	

Date	Lender	Security	Actual loan	Cancellation	Source	Remarks
15 Jan. 1565	Thomas Earl of Sussex	£1,000	1,000 marks	29 May 1572	P.R.O. L.C. 4/191	
15 June 1567	Sir Thomas Gresham	£700	£500	24 Oct. 1567	P.R.O. L.C. 4/191	
5 July 1569	Sir Thomas Gresham	£700	..	31 Jan. 1570	P.R.O. L.C. 4/191	
14 Nov. 1570	Robert Robothom	£600	..	31 Oct. 1572	P.R.O. L.C. 4/191	
14 Nov. 1570	Sir Thomas Gresham	£2,000	..	28 Nov. 1571	P.R.O. L.C. 4/191	
14 Nov. 1570	Sir Roger Martin	£2,000	£1,200	28 Nov. 1571	P.R.O. C 54/820	
28 Nov. 1570	Francis Willoughby	£800	..	21 May 1571	P.R.O. L.C. 4/191	
18 May 1571	Francis Willoughby	£1,500	..	31 Oct. 1571	P.R.O. L.C. 4/191	Sir Thomas Lucy surety for Huntingdon's debt
23 July 1571	Francis Willoughby	£3,000	..	1 Dec. 1571	P.R.O. L.C. 4/191	
24 Nov. 1571	Sir Thomas Gresham	£2,000	..	25 June 1572	P.R.O. L.C. 4/191	
27 Nov. 1571	Sir Roger Martyn	£2,000	£1,000	26 July 1572	P.R.O. C 54/883	
11 Jan. 1572	Grace Robotham	£800	£400	..	P.R.O. L.C. 4/191	

329

Date	Lender	Security	Actual loan	Cancellation	Source	Remarks
1 Feb. 1572	Anne Throckmorton	£1,000	..	..	P.R.O. L.C. 4/191	
23 June 1572	John Spencer	£6,000	..	24 Nov. 1573	P.R.O. L.C. 4/191	
28 Oct. 1572	Francis Willoughby	£3,000	..	..	P.R.O. L.C. 4/191	
31 Oct. 1572	Sir James Harington	£3,000	£2,000	27 Nov. 1581	P.R.O. L.C. 4/191	
16 Nov. 1572	Martin Calthorpe	£1,000	..	24 Nov. 1574	P.R.O. L.C. 4/191	
16 Nov. 1572	Nicholas Backhouse	£1,000		24 Nov. 1573	P.R.O. L.C. 4/191	
16 Nov. 1572	Thomas Brasy	£1,000	..	20 Nov. 1574	P.R.O. L.C. 4/191	
16 Nov. 1572	Ambrose Smith	£1,000	..	20 Nov. 1574	P.R.O. L.C. 4/191	
27 May 1574	William, Earl of Worcester	£1,000	£600	7 Feb. 1575	P.R.O. C. 54/947	
31 Oct. 1581	Sir George Hastings	1,000 marks	£500	..	H.A. Accounts and Inventories	£500 to be repaid in 1583
31 Oct. 1581	Sir George Hastings	1,000 marks	£500	..	H.A. Accounts and Inventories	£500 to be repaid in 1585
23 Dec. 1581	Thomas Smith	£800	..	..	H.A. Accounts and Inventories	
31 Jan. 1582	Humphrey Adderleye	£600	..	..	H.A. Accounts and Inventories	

Date	Lender	Security	Actual loan	Cancellation	Source	Remarks
10 Mar. 1582	John Spencer	£1,500	..	Cancelled, no date	H.A. Accounts and Inventories	Two bonds. Connected with mortgage of 20 June 1582?
25 Oct. 1582?	Richard Branthwaite	£1,600	..	..	H.A. Accounts and Inventories	
20 Nov. 1582	Thomas Billingsley	£3,000	..	..	H.A. Accounts and Inventories	
20 Nov. 1582	Thomas Adderleye	£1,000	..	..	H.A. Accounts and Inventories	
26 Feb. 1583	Philip Smith	2,000 marks	..	..	H.A. Accounts and Inventories	
20 July 1583	William Becher	£1,200	..	Cancelled, no date	H.A. Accounts and Inventories	
28 Nov. 1583	William Wyseman	£700	£376 10s.	..	P.R.O. C 54/1198	
10 Feb. 1584	William Constantyne	£1,200	£700	..	H.A. Accounts and Inventories	To be repaid 1 May 1587
28 Feb. 1586	Sir John Harington	£2,000	..	Cancelled, no date	H.A. Accounts and Inventories	
6 June 1586	Philip Smith	£2,000	..	..	H.A. Accounts and Inventories	
9 June 1586	Thomas Hasell	£1,300	£650	..	H.A. Accounts and Inventories	To be repaid in Aug. and Nov. 1592

Date	Lender	Security	Actual loan	Cancellation	Source	Remarks
9 June 1586	Thomas Hasell	£1,300	£650	..	H.A. Accounts and Inventories	To be repaid in Aug. and Nov. 1593
1 July 1586	John Spencer	£7,000	..	..	H.A. Accounts and Inventories	
18 July 1586	Francis Smith	£1,000	..	..	H.A. Accounts and Inventories	
18 July 1586	Edward Unton	£4,000	..	..	H.A. Accounts and Inventories	
3 Aug. 1586	Nicholas Moslie and Hugh Henlie	£2,000	..	..	H.A. Accounts and Inventories	Henry Earl of Derby surety to Moslie and Henlie for these debts contracted by Huntingdon
28 Nov. 1590	Sir Henry Constable	£1,000	..	..	H.A. Accounts and Inventories	
2 May 1591	Roland Warten and Bartholomew Quyuy	£3,000	..	..	H.A. Accounts and Inventories	

* Recognisance Books (P.R.O. L.C. 4—) wanting from 1573 until 1591. No known bonds to perform covenants in indentures of even date have been entered on this list. Nevertheless, in many cases the purpose of the bond is not revealed and these bonds have been included.

Annuities granted by Huntingdon

Date	Annuitant	Property charged	Term	Payment	Source
5 Oct. 1562	*Katherine, Dowager Countess of Huntingdon	Annuity of £960	Fifty years (apparently cancelled 1 Dec. 1564)	In exchange for grant of all her lands in Herts, Som, Devon (except Plymtree), Cornwall, Wilts. and Hants and for promise to pay additional £1,000 to Ladies Elizabeth, Mary and Frances Hastings on their marriage	H.A. Family Papers, and Cornish deeds
20 Feb. 1564	*Katherine, Dowager Countess of Huntingdon	Further annuity of £100	Fifty years	£400 And in exchange for grant of Aller, Som. and release of other rights	H.A. Deeds Various
28 June 1568	Thomas Wood	Annuity of £80 charged on manor of Lubbesthorpe	[In 1577 for lives of Agnes Wood, widow, and 2 sons]	[Bond for 2,000 marks]	H.A. Seals 225, Accounts and Inventories, Leics. deeds

333

Date	Annuitant	Property charged	Term	Payment	Source
12 May 1572	John Spencer and wife	Annuity of £500	..	..	H.A. Accounts and Inventories
8 May 1574	Katherine, Dowager Countess of Huntingdon	Annuity of £33 6s. 8d. charged on manor of Ashby	..	In exchange for release of dower in Ware Park	H.A. Leics. deeds
15 Dec. 1575	Lady Mary Hastings	Annuity of 100 marks charged on Loughborough Park	Life	£500	H.A. Leics. deeds
4 Apr. 1580	Roger Bromley and Katherine Harware, widow	Annuity of £50 charged on manor of Ashby	Life of longest liver	..	H.A. Leics. deeds
15 May 1582	Richard Branthwaite and Christopher Southouse	Annual rent charge of £14 18s. out of manor of Kirby	For ever	..	H.A. Leics. deeds
15 May 1582	Richard Branthwaite and Christopher Southouse	Annuity of £5 2s. out of land in Kirby	For ever	..	H.A. Leics. deeds
... 1585 ?	Thomas Hasell and Julian his wife	Rent charge of £40	For their lives	..	H.A. 5393

334

Date	Annuitant	Property charged	Term	Payment	Source
8 Mar. 1589	John Stafford and his wife	Annuities of £50 each charged on manor of Ringwood, Hants.	Life	£600	P.R.O. C 54/1321

* Dec. 1564 in exchange for grant of manors of Botleat and Holton and lease of manor of Stokenham Huntingdon reassigned his term of years in the possessions of the dowager countess in Somerset and Devon. (H.A. Cornwall deeds)
Soon after Huntingdon died it was claimed he had granted annuities amounting to £560 p.a. for which recognisances were held. (Bodl. Lib. Carte 78, 246)

z

Huntingdon's bonds and mortgages to the crown

Date	Bond or land assured	Purpose of mortgage or bond	Cancellation	Source
c. May 1562	Bond for £200	To pay £150 at Michaelmas next, part of debt of £921 12s. 8½d. of Francis, second Earl of Huntingdon to the crown	..	P.R.O. E 159/345
c. May 1563	Bond for £200	To pay £150 at Michaelmas next, part of above debt	..	P.R.O. E 159/346
c. Jan. 1566	Bond for £200	To pay £150 at Michaelmas next, part of above debt	..	P.R.O. E 159/352
21 Sept. 1573	Bond for £200	To pay 200 marks at Michaelmas next, part of debt of £1,797 14s. 3½d. owed by Edward, Lord Hastings of Loughborough to the crown	..	B.M. Harl. 3881.54
28 May 1565	Manors of North Cadbury, Som., Evington and Bosworth, Leics. and Henley, Oxon.	To satisfy debt of £4,000 owed by Sir Thomas Lodge to crown. Half sum to be repaid in 1570, remainder in 1571	6 Nov. 1570	H.A. Deeds, Som. and Various
3 Nov. 1570	Manor of South Cadbury and Holton, Som., Kirby and Packington, Leics. and Henley, Oxon.	To satisfy Lodge's debt of £4,000 within ten years	4 Jan. 1582	H.A. Seals 231

Date	Bond or land assured	Purpose of mortgage or bond	Cancellation	Source
8 Apr. 1574 25 May 1574	Fifty years' lease of Park of Ware, Herts. to Thomas Fanshaw, Remembrancer of the Exchequer	To pay into the Exchequer £191 12s. 2¼d. annually until [Hatton's] debt of £1,149 13s. 2d. to crown is repaid. (For last twenty years of lease 100 marks p.a. to be paid to dowager countess and to Huntingdon)	[4 Jan. 1582?]	H.A. Herts. deeds
4 Jan. 1582	Manor of Lubbesthorpe, Leics.	To satisfy within 4 years, debt of £10,685 19s. 9d. to crown—made up of £4,000 owed for Lodge's debt, remainder of £958 0s. 11¾d. owed for Hatton's debt, £3,480 4s. 5¾d. for exporting woollen cloths, £450 for debts of second earl, and £1,797 14s. 3½d. for debts of Edward, Lord Hastings of Loughborough	*	H.A. Seals 242
16 Feb. 1586	Manors of Ashby, Alton Grange, Packington, Knighthorpe and Braunstone, Leics.	To satisfy within eighteen years Lord Lumley's debt of £11,400 to crown —paying £600 p.a.	*	P.R.O. C 54/1251

* When Huntingdon died £2,398 was still owing, charged on the manor of Lubbesthorpe, while for the manor of Ashby, Huntingdon owed £5,400 plus a further £5,400 for the £600 which would become due for each of the next nine years. These two sums alone made up £13,198, the major part of Huntingdon's total debt to the crown on his death of £18,044 9s. 5½d. (P.R.O. E 368/486, m. 125).

Royal grants to Huntingdon

Date	Grant	Term	Payment	Source
27 June 1561	Office of Master of the Hart Hounds	For life	..	B.M. Harl. 3881,51
4 Apr. 1562	Manor of Packington, Leics.	In perpetuity	(c. £650)	C.P.R. Eliz. 1560–3, p. 290 P.R.O. C 54/639, P.R.O. E 371/416
8 Nov. 1564	Next presentation to Terrington church, Norfolk	..	..	P.R.O. C 66/1006
31 May 1569	Wardship of Henry Kendall and annuity of £10 out of his lands in Leics. and Derbyshire	..	..	P.R.O. C 66/1040
12 Feb. 1574	Lease of woods in Deighton and Riccall, Yorks.	21 years	Rent of £10 10s. p.a.	P.R.O. C 66/1117
8 Aug. 1576	Monopoly of exporting 8,000 broadcloths with grant of half the profits otherwise due to the queen	4 years	Normal customs duties	P.R.O. E 159/371
12 June 1579	Lease of Enderby rectory, Leics.*	21 years	Rent of £9 6s. 8d. p.a.	P.R.O. C 66/1176
12 Aug. 1583	Lease of lands in Sheriff Hutton, Yorks.†	21 years	Fine of £60 Rent of £35 15s. p.a.	P.R.O. C 66/1234
12 Aug. 1583	Lease of four mills in Christchurch, Hants.‡	21 years	Fine of £14 Rent of £14 p.a.	P.R.O. C 66/1234

Date	Grant	Term	Payment	Source
June 1588	To Richard Branthwaite and Roger Bromley at the request of Huntingdon of various parcels of land in England and Wales in fee farm and fee simple	In perpetuity	Valued at £138 4s. 0¼d. p.a.	P.R.O. C 66/1319
11 Feb. 1589	To same, further parcels of lands	In perpetuity	Valued at £77 2s. 6½d. p.a.	P.R.O. C 66/1238
4 Apr. 1589	To same, further parcels of lands§	In perpetuity	Valued at £179 9s. 1d. p.a.	P.R.O. C 66/1332
	In exchange for manor of Bradbury worth £310 13s. 6d. p.a. and manor of Hilton worth £141 2s. p.a. to be accepted as worth £400 p.a.	→	£394 15s. 7¾d. p.a.	H.A. Egerton 1264 (c). f. 38
12 May 1591	Wardship of Thomas Waterton and annuity of £6 13s. 4d. out of his lands in Yorks.	...	...	P.R.O. C 66/1364

* Alienated to Sir George Hastings, 1591. (P.R.O. C 54/1408.)
† Alienated to Henry Hall, 1586. (*V.C.H. Yorks. North Riding*, ii. 182.)
‡ Alienated to Edward Dull, 1590. (P.R.O. C 66/1234.)
§ Exchange lands sold in entirety.

Lands acquired by Huntingdon—excluding leases from the crown

Date	Alienator	Property	Consideration	Source
2 Jan. 1562	Edward, Lord Hastings of Loughborough	*Manor of Market Bosworth*—mortgage, not redeemed	£2,625	H.A. Leics. deeds P.R.O. E 368/370
10 Feb. 1562	Sir John Parrott	Kingswood in Belton, Leics.	£440	P.R.O. C 54/606
4 Apr. 1562	The queen	*Manor of Packington, Leics.*	[*c.* £650]	P.R.O. E 371/416
16 May 1565	Robert Brokesbye	*Manor of Shakeeston, Leics.**	£360	H.A. Leics. deeds
16 July 1566	William Barford	*Manor of Newbottle, Northants.†*	[£1,000]	H.A. Middlesex deeds P.R.O. C 54/722
28 Oct. 1566	Thomas Barrington	Residue of thirty years' lease, granted in 2 Ed. VI, of Baron Park, Loughborough, Leics.	£100 (reserved rent of £12 p.a. to crown)	B.M. Harl. 3881, 52
25 Apr. 1569	The queen	Reversion of *manor of Loughborough*, Leics. on death of Edward, Lord Hastings of Loughborough	.. (rent of £115 16s. 6d. p.a. to crown)	P.R.O. C 66/1054
4 July 1570	John Hastings and George Carleton	*Manor of Puddletown, Dorset*	£2,500	P.R.O. C 54/820
6 July 1570	John Browne	Two parts of *manor of Canford, Dorset*	£1,612	P.R.O. C 54/820
15 Mar. 1572	Sir Christopher Hatton	Site of Abbey of St. Mary, Leicester	£1,149 13s. 2d.	P.R.O. E 159/367 H.A. Leics. deeds

Date	Alienator	Property	Consideration	Source
20 Oct. 1574	Feoffees of Walter, Earl of Essex	Reversion of *manor of Newbold Verdon*, on death of Margaret, Lady Willoughby	£3,000	P.R.O. C 54/961
22 Apr. 1575	Sir Valentine Browne	Messuage and lands in Sheriff Hutton, Yorks.‡	..	P.R.O. C 54/971
1 Apr. 1579	William Whyte and wife	Messuages and lands in Christchurch, Hants.	..	P.R.O. C 66/1181
14 Jan. 1580	Thomas Poker	House and garden in parishes of St. Martin and St. Peter, Leicester	..	H.A. Leics. deeds
31 Jan. 1586	Sara, widow of John Hastings	Remainder of lease of fishings in Christchurch, Hants	..	H.A. Dorset deeds
14 Jan. 1587	William Bowes	*Manor of Hilton*, Durham.§	£2,000	H.A. Dorset deeds
16 Feb. 1587	Richard Gresham for William Bowes	*Manor of Bradbury*, with Hilton, Durham§	..	P.R.O. C 54/1268
9 Jan. 1593	John [Piers] Archbishop of York	Twenty-one years' lease of Whitby parsonage, Yorks.	Rent of £50 p.a.	H.A. Yorks. deeds

TOTAL MINIMUM PRICE OF LANDS ACQUIRED (minus exchange manors of Bradbury and Hilton) £13,436 13s. 2d.

* Alienated 8 July 1566 to William Barford. (H.A. Leics. deeds.)
† Alienated 14 June 1568 to William Saunders. (P.R.O. C 54/772.)
‡ Alienated 3 Sept. 1577 to William Wanton? (H.A. Yorks. deeds.)
§ Alienated 8 June 1588 to the queen—the exchange of lands. (P.R.O. C 66/1319.)

The claim of Henry, Earl of Huntingdon to the English throne

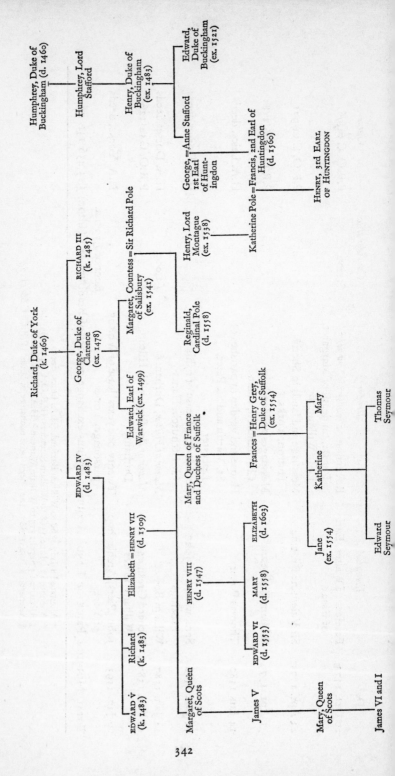

Connections between the families of Hastings, Devereux, Dudley, Sidney and Russell

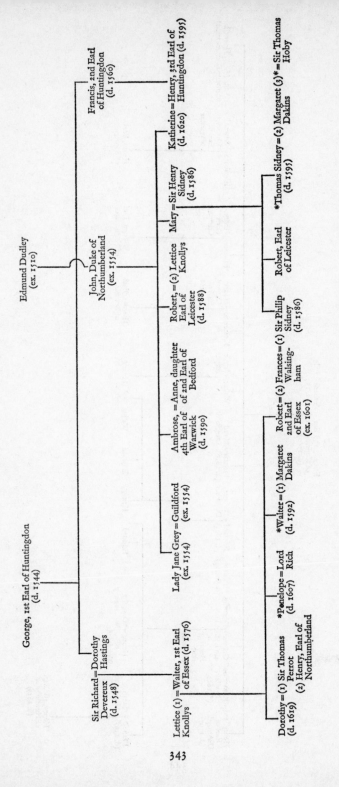

343

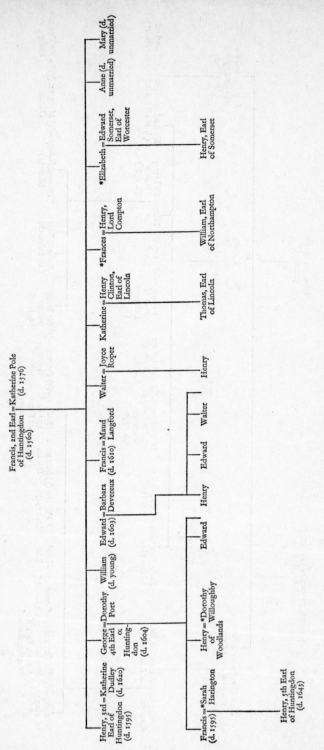

The Hastings family in the lifetime of the third Earl of Huntingdon

* Marriages arranged by the 3rd Earl of Huntingdon.

INDEX